Konkan Economy and Society in Transition (1818-1920)

KONKAN ECONOMY AND SOCIETY IN TRANSITION (1818-1920)

(With Special Reference to Ratnagiri, Malvan and Vengurla)

Dr. Sheela Mohan Nabar

Principal

K.B. College of Arts and Commerce for Women
Mith Bundee Road, Kopri, Thane (E),
Mumbai.

SERIALS PUBLICATIONS

New Delhi

First Published—2005

ISBN : 81-86771-68-9

Published by

Head Office : **SERIALS PUBLICATIONS**
4, B.S.S. Hall, Khyber Pass Market,
Civil Lines, Delhi-110054 (India)
Fax: 91-11-23812678
Phone : 23245225
e-mail : serials@satyam.net.in

Branch Office : 4830/24, Prahlad Street, Ansari Road,
Darya Ganj, New Delhi-110002 (India)

Printed at : R.K. Offset Process, Naveen Shahdara, Delhi-110032

Dedication

In Cherished Memory of
Dear Husband

November 1, 1940 - October 24, 2001.

Though you are not with me in person
The enormous perseverance
You instilled in me goes on
And through if you continue to live.

ACKNOWLEDGMENTS

I express my deep sense of gratitude to my research guide Dr. Mariam Dossal for her inspiring guidance and persuasion.

I am extremely thankful to the entire staff of the Directorate of Archives, Maharashtra State for the assistance they gave me in my research work to obtain access to the unpublished Government Records and Documents. I owe my special gratitude to Mr. A.K. Kharade, Chief Archivist and Mr. D.D. Pawar who lent their helping hand whenever approached. Their cordiality and assistance made the Archives more than a temporary place of study and made the collection work simpler in innumerable ways.

I wish to express my thanks to the staff of the Asiatic Society of Bombay, Jawaharlal Nehru Library, Fort Library, Indira Gandhi Institute of Development and Research in Mumbai, Gokhale Institute of Politics and Economics, Deccan College, Pune University, Bhandarkar Oriental Research Institute and Aitihasik Samhodhan Mandal in Pune for their help rendered at all times by passing on their research material to me.

My sincere thanks are due to Prof. J.V. Naik, Dr. M.D. David, Dr. Arvind Ganachari for their constant encouragement and their steadfast support. I am indebted to Dr. S.D. Pawar and Dr. S.S. Narwade, for their help mixed with extraordinary kindness.

Dr. Swapna Samel, Ms. Anuradha Ranade, Ms. Madhuri Kulkarni and Mr. Ramachandran's valuable friendship and timely advice enhanced my interest in research.

A debt of gratitude is owed to all my family members who endured this long process with me always offering support and love. My nearest and dearest Satyen, Ashwini,

Chetan and Manasi took a great sense of pride in my perseverance and me and enveloped me with love and respect. Warm thanks are due to Mr. Ramakant Malvankar, Mrs. Shaila Malvankar and Mrs. Sudha Varde for helping me in my last minute odd jobs. My parents, sister Medha and brother-in-law Ajit, and Dr. Lalita Deodhar and family deserve a mention of recognition for their tacit but positive encouragement.

Needless to mention the tremendous influence my dear husband Mohan had on me throughout my life. His desire for learning was shown in the form of support and inspiration in all my academic endeavors. It was combined with virtues like affection, patience that he possessed and this alone awakened me to pass the tests of God, accept challenge and complete the task ahead of me with determination. I must here acknowledge the steadfast support of all those who stood by me when I was shaken by the sad demise of my dear husband during the course of my work and for helping me directly or indirectly in achieving my goal.

Last but not the least, my sincere thanks are due to my Mr. S.K. Jha is for his willingness and co-operation to undertake the publication of this work.

SHEELA MOHAN NABAR

PREFACE

My research on 'South Konkan Economy and Society In Transition' (1818-1920) examines the impact of British rule on this region over a period of one hundred years. The focus of my research is on Ratnagiri and Malvan talukas including Vengurla, which was a petha converted to a taluka in 1879. During this period, the South Konkan witnessed a number of administrative, economic and social changes. My research focuses on issues related to khoti, agriculture, trade, industry, forests, and migration, after the British established their control. It evaluates the extent and nature of the incorporation of the South Konkan into the British Indian capitalist economy.

It is my firm conviction that Western Coast is an excellent area to investigate. Each port city will have a market at home and abroad and each market will have a story to narrate of itself. So I chose to explore the Konkan coast. South Konkan being a coastal region had celebrated ports such as Ratnagiri, Rajapur, Malvan, Vijaydurg, Bankote and Vengurla. Commodities to these ports were imported from abroad and carried into the interior through the ghats and vice versa. Pepper from Deccan, saltpeter, spices from Malabar, Ceylon, Indonesia, metals like tin; copper from Malaya, were brought to these ports. Here resided many wealthy merchants who brought and sold agricultural products, textiles, copper and other goods. The economy of the South Konkan also relied upon on saltpans, fishing yards and agriculture.

The East India Company was a British trading Company with political aspirations. It was keen to control the Konkan ports, which would serve their political and economic interests. The British acquired Konkan in 1818 after defeating the Peshwas in the Third Anglo-Maratha War. They shifted the headquarters of the South Konkan from Bankot to Ratnagiri in 1819 for administrative convenience. Since then the South Konkan was also called 'Ratnagiri Collectorate'. My research explores the changes that were observed in the economy and society of the three regions under review. It finally examines the causes of the region's decline during this period. I would like to mention one thing in this context. The theme I did not try to explore in depth was that comparing the area where Konkan stood with other areas of the subcontinent. Certainly there was many an area of growth, which will match this area of decline. But the mathematics of profit and loss, which will be essential for widespread conclusions, has not been worked out.

My research is chiefly based on Archival Records available in the Maharashtra State Archives, Mumbai. The primary sources such as Political Department Diaries, Public Department Diaries, Secret and Political Department Diaries, Revenue Department Volumes, General Department Volumes, Home Department Volumes, Judicial Department Volumes provide comprehensive data relating to my research. Official Publications such as, The Census Reports, Gazetteers, Native Reports and Selections from the Records of the Bombay Government, Crop Reports, Annual Trade and Navigation Reports have proved useful in my thesis. I had a chance to refer to the archival records in the Karnataka State Archives, Bangalore, University Library at Goa and Kolhapur Archives, Kolhapur.

The libraries I have extensively used for the purpose of secondary sources at Mumbai are Jawaharlal Nehru University Library, Fort Library, Asiatic Society of Bombay, Indira Gandhi Institute of Development and Research, Mumbai Marathi Grantha Sangrahalay. I availed of the opportunities provided by the libraries at Pune. They are Bharat Itihas Samshondhan Mandal, Deccan College, Gokhale Institute of Politics and Economics and Pune University. I also visited University of Goa library and referred to a few secondary sources. Unpublished, Published thesis and articles are referred to at libraries in Mumbai, Pune and Goa.

Several works have been written on Western India, which focus on various aspects of Konkan economy. Works by contemporary writers which proved helpful in my research are A.K. Nairne's *History of Konkan (1894),* Alexander Rogers' *The Land Revenue of Bombay,* Vol-III *(1993),* B.H.Baden Powell's *Administration of Land Revenue and Tenure in British India (1907),* T.B. Jervis' *Geographical and Statistical Memoirs of Konkan (1840), A Report of the Weights And Measures of the Konkan Province (1929),* Mountstuart Elphinstone's *Territories conquered from the Peshwas (1838),* Arthur Crawford's *Legends of Konkan (1909),* Da Cunha's *Notes on the History and Antiquities of Chaul and Bassein (1870),* E.T Candy's, *Khoti Tenure, Selections from the Records of the Bombay Government* (1873), R.E.Enthoven's *The Tribes and Castes of Bombay (1915).*

The secondary sources include A.R.Kulkarni's *Medieval Maratha Country (1996), Medieval Maharashtra (1996),* R.D. Choksey's The *Ratnagiri Collectorate (1821-1829)* (1958) *The Malwan Residency (1812-1819) (1956), The Economic Life of the Bombay Deccan (1818-1939) (1960), Economic Life in the Bombay Konkan* (1818-1839) (1960), *The Period of Transition (1818-1826) (1945), Early British Adminstration (1817-1836) (1964), Mountstuart Elphinstone: The Indian Years (1796-1827) (1971),* B.K.Apte's *A History of the Maratha Navy and Merchantship(1973),* C. D. Deshpande's *Western India, a Regional Geography(1948),* Indu Banga's *Ports and their Hinterlands in India(1992),* V.P.Chavan's *The Konkan and the Konkani Language(1924), Ashok Mehta's Indian Shipping,(1940),* Radhakumud Mookerji's *Indian Shipping, A History of the Sea Borne Trade and Maritime Activity of the Indians from Earliest Times,*(1912).

Marathi works which have been useful in the construction of my thesis have been V.G.Khobrekar's Maharashtrache Arthik Va Samajik Khacchikaran (1958), and Konkan: From the Earliest Times to 1818 A.D. (A Study in Political and Socio-Economic Aspects), T.S. Shejwalkar's *Konkanachya Itihaschi Parshvabhumi (1883),* Murlidhar Katdhare's *Marathe Kaleen Adhikari ani Tyanche Gairvartan (1995),* Anant Vasudev's Marathe's *Vengurle Mahal Va Parisar (1961),* Narayan Ganesh's Musale's *Ratnagiri Zillah, Kal, Aaj va Udhya (1958), A.S.Altekar's Shilaharancha Itihas* (1935).

The use of vivid illustrations in the form of maps, tables,

pictures and figures furnish a visual feeling and make concepts clear. The illustrations are drawn from various sources - published work of others, Institutions, Archives who deserve special thanks.

CHAPTER SCHEME

Chapter 1 : Historical and Geographical Background of the South Konkan Region

The chapter provides a historical and geographical account of the Konkan, focussing on the South Konkan. It discusses the etymology of the name 'Konkan' and the debates, which surround it. Information about some of the commercial ports of importance, rivers, forts and ghats of the South Konkan are provided here. It details the manner by which the British acquired the region. The chapter describes the East India Company's activities in the Konkan, beginning with the establishment of a factory in Rajapur in 1637-38 and concludes with the political acquisition of the Konkan in 1818.

Chapter 2 : The Khoti Tenure and British Rule (1818-1920)

The chapter examines in detail the role of the khots, the khoti tenure and the rights of the khots in agricultural lands and forest reserves of the Ratnagiri Collectorate. It probes into the economic viability of the origin of a class called the khots who had grown to be a vital part of Konkan society.

Reports by various Collectors of Land Revenue provide detailed information on the khoti system. Since collection of revenue was so central to the British Government, they relied heavily on the khots who acted as intermediataries. The chapter examines the changing political equations between the British and the khots over a century.

A number of settlements and legislations enacted on agricultural lands and forests are analyzed in this chapter. The responses of the people to these laws are also detailed here.

Chapter 3 : Konkan Economy and Society in the First Forty Years of British Rule (1818-1860).

The chapter provides information on the administrative changes brought about by the British after its acquisition. The shifting of the Headquarters of South Konkan from Bankote to Ratnagiri in 1819, labeling it as 'Ratnagiri Collectorate' and listing out the talukas and mahals falling under this territory are detailed here.

To obtain first hand information, the British appointed officers to assess the yield and quality of lands. Surveys provided them with vital information regarding the nature of the agricultural produce of the land, the prevailing prices, the existing trade routes, the weights and measures in use, common currency in vogue. This enabled the British to establish effective control over the region.

English and Marathi primary schools were started. This was to enable the British with a class of educated persons who would assist in the lower rounds of administration. This chapter analyzes the caste composition of students and the extent of spread of education here.

Chapter 4 : The Second Phase of the British Rule in the Ratnagiri Collectorate (1860-1920)

For purpose of closer examination, the chapter focusses on the three regions separately. They are Ratnagiri taluka, Malvan taluka and Vengurla Petha. The chapter evaluates the changing policies of the British in the three talukas from 1860 to 1920.

To increase agricultural produce, solve issues related to khoti, land revenue settlements were conducted in Ratnagiri and Malvan talukas. The Revenue Settlement introduced in Vengurla is also studied after it was converted to a taluka in 1879. The experiments done in agriculture, co-operative credit societies established, the improved transport systems made available to bring changes in agriculture and volume of trade are studied separately in each section.

Yet, the picture that emerged was one of stagnant agriculture (with certain exceptions), unable to increase either the area cultivated or the productivity of the land, resulting in the decline of trade in general in each region. The expectations of the British for its development in the early years of their rule were belied. A critical study of the lack of state support in the three talukas resulting in their decline is carried out in the chapter.

Chapter 5 : Migration from Ratnagiri Collectorate and its Impact on Konkan Economy

The chapter examines the pattern of migration from Ratnagiri Collectorate to the cities, primarily Bombay. Mounting agrarian tensions, increasing population, growing unemployment problems leading to migration are examined.

The South Konkan or Ratnagiri Collectorate, being a periphery of a metropolitan city, could not escape the adverse impact of centripetal forces that set in during the growth of metropolis, namely Bombay. The region witnessed four categories of people migrating. They were the higher class (absorbed in Government jobs), traders, specialized artisans, and labourers. Emigration to the newly sprung mills and other industries of Bombay, the newly created administrative posts in the British Government, the rewarding opportunities offered in trade, and the necessity of other menial jobs in the growing commercial city of Bombay, causing a rapidly escalating exodus of people from the Ratnagiri Collectorate creating a satellite economy and turning it to a money order economy is detailed here.

Chapter 6: Conclusion

A brief summary of the important aspects of chapter I to V is presented in order to draw conclusions from the study. In a span of a hundred years of my study, an economic decline of Ratnagiri Collectorate is witnessed.

A number of factors are responsible for the decline of the region. The rise of Bombay as a commercial center adversely affected the growth patterns of the Konkan. The silting of its ports made them unfit for the use by the larger ships. The experiments in agricultural fields failed. The problems related to the khoti system were long drawn. The forests were of limited use. There was lack of Government support.

All this led to the decline of the once famous regions turning it into a dependent money order economy.

The role of the state is vital in the growth or decline of an economy. Whether the region is a periphery or is in the mainstream, it can be developed according its size and ability if the government takes interest. Today slow but steady changes are seen in Ratnagiri, Malvan and Vengurla with the construction of Konkan railway. It is a missing link between India's commercial capital, Mumbai and other coastal parts. The 760-kilometer line, which was flagged off on 26 January 1998, connects Maharashtra, Goa and Karnataka. It has changed the lives of the people associated with it. It has already started giving a much-needed impetus to socio-economic development on the western coastline of India transforming the lives of eleven million people who live there. New agricultural and industrial experiments are being undertaken to develop Konkan region while generating employment to people. Roads are being attended to. The beaches are again gaining importance as a result of the efforts of the Tourism Department of Maharashtra. This will not only fetch good revenue to the Government but also bring back the lost glory of the coastal towns.

SHEELA MOHAN NABAR

CONTENTS

ABBREVIATIONS

A.S.B	The Asiatic Society of Bombay
BGS	Selections From The Records of The Bombay Government
BGS	Selections From The Records Of The Bombay Government (New Series)
BRP	Bombay Revenue Proceedings
DASCR	Department Of Agriculture, Season And Crop Reports
DCP	Deccan College, Pune
DCRIP	Deccan College post-graduate and Research Institute, Pune
FL	Fort Library, Mumbai
G.D.	General Department
GIPE	Gokhale Institute of Politics and Economics
I.H.C.	Indian History Congress
IESHR	Indian Economic and Social History Review
IGIDR	Indira Gandhi Institute Of Development And Research
JBBRAS	Journal of the Bombay Branch of the Royal Asiatic society
JD	Judicial Department
JNL	Jawaharlal Nehru Library, Mumbai
M.P.S.	Malvan Political Secret
MSA	Maharashtra State Archives
P.D.	Peshwe Daftar
P.D.D.	Political Department Diary
Pub. D.D.	Public Department Diary
R.D.	Revenue Department Volume

Sec. & P.D.D.	Secret and Political Department Diary
SPS	Shivakalin Patrasar Sangraha

LIST OF ILLUSTRATIONS

TABLES

FIGURES

MAPS

PLATES

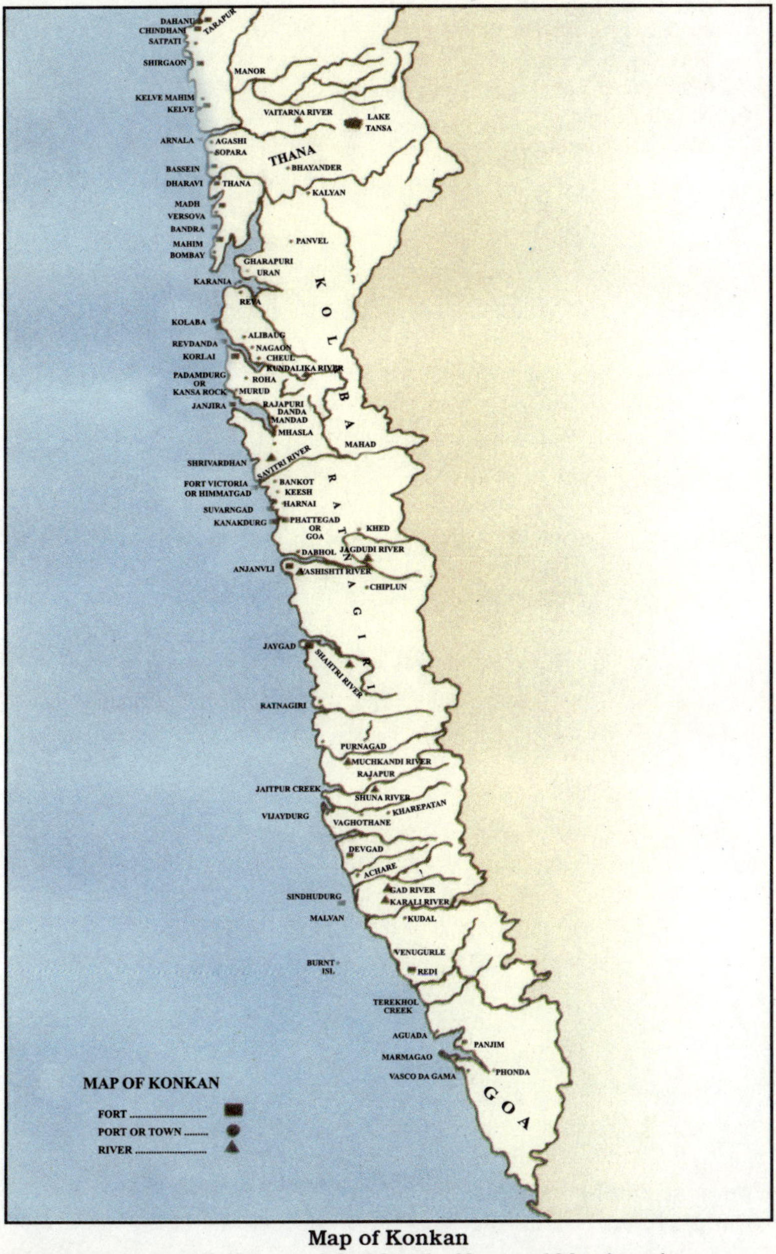

Map of Konkan

Source : B.K. Apte, A History of the Maratha Navy and Merchantships, Bombay, 1973.

CHAPTER 1

HISTORICAL AND GEOGRAPHICAL SKETCH OF KONKAN AND ITS ACQUISITION BY THE BRITISH

The Konkan, a narrow strip of land, on the western coast of India, has a long history but has been overshadowed by the Gujarat coast in the north and the Malabar coast and the Canara coast in the south. According to S. Arasaratnam, the hinterlands of Konkan coast were not conspicuous and therefore were not able to compete with the estuary towns of the western coasts of Malabar and Gujarat[1]. If one goes through the pages of history, this coastal region though poor in its economy, has played an important role not only in the political field, but also trade and has always been a zone of contact between India and the West.[2]

The Origin of the Term Konkan

Various speculations are made about the origin of the word Konkan. There are also a number of explanations given for the term. The legendary stories woven around the term may or may not be reliable, but are interesting.

There is frequent mention of the term Konkan or *Aparanta* in the Puranic and the early Hindu literature.[3] *Aparanta* meant 'the country near the western end.' The term is mentioned in the Mahabharat.The reference to this term is also made in the 5th Girnar inscription of Ashoka. Kalidasa used the term *Aparanta* in the Raghu Vansha. King Solomon during the period 1016-976 B.C. halted at the Konkan ports and the region was called as *Aparanta.*

In fact the common language Konkani is a dialect of Marathi which is of a Dravidian language. The word 'Konkan' is mentioned in the Chalukyan inscriptions in 1034 A.D. (the Shaka year 956). In this inscription, it is stated that the Chalukya king Jay Singh III had attained victory over Sapta Konkan during which time it was given the name.[4] The Chalukyas under the leadership of Kirti Varman conquered Konkan in the latter half of the sixth century. In the first half of the sixth century, i.e. during the rule of Varahamihir, the word Konkan was already well established. If this was the case then the legend that the Dravidians gave the name Konkan is quite unsatisfactory. Although the legend may not be fully accepted, yet in the old writings it was called as Kunkana. (Kunkan vishayat purvena vanavasa vishayam-Kamasutra).

There is also another version and that is the belief that the term Konkan belonged is of Aryan origin. In Sanskrit *Kim Kinvam* means what is this intoxicating drug? (Toddy). The Aryans, when they came to Konkan for the first time found a luxuriant growth of palm trees, known as toddy trees. These trees were often cut down by the colonizers so that they could make room for themselves. Toddy was a juice extracted from the trees. When fresh, it was nourishing and when fermented, it became an intoxicating beverage. In Sanskrit, Kinvam meant a drug or a seed used to cause fermentation in the manufacture of spirits. The Aryans curious to know about it questioned *'kin kinvam'?* meaning what is this intoxicating drink? Later the word changed from *Kim kinvam* to *kim Kikinam,* later to *Konkanam* (derived from the Tamil word meaning at the corner) and finally to Konkan. This happened by the natural phonetic change.[5]

Scholars of ancient history claim that the word Konkan originated from the then tribal inhabitants.[6] The name of one of the aboriginal tribals was *Kong van* means a forest tract inhabited by *Kong* tribals.[7] There is an interesting interpretation that can be seen from an excellent monograph on ancient history of Konkan based on the copper plate of 584 A.D. It refers to Puri as the capital of Konkan. It was named as a region of mountains and minerals. Therefore it was called as *koha khana* meaning a region of mountains. i.e. mountains (koha) and minerals (khana).[8]

The thirteenth volume of Skandapurana mentions the divisions of Konkan being *Laghu Konkan, Konkan, and Suparaka.* It comprised of a number of villages. They were 63,000, 1,42,200 and 10,000 respectively. Puri according to the Jatakas was supposed to the capital of Konkan. The second volume of Sahyadri khand in the Skanda Purana mentions that *Sapta Konkan* is comprised of seven *Konkanas* (Sapta Konkan) a region that stretched from the Malabar coast to Bharoch. These seven divisions were *Barbar (Berber), Konkan (proper), Saurashtra (Saurashtra),Karhat (Karhad),Karnat (Karnatak), Tulang (Andhra),Karhat or Keral* (Malyalam). Barber was the name given to the forest tracts that lay on the northern and western boundaries of the present Kathaiwar. It got the name because of an aboriginal tribe called Barbar lived here. This tribe came from Hastinapur or the present Delhi. Saurashtra was inscribed as a good country with a good government. It was well-known for its prosperity. It was situated in the present *Kathaiwar, Karhat, Tulang, Karnat* and *Keral* may be identified with the present *Karhad, Andhra, karnatak* and *Malabar* respectively.[9]

Based on the epigraphical evidence namely, ' Karatam Cha Viratam Cha Maratam Konkanam Tatha Havyagam Taulavan Chaiva Keralam Cheti Saptakam' the Konkan can be split up into the following division: The Payve or the Hayve-500 in north Kanara; the Konkan-900 which encompasses Goa; Revatidvipa or modern Redi; Iridige including Sawantwadi and a part of the Ratnagiri district; Konkan-1400 around Thana, part of Salsette and Kolaba; Kapadikdivpa or Kavadidvipa around Salsette and the adjacent land; and Lata or Variair-116 including Surat with the adjoining part of the erstwhile Baroda state.[10]

There is also a Canarese and Persian version to Konkan. In Canarese the *konku* means an uneven ground. It is very often mentioned or known as *kemkem*, komkam by the earliest geographers but its meaning as the name of a country is not very clear.[11] During medieval times, the region was known as "*Konkana* or "*Kunkana*".[12]

In Persian *koh kund* means a mountain (koh) and a ditch (kund). Putting the two words together, *koh kund* it may be interpreted that the word meant a ditch or a low

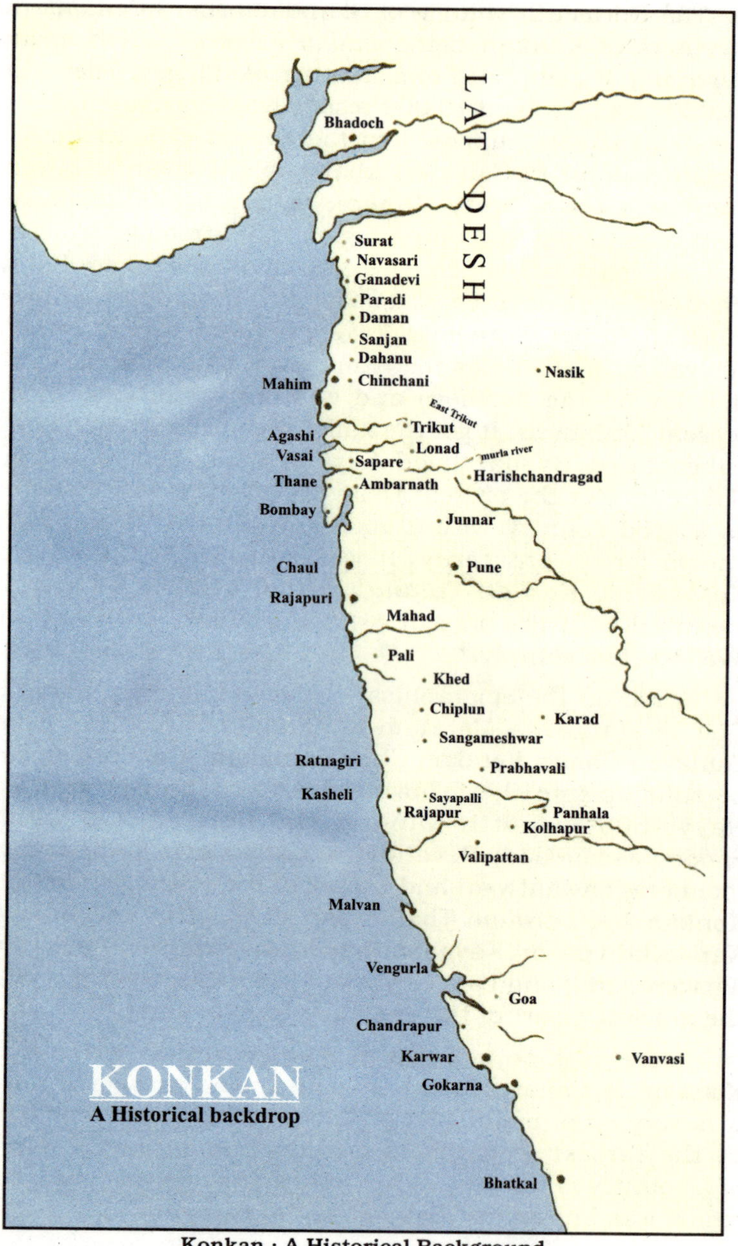

Konkan : A Historical Background

Source : A.R. Kulkarni, Medieval Chaul In Stvdia Journal, Lisbon, 1989.

ground below a mountain. The Persians were merchants who halted at the Konkan ports. But they neither visited the Konkan ports in large numbers nor were they the conquerors that they originated the name.

A mention of Konkan is made by the Chinese traveler Yu-An-Chingin during the same period in his book of travels and he calls it as *Kong-Kina-Pulo* corresponding with name *Konkanpur.*[13]

It is indicated by the ancient author that the west coast was a scene of great commercial and maritime activity especially from the 6th century B.C. From the evidence of Bible, Jatakas, the Periplus of Erythrian Sea, Pliny it is clear that India had flourshing trade with Babylonia, Egypt, Greece and Rome. These ports served as warehouses for the products of the whole of India...The famous city *Ophir* known for its gold and precious stones, sandalwood and peacocks is located somewhere in western side of India and is identified with ancient Sopara near Bombay.[14]

The other ports were *Mandgora*, probably *Bankot, Palai, Patmai Probably Dabhol, Melizigara*, probably *Jaigad, Togarum*, probably *Devgad, Byzantium*, probably *Vijaydurg* and *Auranoboas* or *Tyrannoboas* probably *Malvan* or *Aranyavaha.*[15]

Although the exact origin or the meaning of the term Konkan may be difficult to know but one thing can be undoubtedly said that the Konkan ports were an outlet for the trading articles. As maritime communications increased in volume, these names were replaced by the names of some of the ports, which became important trading centers. They were *Nausaripa (Navsari), Sopara, Bourgaza (Broach), Chaul, Kalyan* etc.

Historical Background and its Importance

Historically Konkan has been a zone of contact between India and the west. To begin with, the earliest centuries witnessed the rule of local Hindu dynasties. The important dynasties, which ruled Konkan region from 1st century to the early 14th century, were the *Mauryas, Satavahanas, Abhir-Traikutakas, Chalukyas of Badami, Rashtrakutas Kadambas, Shilaharas and Yadavas of Deogiri.* The trade of the Konkan coast with European countries is mentioned in

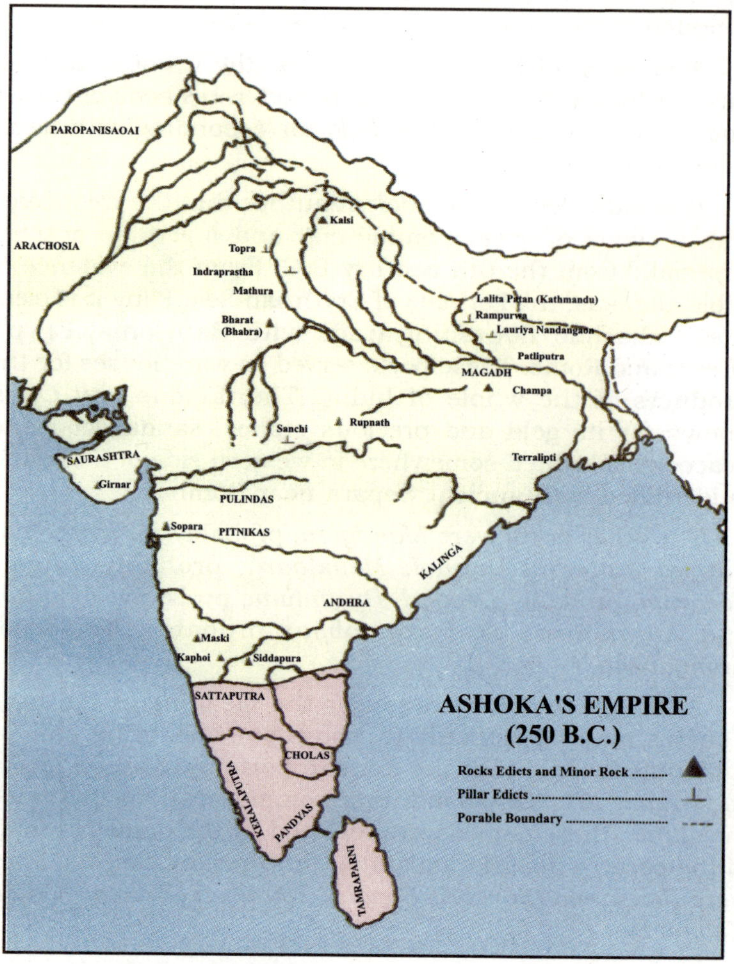

Map of Konkan during Ashoka's period (250 B.C.)

Source : C. Collin Davies, in Historical Atlas of the Indian Peninsula

the earlier phases of the Greek and the Roman civilizations. During this period, the travelers popularly knew Sopara, Thane, Kalyan, and Chaul as the Gate Way of India.[16]

The history of Konkan before Ashoka is shrouded in mystery because of lack of sufficient sources. There is a mention in the Mahabharata that the Aryans visited Konkan then called as Shurparaka.[17] It was during the period of Ashoka that north Konkan was known as *Aparanta.* From the Mauryan period there is an evidence to reconstruct the political history of the Konkan. The dynasty from 234 B.C. to 207 B.C was under Ashoka's sway and enjoyed a semi-independent position.[18] Aurannobboas (near Malvan) and Sesecrienae (Rocky Islands from sea town to Vengurla) were under his control.[19] The only edict of Ashoka found in Maharashtra was discovered at Sopara, which was the main city of the Konkan region during those days.[20] Besides this, remains of the Buddhist stupa, which was said to have been constructed by Ashoka himself, have also been found at Sopara.[21] From these evidences it can be definitely said that the Konkan region formed a part of the Mauryan Empire. The Mauryan Emperor Ashoka had deputed a Greek monk named Yavana Dhramarakshita to Aparanta to spread the teachings of Buddha.[22]

The Mauryan period marked a rapid growth in India's trade relations with the western world. Several ports such as Sopara (*Suparaka*), Kalyan (*Calliene*) and Chaul (*Simulla*) through which the foreign trade of India was carried were situated in this region.[23] Due to this reason, the Mauryan Emperor must have shown keen interest in the establishment of his direct rule over Konkan. The other famous ports of this period were modern Broach (*Barygaza),* Manmad (*Mandagora*); Dabhol (Palsepatmae) *Togarum.* Roman ships often visited these ports. Some of them were busy trading centers. Malvan and the Southern Konkan had become famous for piratal activities.[24]

The Mauryas were succeeded by the Shungas and Kanvas in north India and the Satavahanas in the Deccan. There is a controversy about the exact date of the rise of Satavahanas. The Satavahanas came to power during the

3rd century B.C. An inscription of the second Satavahana king and the brother of Simukha, Krishna has been found at Nasik. These inscriptions indicate that Nasik and Junnar area were the main centers of political activities of the early Satavahana kings. This region is not only adjacent to the Konkan but was a part of the Konkan in those days. That the region was conquered by the Shaka Kshatrapas has been confirmed in several inscriptions. One such inscription at Junnar belongs to the minister of Shaka Kshatrapa Nahapana. The Shaka occupation of the Konkan lasted for about half a century.

The Shaka Kshatrapas were ousted from Konkan by Gautamiputra Satkarni the 23rd king of the Satavahana dynasty. Again Konkan became a part of the Satavahana empire. This re-conquest of the ancestral kingdom by Gautamiputra Satkarni has been mentioned in the Nasik inscriptions of his mother Gautami Balashri.[25] In this inscription, the queen has described all conquests made by Gautamiputra and they include the territory of *Aparanta* in Konkan.[26] The Satavahana rule lasted for about four centuries. During this period, trade relations between India and the Roman empire were enhanced. It was probably due to this reason that they attached special importance for the conquest of the Konkan. Several ports and trading centers in the Konkan, Sopara, Kalyan and Chaul prospered.[27] The Abhiras were the rulers of Konkan who followed the Satavahanas. The next dynasty, which held sway over the North Konkan was the Chalukyan dynasty. It was conquered by Pulikesin II in the first quarter of the seventh century and remained in their hands up to eighth century. The sovereignty of the Deccan passed into the hands of the Rasahtrakuta dynasty in the middle of the eighth century. Dantidurga was the founder of this kingdom who conquered it from the Chalukyas of Badami. This is substantiated by the Manor Copper Plate Grant of Dantidurga dated 749.[28]

The Chalukyas of Kalayana were the successors of Rashtrakutas in the administration of the Deccan. As a result of this, Konkan became a part of their dominion. Amidst the fights between the Chalukyas and Rashtrakutas there came into prominence a new dynasty named

Silaharas who controlled the region from 810 to 1260 A.D.[29] During the period of South Konkan Silaharas, Arab traders settled at Goa.[30]

Mention may be made of the next important dynasty namely, the Yadavas of Deogiri who held control of Konkan from 1270 to 1318 A.D. Their capital was invaded by Malik Kafur, the General of Alla-Ud-Din Khilji, the Sultan of Delhi. An inscription discovered at Andheri dated 1377 mentions the name of the ruler of Konkan of that time as Nasira Raya.[31] According to Dr V. B. Kolte he was a prince belonging to the Tughlak Dynasty of Delhi. The inscription also mentions the names of Alunaka and his son Hamarana who were the Governors of the Konkan under the Sultans of Delhi. The name of Alunaka Rana has been mentioned in his Dombivili inscriptions also.[32] On the basis of this, it can be said that after the conquest of the Deccan by Sultan Alla-ud-din-Khilji, the Konkan region was placed in charge of a Muslim Chief, who belonged to the Nayata Muslim family which had already settled in the Konkan. Following the downfall of Yadavas and Silaharas, the Konkan came to be ruled by the Nayata Muslim Chiefs till the end of the fourteenth century. An inscription dated 1367 A.D.which provides the information was discovered in Nagaon. A chief named Hambirrao engraved this inscription. In this inscription, the Hindu date of the *Shaka Era* 1289 as well as Muslim date of *HijriEra* 769 have been mentioned. According to Dr.V.B.Kolate, Hamirrao was a Muslim ruler belonging to the Nayata family of Alunaka. Worth mentioning names of the Islamic period from 1318 to 1660 were Alla-Ud-Din- Khilji, his son Mubarak, the Bahmanis, (Mohammad Shah, Nizam Shah Adil Shah) and Mohammad Begada. Their chief ports were Mahim, Thane, and Salsette.

During the time of Bahmani kingdom, the southern ports of Konkan were divided among the Muslim rulers. North Konkan (Kolaba) was under the domination of Nizam Shah and South Konkan (Ratnagiri & Goa) was under the domination of Adil Shah.[33] Throughout the period of Muslim rule, increasing contact with Arabia and Persian Gulf was established through Konkan ports.[34]

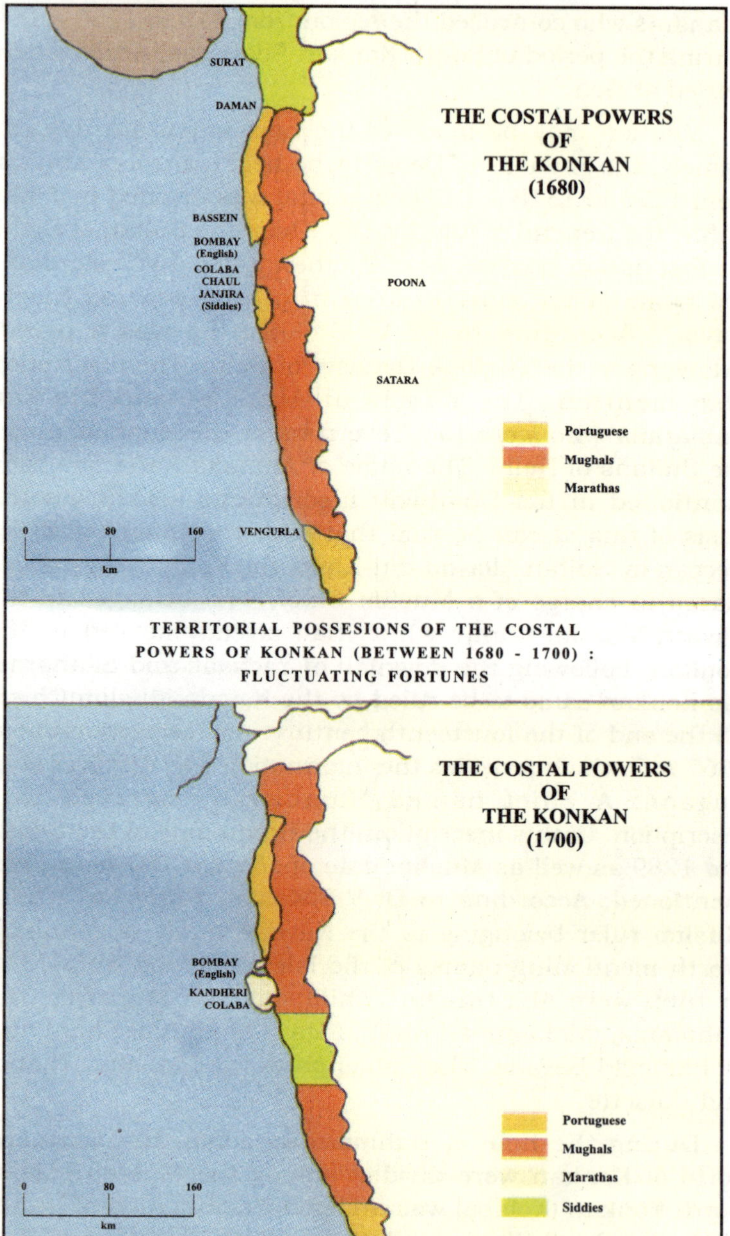

Coastal Powers of Konkan, 1680-1700

Source : C. K.R. Dikshit, *Maharashtra in Maps*, Bombay, 1986.

There is a remarkable convergence of epigraphic data and Arab accounts on the excellent relations between various merchants settled in the Konkan coast and the Rashtrakuta rulers. (almost up to 9th and 10th century) The Rashtrakutas were highly praised by the Arab authors.[35] The most eloquent testimony to this is furnished by a bilingual (Arabic and Sanskrit) inscription of 1264 A.D. found from Somnath, the famous Hindu shrine in Gujarat. It tells about the close of friendship between Nuruddin Firuz, a Muslim ship owner from Hormuz and Chada, his Hindu friend. These two different merchants belonged to two different faiths. They were both prosperous merchants and rose above all religious barriers and placed before their contemporaries a remarkable testimony of toleration, amity and friendship.[36]

The seventeenth century was an important period and geographically Konkan occupied a very strategic place during the Maratha rule. The entire Konkan region was a nodal center for the movements of Maratha navy. Shivaji used the Konkan ports to the best of his advantage. His domination over Konkan remained unchallenged till the end of his life in 1680. Thus the Marathas were able to move in the northern and southern parts of the Deccan without much interruption. Thus they always tried to retain their hold on Konkan region.[37]

Every subsequent stage in oceanic navigation marked a corresponding growth in the importance of Konkan. On account of its maritime position the real contest began with the arrival of western powers to India. The Portuguese made the initial foray into the Indian Territory. They occupied Goa in 1510 A.D. An event, which was a landmark not only in the history of the west coast but of India itself. The establishment of their rule in this part laid the foundation of a great commercial empire in the east.[38] Bassein, Asheri, Tarapur, Mahim, Daman Chaul, were fortified by 1560. Thane was famous for shipbuilding.[39] By 1570 A.D., the Portuguese firmly established their hold on the west coast. It was almost a century after the Portuguese that the English East India Company sought to establish its factories, trading settlements on the west coast. In this rivalry for supremacy in India, the British were most successful as empire-builders.

Geographical Background

The Konkan is a narrow coastal plain lying between the Arabian Sea and the Sahyadri range of Mountains stretching from Daman in the north to Goa in the south. The narrow strip of land is not flat throughout but is a series of estuarine lowlands that are separated by many hill ranges projecting towards the western ghats known as the Sahyadris.[40] The width of the course varies from south to north. It varies from 52 to 60 kilometers in south Konkan while it is approximately 100 to 110 kilometers in the north.

It has general features of relief, climate and vegetation that are common to almost all parts. The coastline has creeks, inlets, and harbours. The tides that penetrate into the sea favour the growth of a number of littoral ports, which are naturally protected. The local topography is much influenced by the vast consequent river erosion and deposition taking place after a long period of quiescence.[41] The rivers though many in number are short, narrow and dependent on the rains. During summer, many parts of Konkan suffer from severe drought. monsoonal rhythm in climate guides all human activity. Throughout its length, it is dominated by the tremendous scraps of ghats. They rise from 3000 feet in a mile or two, fretted into canyons at the valley heads.[42] These ghats act as barriers between the land and its ports. Yet man through a long history of settlement has made it possible to pass through the barrier and establish contacts with the plateau region. Therefore the economic life and human development in Konkan varies from one region to another.[43]

According to Grant Duff, the Konkan region extended along the coast from Tapti River to Sadashivgad and inland as far as the lands of the open plains of the Deccan. This included parts of Gujarat, Canara and the country above the ghats. It was called as *Konkan Gatha Matha* as against the *Tal Konkan*, which was situated on the lowlands (tal means below). In his opinion it was the Muslims who named the lowlands.[44] Ferishta named Konkan as *Tal Ghat*.[45] Khafi Khan called it *Tal Konkan*. According to these scholars, the narrow strip of land situated above the ghats

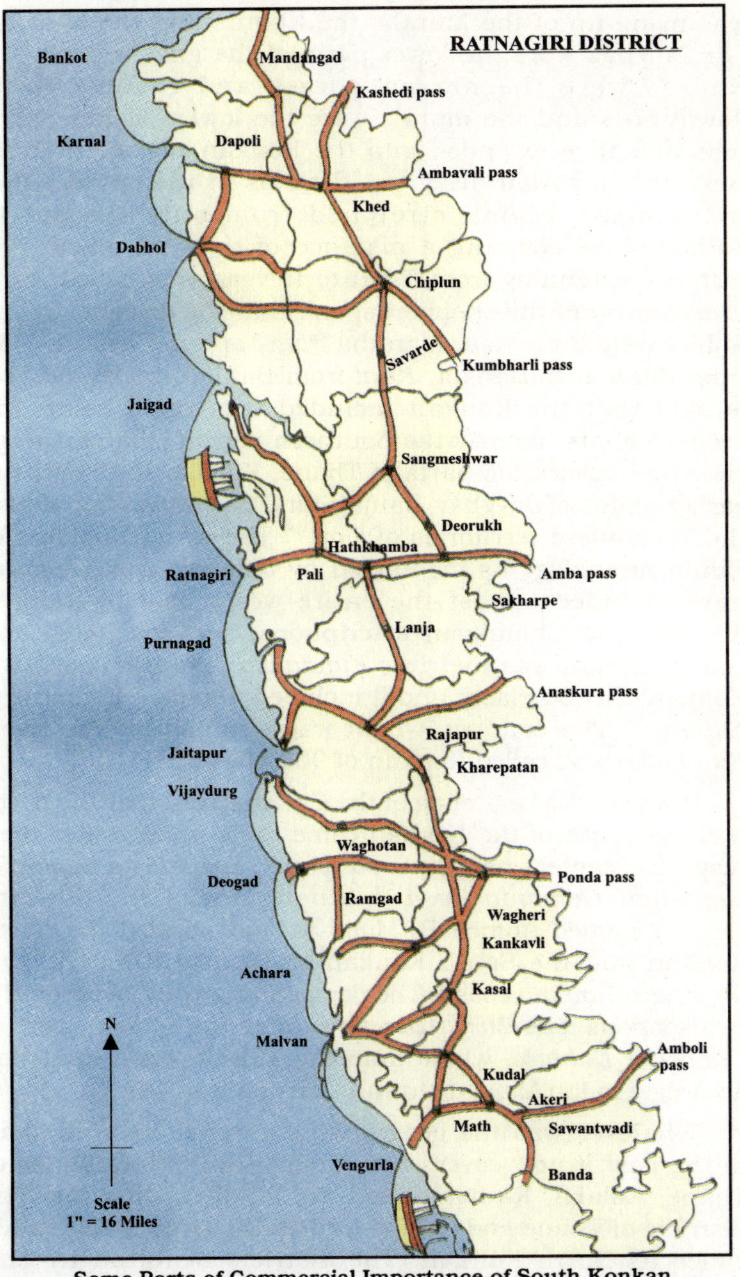

Some Ports of Commercial Importance of South Konkan

Source : Moreshwar Rege, "The History and Survey of Education In The Ratnagiri District", Ph. D. Thesis, Bombay, 1961.

was made up of the Murals, the Khords and the Murhas. The Murhas were the lower parts of the ghat section, the Khoras were the narrow gorges and ravines going downwards and the murals were the lowest slopes of the hills and they extended into the Konkan region.[46] James Bird, the historian disagreed. He was of the opinion that the Konkan region stretched from only Devgad to Sadashivgad covering a distance of only 90 miles. The territory extending from Tapti to Devgad was called *Abhir* (the country of the shepherds) and that the divisions of the Abhirs were Berbera or Maratha from Tapti to Bassein, *Virat* from Bassein to Bankot, *Kirat* from Bankot to Devgad.[47] It is said that the Konkan included the tracts below the western ghats, namely the Southern part of Dhamanganga river and covers the parts of Thane, Kolaba, Ratnagiri the earlier states of Javghar, Janjira, and Sawantwadi and also the Portuguese territories of Goa.[48] The seven Konkans of Hindu mythology as mentioned by John Wilson seems to have included almost the entire west coast of India.[49] According to Chalukyan inscriptions, between north and south Konkan was the river *Kundalika* and was called the Konkan of 1400 places and it included *Thane, Nagamu, and Supara.*[50] The country, which was situated on the river, *Kundalika* was called Konkan of 900 places.[51]

It was at the beginning of the Christian era that the north and the south of the Konkan came to be known after their respective centers namely *Supara* and *Gomanta* as *Suparaka Desa* and *Gomanta Desa.*[52] A navigator of the fifteenth century named Ahmed B. Majid-al-Najdi divided the North Konkan and the South Konkan and called it as '*Tulwan*' (Southern Konkan coast). The demarcating point between the two sections was *Mirya Donghur,* after the famous port of *Dabhol or Dabhole,* where from the Tulwan coast stretched according to Ibn Majid to Juwah - Sindabur or Goa.[53]

Whatever was the geographical extent of the Konkan in the past it now covers the administrative boundaries of Thane, Kolaba, Ratnagiri and Sindhudurg Districts. The districts of Thane and Kolaba formed the stretch commonly called as North Konkan. The districts of Ratnagiri And Sindhudurg are popularly known as South Konkan The Bankot creek separates north and south Konkan. This whole strip of Konkan lies between 72.8 and 73.8 East longitude.[54] The entire land is sandwiched between the Arabian Sea on the west and a steep mountain wall of the western ghats on the east.[55]

The South Konkan

South Konkan, a rocky and rugged portion of the territories conquered from the Peshwas is situated between the Sahyadri range of hills on the east and the Arabian Sea on the west. It lies between 15°36', and 18°5', North Latitude and 73°5' and 74°36' East Longitude.[56] The length of the district from north to south is 180 miles.

The river Savitri forms the northern boundary of the Ratnagiri district. Excepting Mhapral the northern most part of the district, the boundary follows an irregular course on account of chain of hills that run south- east and end into the Sahyadri range at Hatlot pass. The pass divides the district from the southern most part of the Kolaba district. On the western Side, the Arabian Sea gave the Ratnagiri district a seaboard of about 160-180 miles from Bankot on the west (Fort Victoria) to some two miles south of fort Redi. In the South, the district is divided by the territory of Goa.[57]

The district has peculiar characteristics. The valleys are open near the Sahyadri hills. The hills not so rugged as those at the center of the district, these again towards the coast, fall into nearly level plateaus, in great part made barren by a capping of laterite rock, cleft by deep narrow steep sided valleys and ravines through which rivers and streams find their way from the Sahyadri hills to the sea. Those rivers, tidal and navigable, have on their banks, the chief ports and nearly all-fertile lands of Southern Konkan, otherwise the remaining district has poor soil.[58]

Some Ports of Commercial Importance

Viewed from the sea, the Konkan coast presents an apparently unbroken line of hills. At some places the massive boulders erupt from the surging water while at some places we see a thin line of sandy beach intervening the towering rocks and buffeting ocean. But appearances are deceptive because the rocky rampart is often broken by estuaries and creeks. The small places close by easily make place for fortification.

The famous stronghold of Chaul also called as Revadanda which once upon a time could boast of a commodious harbour provided a safe retreat for the Portuguese fleet. It lies on the right bank of the Kundalika River. The creeks and estuaries multiply towards the south along the coast of the modern Ratnagiri coast.

Next, on the south shore of the estuary of the Savitri River lies Bankot also called as Fort Victoria. They are followed by the famous strong holds, namely Dabhol on the northern and Anjanvel on the southern banks of the Vasisthi, Ratnagiri on the Bhatiya, Jaitpur at the entrance of the Rajapur River. Further down is Devgad with its land locked harbour, Malvan and Vengurla, which deserve special mention. These ports and harbours, creeks, estuaries, gulfs and bays played an important role from ancient to modern times on the west coast of India. The west coast had trade relations with the Greeks, Romans, and the Arabs. It is mentioned in the inscriptions found at Brahmapuri in Kolhapur in Maharashtra.[59]

Most ports of commercial importance on the Konkan coast namely Sopara, Chaul, Bassein, Dabhol, Thane, Kalyan in the North Konkan and Rajapur, Ratnagiri, Malvan, Vengurla in the South Konkan with their long and convenient coastline gave ample scope for maritime activities related to ship building, fishing, salt-manufacturing.

The southern coast stretching between Savitri estuary and the Terekol creek is by and large a hilly coast with rocky headlands 20-80 meters high and narrow tidal inlets, small cones and bays and presents on the whole a ria type appearance. The lateritic uplands descend through sheer cliff walls to the coast except in the tidal inlets and estuaries. The continental shelf right up to the shore is quite deep. However the shores are at many places rocky. Most of the tidal estuaries are bar ridden as a result of which entry into the estuaries is blocked by the bars. This gives rise to the necessity of local pilotage. The coast around especially Malvan and Vengurla and the immediate neighborhood of Ratnagiri is very rocky. Tom Pires (1512-15) in his writings about various ports on the west coast said, *"If you sail from Mahim to the kingdom of Goa, the ports in the kingdom of Deccan are as follows: Chaul, Dande (Danda) Mateleni, Dabhol, (Dabuli) Sangameshwar (Sangizara) Kharepatan (Curapatanam)."*[60]

The other minor ports of South Konkan were Kelshi situated at the mouth of the Kelshi River, south east of Bankot,[61] Anjanvel, situated on the shore of the entrance to the Vasisti river, Jaigad situated on the south shore of the entrance to the Sangameshwar river,[62] Sangameshwar a small port on the coast of Shasti river, Achra port on the north west boundary of the Malvan Taluka, Vijaydurg also called Fort Victoria, a minor port on the south shore of the entrance to the Vagothan river 200 Kilometers south of Bombay, Devgad, a minor port on a flat rocky peninsula about 20 Kilometers south of Vijaydurg, Ade situated on a small rather deep creek 5 kilometers south of Kalchi, Mhapral situated on the Savitri river about 35 Kilometers away from Bankot and 12 Kilometers away from Mahad in the district of Kolaba,[63] Bankot lying on the foot of the rocky headland called Panbraj. A few more minor ports are *Chiplun, Harnai, Jaitpur, Banda, Redi, Vagotan,* and *Burondi.*

All these ports handled a good amount of trade, local and foreign. In fact not a single port along the Konkan coast is major in the real sense of the term and of the existing ports namely, Vengurla, Malvan, Achra, Devgad, Vijaydurg, Jaitpur, Ratnagiri, Jaigad, Dabhol which are about a dozen in number can be conveniently called minor and many more, about a hundred in number may be called as Sub-ports.

Table 1.1 showing the names of the minor ports along with their sub-ports.

It may be noted here that besides the ports and their subports given, there exist many more ports, which are situated in the small creeklets where it is difficult for the cargo vessels to enter. Yet they act as small fishing centres. P. Ford and J. Bound have rightly remarked thus:

"Some of the small ports are points of exports of the products of their region. Even when they are subsidiary members of the cluster surrounding one or more larger ports, they perform a distinct and an intelligible function in that cluster."[65]

Table 1.1

Minor ports	Sub-ports
Vengurla	Nil
Malvan	Sarjekot, Phondavi, Hadi, Kalavi, Masura, Bandivada, Maldi
Achra	Nil
Devgad	Wada, Mand, Vanivade
Vijaydurg	Vaghpur, Panjera, Danda, Ansur, Vada, Sagave, Jambhari kutali, Igalwadi, Taral, Upte, Kunkun, Tirlot, Navangar, Abheri, Vaghotan, Dhalvel, Matat-Manche, Korle, Kharepatam, Vijaydurg.
Jaitpur	Tulsunde, Ambulgad, Rumipur, Vaghr, Jambhate, Karel, Chavanvadi, Viliye, Dongre, Kaneri, Shade, Abhyankar, Gothane.Devhale, Vanala Dhopeshwar, Rajapur
Ratnagiri	Harcheri, Tondale
Jaigad	Dhaman-khol, Vambhari, Mubar hate, Raveshi, Phumgis, Makhjan, Kurdandha, Sangameshwar.
Dabhol	Anjanvel, Veldur, Sakhri Trishul, Chiveli, Pavekarul, Vaghivra, Gangra Donacvali, Matdole-Karbone, kalhude, ·Govalkot, Chiplun, Onavare, panjari, Dabhil, Panhale, Haji Shirvane, Bhadavale, Palange, Tumbhad, Savnas, Khed.
Bankot	Umroli, Nigdi, mhaprali, Dasagaon, mahad, Goregaon, Mahad, Goregaon
Revadanda	Ramraj, Nhava, Achalbag, Roha
Karanja	Revas, Nagothane, Anthora
panvel	Taloja, Vaghivadi, Divala, Chinchbunder, Belapur Ulva.

The importance of ports be they major, minor or sub ports along the Konkan coast cannot be under estimated. These not only handled a substantial amount of trade but also served as good links between the ports and the other regions.

Important rivers of South Konkan

The general flow of the rivers is from east to west. They are small in size and volume, ill suited for irrigation, yet one of value to the district because their deep tidal channels, navigable for twenty miles or more when supplemented by good roads between the sea-board and the

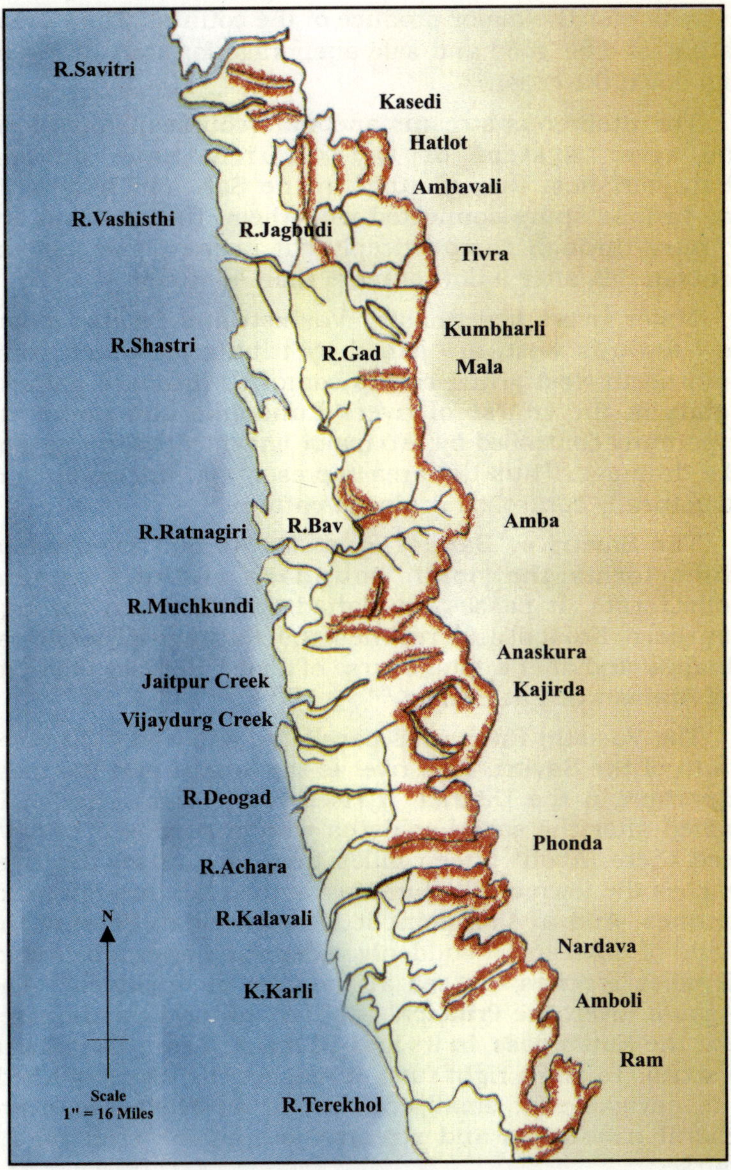

Rivers and Ghats joining the Desh

Source : Moreshwar Rege, "The History and Survey of Education In The Ratnagiri District", Ph. D. Thesis, Bombay, 1961.

Deccan afford an easy means of communication and provide an outlet for the major produce of the country. Their broad estuaries offer good and safe anchorage for craft plying up and down the coast.[66]

The numerous streams and watercourses, which form the river system of the district, have general characteristics. Rising either in the Sahyadri hills or in the various spurs connected with them, they traverse the country through narrow deeply cut ravines, and join the Arabian Sea after a flow of more than 40 miles.

Major rivers like Shastri, Vashisti and Savitri, which flow towards west, are joined by tributaries which come from north-west giving rise to contorted drainage pattern. Bends in the course of rivers Kundalika and Amba are apparently controlled by two major lineaments forming loop like drainage. Thus the area represents a fine example of structurally controlled drainage pattern.[67]

The Savitri or Bankot River for its last twenty-four miles forms the north boundary of the Ratnagiri Collectorate. It passes by Mahad and Dasgaon through Southern Kolaba and reaches the Ratnagiri District at Mhapral and after a total course of about 50 miles falls into the Arabian Sea at Bankot.[68]

The Vasisthi River runs parallel to and about 30 miles south of the Savitri. This river is the largest and the most important in the District. It rises in the Tivra Pass. It is named after the sage Vashistha who is supposed to have lived there. About fifteen miles from its course, the river reaches the town of Chiplun after a rapid fall through rocky routines. And at this point it becomes tidal. Passing the island of Govalkot, it suddenly widens and after a course of 25 miles reaches the sea at the port of Anjanvel.[69] The Jagbudi River, the Principal tributary of the Vasisthi, rises near the Hatlot pass. In its first 12 miles, it runs from north to south. Taking a right turn, it reaches the towns of Khed. It is navigable for small craft as far as Khed. There are several tributaries and streams joining the river on its course.[70]

The next important river in the district is Shastri. It rises on the slopes of Prachitgad and meets the tidal wave at Sangameshwar. The mouth of the river is crowned with the fort of Jaigad.[71] It has a total course of about 40 miles, it falls into the sea at Jaigad, a rocky promontory. The Bav River is a tributary of the Shastri and rises in the Sahyadri range near the Amba pass. Its course is 35 miles and flows through a comparatively fertile valley, joins the Shastri on its left bank at Phunagus about 25 miles from the coast.[72] Another tributary of the river Shastri, the Gadnadi has its source in the Mala pass and meets the Shastri on its right bank. The river being small is useful for small crafts as far as *Makhajan.*[73]

The Ratnagiri River is not important because the mouth of the river is very narrow and on the south side, it is guarded by a large sand bank. It rises in the Amba pass and falls into the sea after a course of 40 miles.[74] The Muchkundi rises at Machal. Small crafts navigate in the river. It flows into the sea with the fort of Purangad on its northern bank.[75]

Another creek of Ratnagiri district is the Jaitpur, which rises in the Anaskura pass. It reaches the ancient trading town of Rajapur after flowing for about twenty-five miles as a mountain stream. Here it meets the tidal wave and after its course of another fifteen miles it reaches the sea of Jaitpur.[76]

Vijaydurg creek or Vaghothane River has its mouth four miles south of Jaitpur. Rising in the Kajirda pass and flowing south east for 15 miles, it reaches Kharapatam. It reaches the sea at Vijaydurg. The Vijayadurg fort stands on the promontory on the southern side of the estuary. The river has no bar. The creek is navigable for vessels drawing 7 feet up to village Vagotna, where quays have been built. Small crafts can go up to Kharepatan 12 miles inland.

The Devgad River rises in the Sahyadri and after a straight course of about 35 miles from east west reaches the sea at the fort of Devgad. Several small islands have been formed in the bed of the river in its tidal section. The Achra river rises in the Sahyadri range near the Phonda pass. Small crafts can pass as far as the Achra town, 7 miles team the mouth. The Kalavali, the Karli, the Terekol are the other rivers of Konkan.

Passes or Ghats joining South Konkan and the Desh

On the eastern horizon of the whole district, lie the Sahyadri hills. The whole Sahyadri range consists of large

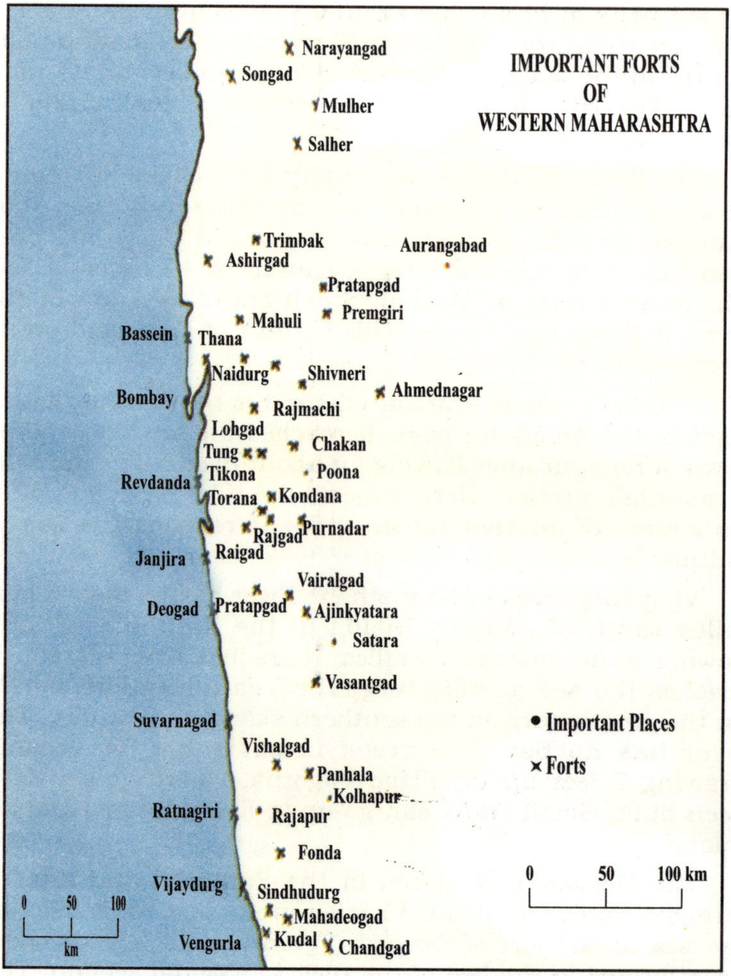

Important Forts of Western Maharashtra

Source : C. K.R. Dikshit, *Maharashtra in Maps*, Bombay, 1986.

massive basaltic rocks. These hills are crossed by numerous passes, which form the only means of communication with the Deccan. From north to south, their names are the Kashedi, the Hatlot, the Ambola (Ambavli), the Tivra, the Kumbharli, the Mala, the Amba, the Anaskura, the Kajirda, the Phonda, the Nardava, the Amboli, and the Ram. The hills rise three or four thousand feet high, and are covered with trees except where the huge black rock is found. The rock is hard and solid and so it is difficult for the hardest shrub to take root. So rugged and hilly is the whole district, that no detailed account of its innumerable spurs and eminences is possible.[77]

Forts of South Konkan

The entire Ratnagiri coast is hemmed with forts and they are of three types namely inland, headland and island. They have played a prominent role in the history of Konkan.

Suvarnadurg is an island fort probably built by the Bijapur kings and later strengthened by Shivaji. It became Kanoji Angre's strong hold in his early sea career. A Dutch record on 1664 says that shivaji built the marine fort on rock island near Harney port. He had forty *galbats* well equipped.[78] Shivaji was known as a great fort builder. He was born in fort and died in fort.[79] To him fort was the essence of the kingdom. He made maximum use of lands and hills in his territory for building forts. Himmatgad later named, as Fort Victoria by the British is a fort now in ruins.

Another fort of importance is the Ratnagiri fort and is like a horse's hoof being divided into two parts by the two hills. Purangad fort lies below Ratnagiri and is built at the mouth of the Muchkundi River. Yashwantgad stands on the Jaitpur harbour, which was an important fort during the Maratha times. Vijayadurg called Gheria stands on a hill on the Vaghotane river shore. It was called the *'Gibraltar of Konkan'* as it withstood the attacks of the Europeans and the Siddis for over half a century.[80] There is a temple of Lord Vijeshwar after which the fort of Vijayadurg was named. Cut out of the solid rock on the waterside, it has witnessed a number of struggles.

The Devgad fort built by Kanoji Angre in 1705 protects the harbour. Sindhudurg fort was one of the achievements of Shivaji. The British named it as Fort Augustus after its capture in 1765. The island fort of Pandavgad lies close to Malvan and was used for shipbuilding by Shivaji. The other forts are Anjanwel, Bhagwantgad, Gopalgad, Kanakdurg, and Phatehgad.[81]

Ethnic Groups of South Konkan

The pattern of land and climate has shaped the distribution and type of human settlement. South Konkan was inhabited by several groups of people of various castes and creeds but it was dominated by the ancient Hindu system of *Varna.* In fact so much was the impact of the Hindu culture and habits in the Konkan society that even after their conversion to Christianity or Islam, the Hindus could not get rid of the systems that prevailed. The population was divided into different groups. They were priests, traders, cultivators, manufacturers, artisans and tribals.

The Brahmins occupied the first position in the South Konkan. The Brahmins in general performed priestly duties, engaged in commercial pursuits, held good posts in government offices, acted as landlords and therefore enjoyed a superior social and economic status in the village community.

The sub castes among the Brahmins were C*hitapavans* commonly called *Konkana*sthas, the *Desasthas*, the *Karahdes*, the *Devrukhas*, the *Shenvis* or *Saraswatas*. The *Konkana*sthas were greatly favoured in the court of the Peshwas who with their distinguished chiefs- Patwardhans, Gokhales belonged to their caste. Ratnagiri was the habitat of *Chittapavans*. These Brahmins were the leading intellectual and literate class of Ratnagiri and of Konkan in general.[82] A number of them bore the designation of khots and were hereditary farmers of land revenue in the villages.[83] The *Karhade Brahmin* also was found in Ratnagiri district. Their surnames like *Desai, Sardesai, Deshmukh, Sardeshmukh, and Phadnis* show that they held high posts in government. The *Prabhus* were writers and had little interest in trade. The *Saraswats* were better at trade than the rest of the Brahmins.[84] The Saraswat Brahmins leading in various fields like literature, arts and trade competed with their rival counterparts, the Chitapavans.

Another group of people that dominated the South Konkan scene were the cultivators called the ryuts. They were nine in number namely the *Marathas, Bhandaris, Shindes, Malis, Pharjans, Ghadis, Meet-Gavadasa, Gavadas, And Kunbis*. The *Kunbis* were also *Marathas* but were of a lesser status than the pure Marathas. The *Bhandaris* got this name because they guarded the royal treasury namely the *Bhandar*. The *Malis* were gardeners.[85]

There were many other professions like the *Telis* (oil pressers), weavers like *Koshti*, the *Sali*, and the *Sangar*. The *Delvi* was a peculiar class and were the male off springs of the female servants of the Zamindars and they were found in the port towns of Vengurla, Malvan and Devgad. They generally worked as servants, drummers and actors in village temples. Another group of village servants namely the balutedars were *Sutar, Sonar, Lohar, Kasar*, who formed an important section of the society.[86]

Coastal Trade of Konkan-Northern and Southern

The topography of the Konkan coast is good for settlement. The settlement pattern of this region is closely connected with both littoral and estuary ports and unique by itself. At points where the tides carry the boats two or more settlements are formed. At no other part of western coast is this parallelism so obvious.[87] The narrow and broken coastline results in the formation of creeks and inlets. This again helps in the growth of a number of littoral ports that are well protected. Jean Deloche said ' This is one of the few areas in either of the sea-boards of India that is sheltered from the sea'.[88]

As a result, the Konkan area came into prominence in the commercial history of India from the early centuries of Christian era to the 13th or 14th centuries. The Periplus of the Erythrean Sea (1st Century A.D.) or the sailing guide of the Erythrean sea is a unique text by the anonymous author who was probably a merchant with experience in sea trade. The Periplus mentions several ports and coast towns such as *Barygaz, Ozene, Sopara, Kalayana*.[89] The writer of the periplus in 247 A.D. said that Ratnagiri Port was a local trade center. From here goods was exported to places like Africa and Arabia.[90] Al-Masudi confirmed that ships were made of Indian teak. Indian teak and coconut wood were in demand by the Arabs for constructing ships.[91]

First Century to the fourth century witnessed brisk trade between India and Rome.[92] During this time, the Red Polished Ware (RPW), a peculiar kind of pottery was found at several sites of northern Konkan coast. The same kind was also discovered from the sites of Gujarat coasts, the Makran coast, Iran coasts and India's Delta. It was clear from the findings of the archaeological sites that there was coastal network going on here.[93] According to N.P.Orton, Red Polished Ware vessels forms were strictly Indian in character.[94] The Indo-Roman trade declined in the fourth century but this did not affect the coastal voyages. The Christian topography of Cosmas Indicopleustes of the sixth century gives details of the commercial contacts between the Konkan port and the Byzantine Empire.[95]

The next phase of a regular network of overseas trade was seen from the seventh century with the Arabs coming on the scene. The Chalukyan king Pulakesin II had commercial contacts with the Persians from 610-642 A.D. He made the Chalukyas the most formidable regional power in the Deccan.[96]

The next to trade with the Arabs were the Rashtrakutas. They appointed Arabs as local Governors over Sanjan.[97] The tenth century witnessed the rise of the Silaharas to power. The trading activities increased at this time. That the coastal trade and merchants were given importance is seen from the various references and the official records of the period. One such grant given by the Silahara ruler Aparajita in 997 A.D. shows how the rulers wished to have a better understanding with the traders and their trading activities. A village named Bhadana was granted to the merchants. It was in favour of the Lord Lonaditya. It said that Udranga and parikara were exclusive of the gifts previously made to Gods and Brahmanas, together with deposits, together with right to levy fines for major and minor offences such as crimes against unmarried girls and the right to property of persons who would die without leaving a son.[98] The merchants Ambu-Sresthin and Vappaiya-sresthi-vanik, the Bhojaka Celapaiya, the Brahamana Govanaiya and others were offered this gift with the libation of water in the hands of these merchants. Sresthi denotes a rich merchant while vanik denotes a trader.[99]

The sreshti -vanik also had the license to mint coins and acted as a moneylender. That he was the financer in the mercantile activities in the Konkan known as trading center of the time tells that he was held in high esteem.

The Chinchani plate of Chittaraja in the year 1034 records three names of the merchants *Alliya, Maharata and Mahumati* (Muhammad). These being Muslim names and the area where the Rashtrakutas had appointed the Arabs as governors, it can be conveniently concluded that the Arab merchants continued to trade with Konkan up to 11th century.[100]

The Kharepatan plates of Anantadeva dated 1008 depict that *Durgasreshti* was a rich merchant of *Balipatana* (*Kharepatan*) his sons owned vessels, which sailed for trade to *Sristhanaka (*Thane), *Shuparaka* (Sopara), *Nagarapura* (Nagar), *Cemulya* (Chaul). His grandsons were also called *Sreshtis*. This shows that the profession was hereditary and they must have acquired a considerable amount of wealth.[101] Merchants or *Sreshtis* were also called as *Prabhu, Setti, Caudhore, And Caudhuri.*[102]

The Siyadoni Inscription refers to the cess levied on eighteen types of grains, spices like pepper, ginger, areca nut and salt. The records also give information on the taxes levied on various articles, and the types of retail merchants like the *vaidehaka* (pedlar) *sartavaha* (Caravan trader), *Apanika* (retail dealer*), Naigama* (trader living in the town).[103]

A mention is made of *Venugrama* (Modern Belgaum) which was a trading center where merchants gathered to exchange goods. Articles of trade mainly consisted of husked rice, black pepper, aesafoetida, green ginger, betel nuts, turmeric, areca nuts, coconuts, palm leaves, grass, sugarcane, coarse sugar, plantains, cotton and finished cotton cloth and perfumery. Daily necessities including different type of agrarian products in the Konkan are also mentioned therein.[104]

The Southern Konkan littorals began to gain importance from 11th Century onwards. Trade in Southern and Northern Konkan and Gujarat - Kathaiwad sea boards and Malabar also prospered.[105]

After the Konkan was occupied by Alla-ud-din most coastal as well as long distance trade with Malabar, Bombay, Kathaiwar, Goa, Arabia, Persia and Europe expanded considerably. In the 14th century, South Konkan became a seaboard for Bahmani rulers. Dabhol became a major trading center. Ibn Batuta, the Arabian Traveller, in the 14th century, described Thane as one of the ports from where ships used to ply to Aden. He further mentioned that the Arabs not only had the monopoly of the trade between Arabia and Malabar but they also settled on the coasts of Malabar and the Konkan.[106]

The other ports were Malvan, Vengurla, Rajapur, and Ratnagiri. This gave a boost to the export of products from the Konkan soil. However continuous wars in the region between these rulers became an obstacle to the development of agriculture and slowly but steadily the cultivable lands turned to waste lands.

By the end of the 15th century, Konkan was occupied by the Adil Shahi dynasty of Bijapur. Adil Shah realized the importance of agriculture in maritime commerce. Therefore he introduced certain measures, which would not only protect but also improve the agricultural conditions here. Constant warfares had forced the farmers to vacate their homes and migrate. Adil Shah understood the importance of bringing the wastelands under cultivation so that the farmers settle here. Keeping this in mind he introduced the Khoti system in Konkan. This not only facilitated the collection of revenue but also restore cultivation in villages, which were deserted. Adil Shah's rule did not survive long to enjoy the fruits of those measures as the area was invaded one by one by the European powers by the beginning of the 16th century. During the rule of Akbar, the systems prevalent in general were direct dealings with the tenants of its own lands. This is what came to be called as the ryotwari system. But the Majumdar, the hereditary accountant of the times did not keep any systematic records whatsoever. The method of collecting taxes adopted by the Marathas through the tax gathering army by attacking the parts within striking distance especially during the harvest season was usually called as *Mulk-giri* meaning country seizing.[107] The other times the head of the estates would come to terms with the army by bribing armed opposition or some such device and so the army would pass on to the next victim.

The Portuguese discoverer Vasco-Da-Gama set foot on the soil of Calicut in 1498. The Portuguese further occupied Goa in 1510. The next in line to enter the Konkan ports were the British and the Dutch. The coastal areas were further strained because of the renewed interference of the newly arrived rivals like the British and the Dutch.[108] During this time Southern Konkan was an exporting district. In 1660, ships coming from Batavia, Japan, Ceylon, Persian Gulf and Red Sea used to call at Vengurla.[109]

In the year 1635, the British captured Dabhol. Rajapur was captured in 1638. In the same year, the Dutch traders established their commercial settlements at Vengurla. Such fresh invasions, their rivalries caused a considerable loss to the ports as well as to agriculture. By 1672, Kalyan, Chaul were in a ruined condition. Dabhol was burnt several times since 1508. Bassein in the Thane District was also gradually declining. Rajapur in the Ratnagiri district was the only one that was prospering.[110] The frequent wars between the local powers and foreign powers showed a dismal picture. However the economy was slowly restored by the new foreign powers. Therefore even in the mid seventeenth century, the Konkan region was a rich commercial center and agricultural products were in demand for internal and international trade.[111] Meanwhile, Shivaji after the conquest of the region in 1659 took interest in improving the conditions of agriculture. He provided cattle, seeds and even financed them. He assessed only those lands, which were under actual cultivation. He also revised the khoti system so that it would create conditions conducive to efficiency in agriculture. Shivaji died in 1680.

The coastal regions were affected by the conflicts between foreign and local rulers and the Moguls. Just at this time, the English took the opportunity provided by the Peshwas and succeeded in establishing their foothold in Bankot in 1755.[112]

The exotic products of the East namely Pepper, spices, indigo, skins and finally textures had long been heard of in English markets.[113] Konkan had several *'mart cities'*.[114]

From these mart cities rice, green ginger, sugarcane, sesame oil, wheat, jackfruits, mangoes, coconuts, arecanuts were exported. Chinaware mirrors, gold and silver ornaments were imported from Venice.[115] During the sixteenth century, coconuts were exported in large quantities from Chaul, while dates and horses were imported. Chaul was famous for its cotton fabrics. Silks were in great demand beyond the seas. In the seventeenth century, spices, coconuts, timbers, roofing tiles were exported from Konkan coast to Sindh and Kathaiwar. On their return journey the merchants brought back dry fruits and horses.[116] All this attracted the innovative entrepreneurs of England to form the East India Company in 1599. The following year the Company of traders was granted a Royal Charter from the Queen of England, which gave it the exclusive rights to carry on English trade in the East.[117] Little did the East India Company know that it was destined to be the 'Mistress of India.'[118]

South Konkan- It's Acquisition by the East India Company

The first to land in the Indian waters were the Portuguese. The other maritime nations became conscious of the fruitfulness of the new venture of these adventurous traders. The Dutch were successful in breaking the Portuguese monopoly by following an entry into the Indian waters. The French soon followed suit. This kindled the English spirit of defiance. The English had to compete with the Portuguese, the Dutch, the French who had already conquered certain parts and established their base on the west coast. There were also strong local forces like the Marathas, the Siddis, and the Angrias who had to be dealt with. But within a span of 150 years, the British who came as traders established themselves as political masters and finally became the empire builders.

To establish themselves, the British had to put in tremendous efforts. But at the same time, the fact cannot be ignored that partly circumstances, partly European rivalry and greatly luck favored the Company to establish itself as a Political power.

Surat was the first possession that put the company on firm footing. It was made available to the East India

Company about 1609 after bartering English goods carried by the Surat vessels passing the straits. The Portuguese were strong at this time in Surat. The Portuguese did not allow Jehangir to give firman to the East India Company to start trade in Surat. Angered by Jehangir's refusal to give firman Sir Henry Middleton sailed to the straits of Bab-el-Mandeb in the Red Sea and by force bartered English goods for those carried by the Surat vessels passing the straits. Further he extorted huge sums before he set the vessels free. J.C.Powell rightly said 'What could not be obtained by diplomacy was now gained by a display of what sea power meant.'[119]

On October 20,1612, The East India Company concluded a treaty with the Governor of Ahmedabad and the Nawab of Surat for the establishment of commercial relations on the western coast of India. This treaty was further confirmed on January 6, 1613 by the Moghul Emperor Jehangir by sending a firman to the Governor of Ahmedabad.[120] Thus the British trade with India almost from its inception became the monopoly of a Corporate body-The East India Company. On June 23, 1661 the King of Portugal gave to Charles II, the king of Great Britain the Port and island of Bombay as a marriage dowry of Infanta Catherine. The island was rented out to The East India Company and this increased the importance of the island and the Company.[121] This was the first actual possession of the Company in India.[122]

Need for Supremacy in Shipbuilding

When Bombay became the main British entrepot on the west coast, the accession of the ports on the west coast was necessary for the establishment of the British marine supremacy on the sea. The Bombay government had to make efforts to extend the area of its settlements on the coast of Konkan in its attempts to secure trade. From the political point of view of geographical contiguity, the East India Company's closest neighbours from Bombay were the Marathas, the Siddis, and the Portuguese. It is these powers, which had the hold on Konkan. North Konkan was under the control of the Portuguese, while the Dutch and the French who had established them in the Seventeenth Centuries dominated South Konkan. Shivaji, the Maratha ruler had chosen a Konkan hill-fort as his capital. After the decline of the Maratha Power the *Konkanasth Brahmins* also called as *Chitapavans* inherited Konkan and Deccan. Thus although Konkan by itself was no more than a coastal region, yet played a significant role because it possessed one of the greatest centers of modern commerce due to the proximity to Bombay. When some territory of Konkan was to be acquired from Bajirao Peshwa II, the last of the Maratha rulers in 1817, Mountstuart Elphinstone told Evan Nepean, the Governor of Bombay that the most desirable area to be acquired was the Konkan coast. He said that

'It (Konkan) was geographically closer to Bombay, it had the men who could be recruited for the Bombay army, it was the strong hold of Peshwas and above all, its acquisition would help the East India Company control of the entire west coast of India.'[123]

There were constant rivalries between the Marathas, the Angrias and the British in the power politics of Konkan. They had to face other European rivals also. With the growth of power on the western coast, their progress in the overseas commerce would speed up. With the vulnerability of British shipping to attacks by belligerent raiders and the local rulers, the Company's defense commitments increased.[124] Thus these Pacific traders found it necessary to indulge in warlike activities, to annex territories, conclude treaties establish settlements to rule over their enclaves to ensure commercial gain. The Company's Charter was also modified by King Charles II to suit their changed policies.

'Power was given to the Company to seize and send home interlopers; to wage war and conclude peace with non-Christian princes and to appoint Governors who in conjunction with their Councils were to exercise civil and criminal jurisdiction at the various settlements'.[125]

The year 1613 also marked the beginning of an era of British progress in their chequered establishment of their empire in India. It was during this year that the East India Company's Marine with armed merchantmen manned by sailor-cum-traders was born.[126] The history of the Bombay Marine began when a squadron was formed.[127] Its main objectives were to protect the interests of the East India

Company from the threat posed by the Dutch, the Portuguese, and the so-called pirates of the western coast of India.[128]

The Bombay Marine was an important adjunct of the military establishment of the Company. The duties of the service were distinctly defined. In peacetime, it protected trade, suppressed pirates, convoyed transport and troops and carried out maritime surveys. It was however the main bulwark against the enemy attack during wars. The ships built were useful both in wars as well as in commerce.[129] The Company at first chartered ships but later decided to build its own. It was necessary to take this step because the ship owners in London charged extraordinary rates. Great Britain had to prove to the world that it was a sea power and shipping was its lifeline. Ashok Mehta said, 'The British came to India as traders and remained as rulers, but in that magical metamorphosis they never relaxed their hold over the sea-the carrying trade had to become their Monopoly' and this led to their shipping interest and more and more ships were built time and again.[130]

'Scaleby' was the first ship that sailed to Great Britain in the Company's service loaded with rice and food grains. It impressed the British Government so much that it authorized the Company to build ships from Indian teak.[131] India offered every resource for shipbuilding. Large quantities of teak wood were available in many parts of western India. Pegu or Moulmein teak was also available in Calcutta. Teak timber was good for Wales, clamps, spirkitting, plank-sheet of the topsides and bottom of ships. Saul timber was useful for the outside plank and plank of the decks. There was yet another type of timber, namely, the Morang Saul and it was useful for keels, sternposts, and beams. Sisoo was suitable for parts where it could be kept dry or where toughness was required, such as caps, drum heads of capstands. *Jarool, toon, poon*s also were suitable for shipbuilding. Coir was famous for its elasticity and lightness. *Ejoo* was praised for its durability. *Sunn* was well known for it's over all superiority.[132]

The next hundred years witnessed ups and downs in shipping by the Company as a complex of forces worked to end their monopoly. Some of the obstacles were as follows-the problems created by the ship owners of London, increased cost of shipping, constant struggles with the rivals both local and European, internal problems in the company and such several others. But they set forth preparing against all odds to accomplish their interests in future.

In 1735 under the Company's patronage, shipbuilding was started in Bombay. Timber was procured from the nearby forests of Ratnagiri, Salsette and Thane along with the Malabar and Canara forests. Lowji Nussarwanji Wadia, the first master builder of Bombay dockyard, was brought by the Company from Surat. After him, his family contributed to the ship building industry and between 1735 and 1837, the Company appointed Lowjee, Mansekjee and Bomanjee, Jamsetjee and Ruttonjee, Janmsetjee and Nowronjee and nowrojee and Cursetjee thus making the master builder's office a hereditary one.[133] By the beginning of the nineteenth century, the Bombay Government with the help of the ship building establishment spared no pains to increase its *fleet, ships, grabs, galleys, sloops, frigates, manchuas* to suit various requirements of the Company.[134]

The Growth of British Power in South Konkan

Rajapur (1637-38)

The political accomplishments started by the British in a few isolated places in the Konkan since the seventeenth and eighteenth centuries continued unabated. It was in about 1637-38 that the East India Company started its activities in Rajapur in Konkan. Rajapur was in those days described as a place, which lay up a long tidal creek, in the independent Kingdom of Bijapur about half way between Goa and the modern city to Bombay.[135] During mid eighteenth centuries, the Arab traders with Rajapur were carrying off all the best timber near Ratnagiri and along Muchkundi River to Zanzibar and the African coast.[136] The British opened a factory at Rajapur for its cardamom and pepper trade in about 1649.[137] But again because of the Maratha and Mughal problems they had to abandon the factory in 1678-79.[138] It then became a strong hold of the Angrias but was invaded by Khemsawant who burnt four of Angria grabs that sunk in the Rajapur River.[139]

Suvarnadurg (1755)

The activities of The East India Company slowly but steadily started increasing. In 1755, Commondor James was deputed to root out the nests of piracy that lay along the Maratha coasts. The expedition began with a plan to bring the island fort of Suvarnadurg under its control. Commondor James set sail for Suvarnadurg from Bombay on 22 March 1755 with the ship *Protector.* It had 44 guns, a ketch of 16 guns and two bomb vessels. The Maratha fleet had *gurabs* and *galbats* and had 10,000 men. The *Protector* chased the Maratha fleet for a long distance yet the *gurabs* and the *galbats* could sail faster than the English ships because of their skills at the oars. After a tough fight, the Angrias surrendered on 8 April 1755 with the ship *Protector.* It had 44 guns, a ketch of 16 guns and two bomb vessels. The Maratha fleet had *gurabs* and *galbats* and had 10,000 men. The *Protector* chased the Maratha fleet for a long distance yet the *gurabs* and the *galbats* could sail faster than the English ships because of their skills at the oars. After a tough fight, the Angrias surrendered on 8 April 1755. Thus Commondor James succeeded in capturing Suvarnadurg situated a few miles south of the Bankot River. After the capture of Suvernadurg, two Company's cruisers were employed on the coast for the protection of trade. These cruisers were used mainly to cruise between Suvernadurg and Malvan.[140]

Vijaydurg, Himmatgad (Fort Victoria at Bankot), Ratnagiri, Rasulgad (1756)

Fort Victoria at Bankot at the mouth of the Savitri had ravines and watercourses and was clothed with fine teak. Curved teak logs highly priced as 'Bankot knees' were largely exported to Bombay. The Angrias had large ship-building yards.[141]

The Angrias, the chieftains of Kolaba, had the iron grip on Vijaydurg and Himmatgad (Fort Victoria). They were also strong on the western Indian coast and their acts of piracy hampered the trade of the British. They were, according to the British reports a stiff-necked race, born and begotten of sea and filled with energy.[142] Angria's exploits were always a threat to the British trade. They had to keep a special fleet to act against the Angria attacks on sea and

The Maratha Admiral Kanhoji Angre

Source: K.Shridharan, *A Maritime History of India*, Publication Ministry of Information & Broadcasting, New Delhi, 1965.

it cost them about 50,000 Pounds a year.[143] In 1748, a sloop for the factory at Anjengo was built. In 1749 the marine force had to be made strong to protect its trading activities on the Malabar coast against the Angrias. *'Revenge'* was a cruiser built in 1755. The Bombay Council informed the Court of Directors in London that the *'Revenge'* commanded by William Dicks sailed even better than the *'Bombay Grab.'* In the same year the *'Kent'* and the *'Cumberland'* were repaired ready to face the enemy on the sea.[144] Some other ships of the time were *Success, Charlotte, Bombay, Bengal, Derby, Restoration, and Ockham.*

The ship *'success'* was seized by Kanoji Angre in 1717 when Capt. Charles Boone attacked the naval force at Vijaydurg. The British ship being heavy could not enter the harbour and at last Kanoji's forces repulsed his attack. Kanoji also seized *Charlotte,* the British vessel in 1720. The British joined hands with the Portuguese yet the combined

Ships of Marathas

forces could not hold on before the Angre's ships. Kanoji's power thus on the Konkan coast was unchallenged. The *Derby,* the *Restoration,* the *Severn,* the *Pilot,* the *Augusta,* the *Dadabhoy,* the *Rose,* the *Anne,* the *Fatte Daulat,* the *Bombay,* the *William,* the *Ockham* and several others were lost in quick succession between 1728 and1738.[145] Kanoji died sometime in 1728 (There is a controversy regarding the date of his death.) But after his death, Sukhoji and then Sambhaji carried on the warfare. Later it was Tulaji who put up a brave fight till he was forced to surrender because of the alliance of the Peshwa with the British.

Thus it is found that the Maratha Navy, which was not a threat to the British at sea in the initial stages, soon overcame its teething troubles and started operating off the Konkan coast with increasing success. Many *grabs, gallivats, galbats* were built. These were the unique Maratha war ships and were built by the Angrias. Some of the types of ships were *galbat, gurab, machava, pagar, pal, toru.* They were the war ships having masts. The *gullivats* were large rowboats built like the *grabs* that did not exceed 70 tons.[146] The pals were the biggest Maratha ships. There were the *Sibadis* also ships built at Jaygad, Vijaydurg sailing from Malabar and Bombay ports carrying goods from Konkan and returning with timber. During the rainy season they would take shelter at Ratnagiri. The crew often belonged to the Bhandari and Muslim community. The *sibadis* were smooth sailors in wild weather. So they accompanied the *pals* and *gurabs* in case of action with light armaments. If the ships were built at Malvan or Devgad, they would be named after the place namely ship of Malvan or ship of Devgad.[147]

Below are given some of the extracts taken from the unpublished documents in the Peshwa Daftar and show the naval fights on sea and acts of piracy:

> *'Naval Subha of fort Vijaydurg in charge of Anand Rao Dhulap, debit as Durbar expenditure. Pals, gurabs and galbats were sent on an expedition to the South. They came across some English ships of Bombay near Ratnagiri. An engagement took place lasting for three hours. Some of the Maratha ships were damaged and lost their war material...later they were weather beaten...'*[148]

Another extract shows the attack of the Marathas

'English ships of Bombay were proceeding to Karnatak. They were attacked by the Marathas near Ratnagiri. In the engagement the Marathas captured five ships of the English along with the Captain and the Councillor (kosildar)...'[149]

Thus Vijaydurg or the Gheria was the stronghold of the Angrias and Tulaji Angria as described earlier was the most dreaded Admiral on the west coast. Therefore the Europeans called Vijaydurg as the *'Gibraltar of Konkan'*. After capturing Suvarnadurg, the English with the help of the Peshwas turned their attention towards the reduction of Vijaydurg. Meanwhile the Peshwa had shown keen interest in the possession of Vijaydurg. At last under the leadership of Admiral Watson, Gheria was attacked on 12th February 1756. With the capture of Gheria, the power of the Angrias was finally crushed. The fleet of the Angrias consisting of three masts ships carrying 20 guns each, nine two masted ships carrying 12 to 16 guns, 13 gullivats carrying 6 to 10 guns 30 others were involved by the Bombay Marine.

The letter written by the Bombay Council to Robert Clive and Samuel Hough shows the infuriation the Angrias gave to the British shipping.

'It is probable that Toolajee Angria may offer to capitulate and probably offer a sum of money; But you are to consider that this fellow is not on a footing with any prince in the known world, he being a pirate in whom no confidence can be put, not only taking, destroying ships of all nations, but even vessels belonging to the Natives, which have his own passes, and for which he has annually collected large sums of money. Should he offer any sum of money, it must be a very great one that will pay for the many rich ships he has taken. Besides the innumerable smaller ones, we will remember the 'Charlotte' bound from hence to China, belonging to Madras; the 'William' belonging to Bombay, from Bengal; the 'Severn' a Bengal freight ship for Bussorah, value nine or ten lakhs of Rupees: the 'Derby' belonging to the Honorable Company with the grab 'Restoration', value Rupees 5,22, 743; the sloop 'Pilot' and the 'Augasta'; also the 'Dadabhoy' from Surat, the 'Rose' from Mangalore, grab'Anne' from Gomroon, the 'Benjimolly' from the Malabar coast and the 'Fatte Dawlalat' from Muscat'.[150]

Meanwhile Siddis of Janjira who were the Admirals of the Nizamshahi and then the Adilshahi finally to be the

Moghul Admirals were interested in parts belonging to the Marathas. There were constant fights between the Siddis and the Marathas over the territories of Kolaba in the north and Chiplun and Anjanvel in the South. It included important Raigad and some important coasts such as Chaul, Thal, Rewas, Bankot, Dabhol and Anjanvel.[151] They laid siege to Bankot in January 1734. But the Maratha Udaji Pawar recovered Bankot on 8 March 1734. At various internal struggles the English and the Portuguese came to the help of the Siddis, as they did not want the Marathas to become powerful in the Konkan.[152] On 19 March 1755, in return for the possession of Vijaydurg, the Marathas agreed to hand over the villages of Bankot (Bankot) and Himmutgur (Himmatgad or Fort Victoria as it was called in 1756).[153] Thus Bankot fell into the hands of the British.[154] But it was only on August 5, 1803 that Bankot and its dependencies were finally given to The East India Company by the Marathas. Ramji Pant, the Subedar who was deputed on the job, took possession of Bankot and called the upper fort as Fort Victoria. At the same time Ramji Pant informed that Anjanvel, Ratnagiri and Rasulgad surrendered to him.[155]

A treaty was signed between the British and the Marathas and it shows how the Peshwa, to a great extent was responsible in making the Maratha fleet weak. In his rivalry with Tulaji Angria, the Peshwa took the help of the British to settle matters, instead of dealing with the enemy himself. The following were the Articles of Agreement for an expedition against Tulaji Angria settled in 1755 between R.Bourchier, Governor of Bombay and Ramjee Pant Subedar on behalf of his Master Nana (Balajee Baji Rao) Pandit Pradhan, General of the Marathas. The terms of the treaty that proved ruinous for the Peshwa were as follows.

1. That all the Marine shall be immediately under the command of the English and the management of all affairs both by land and sea, carried on by the approbation of both parties.
2. All vessels whatever that may be taken from Toolaji Angria shall be equally divided between the English and the Marathas, except the 'Restoration', which is to be the sole property of the English.
3. Bankot and Himmatgad, with the river belonging thereto and with 5 villages to the Southward of the said river, to be diverted to the English as the

Maratha Grabs and Gallivats attacking an English Ship

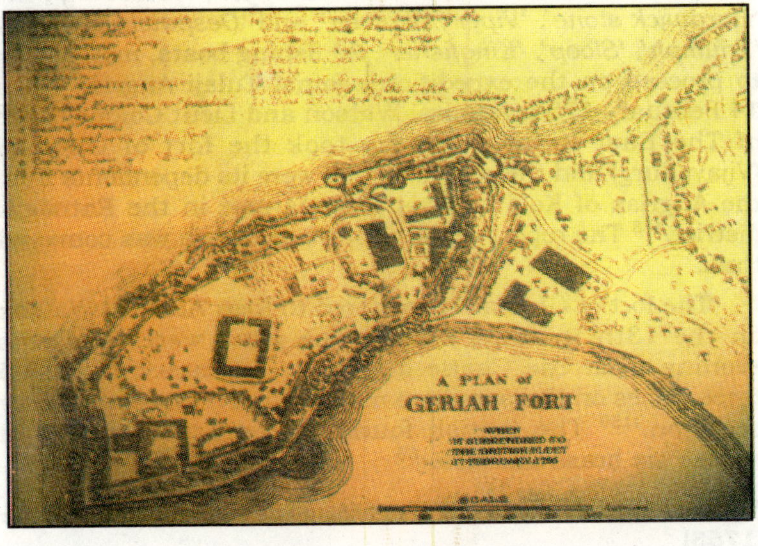

Surrender of Gheriah or Vijaydurg Fort by Capt. Watson in 1756

Source: B.K.Apte, *A History of the Maratha Navy and Merchantships*, State Board for Literature and Culture, Bombay, 1972.

Honorable Company's property for ever and the Marathas not to levy any additional inland duties.

4. The English engage to keep the sea, and prevent Angrias' fleet from throwing succours into any place that may be attacked but at this season only Soovernadroog, Unjanvel, and Vijaydroog.
5. All ammunitions, guns and other stores may be taken in the several forts of the Angria territories to belong entirely to the Marathas.
6. If Manajee's territories are jointly attached, the fort of Khuderee with its harbour to be delivered to the Honorable Company with villages Revas, Ranjunkar, Sarul, Shamy, Kolgaon, Donbaren, Kihim and Avas.
7. Any other Article that may be necessary to be agreed upon, to be settled between the government and the Nana Pundit Pradhan.

The job of acquiring Gheria was given to Commondore Watson. About 8 in the morning Rear Admiral Watson and Rear Admiral Brook sailed with the *'Tyger'*, *'Salusbury'*, the *'Hardwick stone'*, *'Viper'*, *'Warren'*, and *'Despatch Kethches'* *'Triumph'*, *'Sloop'*, *'Kingfisher'*, 20 fishing boats, men of war to proceed on the expedition against Tulaji Angria.[157] On 14 February 1756, Admiral Watson and Lieut Colonel Clive of The East India Company took the fort of Gheriah (Vijayadurg) and the places, which were its dependents from the Angrias of Kolaba. This place is now in the Ratnagiri district.[158] The report of the capture of Gheria was conveyed thus:

'The fort of Gheria surrendered to Rear Admiral Watson on the 13th instant. Twenty one guns were fired this evening from the Castle and their military discharged three vollies on the parade to manifest our joy on this happy occasion.'[159] The British found 250 guns, ten lakhs of rupees six brass mortars.[160]

Malvan (Sindhudurg or Fort Augaustus) and Vengurla (1765)

The capture of Gheria or Vijaydurg, the strong hold of Angres on 14 February did not entirely remove the menace of the Maratha sea power on the Arabian sea. The *'Malvans'*, the so-called Piratical Associations according to the British (Its sea-faring community derived from it the appellation of '*Malvans*' and other foreigners attained considerable power and committed piracies especially from the forts of Sindhudurg, Padamdurg (water fort of Kansa) and Redi (the fort that lay on the rising ground 20 miles south of Malvan and the Vengurla rocks and 16 miles north of Goa.[161]

About Sindhudurg fort, L.Smith wrote that though the fort was small yet, its possession would give the government an influence over the immediate chieftains below the ghats while it would effectively prevent piracy in all the neighbouring ports.[162] About Rajekot, he said that it was situated on the main point of the bay of Malvan and commanded the beach and town on three sides. Vengurla, he said, embraced a circle of six hundred yards but was important. Newty was a port on the point between and in sight of Malvan and Vengurla. Although the territory of Malvan from its inconsiderable extent could not be of great importance as a settlement to Bombay, yet it would be a check upon directions from the native armies and would prove to be a depot for recruiting.[163]

The Angrias had built ship building yards and even docks at Malvan. As early as 1680, Kanoji Angria had sown the teak called *Bandh Tiwra*. He had also taken care to preserve the forests at Malvan, Dhamapur, and Pendur.[164] These yards built small crafts only and were valuable to the service in the growth of teak, coir and hemp. Masura in Malvan was famous for rice, Varada grew rice and dry grains, and Malundy grew dry grains, hemp and some rice.[165] Therefore besides the suppression of the Malvans, there was one more motive behind capturing the Fort Augustus. A very important view in settling at the Fort Augustus was to promote trade. This in particular would help sale of woolens and Europe staples and give every possible encouragement to the merchants who lived there.[166]

Khem Sawant was the Chieftain of Malvan in 1755. As a young leader, he engaged himself in struggles with the Portuguese, the Kolhapur Raja and other powers. The East India Company eventually decided to root out the Malvans. The following armed forces were to be employed in this expedition.

(a) Military Forces: 470 European Infantry, 100 Lascars, 271 Native Infantry, and 70 Artillery.

(b) Naval Forces: The Revenge Cruiser -24 guns, the

Bombay Grab Cruiser- 28 guns, the Asia Europe ship, the Eagle Snow with 10 inches mortar, two Drake Ketches with an 8 inch mortar each, 3 Gallivats, the Euphrates sloop, a Protector's Launch with 4 1/2 inches cohorn, 2 flat bottomed boats, 1 Scooner, and 1 hospital and store ship.[167]

Major Gordon and Commander Watson were appointed for the Expedition against the Malvans. They proceeded on January 12, 1765.[168] These two Officers were instructed to inform the government if keeping the possession of the Malvan fort would be of any public utility and if so what would be the expenses involved to maintain it.[169] They were also asked to report the expenses of demolishing the principal fort if it was not beneficial.

It was reported by J.Watson that a considerable trade might be carried on here, as it lay most conveniently situated for the trading towns of the interior parts of India. Vittul Pandurang who kept the accounts perfectly acquainted with the other Subedars and neighbouring powers felt that demolishing of the fort would prove a work of labour and expense. The expense of demolishing moreover would amount to 1,30,000 rupees and it would also require about a year to get the work finished during which time 1,200 barrels of gunpowder would be required for the demolition.[170]

John Gordon further said that he collected information from various sources and was told that the *Juggar* or revenue of the tract of territory amounted to about 20,000 Rupees a year, 1,000 candies of rice and wood, straw for the fort. Both the officers felt that it was not advisable to demolish the fort.[171]

In 1765, the Company captured Sindhudurg Fort also known as Fort Augustus with its dependencies at Malvan from the Kolhapur Raja. They also took Redi or Rairi from the Sawantwadi rulers.[172] But on 12 Jan 1766, the Sindhudurg fort was returned to the Kolhapur State on condition to desist himself from obstructing British commerce and navigation and by the payment of Rs. 3,82,896 with permission to start a factory at Rajkote (Rajkote).[173] At the same time Rairi or Redi was returned to the Sawantwadi rulers on payment of Rs. 2,00,000 and with a permission to construct a factory at Redi.[174] However, the treaty signed was not followed and new settlements were made. The Malvan fort was evacuated in May 1766 and Fort Redi at the beginning of 1767.[175] The trading activities were started by the Company. The British started settling in this part. This provided ample opportunities for them to know the economic and political conditions at close quarters. They could get first hand knowledge of the methods of revenue collection.

On 1 October 1812, the Kolhapur Raja gave full sovereignty of the harbour of Malvan. This included the fort and island of Sindhudurg, the fort of *Puddumghur* (Padamgadh), *Rajkote,* and *Surajcote* (Sarjakot) with their dependencies, now in the Ratnagiri districts. In return the Company agreed to protect the Raja of Kolhapur if he ceded the territories of Malvan, Sindhudurg fort, Paddumgad fort and Sarjekot fort. It was also agreed that the revenue collected from the locals as well as the neighbouring territories would go to the Company's treasury. The terms of the treaty were notified to the people. To the people's queries as to where they should go if the forts had to be vacated, he replied that they could go to the nearby places and settle at Rangan and Bhudargad if they so wished. There were four ships which belonged to the Raja. They were sold to the merchants with the permission of the Company. It was L. Smith, the officer who took charge of the Malvan.[176]

The strategic importance of Malvan was reported that its inconsiderable extent could never be of great importance as a settlement to Bombay, yet it had some objects of consequence. It acted as considerable check upon directions from the native armies and was likely to prove as a good dèpot for recruiting. Although as maritime station it had not so many advantages, affording safe approach and anchorage to small crafts only, it was valuable from the point of growth of teak, coir and hemp and possessed some articles which were capable of being increased. So a non-commissioned officer's guard was establish on the bank of Karli creek which would afford the best means overawing the Newty boats, preventing any forbidden ride and securing Malvan duties.[177]

An army was stationed in the Malvan. Thus The East India Company's politics from 1812 to 1818 revolved around Malvan. Among the Residents appointed by the government, the most important were L. Smith and J.J. Sparrow. These Residents were given exclusive rights of the territory. During the tenure of L. Smith great help was rendered by a local lawyer by name Devji Naik and therefore on the recommendation of L.Smith, the government appointed him as the right hand of L. Smith.[178]

L. Smith, as the Resident of Malvan gave a detailed account of the establishment, the custom duties collected, the imports and exports and the population and traders of Malvan. It is as follows:

The following establishment was provided when L.Smith was appointed as the Resident of Malvan. 2000 armed forces, 130 tanks, 6 tanks of 9 pounds at Sindhudurg, 1 tank of 6 pounds at Rajekot, 12 European Officers-in-charge of the tanks at Sindhudurg to protect the port towns of Malvan and Vengurla. This shows the interest the Company had in acquiring places. They did have a good trade and yielded handsome revenue to the government. Besides this, the Company wished to control the pirates who hampered the trade.[179]

Land Customs, exports[180]

Table 1.2

		Qrs	Ans
Bombay salt per bullock.	@	-	2
Malvan salt per bullock but 25% to be deducted.	@	-	-
Kopra or dry coconut per bullock load	@	1	2
Supari per bullock load.	@	1	2
Dry dates per bullock load.	@	1	2
Allum bullock load.	@	1	2
Dum sole(?) bullock load.	@	1	2
Coconut bullock load.	@	1	-
Kaut bullock load.	@	1	-
Coir bullock load.	@	1	-
Kuped kar (?) bullock load.	@	1	-
Putting wood bullock load.	@	2	-
Sugar bullock load.	@	2	-
Black pepper bullock load.	@	2	-
Ginger bullock load.	@	2	-
Sandle wood bullock load.	@	1	-
Brimstone bullock load.	@	1	2
Kavaul Bullock load.	@	1	-
Hulud or turmerick bullock load.	@	1	-
Golaol bullock load.	@	1	-
Ambi halad bullock load.	@	1	-
Plumbs bullock load.	@	2	-
Kismis or raisin bullock load.	@	2	-
Almond bullock load.	@	2	-
Ackrood or dry walnut bullock load.	@	2	-
Chin owun(?) bullock load.	@	2	-

Three percent upon valuation amount was added Cloves, nutmegs, mace, silk thread, lead, copper, iron, steel, hing, ivory, or elephant teeth, and vermilion, @ rate of 3 percent upon the amount of valuation was added.

Duty upon the import and export goods by sea @ 2 % valuation or upon the market price of Malvan.

Table 1.3

	Rs.	Qrs.	Ans.
Import duty on Bombay salt per ana	0	3	0
Malvan salt export duty per Bhara	0	1	0

Table 1.4 : Land Custom Imports[181]

	QRS	ANS	PICE
Sandle Wood And Black Pepper.	@	1	2
Bang Per Bullock Load.	@	1	
Cotton Thread Per Bullock Load.	@	3	
Cotton Per Bullock Load.	@	3	
Salt Petre Per Bullock Load.	@	1	
Coarse Cloth Upto 15 Rs Value To Be Charged Half Duty		1	
The Same Cloth When Bought By The Merchants Of This Place Only To Be Charged Half Duty Or			
Chilly Per Bullock Load.	@	1	1
Jaggery Per Bullock Load.	@	1	2
Tobacco Per Maund.	@	1	2

The above tables regarding the produce of export and import had been trifling as its harbour was blocked throughout the year. The duties indeed, upon all trade appeared to be anticipated and sold as temporary supplies of money. The arrack of tobacco farms alone may be calculated at Rs 5000. The saltpans were government property and were annually repaired and let out upon profit of about 1/3 of the produce. The coconut trees also were government property in some places like Sindhudurg.

The next Resident of Malvan was J.J. Sparrow who took office on 25 January 1813, when he wished to extend the power to *Masure, Pat, Varad tarfs.* These tarfs were under the control of the Sawant Wadi State. Col. Docksey marched against *Masura, Varad, and Maland* and defeated the Rani's army. Further, his army was stationed there till 14 March 1814 to avoid any disturbances.[182] Thus by 1814 almost all parts in and around Malvan were taken over by J.J.Sparrow. They were as follows:

- Tarf Masure (11 villages): Masure, Kandalgaon, Chaufe, Amberi, Ambdos, Salel, Malvan, Salgaon, Khed, Verale, Idi, Devli.
- Tarf Maland (17 villages): Maland, Dagmode, Borliye, Aasorde, Vadache Pat, Kirlok, Shiravde, Khotle, Chunavare, Asgani, Hendul, Popiya, Masde, Rativade, Hivale, Golvan.
- Tarf Varad (8 villages): Varad, Kalase, Talagaon, Nandos, Dhamapur, Pendur, Parad, Kuvabe.
- Vengurla Port.

The 37 villages were brought under the district of Malvan. Till 1814 the Officer was designated as the 'Resident'. When it was made a taluka, the designation was 'Resident and Collector' and he was authorized with both civil and military powers.[183]

As early as 1814, The Company inserted an advertisement about its rights over the ports. An advertisement inserted shows how the Company wished to control the trade of the ports and land. 'Europeans of whatever rank, description or country, who shall be discovered passing through the territories under this Presidency, without being furnished with passport will be taken into custody, and confined until pleasure of government shall be known...' This was published by the order of the Honorable the Governor in Council, W Newnham, Secretary to government on 30 June 1814.'[184]

The Interference of The East India Company in the affairs of the Malvan greatly annoyed Rani Durgabai who wished to have the Malvan territories for herself. But the Company was hell bent upon taking them. The Rani did not give up her territories easily and there continued correspondence between the Rani and the Company. Piracy also continued despite the caution taken by the Company.

D. Bhosale informing J.A. Dunlop that Rani Durgabai Should hand over the person imprisoned to the East India Company

ले. १४५
No.

श. १७३६ मार्गशीर्ष शु. २
इ. १८१४ डिसेंबर १३

अजम ज्यान आद्रेव दंडलोप रिसिडेंट
सुभा जंजिरे सिंधुदुर्ग दाम मोहब्बतहू

मोहिबानपन्हा मखलिसानदस्तगाः

आजी दुर्गाबाई भोसले सरदेसाई प्रांत कुडाल व माहालानिहाये येथील नेकी जाणोन मोहिबी आपली कारनेकी करीत जावें दिगर मोहिबी खत पाठविलें तें पोहचून कलमी केला मजमून मालूम जाहाला अर्जुन फटकुरा व कृष्णाजी निर्गुण व बाबू सारंग वगैरे याणी समुद्रांत चोरी केली त्यास निर्गुण यास येथे कैदीत ठेऊन फटकुरा व बरकंद सिपाय यांचे स्वादीन करावे म्हणोन कलमे केले आशास कृष्णाजी निर्गुण याणें गोव्यात चोरी केली असे बामणो गोपाळ यास समजल्यावरून त्याणे कैद करून ठेविला आहे फटकुरा गेल्या च्यार रोजांत वाडीत आला होता असा पत्ता लागतों परंत तो येथे राहिला नाही निघोन गेला त्याजकडेस चोरीचा कज्या असे समजांत आल्यास दस्त होता बाबू सारंग व राम सारंग व सातरडेच्या किरिस्तांव व आणिखी कुठे तं चोरीस असतील त्याची चौकसी सातरडे वगैरा गांवी दोन रोजांत केली परंत त्याचा पत्ता लागत नाहीं .... ही शोध करीत आहों मिलाल्यास कैदीत ठेऊन मोहिबांस मालूम होईल मोहिबांकडील आदमी इंग्यानिशांच्या आमलांत फिरत आसतात त्यास ते चोर सापडल्यास दस्त करून त्यांचे इंग्यानीचा तर्फेने अटक पडणार नाही कृष्णाजी निर्गुण कैदीत आहे त्याजकडेस रुजवातीचे कारण पडल्यास कलमें व्हावें म्हणजे रवाना होईल चोरास आश्रय इंग्यानीत देणार नाहीत हे दिलात आसावें वेंगुर्लें येथील बागायती * ठिकाणास आटक जाहल्याच मार पेशजीच्या खतात कलमे केला आहे त्याचा जबाब ठिकाणाची मोकलीक होऊन पाठवावा रा। छ ३० जिल्हेज (?) ज्यादा काय लिहिणें महबत असों दीजे हे किताबत

True copy signed J- A: Dunlop Resident
True copy signed J. A. Dunlop Resident
C. Schengler Envoy.
1815 In a letter from Envoy at Goa dated D 31st May R 23d June

Exchange of Letters between Rani Durgabai and EIC Letter No.145

Source: G.H. Khare, *Aithihasik Marathi Sadhane,* Bharat Itihas Samshodhan Mandal, Pune,1983

The Company blamed the Rani and wrote to her to punish the culprits but the Rani would convince the Company by writing back to them that the peóple of her territory had no hand in it. One such letter is given below.

> *'I have sent an answer to Mountstuart Elphinstone's letter in regard to the acts of piracy at Rairee. I can assure you that nothing of the kind will take place, this you will recollect the boats which are fitted out there for the purpose of transporting my people from thence to Wadi likewise from Newtee to Rairee on account roads being stopped between the two places by the disputes existing in my country. It will be in your recollection that my ports are free for trade...'*[185]

Another port that interested The East India Company was Vengurla. Vengurla sometimes called those days as *Vingorle, Vengurla* was an important Port of cali for ships coming from places like Japan, Ceylon, Bantam, Persian Gulf during the mid-seventeenth century.[186] It embraced only a circle of six hundred yards but was of a strategic importance. Newtee was a port of point between and in sight of the Malvan and vengurla. In 1766, the fort of Vengurla was ceded to the Company for a period of 13 years. The taking possession of Vengurla was reported thus:

> *'Mr. Mostyn, his having embarked 50 sepoys on board the Eagle previous to which he had ordered Colsim Naiques to go, but after asking them singly, only four were willing, he had therefore discharged the rest which he hoped he would approve and acquaint us of his having the 5th instant gone to Vengurla and took formal possession of it in the Honorable Company's name leaving English colours and 20 sepoys confirmable to the treaty with the Bouncello (Bhonsales)' Again on 4 June 1780, the State of Sawantwadi took back the fort of Vengurla.*[187]

It is found that the isolated parts of Konkan and their forts were shuttling between the Company's and the Maratha's Power. The company benefitted a great deal because it made money in this process.[188]

The British were vexed by two characters who were notorious according to them by name Babji Gopal and Sambhaji Govind who belonged to Vengurla and became an

J.A. Dunlop informs Rani Durgabai Bhosale that for the continuation of the friendship between them, everybody must abide by the Mutual agreement.

ले. १३६ }
No. }

{ श. १७३५ फा. वद ६
{ इ. १८१४ मार्च १२

अजम दुर्गाबाई भोसले सरदेसाई प्रांत कुडाळ व मालवण ताजे सलाम मोहबत
व मोहिबानम्हा: मुश्फिशानदस्त गांहा———आजी दिक बेलयस
ज्यान अद्रेव दडलॉप रिसिदेंट मुंबई बंजिरें सिंधुदुर्ग येथील खैरखुशी नेकी जाणोन
हमेस्त्या कळले करीत गेले पाहिजे दरीविलो मोहिबाकडील लोक म्हणोन मोहिबाचे
नाव सांगोन मोहिबाकडील सरदार यांचे लोक तर्फ वराड व तर्फ मालोंडी येथे बहुलत
म्हणोन येतात आण गावकर व रयेत यासी सांगतात जे सरकार कुंपनीचें हुकमतीने
तुम्ही चालल्यास तुमचे बरे होणार नाही येसे धमकाऊन सांगोन जातात मोहिबाची
व सरकार कुंपनीची दोस्ती त्यापेक्षा येसे मोहिबाकडील लोक येऊन करितात तेव्हां
उभयेता सरकारामधे दिलगिरी होईल त्याकरिता दोस्तीचे जागां म्हणोन हे वर्तमान
तुम्हास समजावे या भावे कळवें केलें आहे तर्फ वराड व तर्फ मालोंडी हे येक
तर्फ करावे हे सरकार कुंपनीस जरूर आहे यांविसीचा सूर्ये हा मजकूर अजम
इस्कालेर साहेब यांणी मोहिबास पेसजीपासून दखल करीतच आले आहेत याकरिता
हा मजकूर फिरोन मोहिबास ईजानेबानि. लिहोन कळवावे येसे नाही एस येत
येस जो आम्हास आहेस आण सरकार कुंपनीने वचन दिले से मागे [illegible]

नाही हे सर्वांस जाहीर आहे [illegible] जाहीलोमें तर्फ वराड व तर्फ मालोंडी
येथे गांवगनामी देणेविसी ईजानेबास सरकारचा हुकूम आला होता त्या आदेशाचेची
तालीक मोहिबाकडेस पाठविली आहे त्यावरून मालूम होईल बंजिरेचा [illegible] तर्फ
घाट व तर्फ हवेली येथे आहे तो मोहिबानी घ्यावा आण तर्फ वराड व तर्फ
मालोंडी येथे मोहिबाकडील येवज आहे तो बंजिरा घ्यावा जाजती येवज मोहिबाचा
जाहालेस नाहि घ्यावा येसेहि होते [illegible] आमची काही दुसरी [illegible] नाही
[illegible] मोहिबाचीहि [illegible] होईल——— आमचे [illegible]
बदोबस्त [illegible] केला तो सदरहू [illegible] लिहिला आहे त्याजवरून [illegible]
मालूम होईल जो बदोबस्त जाहाला तो जाहालाच आण बाउपर मोहिबाकडील
दरबारची [illegible] आमचे सरकारची खुशी आहे सरकारचे दोस्त आहेत
त्यासी व सरकारचे रयेतेसी बदोबस्त केलाप्रमाणें येथास्थीत चालोन [illegible] न
केलेस त्यात उभयेता सरकारचा नफा आहे आण सरकारचीहि दोस्ती राहून दिवसे-
दिवस दोस्ती ज्यादा होऊन महबत ज्यादा होईल आमचे सरकारची व मोहिबाची
दोस्ती कसी चालावी ते सदरहू लिहिले आहे व हालीहि लिहितो जे त्याप्रमाणें
न करितां मोहिबी दुसरे तरेने चालोन कर्तव्य केलेस तुमची बहुत खराबी होईल
का जर सरकारची हद आहे त्यात मोहिबाकडून कांहिमात्र हरकत आमचे सरकार
होऊ देणार नाही मोहिबाकडील लोक तर्फ वराड व मालोंडी येथे बहुलतीस
आले होते. ते सरकारचे लस्करात लागले त्यास केदीत ठेविले आहेत ते लोक आपले
सोडून करें म्हणोन अजम रामचन्द्रराव खानोळकर हे मोहिबाचे [illegible] त्याचे
पत्र ईजानेबास आले होते त्याजवरून त्याजकडील लोक येसे समजले आण त्यास
पत्राचे उत्तर पाठविलें की मुंबईस सरकारांत लिहोन पाठविले आहे तेथून हुकूम
येईल त्याप्रमाणे होईल येसे उत्तर पाठविले त्यास मोहिबास लिहावयासी कारण की
येसे बंद काम दुसरेने कोणाकडून होऊ नये का म्हणाल तर मोहिबाचे हुकमानें
येसे काम जाहलेस इंग्रेज सरकार मोहिबाकडून आंदेसाउ भरून घेईल आगर तुमचे
हुकुमासिवाई मोहिबाचे रयतेनें अथवा लोकानें येसे काम केलेस त्याचे तारिफव
करणेंस मोहिबाकडेस आमचे सरकार मागेल आमचे सरकाराने बदोबस्त केला
त्याप्रमाणे तुम्ही राजी होऊन सर्वत्र लोकांस सदरहू प्रमाणे तालीद करून बदोबस्त
केल्या याप्रमाणें उतर येईपर्यंत मोहिबाचे पत्राचा मार्ग ईजानेब पाहात आहे ता ६
१९ माहे [illegible] ज्यादा काय लिहिणे प्यार मोहबत असो दीजे हे किताबत
मालवणचे बो कापी नकल [illegible]
यशवंत पांडुरंग निविस्ता शुद

Exchange of Letters between Rani Durgabai and EIC Letter No.136

Source: G.H. Khare, *Aithihasik Marathi Sadhane,* Bharat Itihas Samshodhan Mandal, Pune,1983

obstacle in the trade of the Company. A complaint was sent to Rani Durgabai by Mountstuart Elphinstone in which he informed her that Sambhaji Sawant Subedar Chandroba and Baubno Gopal Subedar had posted a party of sepoys at Console in the Bandive taraf for the purpose of levying a tax called *nandose zakat* from the merchants and interfered with the lands dependent on the fort of Nasirgadh which belonged to the Raja of Kolhapur and an ally to the British Government. It was further said that Baubno Gopal's people seized ill-treated the dak runner of the British Government. The British Government alone was entitled to collect the zakat of Nandose. The Rani was requested to withdraw her people from there and allow the British Government to collect the zakat. Thus many such complaints were lodged at various occasions.[189]

To put an end to the constant problems, the Company started negotiating with the Sawantwadi Subedar Chandroba. A letter regarding this shows the diplomacy of the British. The letter tells that Vengurla, an important port should be exchanged for a less exposed one.

'It appears that most of the outrages complained of, have been committed by the dependents of the chiefs of Rairee and Newtee and the scene of them has generally been the districts of Vengurla which is surrounded by the possessions of the Waree State. If this be the case it might be sufficient to require the dismission of the two chiefs complained of and the exchange of Vengurla for some less exposed territory...'[190] At last a treaty was signed on 30 October in which the Sawants were to surrender the artillery that belonged to them, the choukies, along with war ships.[191]

A treaty was signed on 3 Oct 1812. Phond Sawant, the Sawantwadi ruler by which he ceded full sovereignty of Fort Vengurla with its port to the Company, signed it. By 5 May 1813, the rest of Vengurla also was ceded to the Company.[192] These territories were later on included in the Southern Konkan district.[193] This was followed by an agreement on 1 May 1813 between the Rani Doorgabai to Colonel Dowse in which the Rani Writes, 'I am willing to give up the village of Vengurla and now I inform you that I have dispatched the Sunnud for that purpose to Davy Naigum Moodeliar, Agent,

'...You have been much my friend and I trust in a continuance of your friendship but if you do not march your army up the ghats, I will not return to my country...'[194]

From this time onwards the Bombay Government kept civil and military establishment at both Malvan and Vengurla to see that no pirated vessels made use of the ports.[195] The occupied ports were considered very important not only because they could prevent admission of foreign enemies but also because those that could yield revenue. As maritime stations they had no advantages, affording safe approach only to small crafts but were considered valuable because of the growth of teak, coir, hemp and other articles[196] and because of military importance.

The Company laid systematic rules for the duties to be imposed on the imports and exports. The duties imported and exported were to be collected by the local officers of revenue at the ports respectively, the customhouses being open each day Sundays excepted from ten in the morning till four in the evening. The local officers were given instructions as to keep a complete record of the goods and merchandise on board, give details about the vessel specifying at what port they were received, to whom they belonged and all other required information.[197]

The local officers of revenue were expected to keep a daily register of the quantity and the value of goods. Strict rules were laid down for the permit for trans-shipping goods, which were to be signed by the local officers of revenue.

'Goods trans-shipped without permission first had been obtained from the local officers of revenue or shipped or attempted to be shipped upon any other vessel than that for which they may have been passed shall be charged with double duty. The local officers of revenue shall register the value and quantity of articles exported free of duty. The exporter of goods on which an export duty has been levied shall be entitled to a certificate of the amount of duty paid.'[198]

Despite all the systematic rules and all the care taken by the East India Company in the achievement the Konkan territories, there were instances when the officers of the Company showed their dissatisfaction in many ways. They regretted that more military establishment was necessary to suppress the Peshwa power. Sir Evan Nepean wrote that '*The Southern Concan is studded with strong fortresses...*'[199]

He further said, '*Impressed with the importance of the Southern Concan your Lordship we have no doubt will give us full credit from the regret we have experienced in finding from the state of our military resources that we unable to acquire those advantages which its possession would have secured in having received information however from the Resident at Fort Victoria that the enemy was preparing their vessels at Severndroog for the purpose of annoying our trade ...*'[200]

It was thus found that after the cession of Malvan and Vengurla, the Company could not free itself from internal quarrels with the State of Kolhapurs and the State of Sawants for the next several years nor was it successful in putting an end to interference in their trade. The Company had to face Sawantwadi Rani on one side and the Kolhapur Raja on the other side. Things had to be handled diplomatically. A letter from the Collector in the Southern Konkan exposes the constant rivalry between the Raja of Kolhapur and the Company.

'*The Vishalghur Pratinidhi being the chief of the hereditary officers of the petty states of Kolhapur and notorious for harbouring plunderers; the Honorable Governor-in-Council requests you will expostulate with the Raja of Kolhapur and explain the necessity of his immediately suppressing any bodies of banditti... The necessity of settling the district our self may be held out to stimulate the Rajah. It will require to be managed cleverly as probably the Rajah may wish to reduce our territory and then restore it to his government and this should be avoided...*'[201]

All was not too well between the British and Rani Durgabai either.[202] Frequent disturbances, plundering of the villages in the Company's territories by the locals was a common cause of complaint. It is seen from the following letter from M. Elphinstone to the Rani of Sawantwadi.

'*Frequent disturbances have taken place, accounts of which were forwarded to me and which I brought to your notice in a friendly manner. But notwithstanding this, fresh outrages have been committed, of which information has been sent to me by the Resident at Malvan...Parties have entered and plundered the village of Vengurla four times. In this manner do your people continue to commit depredations in the Honorable Company's districts whilst you write expressing your desire to preserve friendship.'*[203]

The Rani's reply was always a cordial one in which she would convince them that the culprits if found would be severely punished and her intentions of friendly relations with them remained unchanged.[204] Thus during the entire exercise of capturing Konkan territories many treaties were signed, territories were transferred from one to the other for fixed periods, made one strong and the other weak in turns.

Konkan, Deccan, Karnataka (1817)

By November 1817, the Peshwa power was almost overthrown and most of the territories belonging to them at Bombay Karnataka, Deccan, Gujarat and Konkan fell into the hands of the British.[205] A letter here throws light on the letter written informing the defeat of the Peshwa.

'Brigadier General Smith's division joined forces at Poona on the 13th instant. That an action took place on the 16th in which the enemy were completely defeated and dispersed, and the British flag hoisted on the palace. The Peshwa fled to Poorunder and General Smith had marched to lay seize to the fort.'[206]

Remaining territories. (1818)

Early in 1818 *Mandangad, Ramgad, Palgad, Rasalgad, Pali, Bharap, Salshi, Devgad, Siddigad, Bhagvantgad, Achra, Chiplun* and other small parts were captured.[207] The conquests of the British were completed with the surrender of fort by Deshmukh of Ratnagiri and of Vijaydurg by Dhulap. Meanwhile on 11 February 1818 a proclamation was issued by General Munro announcing the annexation of all the territories of the Peshwas. Thus by 2 Sept 1818, The East India Company took political control of the Peshwa territories bounded in the north by the Apta river and on the south by the Karli or Malvan river and areas trying between the ghats and the sea.[208] Two most important prepositions made to Bajirao Peshwa on 1 June 1818 were as follows:[209]

(1) That he shall resign, for himself and successors, all

right and claim over the government of Poona or to any sovereign power whatsoever.

(2) That Bajee Rao shall immediately come with his family and a small number of his adherents and attendants to the camp of Brigadier General Malcolm where he shall be received with honour and respect and escorted safe to the city of Benaras or any other sacred place in Hindoostan, that the Governor General may at his request, fix for his residence.

This was the fate of the Peshwa in 1818. A trading company which had signed an agreement not to interfere in either political or economic affairs of the Peshwa, took control of the entire territory in less than a 100 years. The Article of 1739 I had been as follows:

The English shall only issue passes to the Company's vessels, the merchants or servants dependent, belonging to the Island of Bombay or other places where the English have settlement. And the English will not interfere with Bajee Rao's fleet nor give convoy to foreign vessels...[210]

On May 17, 1820, the villages of Redi, Arowlee and Seerowdee of Ajgaon tarf and Daboli, Kanoli, Kayloos, Konchrey, Mahapun, and Purolen of Pat turf, on the sea coast, which were ceded to the Company on February 1819, were included in the district of South Konkan and laws and regulations in force in the district of South Konkan were to be in force in the above mentioned villages from 17th February 1819 being the date from which the authority of the British Government had effect in those territories.[211]

Thus, in this struggle for power, The East India Company had to face not only the internal enemies but it had to face the Europeans who had settled in parts of Konkan much before their arrival. The Portuguese enjoyed supremacy in trade, in the fifteenth century because they were the only European power plying in the Indian Ocean. They had to cope with an opponent in the first decade of the seventeenth century when both the English and the Dutch established their Joint Stock Companies. However, these European powers lent a helping hand as and when necessities arose in their struggle against the local rajas or sometimes in their own internal problems. The English got the support from the Portuguese against the Dutch and the increasing maritime Strength of The English East India Company was a favorable factor, which finally resulted in the English supremacy over the Dutch in Indian waters.

It took greater time and energy for The East India Company to occupy parts of South Konkan as compared to North Konkan. Mountstuart Elphinstone in his report stated that the Company took great care lest the Peshwas or his people rebelled again. This is seen from the letter written below from Hale, Secretary to government to the Collector of Malvan.

'A copy of the Proclamation dated 10th instant promising indemnity to all of Bajirow's horses who may now return to their homes and threatening with the punishment of rebels all who may take up arms and care to be taken...[212] *I could not take the lower concan without giving great pain to the Peshwa and what is worse, great disgust to every man about the government. I have therefore, contented myself with the part north of the road to Bombay, which I reckon at Rs. 10,00,000.'*[213]

Ratnagiri in South Konkan compared to the North fell into their hands late because Brahmin families lived here. In this connection Lord Hastings reported that 'Almost all the Principal Brahmin families connected with Poona government came from the Southern Konkan' He further stated that 'almost all of them were of a high caste, intelligent and would not part with their territory so easily'.[214]

They had great loyalty to the Peshwa government. The Peshwa belonging to this caste had held a great part of the coast of the Southern Konkan. But it was also noticed that there was no unity among them. While in another statement J. H. Pelly wrote thus:'The Peshwa officers are already quarrelling with one another for the division of the spoils, each in turn harassing and impoverishing the Peasantry with illegal exactions...'[215]

'Ever since my arrival at this place (South Konkan) on the morning of the 10th. I have been engaged in carrying into effect such measures as in my estimation seemed best calculated for the defense of the public property and inhabitants in the

probable event of our being attacked by the Maharattas, whose fortress are planted all around us and whose villages are intermingled with our own...I have given directions to Capt. Morisson that the public treasure should be conveyed afloat and the utmost vigilance maintained in our villages both to prevent a surprise and to check the ingress of suspicious characters.'

'The precautions became necessary since the recent occurrences at Poona have created a great sensation in the South Konkan, which abounds with Brahmins, deeply interested in the Peshwa welfare and in the stability of his power with which their own is identified.'[216]

The Marathas who were powerful next to Brahmins were physically strong and loyal supporters of Peshwa government. The fishermen who were great in number stayed along the coasts. On the one hand the British tactfully subdued the internal local rivals and on the other they successfully managed to put an end to the power of her European adversaries after a long struggle. The Dutch, the French, the Portuguese, the Arabs, the Siddis one by one could not stand the British challenge and lost their hold on both the Arabian sea and the Indian Ocean. The entire trade between Britain and the colonies in India, it should be remembered, was carried on by the sea routes. It was therefore of prime importance to them- or indeed to any maritime country which depends on sea trade-to ensure the protection of their shipping.

But constant struggles, acts of piracy, wars for a long time between the British and other rivals had hampered the trade of South Konkan. When almost all the territories of Konkan were brought under their control, the British heaved a sigh of relief. Their political and economic domination both in the Deccan and the Konkan would now permit an easy journey to the coast along with free and uninterrupted trade between ports and main lands.[217] Thus began a new era in the history of South Konkan which also came to be called as Ratnagiri District or Ratnagiri Collectorate.

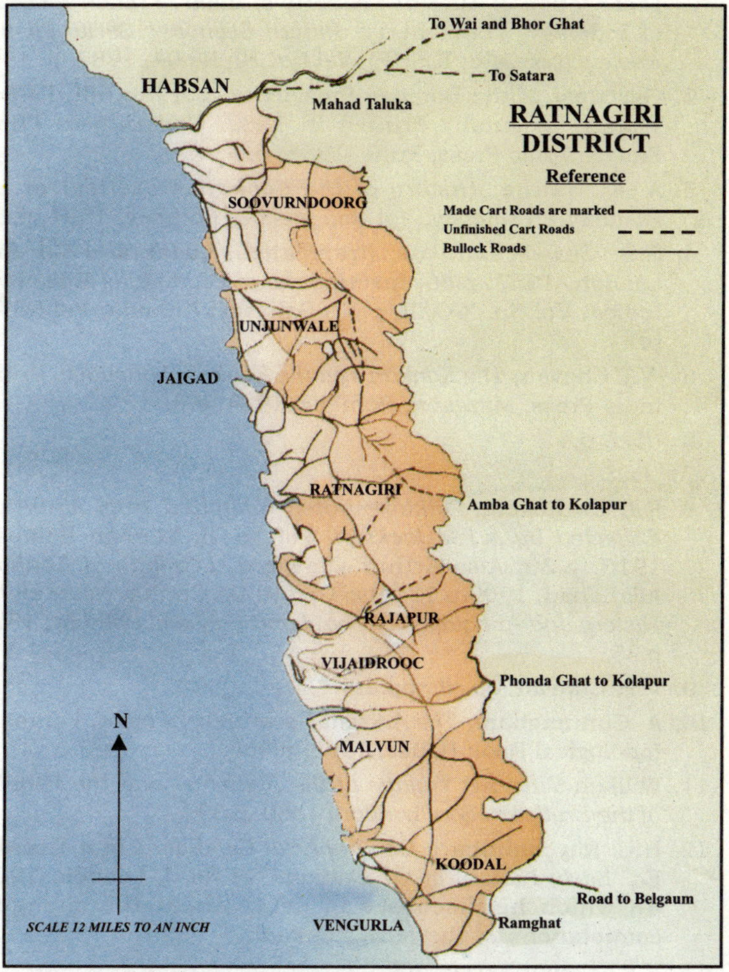

Ratnagiri Collectorate in the early 19th century

Source : MSA, Revenue Department, Vol. No. 60/1878.

REFERENCES

1. Jean Deloche, 'Geographical Considerations in the Localization of Ancient Seaports of India', French Institute of Indology, Pondicherry, *Indian Economic Social History Review* (hereafter IESHR), Vol No. 20, No.04, 1985, p. 439.
2. Gazetteer of the Bombay Presidency, Vol No. XIII, Part II, Thana, Originally Printed In 1882, Government Photo Zincographic Press, Pune, 1986, p. 414.
3. A. K. Nairne, *History of the Konkan,* Gazetteer of the Bombay Presidency, Vol No.I, part II, Bombay, 1894, p.8.
4. E.B. Cowell, *Jatakas,* (translated), Luzac and Co. Ltd, London, 1957, p.86; Inscriptions of Chalukyas Epigaphia Indica, Vol No. XXVIII, p.17; Sahyadri Khanda, Vol No. 2, p.1.
5. V.P.Chavan, *The Konkan and the Konkani Language,* British India Press, Mazgaon, Bombay, 1924, p.6.
6. *Ibid,* p.4.
7. *Ibid.*
8. R.E.Enthoven, *Folklore Notes Compiled from Materials Collected by A.T.M.Jackson,* Vol No. II, Konkan Bombay, 1915, p.30; Also Arthur Crawford, *Legends of Konkan,* Allahabad, 1909,p.12; Also Gerard Da Cunha, *Notes on the History and Antiquities of Chaul and Bassein,* Bombay, 1870, p.35.
9. V.P. Chavan, *op.cit.,* pp.8-9.
10. A. Cunningham, *The Ancient Geography of India,* Varanasi, Indological Book House, 1963, p.466.
11. William Vincent, *Voyage of the Nearchus and the Periplus of the Erythrian Sea,* London, 1880, p.392.
12. H.C. Raychaudhari, *Geographical Conditions in a Yazdani,* Ed *'Early History of the Deccan,* Vol No. I, London, 1960. (In which he discusses in detail about the changing connotations of the term Konkan).
13. V.P.Chavan, *op.cit.,* p.9.
14. M.D.David, History of Bombay, 1661-1708, T.V. Chindambaran publication, Bombay, 1973, p.2.
15. *Ibid.*
16. Gazetteer of the Bombay Presidency, Kolaba and Janjira, Vol No.XI, 1883, p.10; also Ranabhir Chakraborthy 'Merchants of Konkan', *IESHR,* Vol No.23, No.2, 1986, p.385.
17. N. B. Utgikar & V. G. Paranjape, *collected works of R.G. Bhandarkar,* Vol No.III, published by Bhandarkar Oriental

Research Institute, Poona, 1927, p.406.

18. K.Gopal Chari, *Early History of Andhra Country*, 1941, pp.28-29.
19. W.H.Schoff, *Periplus of Erythrian Sea*, Longman, Green and Company, New York, 1912, pp.43-44.
20. Bombay Gazetteer, Vol No.IX, *Thane district*, Government of Maharashtra, Bombay, pp.10-47.
21. *Ibid*, p.44.
22. B.G.Gokhale, *Buddhism in Maharashtra*, Popular Prakashan, Bombay, 1976, pp. 3-7.
23. M.A.Prasad, 'Studies in India's Trade Relations during Ancient Times with special reference to Maharashtra' Unpublished Ph.D thesis, Bombay University, 1989, p.102.
24. *Ibid.*
25. *Ibid.*
26. T.S Thosar, *South Indian Inscriptions and Place Names*, Vol No. XII, Mysore, 1991, pp.22-30.
27. M.A Prasad. *op.cit.*, pp.112-122; V.V. Mirashi, Indian *Historical Quarterly*, Vol No. XXXVI, pp.183-89.
28. N.B.Utgikar, and V.G. Paranjape, *op.cit.*, p.81.
29. A.S. Altekar, *Silaharas of Western India*, Calcutta, 1936, pp.1-4.
30. *Ibid.*
31. V.B.Kolte, *Maharashtratil Tamrapat va Shilalekh* (Marathi), Maharashtra Rajya Sanskriti Mandal, Bombay, 1987, pp.301-308.
32. *Ibid.*
33. Gazetteer of the Bombay Presidency, Surat and Broach, Government Central Press, Vol No.II, New Delhi, 1877, p.438.
34. *Ibid*, p.444. (Arab Geographers of this period describe Bassein, Bombay, Dabhol, Chaul, Panvel, Kalyan and Bhiwandi as prosperous ports during the Muslim period).
35. S.Maqbul Ahmed, *Early Arabic Accounts of India and China* (translations of the accounts of Suleiman and Ibn Khurdabeh), Shimla, 1989, p.33; Ranabhir Chakraborthy, 'Monarchs, Merchants and a Matha in North Konkan' *IESHR*, Vol No.XXVII, pp.189; G.F.Hourani, *Arab Sea Faring, in the Indian Ocean in Ancient and Early Medieval Times*, Princeton University Press, Princeton, 1951, p.17.
36. For the Sanskrit text see D.C.Sircar, *Inscriptions of Ashoka, Delhi,* Publication Division of Information and Broadcasting, Government of India, 1957, p.402; Z.A.Desai,

Studies in India Epigraphy, Vol No.I, the Epigraphical Society of India, Geeta Book House, Mysore, 1977, p.10; Ranabhir Chakraborthy, Monarchs, Merchants and a Matha in North Konkan, *IESHR*, Vol No.XXVII, p.189.

37. V.G.Khobrekar, *'History of Konkan'* unpublished, Ph.D thesis, Mumbai University, p.80.
38. H.H. Dowell *op.cit.*, p. 654; B.K.Apte, *The Maratha Navy and Merchant Ship,* State Board of Literature and Culture, Government of Maharashtra, Bombay, 1973, pp.55-56.
39. B. K Apte, *op.cit.*, pp.55-56.
40. Jean Deloche, *op.cit.*, p.439; Also R.D.Choksey, *Economic Life in the Bombay Konkan (1818-1939),* Asia Publishing House, Bombay, 1960, p.1.
41. C.D.Deshpande, W*estern India, A Regional Geography,* Student's own Depot, Dharwar, 1948, p.181.
42. O.H.K. Spate, *India and Pakistan, A General and Regional Geography,* Methun, London, 1964, p.608.
43. Ranbhir Chakraborthy, 'Merchants of Konkan', Vol No.23, 1986, *IESHR,* Calcutta, 1959, p.385.
44. J. Briggs, *History of the Rise of Mohemmedan Power in India till the Year A.D.1612,Translation from the Original Persian Mohd-Kasim-Ferishta,* Vol No.II, New Delhi, 1981, p.338.
45. A.K Nairne, *op.cit.*, p.8.
46. James Birds, *The Political and Statistical History of Gujarat,* translated from the Persian Ali Mohammad Khan, the Revenue Minister of the province to which are added copius annotation and a historical introduction, London, 1835, p.8.
47. V.P.Chavan *op.cit.*, pp.9-10.
48. Jas Burgess and Faithfull Fleet, Indian Antiquary, A Journal of Oriental Research, in Archaeology, Geology, History, Folklore, Language, Literature, Numismatics, Philosophy, Religion, Vol No. IX, (Microfilmed), The Asiatic Society of Bombay (hereafter A.S.B.), p.47.
49. Indian Antiquary, Vol No.IX p.35; Epigaphia Indica, Vol No-XXVIII, p.17.
50. *Journal of the Bombay Branch of the Royal Asiatic Society,* (JBBRAS) Vol No. IX, p. 297.
51. V.R. Shenoy, *Valavlikar, Goyankarchi Goyabhali Vasnook,* Bombay, p.25.
52. V.G. Khobrekar, *op.cit.*, p.6.
53. G. R. Tibbetts, *Arab Navigation in the Indian Ocean before the coming of the Portuguese*, translated KiTal-Fawai' Id Fiusal Al-Bahr Wa'-L-Gawa', London, 1971, pp.450, 454.

54. V.R.Shenoy, *op.cit.*, Bombay, p.25.
55. Ranabhir Chakraborthy, *op.cit.*, p.385.
56. Ratnagiri District Census Handbook, Board on 1951 Census, Bombay, 1952, pp.4-5.
57. Indian Janaganana, 1961, *District Jangana Nirdesh Grantha*, Ratnagiri, Maharashtra Janaganana Karyalaya, Mumbai-1965, p.1, Deccan College, Pune (hereafter D.C.P.); Narayan Ganesh Musale, *Ratnagiri Jillah, Kal, Aaj va Udhya* (Marathi), Abhinav Prakashan, Mumbai, 1958, p.1.
58. Gazetteer of The Bombay Presidency, Vol-X, Ratnagiri and Savantwadi, Government Central Press, Maharashtra State, 1880, p.2.
59. Armando Coresao (tr) *The Pires Nedeln Liestenstein*, 1967, Vol No. I, p.48. Also A.D Pilot, *west coast of India Pilot Comprising the west coast of Ceylon of Indian from Colombo to Karachi, also the Maldive and Laccadive Islands, Great Britain Admirality, Hydongraphy London, 1926*, p.20.
60. Gazetteer of Bombay Presidency, Vol No. VIII, p.404.
61. Primeiro Roterio Da Costa Da India, *op.cit.*, p.152.
62. Duarte Barbosa, *The Book of Duarte Barbosa* Ed, M.L. Dames London, 1967, Vol No. I, p.165.
63. A.R.Kulkarni, *Medieval Maratha Country Books And Books*, New Delhi, 1996, p.561. (Don Joao De Castro was probably Oligby's authority as they call this place Quelecim) Also Prim. Rot da Costa da India, p.39.
64. *Ibid.*
65. Survey of the Minor ports of India, Report, government of India, Delhi, 1952, p.11.
66. B. G. Wagle, 'Geomorphology And Evolution Of The coastal And Off-Shore Areas Of Maharashtra And Goa', unpublished Ph. D. Thesis in Geology, Goa, March. 1987, p. 72.
67. B. G. Wagle, *op.cit.*, p.72.
68. Bharatiya Janaganana, 1961, Jillah Janagana, *op.cit.*, p. 1.
69. *Ibid.*
70. B. K. Apte, *op.cit.*, p.13. Also M. S. Rege, 'History And Suıvey Of Education', Ratnagiri District, Ph.D. Thesis, University Of Mumbai, 1961, pp. 10-15.
71. *Ibid*, p.13.
72. *Ibid.*
73. *Ibid.*
74. C. B. Joshi, 'The Ratnagiri Taluka, Land Use and

Settlements', Bombay Geographical Magazine, Mumbai. p.5 Also B.K.Apte, *op.cit.*, pp.13-14.

75. *Ibid.*
76. *Ibid.*
77. M. S. Rege, *op.cit.*, pp.10-20.
78. *Shviakalin Patrasar Samgraha* : (hereafter SPS) Shri Shiva Charitra Karyalaya , (Marathi), Vol No. I:1023, pp.272-73.
79. K.S. Behera,Ed, *Maritime Heritage of India,* Aryan Books International, New Delhi, 1999, p.209.
80. B.K.Apte, *op.cit.*, pp.20-23.
81. *Ibid.*
82. Gazetteer of the Bombay Presidency, Kolaba and Janjira Vol No.XI, 1883, p.44; Gazetteer of the Bombay Presidency, Ratnagiri and Savantwadi, Vol No.X, 1880, pp. 111-112.
83. T. B. Jervis, *Geographical and Statistical Memoirs of the Konkan,* Calcutta, 1840, p.75; also John Wilson, *Indian Caste,* Vol No.I, Deep Publication, New Delhi, 1976, p.20.
84. A.R.Kulkarni, *Medieval Konkan, its history, society and economy,* 56th session of Indian History congress(hereafter I.H.C), Delhi, 1996, p.13.
85. *Ibid.*
86. *Ibid.*
87. Ranabhir Chakraborthy, *op.cit.*, *IESHR*,Vol No.23, No.4,1986, p.207; Also Jean Deloche, *op.cit.*, *IESHR*, pp.439-48.
88. Jean Deloche, *op.cit.*, Vol No.20, No.4, Oct-Dec 1983, pp.439-48
89. K.S. Behera,Ed, *Maritime Heritage of India,* Aryan Books International, New Delhi, 1999, p.23.
90. Gazetteer of the Bombay Presidency, Ratnagiri and Savantwadi, Vol No. X, 1880, p.174.
91. G.P.Hourani, *Arab Sea Faring in the Indian Ocean and Early Medieval Times,* Princeton, 1951, pp.89-91.
92. K.A Nilkantha Shastri, ed, *The Comprehensive History of India,* Vol No.II, Bombay, 1957, pp.439-46.
93. D. White and A. Williamson, *Sasanian Maritime Trade,* Iran, Vol No.II, 1973, pp.29-49; also A Catalogue of 'Twelve sites' Vimla Begley and Richard Daniel De Puma, Ed, *Rome & India. The Ancient Sea Trade,* New Delhi, 1992, pp.157-96.
94. N.P.Orton, in Begley and De Puma, Eds, *Ibid,* p.46.
95. S.K Maity, *Economic Conditions in Northern India in the Gupta Period,* Delhi, 1970, pp.170-71.

96. R.C Majumdar, Ed, *The Classical Age,* Bombay, 1970, p.240; also Yazdani. G., *Early History of the Deccan,* Vol No.I, London, 1960.
97. Ranbhir Chakraborthy, *op.cit.*, p.208. The Chinchani Copper plate of Indra III dated 926 A.D. shows that during the rule of Krsna II 878-915 A.D. Madhumati the Tajjika namely Mohammad of the Arab Country was made the Governor of Sanjana Mandala.
98. Ranbhir Chakraborthy, *op.cit.*, p.209, also CII, 6, No.7, pp.36-44.
99. *Ibid,* p.207; also CII 6,no 12, pp.71-75.
100. *Ibid,* p.211; also CII 6,No.40, pp.178-83.
101. *Ibid,* p.212; also CII 6 No.41, pp.183-93.
102. *Ibid,* p.213; also CII 6,No.41, pp. 233.
103. Balarama Srivastava, Trade and Commerce in Anicent India from the Earliest times to Circa A.D. 300, Varanasi, Chaukhamba Sanskrit Series Office, 1968, pp.70-75; CII, Vol No. VI, p. 235, lines 26-32, and 245, lines 22-29.
104. B.D.Chattopadhaya, *Urban Centres in Early Medieval India:* An overview in Sabyasachi Bhattacharya and Romika Mapar; ed situating Indian History for S. Gopal, Delhi, 1987, pp.8-33.
105. Ranbir Chakraborthy, *op.cit.*, p.121.
106. A.K.Nairne, *op.cit.*, p.7.
107. Alexander Rogers, *The Land Revenue of Bombay,* Government of Maharashtra, Government Central Press, 1962, Vol No.I, Low Price Publication, 1892, pp.2-10.
108. E.T Candy, *Khoty Tenure, Selections from Records of Bombay Government,* IOC, 34 series, Bombay, 1873, p.24, S. 'Savur, Ratnagiri-Underdevelopment of an Area of Reserve Labour Force', Sociological Bulletin, 31 (2) 82, pp.182-219.
109. Gazetteer of the Bombay Presidency,Vol No.X, Ratnagiri And Savantwadi, Government Central Press, Maharashtra State, 1880. p.175.
110. A.K. Nairne, *op.cit.*, pp. 66 and 72.
111. *Ibid.*
112. R.D Choksey, *op.cit.*, p.25.
113. William J. Barber, *British Economic Thought and India,* 1600-1858, Oxford University Press, 1975, p.6.
114. Steward Gordon, The *Marathas,* 1600-1800, The New Cambridge History of India, CUP, 1993, p.113.
115. B. K. Apte, *The Maratha Navy and Merchant ships,* State

Board for Literature and Culture, Government of Maharashtra, Bombay, 1972, p.59.

116. Steward Gordon, op cit., p. 22.
117. K.Sridharan, *A Maritime History of India*, Published Ministry of Information and Broadcasting, New Delhi, 1965, p. 64.
118. Ashok Mehta, *Indian Shipping*, N.T.Shroff, Bombay, 1940, p.1.
119. K.Sridharan, *op.cit.*, p.65.
120. D.C.Wadhwa, Agrarian Legislation in India, Vol No.I, Oriental Longman Limted, Poona, 1973, (Vide Articles of 4 to 6 of the Treaty), p.612.
121. *Ibid*, (Vide Article 11 of the Treaty of marriage between Charles II, The king of Great Britain and the Princess Infanta of Portugal concluded between the kings Alfonso VI of Portugal and Charles II of Great Britain), p.612.
122. *Ibid*, Vide His Majesty's Royal Charter, dated March 27, 1668.
123. R. D. Choksey, Mountstuart Elphinstone to Evan Napean, dated 21st May 1817, Bombay S.C. 4 December, 1812, Malvan Residency*(Savantvadi Affairs)*, *op.cit.*, pp.1-2, Kenneth Ballhatchet, *Social Policy and Social Change in Western India*, London, Oxford University Press, 1961, p.141.
124. K.Sridharan, *op.cit.*, p.65.
125. H.H. Dowell, *The Cambridge History of India* Vol No.V British India, Cambridge University press, London, 1929, pp. 95-96.
126. K. Sridharan,' *A Maritime History of India*, Publication Division, Ministry of Information and Broadcasting New Delhi, 1965, p.65.
127. Radhakumud Mookerji, *Indian Shipping, A History of The Sea Borne Trade and Maritime Activity of the Indians from Earliest Times*, Longman Green and Company, Bombay, 1912, p.243.
128. The Gazetteer of Bombay City and Island (hereafter GBCI), Vol No.I, Bombay, Reprint, 1977, p. 273.(The Bombay Marine Forces of Bombay were known by varying titles since their first enrolment.1612-1686 The Hon. East India Company's Marine,1686-1830, The Bombay Marine,1830-1863 Indian Navy,1877-1892 Her Indian Majesty's Indian Marine, onwards Royal Indian Marine.
129. C. R. Manshuramani, 'History of Bombay', unpublished Ph.D thesis, University of Bombay, 1966, p.75; also GBCI, *op.cit.*, pp.389-91.

130. Ashok Mehta, *op.cit.*,p.25.
131. Sir Evan Cotton, *East India Men,* The Batch North Press, London, 1949,p.46; *Scaleby* was built for the firm Bruce Fawcett and Company prior to her despatch to England in coastal trade and voyages to China. About 1805 she disappeared from the list of East India calendar as owned by the Bombay firm because of her sale to William Moffat. Also J.M. Campbell, Bombay Gazetter, Vol No.XXII, Government Central Press, p.363.
132. Victor Rajamanockamkam and Y.Sabbarayalu, *History of Traditional Navigation,* Tanjavur, 1988, p.150. Coir yarn was a made from the husk throughout the Malabar coast; Ejoo was something like horsehair was the produce of a saga palm tree. The Dutch and the Spaniards reckoned it 'far superior to the best European hempen cordage', Sunn according to Dr. Roxburg grew in almost every situation and rope makers in England thought it to be a fine material for ships.
133. Radhakumud Mookarjee, *op.cit.*, p.245.
134. Jagjit Singh, 'History of Bombay' (1705-56) Unpublished Ph.D thesis, University of Bombay,1977,p.59.'Here ships meant naval vessels. They ranged from 300 tons onwards and were protected by guns. Grabs were broad beamed coastal vessels with two or three masts; galleys were low flat single decked vessels using sails or oars. They were useful both in wars and commerce. Sloops were one masted vessel. They were small warships used for police work and general purpose. Frigates were warships used for escort duties. Manchuas were fishing boats and were suitable for coastal use.'
135. B. K. Apte, *op.cit.*, p.61; also Selections from the Bombay Secretariat, Maratha series, Vol No.I, 1854, p.91.
136. Arthur Crawford, Collector, to the Commissioner, Re: sketching a brief history of the forestry in the Ratnagiri, Revenue Department Vol No. 60/1878, (hereafter R.D.) p.42.
137. Gazetteer of the Bombay Presidency, Ratnagiri and Sawantwadi, Vol No. X, Government Central press, p.175.
138. W.W.Hunter, History of British India, Vol No.II, Longman Green and Company, London, 1912, p.128.
139. Chief, Fort Victoria to Bombay Council, 16 February 1756, Public Department Diary No. 1/A/1720, p.246. (Hereafter Pub.D).

140. J.Narons, Chief Secretary, Bombay Castle to V.Hale, Resident in Malvan, 12 December 1817, Malvan Political Secret from(hereafter M.P.S.) 1815-1829, letter No.34.
141. Arthur Crawford, Collector, to the Commissioner, Re: Sketching a Brief History of the Forestry in the Ratnagiri, R.D. Vol. No. 60/1878, p.42.
142. James Douglas, *Bombay and Western India, A Series of Stray Papers,* Vol No.I, Sampson Low Marston and Co.Ltd, London, 1893, p.126.
143. *Ibid,* p.115.
144. Ruttonjee Ardeshir Wadia, *The Bombay Dockyard and the Wadia Master Builders,* R.A.Wadia, Thakur Nivas, Bombay, 1955, pp.142-43.
145. K.M.Panikkar, *India and the Indian Ocean,* p.61; also D.G.Dhabu, *Kulabkar Angre Sarkhel,* Bombay, 1939, p. 215.
146. B. K. Apte, *op.cit.*, p.58.
147. G. S. Sardesai, *Selections from the Peshwa Daftar*(hereafter S.P.D.), Vol No.XXII, letter No.100, Government Central Press, Bombay, 1933, p.34.
148. S.P.D., Extract 61, Rumal No.454/1351, Unpublished, Alienation office, Poona.
149. S.P.D. Extract 62, Rumal No.454/1344, Unpublished, Alienation office, Poona.
150. Ruttonjee Ardheshir Wadia, *op.cit.*, p.143.
151. A.C.Banarjee and P.K.Ghose, *A Comprehensive History of India, The Maratha Ascendancy (1712-1772),* Vol No. IX, New Delhi, People's Publishing House, 1978, p.378.
152. S.P.D., Vol No.XXXIII, 34, Government Central Press, Bombay, pp.149-64.
153. D.C.Wadhwa, *op.cit.*, pp.614-615.
154. Kenneth Ballhatchet, *op.cit.*, p.141; also James Douglas, *op.cit.*, p.117.
155. William Hornby and others at a Consultation, dated 20 and 25 January 1756, Political Department Diary No. 29/I/1756(hereafter P.D.D.), p.51.
156. Thomas Hughes, *Treaties, Agreements and Engagements between the Hon. East India Company and the Native Princes, Chiefs and States in Western India; the Red Sea; The Persian Gulf,* Bombay Education Society's Press, Bombay, 1851, p.475. Maharashtra State Gazetteer Ratnagiri District, Vol No.X, Government Central Press, 1962, p.168; also G.S.Sardesai, *New History of the Marathas sunset over Maharashtra,* Phoenix Publication, Bombay, Vol No.II, 1948, pp.344-45.

157. William Hornby and others at a Consultation, dated 20 and 25 January 1756, P.D.D. No. 29/I/1756, p.65.
158. *Ibid.*
159. Chief, Fort Victoria to Bombay Council, at a Consultation present H.R.Bourchier, C.Crommelin, William Sedquick, Thomas Byfield, dated 19 January 1756, Pub.D No. 29/I/ 1756, p.87.
160. Chief of Fort Victoria, Reporting the victory of Gheria, At a Consultation present William Hirnby, Hugh Symmions, John Spencer, William Sidwick, Thomas byfield, dated 19 January 1756, P.D.D. No. 29/I/1756, publishing 87. Gheria or Giria as called by the Muslims and employed by European writers of last century, for Vijayadurg (Viziadroog) a fortress on a rocky promontory at the entrance of a fine harbour formed by the mouth of the Vaghotna river, on the Konkan coast about 170 miles south of Bombay. It was fortified in 1662 by Shivaji. In 1707 kanoji Angria established an independent sovereignty here and possessed numerous piratical fleet. On 13 February it was attacked by Admiral Watson with three ships of the line, one ship of 50 guns, and one of 44 with some armed vessels of the Bombay Marine amounting in all to forty sail, having on board 800 Europeans and 1000 native soldiers under Clive Angria's fleet was destroyed in a few hours. In return, the company promised to help the Marathas in a joint expedition to suppress the Angria, the Chieftains of Kolaba (vide Article No. 3 & 4 respectively of the agreement between the Governor of Bombay and the Marathas).
161. Dr. G. N. Saletore, 'The Malvan Expedition of 1765 and its Sequel', *I.H.C.*, p.249.
162. Mountstuart Elphinstone to Sir Evan Napean, President and Governor, dated 16 Dec 1812, Secret and Political Department Diary No. 280/ 1812, p.15-19. (Hereafter Sec. & P.D.)
163. R. D.Choksey, Malvan Residency*(Savantvadi Affairs)*, Select Documents from the Ratnagiri Collector's Files, (hereafter S.P.D.), Poona, pp. 2-7.
164. Arthur Crawford, Collector, to the Commissioner, Re: sketching a brief history of the forestry in the Ratnagiri, R.D. Vol No. 60/1878, p.42.
165. *Ibid.*
166. John Gordon, Sindhudurg fort, to the Bombay Castle, re: capture of Fort Augustus, Pub.D No. 44/I/1765, p.150.
167. *Ibid*, p.250.

168. Rawson H. Boddam, Consultation, dated 12 January 1765, Pub.D No 44/I/ 1765, p.20.
169. J.Reyley, R.H.Boddam at a Consultation, dated 29 Feb 1765, Pub.D No.44/I/1765, p.63.
170. John Watson, to Charles Crommelin, President and Governor of Bombay, dated 1 February 1756, Pub.D No.44/ I/ 1765, p.85.
171. John Gordon, Sidhudurg Fort, to Bombay Castle, dated 1 Feb 1765, Pub.D No. 44/ I / 1765, pp. 87-88.
172. D. C. Wadhwa, *op.cit.*, pp. 614-15; Mahrashtra State Gazetteer, Ratnagiri District, *op.cit.*, p.172 .
173. *Ibid*; Grant Duff, *History of the Maharattas*, Vol No. I, London Longman, Bombay, Ed. S.M.Edwardes, Times of India, 1826, p.70.
174. *Ibid*; (Vide article 2, 3 and 5 of the Treaty between the Company and Sawantwadi State); also G. N. Saletore, *op.cit.*, p.252.
175. G. N. Saletore, *op.cit.*, p.252.
176. V.G.Khobrekar, *Konkachi Rajakarane* (1707-1818), (Marathi), Marathi Grantha Sangrahalaya, Itihas Samshodhan Mandalache Traimasik (hereafter ISMT), Bharatiya Itihas ani Samskriti, October 1977, p.53.
177. R. D.Choksey, *Malvan Residency(Savantvadi Affairs)*, S.P.D. , Poona, p.7.
178. *Ibid*, p. 55.
179. List No. 15, Ratnagiri Vol No.40, *Malvan Residency,* for 1816, Ratnagiri Collector's office, M.P.S., p.44.
180. R.D.Choksey, *Malvan Residency(Savantvadi Affairs)*, S.P.D., Poona, 1956, pp.13-14.
181. *Ibid*, p.14.
182. List No. 15, Ratnagiri Vol No.40, Malvan Residency for 1816, Ratnagiri Collector's office, M.P.S., p.45.
183. V.G.Khobrekar, *op.cit.*, p.57.
184. Government Advertisement, Public Department, Bombay Castle , 30 June 1814, published by the order of the Secretary to Government, List 15, Ratnagiri Vol. No. 43, Malvan Residency Correspondence for 1818-19, Ratnagiri Collector's Office, Letter No.19.
185. H.E.Kitabut to the British Envoy at Goa re: translation of a letter from the Ranee Durgabayee to the British Envoy at Goa, List No. 15, Ratnagiri, Vol No. 40, Malvan Residency for 1816, Rumal No.82, Ratnagiri Collectors Office, M.P.S., Letter No.15.

186. Gazetteer of the Bombay Presidency, Ratnagiri and Sawantwadi, Vol No.X, Government Central Press, Maharashtra State, 1880, p. 175.
187. Charles Crommelin, President and Governor, at the Consultation, re: Thomas Mostyn, Fort Rairee on taking possession of Vengurla, dated 14 Nov 1766, Pub.D No. 47, part II, No. 2, 1766, p.776.
188. D. C. Wadhwa, *op.cit.*, p.620.
189. List No.15, Ratnagiri Vol. No. 40 'A' from 1816, Malvan Residency Correspondence, Re: Substance of a letter by M.Elphinstone to Chndroba and Rani Durgabai, one addressed to Chandroba and the other to the Rani, dated 8 December 1816, M.P.S.,Letter No.44.
190. List No. 15, Ratnagiri, Malvan Residency Correspondence for 1818, Ratnagiri Collector's office, General Smith, to Newsham, M.P.S., Letter No.41.
191. List No. 15, W.Davynaigam to R.Hale, re: Vengurla Treaty, Ratnagiri Vol No.43, Malvan Residency Correspondence for 1818-19, Ratnagiri Collector's Office, M.P.S., Letter No. 24.
192. *Ibid*,(Vide Article 2 of the Treaty concluded between the Raja of Sawantwadi and the Company); also K.N. Chaudhuri, *The Trading World of Asia and the East India and Company*, Cambridge University Press, 1978, p.169.
193. *Ibid*, (Vide Clause Second of Section 16 of the Bombay Regulation 2 of 1827), p.625.
194. Cession of Vengoorlah to the Honorable company, dated 1st May 1813, Select Documents from the Ratnagiri Collector's files (S.P.D.), Malvan Residency 1812-19, p.23.
195. W. Hamilton, Vol No.II, *op.cit.*, p.217.
196. R. D. Choksey, *Malvan Residency(Savantvadi Affairs)*, 1812-1819, Poona, 1956 Select Documents from the Ratnagiri Collector's Files, S.P.D., p.7.
197. List No.15, Ratnagiri Vol No.43, for 1818-19 Malvan Residency Correspondence, Ratnagiri Collector's Office, M.P.S., Letter No. 37., re: Regulation for the Department of Customs in the South Konkan.
198. *Ibid.*
199. Evan Nepean, Governor General to Francis Earl of Moira, Governor General, dated 18 December 1817, Pub.D No. 304/1817, p.79.
200. *Ibid.*
201. J.Henderson, Secretary to Government, Bombay Castle, to William Chaplin, Commissioner in the Deccan, from

1815-29, List No.15, Ratnagiri Vol. No. 44, dated 14 July 1820, M.P.S., Letter No. 33.

202. *Ibid.*

203. Translation of a letter from M. Elphinstone, Resident at Poona to Doorgabhye Ranee of Savantwadi, dated 6 August 1817; also R.D.Choksey, *op.cit.*, pp.116-117.

204. Translation of a letter from Ranee Doorgabhye of Waree to the M. Elphinstone, Resident at Poona, dated 13 August of sawul 27 August, 1817; also R. D. Choksey, *op.cit.*, pp.117-119. Refer (Extracts from Aitihasik Marathi Sadhane, Pune, 1983)

205. D. C. Wadhwa, *op.cit.*, p. 626.

206. F.Warden, Chief Secretary, Bombay Castle, 20 November 1817 to V.Hale, Resident at Malvan, informing him of the Peshwa's defeat on the 16 November 1817; also R. D. Choksey, *op.cit.*, p.119.

207. A. K. Nairne, *op.cit.*, p.116.

208. D. C. Wadhwa, *op.cit.*, p.628.

209. Thomas Hughes, *op.cit.*, p.542.

210. *Ibid*, p.471.(Treaty signed on 20 July 1739).

211. D. C. Wadhwa, *op.cit.*, p.634.(Vide Section 2 of Bombay Regulation 3 of 1820).

212. A. Henderson, Bombay Castle, to W.Hale, Resident, Malvan, January 1818, List No. 15, Ratnagiri Vol. 43, Malvan Residency Correspondence for 1818 and 1819, Ratnagiri Collector Office, Letter No. 22.

213. Governor-General to Court of Directors, dated 4 September 1817,1818, Paragraph II, Vol No.XI, 369,pp.45-49; also M. Elphinstone to Nepean, 7-6-1817, Bombay S. C. 25.6.1817, p.357.

214. *Ibid.*

215. J.H.Pelly, The Chief Secretary to Government, Fort Victoria, dated 1 December 1817, Diary to the Collector of Ratnagiri 1818-19, Vol No. I, pp.71-72.

216. *Ibid.*

217. S.M.Edwardes, *The Rise of Bombay, A Retrospect*, Reprinted from Vol No. I of Census, The India Series, The Times of India, Bombay, D.C.P., 1902, p. 244.

CHAPTER 2

A HISTORICAL SKETCH OF THE KHOTS AND KHOTI TENURE IN THE RATNAGIRI COLLECTORATE [1818-1920]

When the East India Company started its rule in the South Konkan in 1818, it found that there existed a peculiar system known as the khoti system. The khots as Collectors of revenue had remained socially influential in the South Konkan for more than four centuries. No other indigenous groups could challenge their position. The physical configuration (hilly and rugged nature) and the problems of agriculture and administration had created a special type of land tenures there. They arose out of the need of reclamation of the waste and uncultivated lands populating the villages by bringing settlers from outside and collecting land revenue on behalf of government. The British needed this class of people to work as agents in the collection of revenue.

The Origin of Khoti System

The sanads issued during the time of Yusuf Adil Shah, the king of Bijapur in 1502 (1498-1510) are the earliest evidences available about the existence of the khoti system. Sher Shah Soor modified it in the middle of the 16th century. Todarmal who was the finance minister of Akbar, the Mogul Emperor perfected it. The revenue system of Todarmal was adopted almost throughout the country.

However, the credit of revenue settlements in Konkan goes to an Abbysinian Malik Amber, the Ahmednagar minister who ruled the Deccan and the Konkan from 1610-

1626. According to Mountstuart Elphinstone, Malik Amber followed the system of Todarmal. But there is a basic difference between the two. While Todarmal divided the soils into three classes, Malik Amber divided it into four classes. They were *Val, Dum, Sim,* and *Charsim.* Todarmal levied the rent in kind and Malik Amber levied it in cash. Todarmal took one third of the gross produce while Malik Amber took one fifth.

The person to introduce a systematic revenue system in the Maratha territory was Dadaji Konddev. He introduced the system to the territories under Shahaji.[1] He called the assessment as the Bigoti system. The Bigha was a measure adopted by both Todarmal as well as Malik Amber. Shivaji modified this system about a century and a half later (1670-1680) and fixed the Royal share as one third of the produce.[2] It was later on increased to half of the produce. That the khoti system was not unknown in the Deccan and the Konkan can be seen from the following statement.

'Many of the khots South of Bankot or Savitri River hold sanads given to them by the Marathas (1670-1786), the Moghuls (1690-1720), or by the Peshwas (1760-1818)'.[3]

During the year 1683, Sambhaji, under the advice of Kavi Kalaush, his close friend and advisor, upset the revenue system and the royal share became about one half to two thirds of the gross produce. The people were not able to bear the burden of taxes and often became robbers and murderers.[4] Rajaram after the death of Sambaji in 1689, tried to bring about changes as the revenue system had fallen into disorder but he could not succeed. In the Konkan, the Arab and African relations had promoted the Habsi community.[5] In 1699, the Habshis who were also called as Siddis conquered Suvernadurg and Anjanvel. In 1744, the Angrias ousted the Siddis and Ratnagiri fell into their hands and remained with them till 1756. The Angrias imposed several new taxes, which included levy on small items like baskets, mats, firewood, brooms, earthern pots and others and the poor farmers were burdened under them. The people could not follow the accounts and began depending more and more on the khot.[7]

The next rulers who brought the South Konkan under their control were the Peshwas. They conquered it in 1756.

In the year 1770, the Peshwas ordered the survey of Konkan. But the actual survey of the South Konkan began in 1781 only after it was to the north of Kalyan. This survey was completed in 1794. The Peshwas deputed a number of officers for the survey of land and some of the important officers were Gangadhar Pant Bhanu, Raghunath Trimbak Barve, Mamlatdar Parshuram Ramchandra Paranjape and others. These officers surveyed Suvarnadurg, Anjanvel, Ratnagiri and Vijaydurg.[8] All the surveys were recorded in the *Pahani Kharda*. It gave a record of the area of all the cultivated lands held by the village renters, khots and peasant holders, dharekarees together with the names of the holdings and the assessment of each. An example of *Pahani Kharda* used is given below:[9]

PAHANI KHARDA

Shri.

Pahani Kharda of the revenue survey of the lands fit for agricultural purposes in the village. Virjoli Prant Ghosle for the year Samn Saban Maya and Alaf 1178 (1778-79 A.D.)

About the field 'Mahar Wawade' by name.

For the last year the extent of this land had been under a mistake entered in the description of the 'Kak' field; and in consequence of that in the current year this field has been separately entered. For that reason, now the following account is freshly prepared for this field of 'Mahar Wawade'. At the time of the present Survey this field stands entered in the name of the Khot himself, while the present tenant in occupation of the land id Ramaji Ghosalkar in addition to Gharatkar.

The grand total of the whole of this field is that the extent in all is of ½ Bigha and 3¾ Pands, out of which the waste piece if the land to be deducted is Nil and remaining portion of the land that is still fir to be cultivated is of half Bigha and three and three-fourth Pands, while the total quantity of rice that has been now fixed as the assessment for this land is of half Khandi and 2 ½ Payalis.

About the field 'Bahule'.

The extent of this filed for the last year was of 4 ½ Pands, out of which the portion that was at that time fit to be cultivated was of 2 ¾ Pands, the fallow ground that had been abandoned being then of 1 ¾ Pands.

Bighas	**Pands**	
0	1 ½	Being made up of 7 Kathis in length and 5 Kathis in width, which make up 1 ¾ Pands, out of which the stony portion to be deducted is of ¼ Pand and the remaining is entered here.
0	1 ¼	Being made up of 5 Kathis in length and 5 Kathis in width
0	2 ¾	

At that time of the present survey this filed stands in the name of the Khot himself while his Ardheli tenants in occupation If this land is Navjee Kude, and at the present time the cultivable piece are as detailed below:

The waste piece that has been abandoned now out of this land is of 1¾ Pands, it being the best part now out of the original waste ground.

The grand total in connection with the whole of this land is that the total extent is of 4½ Pands, out of which the waste piece to be deducted is of 1¾ Pands while the remaining portion of this land that has now been fit to be cultivated is of 2¾ Pands, while the total quantity of husk rice (bhaut) that has been fixed as the assessment for this land is of maund and 2¾ payalis.

It was the Peshwas who left the entire job of the collection of the revenue in the hands of the khots. It was left at the discretion of the khot as to the bargains to be done with the peasants although they were to meet the ever-demanding, ever-fluctuating demands of the government.

They had two duties to perform-namely as farmers of revenue and as performers of duties elsewhere in the hands of Patels or village headmen.[10] The khots enjoyed the privileges because the overall management of the villages was assigned to him. By his right over the trees and gardens the khot could not dispossess the actual holder there. He only exercised his customary right as Watandar.[11]

Thus by the time the East India Company acquired the South Konkan, the office of the khots had become almost indispensable. While in some cases the rents were fixed in khoti lands, in majority cases, the actual quantity of grain to be paid was determined after the *abhavani* or the annual assessment of crops by inspection of the standing crop. Such estimates of crops were made by the khot, the tenant and a third person who was generally a partisan of the khot either through obligation or fear. The result was over-estimation of crops leading to appropriation of the bulk of the tenant's produce. Secondly, most of the tenants were tenants-at-will and so could be evicted quickly. The lands were also cultivated on the basis of yearly agreements or *kabuliyats.* The khot also received a share in the produce of fruit trees planted by the tenants.[12]

Types of Tenures in the Konkan

The khoti tenure differed from the land tenures of Gujarat, interior Maharashtra and other parts of India. The northern parts of Bombay, chiefly the Ahmedabad district afforded examples of a particular system called the talukdars. These talukdars were recognized as landlords paying a fixed tribute. The old rajas used to be replaced by the new ones. Thus the lands turned into revenue paying lands of the conquering power. But the subordinate chiefs who controlled the hilly parts submitted and agreed to pass on the portion of their revenue to the conquered territory. It was found convenient to leave control of these territories under local chiefs who were designated as *Talukdars.*[13] Maharashtra also had a system in which the chiefs were called as *khots.*

The khoti tenures of the Konkan were as follows:[14]

1. The Khoti in the Ratnagiri and the Kolaba districts.
2. The Salsette estates commonly known as Salsette

Khoti in the Bombay suburban districts and Thana district (the former Salsette Island).

3. The Kauli and Katuban tenures in the ex-states of Janjira and Sawantwadi and Kolhapur merged in the Kolaba, Ratnagiri and Kolhapur districts.
4. The khoti in the ex-Janjira and Bhor states merged in the kolaba district.
5. The shilotri tenure in the Kolaba district.

Thus the Khoti system differed in the coastal parts of Maharashtra. After the acquisition of Salsette by the British in 1772-73, the khoti tenure was extended to about 51 villages because the island was depopulated and scantily cultivated. With a view to attract population and introduce cultivation, the British Government gave the right of absolute ownership or to give it on lease perpetual or periodical.[15] However the leases differed according to the exigencies of administration. Powai, Goregaon, Deonar, Bhandup, Chincavli, Maravli, Mahul, Kanjur and Vikroli had estates, which were leased for revenue farming. While the leases in the case of Vile Parle and Juhu were hereditary inams. The motive behind the leases of Ghodbunder, Bhayandar and Mira estates was maintenance of embankments. Kurla and Malad estates were leased for exchange of lands.[16] The lessees paid remuneration to village *Patels* or *Madhvis*. It was also found that many villages were granted to the Parsis as they ventured to develop the villages.[17]

In Kolaba, the Khots had to execute the *kabulayats,* which defined their rights and responsibilities. Accordingly, they had to pay local fund cess to government and recover the dues from the cultivators. The dues could be survey assessment from the dhara lands. They could be customary *khoti faida* in kind or in cash.[18] There were 464 villages in Kolaba district. There were two types of ownership granted to the khots in Kolaba. They were *khoti khasgi* and *khoti nisbat.* The *khoti khasgi* was a private property of the khots, the *khoti nisbat* land was vested in the government. As far as the forest rights were concerned the khots in kolaba were entitled to one third of the net proceeds after deducting all the felling expenses incurred by the government reduced by twenty percent of the amount of the share as it was given in the *kabulayat.*[19]

The khoti system of the Konkan, especially of the Ratnagiri district was created because of the roughness of the country. It was more prominent in Ratnagiri taluka than in the Malvan taluka or the Vengurla petha. It was a difficult task for the British to understand the khoti system of Ratnagiri. This peculiar system was difficult to be grasped for both the administrators as well as the farmers. Were the khots the friends of the farmers? Or were they the supporters of the administrators? Were they originally farmers, or were they revenue collectors? Who were the district officers? What were their functions? The East India Company took many years to understand the issues connected with them.

District Officers

In the administration of land revenue of the Konkan, village communities and administrative officers played an important role both in the collection of taxes and in maintaining the necessary accounts. This was their most important share in village administration. However, it is also seen that the nature of work, their powers, responsibilities and duties were not really well defined and very often found to be overlapping.

The officers were mainly divided into three divisions namely *Paragana watandars, Gaon watandars, Pethe watandars.* The *gaon watandars were Patil, Kulkarni, Chougule,* while *Sardeshmukh, Sardeshpande, Sardeshmukhi, Deshkulkarni, Sarpatil, Desh Chougule* were the *paragana watandars.* The head of the smaller units or *prant* was *Kamvisdar.* Each revenue division as *paragana* or *prant* was under a *Kamvisdar. Mamlatdar* who was a higher authority had eight members under him. *Divan, Mazumdar, Phadnavis, Potnis, Potedar, Chitnis Karkhanis and sabahasad.* Hereditary officers were directly responsible to government, their signatures were necessary on all documents and they were bound to give information of all the misdeeds and malpractices of the *Mamlatdars.*

The head of the village was the *patil.* He was referred to also as *the Mukaddam, Mokadam, Patel, Mukhia, Gram*

Pramukh, and *Gramini.* He used to allot the land to such cultivators who had no landed property of their own. He fixed their rent. He collected the revenue for government from all the rayats, conducted all its arrangements with them and exerted himself to promote the cultivation and the prosperity of the village.

Kulkarni also called, as *Coolkurnee* was the next important officer of the village. He was also called *Gramlekhak or Gramlekhi. Gramlekhi* meant 'the person who looked after the village.'[20] The word kulkarni has its origin from *'kula'* meaning a debtor or tenant and *'karni'* meaning a doer or an agent. To be more precise he was the village accountant. He used to keep records of land revenue of each farmer after surveying the yield of the crops. He had to prepare and submit to the government treasury, yearly statement of accounts of estimated revenue, actual collections, the balance of revenue to be collected from each farmer. Kulkarni was held responsible jointly with patil for the collection of the land revenue.

Thus the officials like Patil, the village headman, Kulkarni, the village accountant, the Deshpande, The Deshmukhs, the Chougula assistant of the Patil, the Shete Mahajan village market officers, and Mahars, the village helpers held the watan tenure. They were given hereditary rights, fixed salaries and presents in kind. Many of them were khots. The *paragana* (group of villages) watandars like the Deshmukhs and the Deshpandes supervised the work of the Patils and the kulkarnis. *Watan*, an Arabic term signifying the grant of land made to a person holding an office was not only a source of income but also a social status to them.[21]

Remarks on the Prevailing Khoti Tenures

In the Ratnagiri district, there were about 952 khoti villages. A khot here got the village by paying to the government *Jama* (which meant paying aggregate assessment of the village). The rights of the khots to these khoti lands were transferable and heritable. The *khoti khasgi* land was a private property of the khot similar to that of the Kolaba district. According to it, the khot was recognized as an occupant, and was called the *dharekari* or *quasi-*

dharekari of the *dhara* land. He was recognized as a permanent tenant in the case of the lands held by them.

In case of the *khoti nisbat* land, a tenant could be in possession of *khoti nisbat* land. If there was no tenant, then the khot was in its possession. The *khoti nisbat* however was a joint property of the khot and the government. He was entitled to one third of the net profits made by the government in the rights of the forests.[22]

In fact not more than about half the villages in the Southern Konkan were entirely managed by the khots. In others the khots were either absent or they were empowered with restricted rights by the superior class of persons known as *dharekaris* (dhara holdings) who enjoyed hereditary occupancy rights. But most of the tenants called *ardhelis* (Paying half of ones crop as rent) were not very fortunate because they seemed to have no right of any practical importance.[23] The following table shows the villages of Southern Konkan having different tenures with less than and more than Rs 1000 annual income.[24]

Table 2.1: Villages Worth Less Than Rs 1000 Annual Revenue

Khoti	1,062 ½
Dharekari	337
Mixed	525 ½
Total	1,925

Table 2.2 : Villages Worth More Than Rs 1000 Annual Revenue

Khoti	38
Dharekari	133
Mixed	106
Total	277

The khot according to Jonathan Elphinstone was an officer appointed by the Peshwa Government to collect the revenue. He said that it was the Peshwas who left the entire job of the collection of revenue in the hands of the khots. It was left at the discretion of the khot as to the bargains to be done with the peasants although they were to meet the ever demanding and ever fluctuating demands of the government.

Local investigations and inquiries also revealed that there were two types of khoti in Ratnagiri. The villages under what was called as khot were khotwar villages. The khot was a farmer of the village and alone was answerable to the government for the rent and the ryuts. Under the *Koolargwar* system each ryut paid for his own field through the khot or the Patel to government. There were also villages where both were mixed and were called the *khichari* and at such places where management was mixed, the khot paid for all the *khotwar* lands and the independent ryuts called *dharekarees* paid their rent directly to the officers of the government or indirectly through the khot.[25]

In the *khotwar* villages, the local collection of the rent was different from the *Pahanee Jummabundee.* The khot alone decided the amount of assessment and he alone was answerable for it to the government. He farmed the lands at that rate and let them out at the best advantage to the ryuts. In letting the lands he was not guided by the rent fixed by the government for each ryut land but got as much more as he could. The ryut also had no right to it except on the terms, which he could agree upon with the khot.[26]

In *koolargwar* villages the *jummabundee* was fixed and the ryut paid the rent invariably for his land until a new *pahanee* took place. He paid it either directly to the government or to the head of the village for government. In such villages there was neither khot nor Patel, the principal officers being the *Wartak, Mahajan, Chougula* and *Kulkarni* who received small allowance from the government. If there was a khot or a Patel, he was only the head of the village and the Collector and not the farmer of its revenue. The Wartak was considered the chief manager and was assisted by the Mahajan. The Chougula and Kulkarni were like the functionaries of the same name as in the Deccan.[27]

The khots belonged to different castes but mostly were Brahmins and soon came to be regarded as de facto hereditary farmers, whatever they may have originally been de jure.[28] The khots also were Muslims, Prabhus, and Marathas.[29] They had two duties to perform-namely as farmers of revenue and as performers of duties elsewhere in the hands of Patels or village headmen.[30]

The Company wished that all social classes mingled together thus checking the prevalence of abuses. The policy seemed to have received official consent because the government in 1822, in its report stated that the Brahmins, the Muslims and the Prabhus had mingled as much as possible in the Government services in all the talukas of the South Konkan.[31] The khots thus who were normally Brahmins, Prabhus, Marathas, and few Muslims had the rights to mortgage them because they rented it out. They received no fees from the government but enjoyed the privilege of one day's labor in eight days from each house. If there was a large family, the brothers took by turns annually to manage the village affairs as khot for that year.[32]

The following articles were exacted every year from persons who did menial labour 4 days in each month during which time the khot gave a meal to them.

Ratnagiri taluka: 2 Fowls, 1 gourd, 1 cucumber, 1 vurleh (A covering used in the rainy season), 2 ½ seers of karvanda (a sort of fruit), 4 bundles of hay, 6 bundles of firewood. Persons bringing the last two mentioned articles were given one meal a day.

Malvan taluka: 1 fowl, 1 gourd, 1 cucumber, 5 seers of karavanda, 1 bundle of hay. The mahars were exempted from giving the above articles but they gave to the khot 1 soop, 1 broom, 1 vurleh, 1 rowlee, 1 bundle of firewood, and 1 mat.[33]

Besides the above-mentioned privileges, they were also granted special rights like *manpan* (On the occasion of marriages and social Functions, the khot was presented with gifts as a mark of honour. This was called manpan), *Hakka* (hakka meant the right or the privilege of the khot to collect fees, fines and others. This was claimable by him under the established usage of the village.), *kanoon Kayade* (kanoon Kayade was the right of acquiring from every man the knowledge about his products for sale; The khot even possessed the privilege of taking a portion of his goods, *lavajima* (The khot was entitled to make use of the village services and village servants like mahar, gurav and others. The word Lavajima in the literary sense meant Retinue),

Vethbegar (The khot had the right to make use of the services of his tenants without any remuneration.), *devdevaski* (Being a man of honour, the khot had the right in the duties which were connected with the worship of villages. For example if any body in the village wished to offer Kowl to the village deity, he could do so only through the Khot.) *gavki* (Gavki was the right of the khot to collect land revenue from the people of the village.) *holipoli* (The khot would be a chief guest at the important festival, namely holi faida farmas The produce in the fields had to be partly given to the khots. In fact it was his right to take the produce.) *asthadikar* (The khot had the right over the eight officers of the village.) The khot enjoyed the above privileges because the overall management of the villages was assigned to him. By his right over the trees and gardens the khot could not dispossess the actual holder there. He only exercised his customary right as Watandar.[34]

Some of the khots were described as Watandars and others as having acquired the khotship by mortgage of various kinds. The first of watandars were purely farmers and were principally found in the villages along the ghats. They were said to have had their rise from the distracted state of the province, the revenue of which was divided between the Wadi, Kolhapur, & Angria's Government.[35]

The British initially felt that it was utmost necessary to have a powerful agent like the khot, who could help them in performing the duties of the revenue collection. Considering the long period during which the khot had officiated as the head of the village, he was probably viewed by them as the fittest agent to be entrusted with the same revenue and police duties as were inherent in the patel.[36] His position was that of a middleman between the ryot and the state. He had to collect rents from his village and pay a lump sum to the state. Usually the amount collected by the khot from the tenants was called *Khanda* in the Southern Konkan and the same was called *matka* in the northern Konkan region.[37] Sometimes the khots bore the burden of payment of the revenue for the entire village.[38] It was often found from the different cases that reached the courts that the khoti was an estate, which paid revenue to the government upon which an assessment was temporarily settled and it was the khot who normally paid the revenue for the entire village.[39]

It is no wonder then if it appeared to J.J.Sparrow in 1821 that the villages in the Konkan had not only ever possessed the municipal establishments but the whole control concentrated in the khoti. He further felt that the authority of two of the most useful village agents, the Patel and the Kulkarni had been entirely suspended because of the influence of the khots.[40] It was therefore not at all surprising that as the whole revenue settlement and management of the accounts as well, relations between him and the ryut and the government rested in the khot.[41] In another report it was stated that he had an uncontrolled power, which exercised over the affairs of the village.[42] Moreover, it was difficult for the British to understand the system because of the imperfect accounts managed in villages by the kulkarnis and other village officers. The accounts kept on loose papers, not informative, liable to be altered and untraceable created confusion. D.Blane, Assistant Collector was deputed to report on the existing system and recommend new methods that could be introduced. The new mode of keeping account was referred to by D.Blane was to have a simple method of double entry, all receipts and disbursements entered in a day book and then transferred to another book containing several accounts of the district, villages or persons as the case may be with reciprocal references to the pages of each entry for all the payments and disbursements.[43]

J.H. Pelly, J. A Dunlop and others however, found it difficult to differentiate between the agricultural classes and the khots. The new rulers might well have expected the hereditary officers like the Deshmukhs and the Deshpandes to furnish valuable source of information on such complicated points. But unfortunately, most of these were khots themselves.[44] In order to curb the powers of the khots, J. A Dunlop suggested that more of the superior class of tenants namely the *dharekaris* should be established in the villages where the khoti system prevailed. This in the long run would turn the khots into some sort of agents like the Patels who were more important in other parts of the Konkan. A revenue survey would also enable him to draw up a scale of pay for the khots proportionate to the produce of the village. He suggested that accountants were to be appointed to get correct information on the produce. An incidental advantage of this, he thought, would be to absorb the crowds of discontented Brahmins who were so numerous.[45]

One thing was understood by the Company that they needed the khots for their administrative convenience and also because they could not do away with them. Whatever may be their origin they were a vital part of the villages in the Ratnagiri district. J.A.Dunlop, therefore, believed that they appeared to have acquired a right and it was not possible to interfere.[46] But at the same time he felt that it was necessary to curb the powers of the khots by holding a survey to find out if there was any way the ryuts could be protected by the government.[47] This was not an easy task. The only way that was thought feasible by the court of Directors was to find out by methodical surveys, the demands of the cultivators and the rights of the khots, as it was too early for them to obstruct the rights of khots.

J A Dunlop visited the Paros Mahal in the Ratnagiri taluka where almost 20 villages belonged to the khots. He also found that these villages were the most productive in the district and yielded considerable profit to the khots. He, therefore, sent orders to the khots that if they did not immediately give consent to furnish security, he would legally take charge of their villages. He succeeded in doing so by sending the karkoons to proceed and take charge of the villages if the security was not given. He gave the names of the khots who gave security to the government.[48] He reported the names of nineteen out of twenty khots who gave security. Some the names are as follows. *Shivram Prabhoo Desoy of kusba Huchree, Ganajee Hurrey Mosley of Massurah Vessoorlah, Chandakurs of Mauja Chandoor, Amburdakar of Mauja Koortadah.*[49]

Lieutenant Dowell in 1829 gave a description of the khoti system as it then existed in the southern Konkan and as understood by him. He said that there were 345 villages in the Ratnagiri taluka itself and they were divided into *khoti, koolargi* and *khicheri.* 271 of them were khoti, 66 *koolargi* and 8 *khicheree* villages. Some villages according to him had become khoti within the last eighty years, and that the khots were farmers of the village revenue, who toiled and suffered to remain till the tenure became hereditary. The *koolargi* villages were those whose lands were held by the *dharekarees* or the so-called independent proprietors. Even in these villages the Khots and the Mahajans settled but they did not have propriety rights over the lands of the *dharekarees.* The *khicheree* or the mixed villages wherein portion of the land was in the hands of the *dharekarees* and the remaining lands were in the hands of the khots. The khot lands, on the other hand had no independent proprietors at all.[50]

The profits of the khots depended on chiefly rice lands and their location. For example the *Sur Desai* who was a khot of 11 villages in Sangameshwar let out all his best lands and got an annual rent of Rs. 1500 or 2000 above the jummabundee while in Lanje Mahal, the khot got a rent of about Rs 200 above the jummabundee from 10 villages of hilly land. Thus it was difficult for the Company to assess the income of the khoti villages. In the initial years, therefore, the Peshwa's system of measuring and classifying was followed. The Company tried to adjust the assessments however, settlements put forth could not be brought into practice owing to the difficulty of fixing the khot's demands.[51]

The *kunbis* or *kulbis,* cultivators of the soil under the khot, were mostly of that class called *'ardhilee'* (Ardha-half receiving half their produce.) The cultivator could not prosecute the khot in the *adawlat* and neither the collector, nor the assistants had any control over him as long as he paid the fixed rate of jummabundy to government.[52]

Between 1839 and 45 a number of complaints were lodged against the khots by the farmers. Some of their complaints were that the khots collected house taxes while they had been suspended by government, that they refused to give receipts for initial mints of revenue paid, that the khots used false measure, that they made the ryuts pay 18 or 20 pailies instead of 17 pailies for each maund of revenue grain, that they collected *'purson purda'* taxes about which they were ignorant, they extracted *'Varsai'* and *'ath* veth' (Labour exacted without remuneration one day in eight days) from the ryuts when they were abolished by government, that the khots appropriated to their own use government grass lands, that they never gave the ryuts any remissions, that they claimed more than half share of the crops from the ardheli ryuts, that they continued to take all the taxes that had been abolished by the government, and above all they would beat and abuse the ryuts.[53] The complaint also included that under the system of *Veth* or forced Labour, the khots made use of the tenant's family Labour for his domestic needs as well as for agricultural operations on his self-cultivated lands.[54]

G. Guriyale, Superintendent of revenue survey observed that the system of *Ath Veth* had to be abolished. He wrote, 'the total abolition of the customs would in any way be detrimental to the real interest of the khot, though it would probably curtail a little, the parade with which, he now travels, and induce him to substitute a pony or perhaps his own legs for the shoulder of his fellow villagers as a means of conveyance'.[55]

Despite the complaints compiled and reported by the R.A.Bazeth, nothing much could be done against the khots. G.Coles agreed that khots' place in the village was important because according to him, 'the khot furnished the ryot with advances for cultivation and received his rent in kind and thus not only supplied the place of a village to the coonbee but saved him some loss in the conversion of his grain into cash in which part of the government was required to be paid and that same time at an advanced rate above the bazaar price.'[56]

Moreover, he further stated, 'It was doubtful how far it might be just or polite to interfere in the khoti matter. The khots had enjoyed their farms for a long course of years, they had bought and sold, inherited and bequeathed them from generation to generation. The ryuts themselves would even at first dislike the change, they would not know to whom to look up or to apply for advances or for support or redress it would certainly create confusion and distrust to supply the place of the khot by a direct agent of government and considerable time would be required to reconcile all parties to the change.'[57]

But by 1850s, the Company wanted to reduce the powers of the khot. It became imperative for the British Government to make a more searching enquiry into the khoti system. G.Coles, the collector was placed in charge of the revenue survey. He was assisted by Capt. Wingate who was then the Superintendent of the Revenue Survey. G.Coles paid a visit to various parts of the district and spent time in each taluka to gather information about the existing system. His tour was as follows:[58]

Table 2.3

Ratnagiri Taluka:
From 18 Nov - 20 Nov 1848.
From 16 Dec - 21 Dec 1848.
From 6 Feb - 20 Feb 1848.
From 23 Apr - 30 Apr 1848.
Malvan Taluka:
From 29 Mar - 14 April 1849.

These officers also toured some more parts like Vijaydurg, Unjunwell, and Suvernadurg during this period, and the tour lasted for almost 165 days.[59] It was reported by these officers that with the exception of seven villages under the direct government management belonging to Bankot which were ceded to the British Government by the Peshwa in 1754 and 48 villages in the Malvan districts which were received from the Kolhapur and Waree Government in 1812-13, the entire country acquired by the Company from the Peshwa in 1817-18 had the khoti management.[60] The khots thus were the hereditary officers in the district. They had less influence and more power than the Deshmukhs and the Deshpandes of the Deccan.[61]

In 1851 Capt. Wingate suggested that the Government had the right to interfere in its administrative if not legislative capacity to regulate the relations of the khot and the ryut. Capt. Wingate's suggestion was accepted and permission was given to have an experimental survey done with an aim to ascertain to what extent it was desirable to define or modify the relations of the khot and and his tenants by Legislative Act.[62] However, experimental survey was sanctioned in a few villages but it turned out to be a failure. Hence, the Government had to suspend the survey operations.

In 1859, Col.Francis was appointed to further investigate into the powers of the khots and as how to reduce them. (G.R.1892 /19-5-1859) Based on the earlier reports from the other officers and fresh surveys, Col. Francis gave a suggestion that it would be possible to arrive at an amicable settlement, by signing an agreement with the khot himself as a superior holder for the revenue of the village in the gross revenue. He also proposed that the ryuts should be protected by giving them rights of occupancy, thus depriving the khot of his power of exploiting the tenants. Although the Government accepted his suggestions because the ryuts could be protected from the over-exaction on the part of the khot, and the khots would be made to hold the survey rates on a lease of thirty years, yet they realized the impracticality of the policy.

Settlements of Khots and the Khoti Villages and the Reactions of the People

The East India Company Officers had done extensive work from 1818 to 1860, but it had not given any satisfactory solution to the problems of the khots in the land revenue administration. So many reports had been made on the khoti system by the various officers from 1820 to 1860, yet the Government was perplexed about the rights of the khots. However, based on the earlier reports, the Government realized the urgency of incorporating provisions for the settlement of khoti villages. It passed Revenue Settlements Acts, which however were amended time and again. To begin with, the khot was considered as merely a contractor or farmer being regarded for the purposes of Section of Act VIII of 1859 as an 'Estate Paying Revenue to Government'.[63]

During the first few decades of Company's rule, as long as the revenues were collected, little attention appeared to have been given to the individual entering into the annual *kabulayat* (Formal agreements by which the khot engages to make good, the fixed sum at which the revenue is assessed, coupled with two securities for punctual payment of the revenue- Bombay Act of 1865). As a result, throughout the district, barring a few cases, the khots had mortgaged their trusts. In other cases the khots had actually sold their trusts. The management of such villages had consequently fallen into the hands of a class of men whose sole object was to the make the most they could with little regard to the benefits of the ryuts.

But the British Government felt that the interference of the khots had to be minimised for their benefit. At the same time, it had to strike a balance between the khots, the ryuts and the revenue collection. It was a tough job because the khoti had been so much absorbed into the system in Ratnagiri Collectorate that it was difficult to uproot it.

To begin with, it was resolved by the British Government that whatever rights of the khoti may be, the khot of a village cannot choose to sell, mortgage, or give the khotship without informing the Government. Nor could he dispose off the profits or transfer the right to anyone else without the consent and concurrence of the government. Further the mortgaged could not be looked upon as having any claim to the khotship, which may be held to have lapsed by the death of the original khot without heirs and the mortgagees had no further claim to the profits of the management, and this management would be passed on to the government.[64] It was also resolved that it was the duty of the officers making the settlement, to see that the prescribed limit did not exceed in any of the agreements, which the khots brought for registry.[65]

The Survey Settlement Act of 1865 made the dharekarees (dhara-land given in charity thus meaning in favour of tenants) hereditary occupants and they were freed from the control of the khots. It at least seemed so theoretically. This is understood because the British, on the one hand curbed the powers of the khots, and on the other gave special privileges to them. The khots of Ratnagiri were given the right to claim 5% of the share over the tapping of trees. The British employed them for the reclamation of land. This probably had to be done to keep them happy. Such strategies neither made the farmers happy, nor the khots contented. The Act of 1865 proved abortive, for both the khot and the tenant grew discontented with the working of the survey thus newly inaugurated. The khot was dissatisfied because almost all farmers under him were entered as holders or occupants of the land held by them in the survey records. The farmers felt that the new system of punctual payment of cash or kind sometimes to be paid by going to far off places from their destination, with a penalty for default was harsh and obnoxious. Both lodged numerous complaints and the British Government spent a number of years in solving them.

What was astounding here was that it was difficult to understand whether the khots were the friends of the British or the friends of the farmers. The people in the newspapers expressed very contradictory views. One thing is sure that the khots who belonged to the upper strata of society, generally the educated Brahmins probably were their friends, but generally the khots who belonged to the middle class were equally disgusted with the rules and the management of the British administration in the field of revenue collection. This was obvious because the British revenue officers laid rules for their own benefit.

By and large, the bills passed or rules laid by the British often had adverse effects. The rights of the khots were not fixed and led to further confusion. Over assessment of lands was another eternal cry. Vasudev Damodar Juvekar khot's complaint was that the form of the lease to be taken for the year 1868-69 was not in accordance with the conditions of the *kabulayats* and contained matters which were likely to prove detrimental to the Watandari rights. According to him, under section 8 Regulation of 1827, it was not correct to attack a khot as long as he paid the government due. He regretted that the annual *kabulayat* of his village was discontinued under Section 36 of the Act No.1 of 1865 and he wished that the khot be allowed to take the management of the village.[66] Thus he protested against the legality of the proceedings of the Survey Department.

Regarding the discontinuance of propriety right over his land, Gulam Moheedeen Mohommad Ebraim khot of Mauje wrote, *'I state that being wuttandar khot I have full propriety right over my land and that government cannot under the Act of 1865, exercise any control in the matter of interfering with my tenants. But the Government states that I have no propriety right over the lands of the village- that the Act of 1865 is applicable to all khotee villages and that under sections 37 and 38 that they are competent to settle with the tenant of all the khotee villages. The circumstance, therefore, of my having agreed to take up the management of the village according to the terms of the kabuliyat, should not be held to hinder me from asserting my propriety right or bringing in future whatever settlement may come to. On these conditions I have signed these kabuliyats. What I have to say, and what the government has to say is written above but it should be understood that the period of limitation prescribed by law for seeking redress in the civil court, is not hereby affected.'*

The highhandedness of the Survey Department was often described in the Native Newspapers. One such was given in Jagan Mitra, in which the writer signing himself as Sindhvasi exposed the dramatic form of injustice done by the British. *'A Khot is called by the Superintendent. He comes and the superintendent simply informs him of the amount of assessment imposed upon him and refuses to give him any particulars. The khot then leaves the cutcherry with disgust. This is the way in which the settlement is carried on ...'*. He asked whether the survey assessment was a trick invented by the government to seize upon the estates of the khots.'[67]

V.N. Mandlik, a khot himself also published various articles in the Native Newspapers. V.N. Mandlik in his book 'A Brief History of Watandars' gave a detailed account of the origin of the khots of the South Konkan, its system, the rights of the khots, their relationships with the villagers and farmers and their duties and responsibilities. This was helpful to the government while laying down the rules.[68]

Another petition from Gopalrao Chintaman Karandikar, a khot was made. The other khots also signed on the petition. It was said that the assessment of their village as fixed by the revenue survey was heavy in comparison with that of the adjoining villages. He also complained that the Mamlatdar of his village Nuwusjee refused to take the lease prepared, and said that according to the Act of 1865, his villages would be attacked. The petitioner gave the following reasons for not being wrong:

1. 'That I was the Wattandar khot of villages alluded to and that I had a right to make recoveries from cultivators.
2. That the Act of 1865 was not applicable to me.
3. That I agreed to pay the just rate that might be fixed by the Survey Settlement.
4. That I agreed to the sirkar's interference in my internal management.
5. That the present rate was contrary to the usage of the country and the regulations. That I agreed to pay it without relinquishing my right of complaint.
6. That the amount of assessment was ready and the same be received.'[69]

He further said that both the Collector and the Mamlatdar paid little attention to the complaints. Along with the khots, the common ryuts also were unhappy with changes. They objected to the place the revenue officers stayed during the collection period. According to them, the officers maintained their headquarters at Satara instead of Ratnagiri even during the difficult seasons like the monsoon. Many ryuts had to go to Satara with complaints and petitions and it was not at all fair that the farmers were put to inconvenience during the rainy season. The people in the same issue brought to light, the fact, that the cultivating ryuts instead of being happy by discarding the middleman i.e. the khots were sorry to have become direct tenants of the state.[70] Over-assessment was also one of the complaints of the people. The ryuts had requests to make and some of them were as follows:

1. That the *warkasi* land should to be measured by chain, the barren portion of it should be deducted.
2. That if the *warkasi* (ground chiefly hilly) land should be separately assessed, the present rates on the *kharif* (land producing autumnal harvest) land should be lowered.

3. That the warkasi land should be assessed at one or two annas an acre and not at three or four annas as has been done.
4. That the excess of the rates over the superseded ones should be remitted for one year, according to the old practice.
5. That as the government assesses the Warkasi land those who pay the assessment of that land should be allowed to have propriety right in the jungle and other produce of that land.[71]

In a letter complaining against certain acts of oppression and injustice committed by the revenue officers in the Ratnagiri, the khots and the ryuts of the village complained that the rate was too high for the lands assessed. They agreed that the garden lands irrigated by water drawn from the wells and those irrigated by artificial water courses need to be differently assessed. While the former were rated at five or six rupees per acre, the assessment put on the latter was in some cases as high as fifteen or sixteen rupees an acre, the difference in such treatment was unjust.

Such and many more petitions that came in large numbers to the government led them to question the Survey Officers on duty. But the reports by J.T.Francis, Survey and Settlement Commissioner showed that no warkas lands had been assessed at a higher rate than the maximum sanctioned. That the khots had been treated with every consideration by the officers of the Survey and Settlement Department and the assessment was equitable. He further said that the increase or decrease of assessment in the Ratnagiri district was more due to variations in area between the old and recent survey rather than the actual difference in rates. The following statement was shown to prove the nominal increase in revenue in the past ten years.

Average ten years payment	32, 197
Collections for 1864-65	44, 358
Survey Settlement	35, 702

He remarked that the total reduction in the collections of 1864-65 was Rs. 8,656 or about 25%. The increase in the average of ten years collection was Rs. 3,505 or 10%. But if comparison was done on the actual rates charged with those imposed under the survey settlement, it would show how liberally the petitioners were treated and how groundless their complaints were. In some parts of the district, there was as low a rate as Rs. 1½ per acre. The respective rates of assessment were as follows:[72]

Table 2.4

Classes	Old Rates per Beega Shown in Grain Maunds	Value of Grain at the rate of Rs. 20 per Maund	Survey Settlement Rates
First	12	16.6	10
Second	10	13.1	8
Third	8	10.7	7
Fourth	6	8.3	6
Fifth	5	6.8	5

A serious thought had to be given to solve the problems of the khoti system in an amicable manner. Therefore, J.T.Francis and A.K.Nairne, President and member of the Khoti Committee reported the result of the enquiries made by the Commissioner in the Ratnagiri Collectorate. The joint letter was produced on 8 February 1875. It was told that it was the wish of the committee to ascertain by inspection and enquiry on the spot in different villages, how far it was probable to arrive at both, with the khots and the cultivators, an agreement and whether it was practicable :

1. To declare who are dharekarees and the like.
2. To mark out the holdings of the dharekarees both in rice and warkas lands.
3. To declare who are customary tenants with rights heritable but not transferable.
4. To determine the period of prescriptive possession conferring those rights.
5. To fix the amount of rent paid by the customary tenants in produce.
6. To abstain from interference between the khots and the tenants-at-will.

7. To fix the customary rent of the tenants-at-will and give them heritable rights.
8. Precise and definite information on these points to enable government to decide on the proposals to be made to both parties with a view to an adjustment of their differences. Above all the possibility of clearly defining the rights to warkas lands be placed beyond doubt.'[73]

In 1876, the government revived the old and wrong practice of the khot collecting from the ryut, what upon his periodical inspection of the harvest, he chose to designate as his customary 1/2, 1/3, or 1/4 share in the gross produce of the crops grown by the holder himself with his money and industry, the khot himself in his turn paying government assessment in cash. And it was to this Settlement that the legislative sanction was given by the Bombay Act of 1880. The ryuts were unhappy about the oppressive character of this system, which enforced payments in kind, assessed upon periodical appraisements of the crops. Also since the reintroduction of the old practice they had been compelled to pay to the khot five to ten times, what they had to pay under the settlements of 1860 and 1865. In case of their inability to meet the khot's demands then, their lands were confiscated, thus, benefiting the khots. Because the Act declared that the lands thus forfeited was to be their *(Khoti faida)*. The khots, then, were able to impose on the newcomers any conditions that may be favourable to them, if the government was indeed, desirous of settling the complications. The rents of the ryuts ought to be fixed for some definite period and not liable to enhancement every year. And if dependent upon a definite share of crops, they ought to be represented by a money value, so that the ryuts would know beforehand the amount of rent actually payable to the khot for a definite number of years and knowing also that they would not be interfered with the annual inspection and appraisement of what they grew on their lands. This would enable them to live peacefully and concentrate on improvement in agriculture.[74] But such petitions often went unheard. The petitioner would be informed that the Government saw no reason to withhold his assent to the bill.[75]

The Khoti Settlement Act of 1879: According to the report made by Arthur Crawford on 26th December 1878, Ratnagiri Collectorate had altogether one thousand three hundred and thirty six villages. Out of which five eighty one were pure khoti, one thirty two were pure dharekari, four hundred and fifteen were khichari, seventy seven were khoti and khichari under government management but no Bedawas or deeds of reliquishment had been given by the khots, sixty four were inam, sixty three belonged entirely and six partly to the government.[76] The share of government villages in Ratnagiri Taluka was nine. Malvan Taluka had four government villages.[77]

To complete the job, Crawford immediately appointed one-fourth class Mamlatdar with a salary of Rs. 150. His bhatta was fixed at Rs. 25. A head karkoon on a salary of Rs. 30 was appointed and 4 karkoons on Rs. 20 each were absorbed.[78]

In 1877-78, G.W.Vidal settled 42 villages, Mr.Winchester 41, Mr.Hearn 116, Rao Bahadur N.B.Joglekar 171 and Crawford 37 villages. The outturn of the season of 1877-78 was 1,70,086 acres or an average of 34,000 acres per establishment. In 1878-79, the average was 26,726 acres. In the year 1879, the Bombay Legislative Council passed an Act called The Khoti Settlement Act of 1879. The Bill was to regulate the khoti system. The result of all the disputes led to the introduction of another Act. A Committee was formed consisting of Col.Francis and Messers, A.K. Nairne, N.G. Sathye, and N.B. Gole.[80]

Based on the receipts of the reports of the Commission from 1874 to 1878, a new bill was passed in 1879. The Bombay Legislative Council passed an Act, namely *The Khoti Settlement Act of 1879* and ultimately passed as Act I of 1880 which was commonly called as The Khoti Settlement Act-Bombay Act of 1880 and it was extended to all the villages held by khots in the Ratnagiri district.[81]

This Bill was meant to regulate the khoti system. The provisions of the Bill were to confirm the khots in the hereditary enjoyment of their khoti rights, after paying the amount that was fixed by the Survey Department from time to time, to secure tenant rights to all who could prove occupation previous to 1845, to fix the rents payable by the khots and all classes of tenants and to abolish all irregular cesses which had been a source of oppression and dispute. A settlement register was to be prepared under Section 108 which was to the area and assessment of every number and also whether such survey number was held by a privileged occupant or not. If it was to be held by a privileged occupant, the tenure upon which it was held was a *dharekari, quasi-dharekari* or an occupancy tenant. A list of co-sharers if any of the khoti was to be given. The survey officer was to prepare the register on the occasion of the introduction of the land revenue or when the same was revised after the expiry of the guaranteed period, which was generally fixed for a period of 30 years.

The following is a detailed picture of the year of Settlement.[82]

Table 2.5

District	Taluka	The year in which the current Settlement was introduced.	The district becomes open for resettlement
Ratnagiri	Dapoli	1868-69	1898-99
	Chiplun	1871-72	1901-02
	Guhaghar	1872-73	1902-03
	Vengurla	1875-76	1905-06
	Malvan	1883-84	1913-14
	Sangameshwar	1885-86	1915-16
	Rajapur	1890-92	1920-21
	Deogad	1892-93	1922-23
	Ratnagiri	1897-98	1927-28
	Mandangad	1895-96	1925-26

The Khoti Settlement Act was passed in 1880: The Act was extended to all villages held by the khots in the Ratnagiri district. The Act, which came into force on 6 May 1880, confirmed only the settlement already introduced tentatively in 1878-79. A regular Annual Progress Report was submitted to the government as to the working of the Acts. Re-measurement of lands was done.

Ratnagiri Taluka: (Khoti) Ratnagiri Taluka, which had 39,859 acres or 274.5 square miles, was re-surveyed in 1881. The pure dharekari lands increased from 2 to 35, pure khoti from 11 to 27 and khichari from 1 to 10 from the year 1879-80 to 1880-81. A register of new *dharas* was created and the *dharas* created from 1877-78 to 1879-80 in Ratnagiri was 2 in number. As compared to the *dhara* lands created in Dapoli, the number being 71 and Chiplun 65, the Ratnagiri Taluka had a minimum of two, showing the predominant khoti system that prevailed there.

Vengurla

Settlement of *Sheri, Kabutan* and *Gair Dasti* lands of the Vengurla: out of 130 *Sheri Thikans,* G.W.Vidal completed the register and recorded 126 of the rest 3 had been registered. 129 *thikans* had been settled as follows:

- 9 recorded as *dhara* at the survey rates.
- 6 leased for a term of 30 years at the survey rates.
- 3 continued in perpetuity under *kauli* tenure.
- 3 continued on *katuban* tenure.
- 108 continued for a term of 30 years at the *mamul* rates.

The *mamul* (old or customary rates) assessment on 129 *thikans* was Rs.6,246-9-8. The assessment on the same at survey rates was Rs. 4,310-6-1. The financial result of the settlement gave an annual income of Rs. 6,332-15-3 or a net increase of Rs. 86-5-7 over the *mamul* rates. Or Rs 2,022-9-2 over the survey rates.[83]

Katubans (Fixed rent): There were 28 of this class. Of these 18 proved to be of permanent nature. The total amount leviable on the thikhans was Rs. 287-5-8. The survey assessment on the same was Rs. 574. The result of the settlement done in 1880 gave an annual profit of Rs. 87-15-6 over the old rates.

Gair dasti (Improper use of taxable land): There were 19 *gair dasti thikans* actually occupied by 735 tenants in the Vengurla Taluka. A *mamul* assessment rate was Rs. 322-2-1 and the survey assessment was Rs. 628-6-0 thus giving the government a net profit of Rs. 306-3-11 per annum G.W. Vidal, the officer-in-charge of assessing the lands in Vengurla containing large coconut and betel-nut plantations said that the lands were fit for forest reserves, most of them adjoining rice and grass and brushwood for ash manure.

Malvan

There were 1,659 *sheri tikhans* and 315-*gair dasti* in Malvan *Sheri* lands. (Crown lands or lands cultivated for the khot by village ryuts gratis).[84] In 1886, an amendment was made under the section 40 of the Khoti Settlement Act of

1880. In rule no.1, it was made compulsory for the khot to inspect, appraise the yield of the crop of each field before a fixed time. Halwa or nagli on or before 10th September, other halwa crops before 1st October, late crops like harik, kulith, urid, tag and tur on or before 15th November, Rabi like gram on or before 1st March, summer crops like patwa on or before 20th March, hot weather crops like rice, nachni, and jackfruit on or before 20th May. He would have to give the probable estimate yield of the crop in front of two witnesses who were able to read and write. Rule 8 of the same published in notification No.1659 of March 11,1882 was that if the khot failed to keep and *abhavani patrak* or to inspect or appraise the crop at the given time or make the necessary entry, then he would compulsorily accept from the tenant according to the yield of the crop admitted by the tenant.[85] There were many more amendments made on these lines during these few years. The khoti system of Ratnagiri was so complicated that no number of Bills or Acts was helping the British to solve the problems of the region. There were a number of complaints against the Act of 1880 both from the ryuts and the khots.

The ryuts of various talukas of Ratnagiri Collectorate submitted a petition to the Government of Bombay. Their grievance was as follows: The Revenue Settlement was principally made in 1860 and later in 1865 and guaranteed the peasants that it would last for a period of thirty years. The Settlement in general terms was that the holder in the khoti village was to pay a fixed annual assessment on the holdings to the government and a specified quantity of grain to the khot, the middleman for every rupee of the government assessment as his profit called the *khoti faida.*[86]

If the ryuts on one side were unhappy with the Bills and Acts, the khots on the other side wrote innumerable letters in the newspapers against the British autocratic policies. One such complaint was given in the Kaisare-E-Hind, in which, a khot wrote that the rights of the khots were threatened with extinction. And it was because of the trained lawyer and an expert in khoti land tenure, V.N.Mandlik that their perspective rights were not altogether trampled under foot. But for his strenuous struggle carried on single handed, the khots would have been snuffed out of existence. He regretted that settlement arrived in 1880 was again was an unsatisfactory one.[87]

The Reporter of the Dnyan Sagar condemned the conduct of the Bombay Government in instituting a Secret Inquiry into the rights of the khots in the Ratnagiri Collectorate.[88] Another letter said that ever since the British came to the South Konkan, the khoti tenure had been a matter of perplexity to them and since then, either deliberately or through ignorance, the British had treated the khots most unfairly and in this process, the rights of the khots had been curtailed one after the other. It was further written that the khots no doubt existed but it was a mere miserable existence. This unfair treatment was proved by the Survey Act of 1865 and later the Khoti Act of 1880.[89]

Thus, the changing rules sought to bring conflicts between the khot and the ryuts rather than solving them. There was always a group of ryuts who were unable to pay the revenue whatever be the means of collection. In one of the reports it was written by G.M.F.Grant, Acting Commissioner, that 'the district is so over-populated, the soil so sterile and the holdings so minutely sub-divided that the Ratnagiri people must always be poor, and in a good many cases cannot live by agriculture even if they have nothing at all to pay. There will therefore probably always be a certain percentage of ryuts whose failure to pay will be due to poverty.'[90]

As for the reasons why the crop-share system did not work well in Ratnagiri, the chief ones were these. The people were not in the habit of paying a mathematical proportion of the crop. As early as 1830 Capt.W.Dowell had written that 'the *tirdhelis* in the ghat villages paid about one fourth of the crop. Capt Wingate in 1851 said that 'the recognised shares of one half, one-third, and one-fourth paid by the *ardhelis, tirdhelis* and *chauthelis* were seldom those really collected.' The ryut's contribution varied with the fertility of a particular field. And therefore, when he was called upon to pay a full half for the piece of third-rate rice land, he felt aggrieved. But the chief reason why the crop share system was so unpopular and injurious to the ryuts in the Ratnagiri was that it was so overpopulated. It was said that

'Where the demand is a demand was a demand by men for land and not by land for men, there the occupancy and all other rights of the ryuts are bound to become a mere farce unless payments were fixed.'[91]

Thus the government was not able to decide whether the crop share system was to be adopted or fix the occupancy tenant payments. It had to proceed gradually and not ask for too much. This would ensure peace to a certain extent, between the khots and the ryuts and minimise their conflicts.

In 1901, a new khoti Act was passed. The much-needed provision enabling khoti tenants to get their rents fixed in cash was made. The kind of harassment the tenants faced at the hands of the tenants is shown in the report of J. K.N.Kabraji, Acting Collector to the Commissioner. He said, 'A khot in the Mandangad petha was murdered in last March by three of his tenants. The Sessions Judge remarked: Almost all the witnesses state that the deceased who was the managing khot of the village was tyrant and unpopular with which he recovered his rents. The reporters did not want a harsh punishment to be given to the accused'. He further said, ' they were shamefully ill-treated by the khot... to kill him was to their limited understanding their only means of deliverance.' Similarly there was another incident in the Malvan Taluka, when a khot was shot dead by a man because he objected to obey the court's decree. These two cases within a span of six months spoke volumes about the trouble the tenants were in.[92]

Three quarters of a century were spent in experimental surveys, reports and settlements. The relation between the government and the khot and the relation between the khot and the farmer had become unsettled and confusing. The theories advanced were numerous. Very often, these could not be put into practice. The people also suffered because of the continuous surveys. The Acts definitely helped in doing away with some of the main difficulties. They were also partially successful in the smooth revenue administration of the khoti villages of Ratnagiri district.

A Bill in 1903 to amend the Khoti Settlement Act of 1880 was passed by the Legislative Department in Bombay. The reason behind this bill was to substitute cash for crop share rent. According to this bill, the tenant had to pay his rent in cash under certain restrictions. The bill was passed as *The Bombay Act No. III of 1904.* the Preamble of the Act of 1904 was special provision for the settlement and revenue administration of villages in the Ratnagiri District. The Act considered the khot as a superior holder. (This was according to the Bombay Land Revenue code 1879,Bombay V of 1879) He was entitled to settle with the government the revenue of his village. He had the right to hold the village by paying the *jama.* The khot was at liberty to settle his own terms with ordinary tenants. He also was vested with the power to cultivate wastelands in the village. The rights and privileges of the farmers were safeguarded by debarring the khot from exacting any kind of cess, tax or service from them. "It shall not be lawful for any khot to levy *faski, veth, nangarveth, wartala* or any other cess, rate tax or service of any description or denomination whatsoever, from any privileged occupant other than the rent lawfully leviable under the provisions of the Act of 1904."

In addition to the cesses mentioned above, the following cesses used to be levied by the khots: *karsai* (impost of fodder, fruits), *pendhi* (Bunch of tied grass), *fad-farmas* (fad-standing crop, farmas-fruit, vegetables and other petty articles) *dahi handi* (pot of curds), lagna tacca, *potdari patti* (collection in general of land), ambsul patti (cess on a typical sour fruit of konkan), *panchotra, kharedi katha* (rope), *kharedi halad* (turmeric), *dharekari karkun* patti (Dharekari Labour cess), *ghar patti* (cess on house) and others. The 35th section of 1904 did away with all these cesses and the khot could now lawfully recover from them nothing more than what was entered as rent in the survey record. Although the Act made the levying unlawful it did not lay down the penalty for the breach of the rule. However if it was exacted against the will of the tenant, it was punishable as being 'unlawful compulsory labour' under section 374 of the I.P. code.

On 28th May 1913, an Act to amend the Bombay Land Revenue Code 1879, the Khoti Settlement Act 1880, and the Gujarat Talukdar's Act and to repeal the Bombay Land-Record-Of-Rights Act, 1903 an Act called Bombay Land Revenue (Amendment) Act, No.IV of 1913 was passed.

The Khoti Rights & Ratnagiri Forest Settlements

The khots not only had a hold over the agricultural lands in Ratnagiri district but also held exclusively rights in the forest regions. The Ratnagiri was well wooded in the pre-British days. Its forests were cut down for shipbuilding and various other purposes. Lieutenant W. Dowell in 1830 had said that the Ratnagiri taluka was very thick scarcely allowing a horse to pass.[93] Jonathan Duncan's proclamation of 1824 had an adverse effect when the khots and *dharekarees* began cutting the trees recklessly, and started selling timber as fast as they could.

Dr. Gibson, the Father of Western Indian Forestry, had described the South Konkan forests to be unusually adaptable to the growth of fine teak. This was true because the southern parts of the Shastri river with a fine port called Jaygad at its mouth was until Dunlop's Proclamation clothed with fine forests, mostly teak, much of it of even larger size. There were many Muslims who set to work to build native shipping of the largest size for the Malabar coast trade. One of them had not less than 31 *shibadis* ranging from 1,100 candies (nearly 300 tons) burthern, downwards built on Shastri banks. He said that all timber was brought from the riverbank. This was the kind of felling that went on. And when Dr. Gibson visited it in 1857, to his great grief, he found bare slopes and all other timber gone.

The Government, therefore, was compelled to change its policy. It disallowed the cutting of trees. There were two main reasons why it did so. First of all, it wanted to use the wood for its own use and secondly, it wanted to have monopoly over the forests. In Ratnagiri Collectorate, many of the forests belonged to the khots. The rights of the khots in matters of forests were a stumbling block. It was difficult for the government to differentiate between the khoti forests and the private ones. The government had to pass Acts so as to control illegal activities, differentiate between the khoti lands, government lands and bring maximum revenue to the government from the forest resources.

An Act in 1865 was passed to lay down rules for the proper administration of forests. The rules were applicable to the lands.

(1) Covered with trees, brushwood or jungle which were the property of the government, and which were not occupied by the private individuals.

(2) Occupied by private individuals, in which Government had reserves, certain rights with regard to trees, timber or forests.

Government forests were divisible into three classes. Imperial Forest Reserves, Village Forest Reserves and forests and other lands in occupancy of private individuals, where the government had reserves. Exclusively the Conservator of Forests managed the Imperial Forest Reserves. Village Forests were under the management of the Collector in consultation of the Conservator of Forests. In cases where the government had reserves, the Collector under the control of the Revenue Commissioner, exercised the management.[94]

Unauthorized felling, cutting, lopping, marking or injuring of trees was prohibited and punished by fine of maximum Rs.500 on all the roads passing through the Imperial Forest Reserves. In the village Forest Reserves, firewood was free to all with the exception of immature trees. No charcoal burning was permitted within the boundaries of the Village Forest Reserves. The following articles of forest produce were free to the cultivator but it was not for sale.

- Woods for agricultural implements and carts, from unreserved trees only.
- Unreserved thorns, woods and bamboos for fences, floors and stalk floors and cattle pens.
- Leaves and branches of unreserved trees, for manure and litter.
- Grass for thatching.

It was further instructed that all teak, black-wood, and sandalwood was the property of the government and any illegal cutting would be liable to a fine of maximum Rs.500.[95]

In the year 1867-68, a report given about the area covered by the Ratnagiri forests showed that out of the entire area of the Collectorate, which was 24,00,000 acres, the forest area covered was about 99,852 acres. The aggregate area covered with tree growth under the four heads is as given below:[96]

Table 2.6

Taluka	No of Villages	Area of Present Tree Covered Tract									
		Government Reserves		Private Reserves		Coconut Groves		Village Trees		Total Area	
		Acres	Guntas	Acres	Guntas	Acres	Guntas	Acres	Guntas	Acres	Guntas
Dapoli	250	2,756	31	1,802	11	1,681	2 ½	12,500	---	18,740	5 ½
Khed	147	2,488	5	763	20 ¼	88	34 ½	7,350	---	10,690	19 ¾
Chiplun	213	856	28 ¼	639	30 ½	831	38 ½	1,065	---	12,978	17 ¼
Sangameshwar	155	112	14	--	--	4	32	7,750	---	7,807	6
Ratnagiri	146	---	--	202	18	1,575	16	7,300	---	9,077	34
Rajapur	212	2,988	38	0	6	58	12	10,600	---	13,647	16
Deogad	135	--	--	10,448	30	338	4	6,750	---	17,536	34
Malvan	79	2,042	29	6	0	3,315	31	3,950	---	9,314	20

The efforts taken, however, did not always give much result. The Ratnagiri forests were not in the leading list of the British Government. The expenditure often exceeded the income. For example in 1867-68, there was an actual loss of Rs. 800 on cash transactions of the year even after deducting the expenditure on roads and plantations to which were added the check up of the stock in hand by Rs. 2,984 making a total loss for the year amounting to Rs. 3,784.[97]

There were Acts passed between 1865 and 1874 by the Bombay Government, but not all were related to the Konkan. *Act VII of 1869* was passed to give validity to give certain rules relating to the forests in British Burma. *The Act of 1873* amended the law relating to timber floated down the rivers of British Burma. *The Regulation IX of 1874* was passed in the Arakan hill district. But such laws always directly or indirectly had an impact on the other regions too.

A Committee consisting of Arthur Crawford, Collector of Ratnagiri, J.R.Gibson, Deputy superintendent, Ratnagiri Revenue Survey and Mr.Shuttleworth, the Conservator of forests were appointed to report on the forest question and khoti rights. A lot of in-depth study followed in the subject of conservancy of the forests of Ratnagiri. The minutes by the Governor about the forest conservancy in the Ratnagiri district reported that the destruction of forests during the last two generations in the Ratnagiri district, the Principal division of the Konkan was generally understood to have been greater than in any other district of Bombay Presidency. When Jonathan A Dunlop placed the forests at the disposal of the people, he seemed to be confident that they would regard the forests and jungles as being among their best resources, their valued possession and so use them thriftily and husband them carefully. But the proclamation of J.A.Duncun had been regarded as constituting a character for unlicensed, unlimited, unguarded wood-cutting. The proximity to Bombay, the facilities of communication by sea had offered a powerful inducement to people to fell, cut and carry away forest products. Untold quantities of Ratnagiri wood and timber had been for many years sent to Bombay. If all that had been managed scientifically, reasonably, judiciously, there would have been no objection to it. The demand had been at Bombay. The supply had been at Ratnagiri. But the woods and forests, if had been cut and thinned in a manner that left sufficient trees or plants to produce seeds and ensure a constant reproduction, the Ratnagiri forests would have been made to supply the markets and yet might have been preserved for continuous use.[98]

The khoti tenure in its various forms was another hurdle in forest conservancy. The khots of varying degrees had to be induced to reconsider the local arrangements about wood-cutting. The khots had been informed that the government was not doing it for its own profit but to ensure the preservation of the forests. It was necessary to obtain a formal assent of the khots to a code of forest rules.[99]

On his visit to the Ratnagiri coast, Richard Temple found that the navigable streams were gradually silting and the upper courses were being denuded of forest and vegetation.

- Denudation was almost complete at the source and upper course of Savitri River, joining the sea near Bankot.
- Washisti river, rising near Kumbarli ghat and passing near the town of Chiplun, from which point it was navigable to the sea joining the port of Jaygad had started showing signs of silting up.

- Shastri River, rising near Amba ghat, joining the sea at the inland bay of Jaygad was a promising harbour in the Collectorate. The denudation of the once wooded areas of Amba ghat was bad.
- Muchkundi River passed by the town of Rajapur and joined the sea at Vijaydurg. The Baura and the Phonda ghats though were found to be in a better condition than the others yet would start silting if no care was taken.[100]

The Forest Act of 1878 was specially passed for reservation of forests. It was stated that there were 34,769 acres of the occupied land, warkas and rice in government villages, which could be brought under forest protection. In the Malvan Taluka, the Government took steps to reserve all lands selected for forest by the forest officers. All the unoccupied warkas land in the khoti villages in the Collectorate whether surveyed or not surveyed, were to be preserved by the government in the interests of the country and for the benefit of the people. Those forest that were liable for cutting; the government reserved two third and would pay the khot one third of the net profits after deducting cost of management.[101]

The Conservator of Forests established the routes from where the timber could be lawfully conveyed and he fixed the depots, where it would be taken for determining the amount to be paid to the government. Timber and other forest produce could be moved into or from any one of the roads of the given districts of Thane, Kolaba, Ratnagiri, khandesh, Nasik, Ahmednagar, Poona, Satara, Sholapur, Surat, Pancha Mahal, Canara, Dharwar, Belgaum and Kaladgi districts. Any person who broke the rules, was liable for punishment and imprisonment up to six months or a fine that may extend up to Rs 500 or both. The following routes were given permission to carry timber in the Ratnagiri Collectorate.[102]

The government declared Malvan, Olye, Dhamapur, Pendur, Kalsi, Kundalgaon in the Malvan Taluka, and Kelus in the Vengurla petha to be reserved forests in exercise of the powers conferred by Section 34 of the Indian Forest Act of 1878.

Table 2.7

Routes through Passes
Ratnagiri -Poladpur Road.
Harni Bandar.
Khed-Amboli.
Chiplun-Kumbhar ghat.
Amba Ghat-Ratnagiri.
Bhowra Ghat.
Phona Ghat.
Vengurla-Belgaum.
Bankot Bandar.
Anjarle Bandar.
Anjanvel Bandar.
Jaygad Bandar.
Ratnagiri Bandar.
Purangad Bandar.
Jaytapur Bandar.
Viziadurg Bandar.
Malvan Bandar.

There were loopholes in the Act passed especially in the Ratnagiri Collectorate because of the khoti system that prevailed there. The question of reservation of forests was opened in Sir Richard Temple's minute of 31 July 1878, which led to the assembling of the Forest Conference of 1879. The plan suggested by the conference was that since the government was unaware of the extent of its legal rights to reserve warkas land without paying compensation to the khots, the government should compromise the matter by getting the khots voluntarily to give up such lands for forests, on condition, of their getting one third of the value of the forest produce. This, the government felt, was easy to carry out. Special Mamlatdars were appointed whose duty was select:

- Unoccupied lands under khalsa villages or in pure dhara villages held by the khots or in department dhara portion of khichadi villages. (*warkas*)
- Government lands leased for cultivation but resumable at the pleasure of the government. (*khajan*)

- Unoccupied lands in pure khoti or in the khoti portion of the *khichadi* villages. (*Theri*)
- Lands situated in the said villages if uncultivated for 20 years preceding 1st June 1879. (*Gairdasti*)

The special Mamlatdars surveyed the villages of Ratnagiri and selected 11,792 acres of land for forest reserves. Seven villages of Malvan Taluka were surveyed and the area of reserved forests was 3,237 acres. 17 villages of Ratnagiri Taluka had 2,317 acres. It has to be noticed that the forest reserves of both Ratnagiri and Malvan had a less area of forest reserves in comparison with the rest of the talukas of Ratnagiri.

But there were so many complaints lodged by the khots from various corners of the Collectorate as to the rights of the forests that William Logan was appointed as Forest and Demarcation Officer to enquire into and settle claims to lands. William Logan visited seventeen villages of the Ratnagiri Taluka in 1884, all khoti in which the special Mamlatdars had selected *warkas* land for forest purposes and in which the selected lands had been notified in the government gazette under section 4 of the Forest Act. After hearing to a number of complaints and statements under section 7, William Logan found it impossible to proceed for two reasons. First of all he was embarrassed at the imperfect way, in which the Mamlatdars had dealt with the claims and rights and secondly by the peculiar character of the land, which had been selected and notified.

William Logan found that the lands were as a matter of fact, covered with occupants having a status under the khoti Act. It would be necessary to give compensation to these people, if the lands had to be acquired for forests. Such matters had intricate legal problems. Therefore, he divided the lands to be settled into three classes.

- The old forests such as Bandh Tivre, which had been already notified but not settled.
- The Crown lands in Malvan or wastelands in government khalsa villages, which had been notified under section 4 of the Forest Act.
- The lands selected by the Mamlatdars in 1881-82.
- Under agreements with the occupants or khots.

- Under section 41 of the khoti Act.

There were agreements made with khots, with *dharekarees* and *quasi dharekarees.* A resolution was passed that all khoti lands that remained uncultivated between 1859 & 1879 would be brought under section 41 of the Act of 1878. Also the selection of *dhara* lands uncultivated for 20 years was afterwards prohibited as illegal in 1882.[103] It was further informed, that if the khots or ryuts declined to come to terms, the Forest Settlement Officer should refer the question of compensation to the District Court under Act X of 1870.[104]

It was often found that the Forest Department took undue advantage of the rules laid down and harassed the common people. Local people complained in the newspapers about the malpractices of the Forest Department. This is seen from the letter written by a local man requesting the government to look into the wrong doings of the Forest Department Officers in the year 1891. He wished to throw some light on the administration of the Forest Department. He complained that only five types of trees namely, Saag, sisu, Chandan were prevented from being cut especially if the tree had not grown 8 feet above the ground. But even *ain* and *nana* were being hacked without permission. He asked, whether the Forest Department was so blind to the orders of the government. Moreover, he wondered if the government had the right to issue such orders as regards to cutting of the trees that were grown on a khoti land.[105] This shows that the Acts or the rules laid down did not satisfy the people.

On the other hand, efforts were taken by the government in the reserved forests to preserve trees. The Forest Officers as regards the number of trees furnished figures. Forest produce was exported from various ports in the Ratnagiri Collectorate. The following table shows a type of timber called *Myrobolan* was exported more than other types of forest produce from all the following ports during the years 1884-86.[106]

The Collector reported in 1889 that Ratnagiri, Malvan, Vengurla and Rajapur together had about 50,000 teak trees. *Ain, Nana, kumbya* and *Kinjal* formed the principal source of manure. The ryuts lopped off their branches and burnt

Table 2.8

Headquarter	Bundar	Myrobolan		Teak		Other Timber			
		1884-85	1885-86	1884-85	1885-86	1884-85	1885-86	1884-85	1885-86
	Ratnagiri	253	-	-	-	83	66	2	-
Ratnagiri	Jaygad		20,730	-	-	-	-	-	-
	Varvada	11,48,323	-	-	-	-	-	-	-
	Purangad	633	25	-	-	83	66	2	-
	Total	11,49,209	20,755						
Malvan	Malvan	6,223	2,265	-	-	-	-	-	-
	Deogad	213	-	-	-	-	-	-	-
	Achara	-		-	-	-	-	-	-
	Total	6,436	2,265	-	-	-	-	-	-
Vengurla	Vengurla	2,37,925	-	-	77	-	-	-	-
	Nivti	-	-	-	-	-	-	-	-
	Redi	-	-	-	-	-	-	-	-
	Total	2,37,925	-	-	77	-	-	-	-

them on their fields. To stop this process was to stop cultivation. But at the same time, it was necessary to preserve these trees and with least interference possible to the ryuts. Therefore, some of the steps like acquisition of land and its conservation into a reserved forest in villages where teak trees were numerous, selling of all scattered teak trees in occupied numbers, counting of *Nana* and *Ain* in *warkas* land, and strengthening of the existing establishment were taken. The following was the strength of the establishment in 1888.[107]

Table 2.9

Place	Designation and Grade	Amount of pay
		Rupees
Ratnagiri	Forest Guard 6th Grade at Rs 7 each Round Guard 1st Grade at Rs 15 each	21 15
Malvan	Forest Guard 5th Grade at Rs.8 each Forest Guard 6th Grade at Rs 7 each	8 7
Vengurla	Forest Guard 5th Grade at Rs 8 each	8

With the sole purpose of preserving the various classes of trees and to regulate the lopping of reserved trees in the warkas and cultivated numbers of the Ratnagiri Collectorate, care was taken to make rules strict. The government prohibited the following Acts.

1st Group

- The lopping, pollarding (The cutting off of annas portion of the leading shoots or stems) or injuring in any way, of teak.
- The lopping of ain and nana trees within ten feet of their summits.
- The pollarding of ain and nana.
- The lopping off of the branches, exceeding at the cut end six inches in circumference.
- The burning of rab or other matter within a distance of eight feet of any reserved tree.

2nd Group

- Subject to the above mentioned restrictions, it shall be lawful for the cultivator to lop reserved trees on their warkas and cultivated lands for the purpose of manuring their own fields, but no such produce obtained free shall be used for barter or sale.

3rd Group

- Government reserves itself the right to cancel the above rules and privileges at any time.
- The last clause was not applicable to a protected area.'[108]

It was not an easy task to settle such, and many more problems arose as far as the forests were concerned. The Ratnagiri Collectorate was put under the Collector's charge by the Government Resolution No. 4564 of 18th June 1895 and the Revenue Department.[109] By 1911, the total forest area was 12,050 acres, and the district had forests in 53 villages. The area was classed as fuel and fodder reserve. Besides that, the Forest Department had charge of trees in wastelands of khoti villages. There were three Range Officers working on a salary of Rs. 20, 30, 40 respectively each with Rs.10 fixed travelling expenses. Besides these officers, there were the Writer Guards, Tour Round Guards, Beat Guards and Clerks in the Forest Offices.[110]

The Malvan taluka had 624 acres of forests in its seven villages. Ambdos had 57 acres; Dhamapur covered 142 acres, Kalse had 30 acres, Kandalgaon had 190 acres,

Malvan had 21 acres, Owliye had 21 acres, and Pendur had 161 acres. It had no pasture lands fit for grazing. There were approximately 45,000 young trees. The Collector however reported that the number seemed to be over-estimated. There was an experimental rubber plantation at Dhamapur with 71 rubber trees. They were as follows:[111]

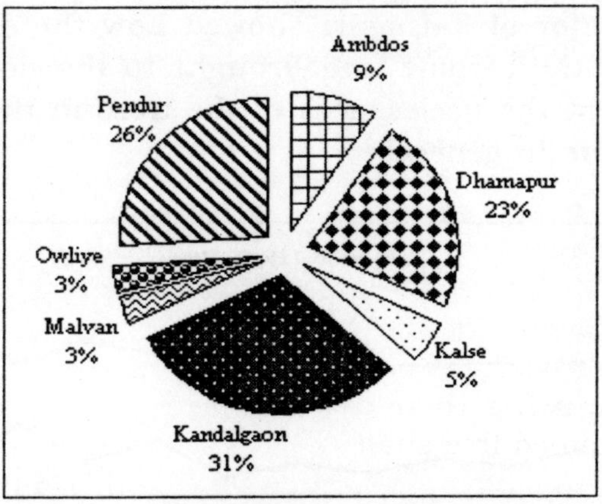

Fig. 2.1

At Tondivli, there were also Casurina plantations and there were over 5,000 trees. About one to two thousand seedlings were sown at the seashore because to grow Casurine, ordinary sand was all that was required to rear the seedlings till they grew two to three feet high. A minimum work of thinning, pruning and cleaning was required in all the Casurina plantations on the coast. Rs.895 were spent on the plantation up to 31 March 1817. The Mamlatdar felt that the plantation would yield about Rs. 1,500 a year. Casuarina was used for sending firewood to Bombay. The Malvan taluka in comparison with the other two mentioned above had more forests. Another advantage of the forests here was that they were not far away from the large town of Malvan and secondly, the trees being at the coast it was easy to transport them to Bombay at a cheap rate.[112]

J.P. Brander, the Collector of Ratnagiri in 1915 wrote that the Ratnagiri forests were not worth keeping as forests.

In Ratnagiri Taluka, there were three forest villages each isolated with a total area of 277 acres. There were trees but were of no great value.

The Vengurla taluka had only 9 acres of forests in one village. There were no valuable trees. It was often found that the Daftar Guards attached to each forest range were not necessary, as they had little work to do. J.P.Brander, the Collector of Ratnagiri showed how the expenditure exceeded the income and brought to the notice of the government the uselessness of the trees in the Ratnagiri Collectorate in general.[113]

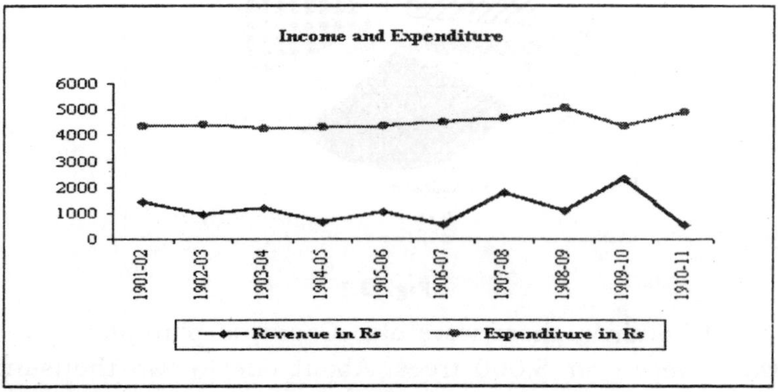

Fig. 2.2

Constant care had to be taken to protect forests from fire. The statement given below shows the areas of forests protected in 1915-16. The total area division in charge of the Forest Department was 12,054. The extent of valuable forest for which continuous protection from fire was desirable was to 2,546 acres. The extent of forests naturally immune from fire was 9,508 acres. Therefore, it was suggested that area except Malvan taluka should deforested and made revenue waste and village officers made responsible for them. The village officers also were also expected to be responsible for government-reserved forests ceded by the Peshwa.[114]

Having shown the loss to the government in maintaining the forests of Ratnagiri, he recommended the reduction in the number of establishment by abolishing the posts of Beat and Round Guards, reducing the number of forest clerks, abolition of the experimentation of rubber and cotton plantations in Dapoli taluka, retention of the rubber plantations at Dhamapur in Malvan taluka and abolition of the Forest Department accounts and procedure by abolishing the post of the clerk.[115] By the year 1918, Plantations such as cotton in the Dapoli taluka and Malvan taluka were ordered to be abandoned at once as utter failures.[116]

T.R.Bell, Conservator of Forests did not agree to J.P.Brander's suggestion that supervision of deforested lands to be done by village officers would lead to deterioration. He felt that it would still pay to protect the inaccessible slopes by making it penal to cultivate, hack, burn or otherwise injure what forest growth may appear on them. According to him, no Mamlatdar would ever look after any plantation well.[117]

It was accepted that the forests in the camp Kadvan in Dapoli and Malvan forests were to be retained as forests but without any Forest Department accounts and returns. All the forest lands with the exception of the Mandangad petha, and the Malvan and Dapoli talukas were to be completely deforested and given out for cultivation. The Collector further proposed that the revenue from the Malvan forests be credited to land revenue and all charges debited to the same head.

Various bills were introduced time and again, but the question of khoti in Ratnagiri was not solved completely. Some bills gave the khots upper hand while some others helped the ryuts but no satisfactory answers were obtained. The questions on the securities for the khots, the assessments imposed on gaothan lands, transfers of occupancy tenancy rights, commutation of produce, and many more remained despite the Acts passed. A.F.Maconochie, the Collector of Ratnagiri said that the vast amount of suffering and discontent that was caused by the khoti system of land tenure indeed was a veritable curse to the district.[118]

By 1918-19 forests of Ratnagiri were transferred to the Revenue Department. All these efforts were taken by the government to have more lands under their control for the sake of getting more cultivable lands and ultimately more revenue. The expenditure exceeded the revenue and the British lost interest in the Ratnagiri forests.

The British Government could not abolish the system and they lost interest in solving the long drawn problems. The evils of the system were felt although efforts were taken to remove them. They were inherent in the managemant of the villages themselves. It was only after independence that the Bombay Khoti Abolition Act of 1949 was enacted and enforced from 15th May 1950 in order to remove the intermediatory khots from the village administration. Yet there were the personal Inam and the paragana watan khoti villages in the Ratnagiri District. These were also abolished under the Bombay Personal Inam Abolition Act of 1952 and the Bombay Paragana and Kulkarni Watans Abolition Act of 1950 respectively and thus the powers of the khots were eliminated after almost a century and a half.[119]

References

1. Grant Duff, *History of the Maharattas*, Vol. No.I, London, Longman, Bombay, Ed. by S.M.Edwardes 1921, pp.57 & 104.
2. T.B.Jervis, *Geographical and Statistical Memoirs of the Konkan*, Calcutta, 1840, p.68.
3. 'Papers Relating to the Revision Survey Settlement of 131 Villages of the Ratnagiri Taluka of the Ratnagiri Collectorate', Selections from the Records of the Bombay Government No. CCCLXXVII -New Series, Bombay, Government Central Press (hereafter BGS), 1898 pp.166-192.
4. T.B. Jervis, *op.cit.*, p.109.
5. Lakshmi Subramanyam, Book review on Anirudha Gupta, Ed. Minorities on India's West Coast-History and Society, *IESHR*, Vol. XXIX, No.3, Jul-Sep.1992, p.383.
6. J.Dunlop's Report, dated 15th August 1824, Bombay Revenue Record, Revenue Department Vol No.121 of 1825 (hereafter R.D.), pp.93-110.
7. T.B. Jervis, *op.cit.*, p.115.
8. S.R. Reid, Lithog papers, pp.10-11, R.D.Vol. No. 121 of 1825, pp.59-61.
9. A.G.Desai, The Khoti Settlement Act I of 1880, Vakil High Court, Bombay, 1913, pp.202-3.

10. The Gazetteer of Bombay Presidency Vol No.X, Ratnagiri and Sawantwadi, Government Central Press, Maharashtra State, 1880, p.226.
11. Varsha Shirgaonkar, 'Conservatism In Maharashtra, Vishvanath Narayan Mandlik', Ph.D in History, University of Bombay, May 1987, pp.182-83.
12. Shri Krishnan, Peasant Mobilisation, Political Organizations and Modes of Inter-Action: The Bombay Country Side 1934-1941, P.G.Regional Center, M.D.University, *IESHR,* Vol No.XXXII, No. 4, Oct-Dec 1995, p.431.
13. B. H. Baden Powell, *Administration of Land Revenue and Territories in the British India,* Ess Ess pub, New Delhi, 1907, p.110.
14. G.D.Patel, *The Land problem of Revenue Reorganized Bombay State,* Pub Tripati Private Ltd, 1957,p. 240.
15. *Ibid,* p. 245.
16. *Ibid.*
17. *Ibid.*
18. G. D. Patel, *op.cit.* 1957,p. 243.
19. *Ibid,* p.244.
20. A.M. Katdhare, *Marathe Kalin Patil,* (Marathi) Poonam Prakashan, Nanded, 1996, p.32.
21. A.R Kulkarni, *Medieval Maharashtra,* Books and Books publications, New Delhi, 1996, pp.56-57.
22. *Ibid.*
23. J. Dunlop, Collector of Southern Konkan to the Secretary to Government, dated 18 December 1820, MSA, R.D.Vol. No. 225/1851, p.65.
24. Kenneth Ballhatchet, *Social Policy and Social Change in Western India,* Oxford University Press, London, 1961, p.150.
25. M.Chaplin, Poona to Francis Warden, Secretary to Government, Bombay, 21 November 1821, MSA, R.D.Vol. No.16/1821, pp.509-10.
26. *Ibid,* pp.511-12.
27. *Ibid,* pp.514-15.
28. Alexander Rogers, *The Land Revenue of Bombay* Vol. II, Low Price Pub, Delhi Reprint 1993, p. 2;also M. V. Chaplin to Francis Warden, Chief Secretary to Government, dated 21 November 1821, R.D. Vol. No. 40/1821, p. 519.
29. W.Chaplin, Commissioner, Poona, to Andrew Burnett, Acting Collector of the South Konkan, Fort Victoria dated 21Nov1821, MSA, R.D. Vol. No. 225/1851, p.129.

30. The Gazetteer of Bombay Presidency Vol X, Ratnagiri and Sawantwadi, Government Central Press, Maharashtra State, p. 226.
31. J.H.Pelly, Collector of Southern Konkan, to the Secretary to Government, dated 23 February 1822, MSA, R.D. Vol. No. 225/1851, p.65.
32. M.V.Chaplin to Francis Warden, Chief Secretary to Government, dated 21 November 1821, MSA, R.D. Vol. No. 40/1821/p.519; also, W. Chaplin, Commissioner Poona, to Andrew Burnett, Acting Collector of the South Konkan, Fort Victoria, dated 21 November 1821, R.D. Vol. No. 225/1851,p.129.
33. H.H.Glass, Collector, Ratnagiri Collector's Office to J.P.Willoughby, Secretary to Government, Bombay, dated 5 May 1837, MSA, R.D. Vol. No 225/1851, pp.365-676.
34. Varsha Shirgaonkar, *op.cit.*, p.183.
35. J.A Dunlop, Superintendent to E.H.Townsend, Revenue Commissioner, dated 30 Jan 1851, MSA, R.D. Vol. No.225/1851,p 38.
36. J.J. Sparrow, Southern Konkan, to Francis Warden, Chief Secretary to Government, Bombay, dated 23 July 1824 folio 850, No.58, MSA, R.D. Vol. No.30/1821,p.485; also Varsha Shirgaonkar, *op.cit.*, p. 183; also J. Elphinstone to the Revenue Commissioner, 61/A/ R.D., Vol No. 421 of 1873, dated 10 March 1873, pp.280-81.
37. Varsha Shirgaonkar, *op.cit.*, p.183.
38. *Ibid.*
39. A.G. Desai, *The Khoti Settlement Act I of 1880*, Vakil High Court, Bombay, 1913, Bombay, High Court Records, Vol No. IV, 1867, Appellate Civil Jurisdiction, pp.148-49.
40. J.J.Sparrow, Reporter to Francis Warden, Chief Secretary to Government, Southern Konkan, dated 23 July 1821 folio 850, MSA, R.D. Vol. No 58 /1824, p.485.
41. *Ibid*, p.486.
42. *Ibid*, p.485.
43. J.A.Dunlop, Collector, Ratnagiri Collector's office to James Farish, Secretary to Government, Bombay, dated 1 August 1823, MSA, R.D. Vol. No. 12/64, 1823, pp.471-473.
44. J.A.Dunlop,Collector of Southern Konkan, to the Secretary to Government, dated 31 December 1822, MSA, R.D.Vol. No. 225/1851, p.147.
45. *Ibid.*
46. *Ibid*, pp. 40-41.

47. A.G.Desai, *op.cit.*, G.R.434/25-2-1823, p. IV.
48. J.A Dunlop to James Farish, Secretary to Government, Southern Konkan Collector's office, Bombay, dated 11 September 1823, MSA, R.D. Vol No. 12/64/1823, pp.600-601.
49. *Ibid*, pp.601-62.
50. W.Dowell, Ratnagiri, Re: Report on the Survey of Ratnagiri Taluka, dated 1 November 1829, MSA, R.D. Vol. No. 225/1851,and p.255.
51. *Ibid*, p.257.
52. M.V.Chaplin to Francis Warden, Chief Secretary to Government, dated 21 Nov 1821, MSA, R.D.Vol. No. 40/1821, p.519.
53. R.Y.Bazeth, 2nd Assisstant Collector to A Elphinstone, Collector, Camp Kheir dated 2 Jan 1839, MSA, R.D. Vol. No. 225/1851, pp.384-85.
54. A.V.Patwardhan and Anant Vinayak, *Serfdom in Konkan*, Bombay, pp.9-10.
55. G.Guriyale, Superintendent, Revenue Survey, Superintendent Office, Camp Sunklipur, Dharwar District, dated 30 January 1851, MSA, R.D. Vol. No- 225/1851, p.69.
56. *Ibid*, p.520.
57. *Ibid*, p.524.
58. G.Coles, Collector, Ratnagiri Collector's office to H.E. Goldsmith, Secretary to Government, Bombay, dated 22 March 1850,MSA, R.D. Vol No. 19/1852, p.119.
59. William Courtney, Revenue Commissioner to H.E.Goldsmith, Secretary to Government, dated 17 February 1852, MSA, R.D. Vol No. 19/1852, p.24.
60. George Coles, Collector, Ratnagiri office, to Capt. Wingate, Superintendent Revenue Survey and Assessment, dated 6 October 1849, MSA, R.D. Vol. 225 /1851 pp.395-96.
61. The Gazetteer of Bombay Presidency, Vol-X, Ratnagiri and Savantvadi, *op.cit.*, p. 226.
62. H.B. Samant, Government resolutions (1) 8 November 1851, 10555, Printed at Belgaum Samachar Press, p.6.
63. R. West, Under Secretary to Government, to the Revenue Commissioner, dated 2 October 1862, Re: Khots and Khoti villages, MSA, R.D. Vol. No. 71/1862-64, p. 205.
64. The Bombay Government to J.W.Robertson, Acting Collector, Ratnagiri, Re: Extracts from the Proceedings of the Government of Bombay, Revenue Department, dated 23 November 1863, R.D. Vol. No. 71/1862-64, p.111.

65. *Ibid*, p.119.
66. U Mayor, Oriental Translator to Government to Oriental Translators Department, dated 10 November 1869, MSA R.D. Vol. No.37/1870, pp.303-304.
67. Jagan Mitra, REPORT ON NATIVE PAPERS For the Week ending with 25 April 1868, Native Press, Poona, office of the Director of Public Instruction, dated 9 May 1868, Bombay Education Society Press, Byculla, p.4
68. V.N.Mandlik, *A Brief History of the Watandar Khotes of the Southern Konkan*, Printed at the Times of India Exchange Press, 1874, pp.1-6.
69. Gopalrao Chintaman Karandikar to the Governor in Council, Re: Substance of Petition, dated 14 August and 27 September 1869, R.D. Vol. No.37/1870, pp.323-24.
70. *Ibid*, dated 28 September 1872, p.5.
71. Sarvodaya, REPORT ON NATIVE PAPERS For the Week ending with 11 July 1868, Native Press, Poona, office of the Director of Public Instruction, dated 9 May 1868, Bombay Education Society Press, Byculla, p.4.
72. J.T.Francis, Survey & Settlement Commissioner, Re: A Report, dated 22 May 1869, MSA, R.D. Vol No-37/1870, p.399.
73. W.Woodward, First Assistant to the Secretary to Government, Bombay Castle to the Collector of Ratnagiri, dated 5 March 1875, MSA, R.D. Vol. No 61/1875, pp.191-92.
74. Daji Krishna Rao Dalvi, Hon Secretary of the R.A Association to Marquis of Hartington, Her Majesty's Principal Secretary of State for India in Council, London, dated 4 August 1880, MSA, R.D. Vol. No118/1880, pp.167-69.
75. C.G.W.Machpherson Acting Secretary To Government, Memorandum, Legislative Department, Bombay Castle, 24 May 1880, MSA, R.D. Vol. No 118/1890, p.170.
76. Arthur Crawford, Collector of Ratnagiri to the Commissioner, Southern Division, dated 8 Feb 1879, MSA, R.D. Vol. No 92/1879, p.317.
77. *Ibid*.
78. Arthur Crawford, Collector of Ratnagiri to the Commissioner, Southern Division, dated 17 March 1879, MSA, R.D. Vol. No 106/1879, p.283.
79. Arthur Crawford, Collector of Ratnagiri to the J.B Piele, Acting Secretary, dated 1 July 1879, MSA, Revenue Department Vol. No 106/1879, pp.341-2.
80. A.Cumine, Assistant Collector to the Secretary to

Government, Ratnagiri Collector's Office, dated 19 July 1882, MSA, R.D.Vol No. 21/1882, p.39.

81. *Ibid,* p.42.
82. A.G.Desai, *op.cit.,* p.66.
83. G.H.D Wilson, Collector and Settlement Officer, Ratnagiri to the Commissioner, Poona, dated 2 July 1881, MSA, R.D. Vol-169/1882, p.66.
84. *Ibid.*
85. J.Nugent, Secretary to Government, Notification-Act and Regulation Proposal to Modify Rules 1and 8 of the Rules Under Clause (A) Section 40 of the Khoti Settlement Act Bombay Castle, dated 21 April 1886, MSA, R.D. Vol No. 17/A/12/1886, p.86.
86. Daji Krishna Rao Dalvi, Hon. Secretary of the R.A. Association to Marquis of Hartington, Her Majesty's Principal Secretary of State for India In Council, London, dated 4 August 1880, MSA, R.D. Vol No. 118/1890, pp.167-69.
87. Kaisare-I-Hind, dated 31 August, New Secretariat at Bombay Office of the REPORT ON NATIVE PAPERS For the Week ending with 2nd September 1890, p.12.
88. Gnyan Sagar, Reporter Sathe, REPORT ON NATIVE PAPERS For the Week ending with 2 September 1890, New Secretariat at Bombay Office, MSA, Bombay, p.13.
89. Native Opinion, Reporter Sathe, REPORT ON NATIVE PAPERS For the Week ending with 2 September 1890,New Secretariat at Bombay office, MSA, Bombay, p.13.
90. G.M.F, Grant, Acting Commissioner to the Secretary to Government Revenue Department, MSA, Poona, dated 28 September 1889, R.D. Vol No.118/1890, p.15. (So it was stated in Capt. Wingate's Survey inserted in the Index)
91. *Ibid,* p.16.
92. J.K.N.Kabraji, Acting Collector of Ratnagiri to the Commissioner, Southern Division, Ratnagiri, dated 12 March 1904, MSA, R.D. Vol. No 26/1905, p.181.
93. Papers Relating to the Revision Survey Settlement of 131 Villages of the Ratnagiri Taluka of the Ratnagiri Collectorate, MSA, BGS, No. CCCLXXVII -New Series Bombay, The Government Central Press, 1898, p.2.
94. Schedule 'A', Re: Rules for the Administration of Forest in the Presidency of Bombay framed in accordance with Section 6 of Act VII of 1865, MSA, R.D. Vol. No 18/1870, p.115.
95. *Ibid,* pp.12-24.

96. Arthur Crawford, Collector of Ratnagiri to the Commissioner, Ratnagiri Collector office, dated 11 November 1878, MSA, R.D. Vol. No 60/1878, p.44.
97. Majesty's Secretary of State for India to His Excellency, Governor-In-Council, Bombay, dated 3 March 1867-68, MSA, R.D. Vol. No 19/1870, pp.3-6.
98. Richard Temple, Re: Minute by the Governor of Bombay, dated 31 July 1878, MSA, R.D. Vol. No 60/1878, p.25.
99. *Ibid,* p.26.
100. *Ibid.*
101. J.B.Peile, Acting Chief Secretary to Government, Memorandum, dated 19 May 1879 forwarding report from the Committee appointed under the Government Resolution No. 6649, dated 26 December 1878 to consider forest question in the Ratnagiri district, MSA, R.D. Vol. No 92/1879, p.375.
102. The Indian Forest Act 1878, Booklet, and Published by the Government of India, Central Printing Press office, Subject: Forests, R.D. Vol. No 16/1886, p.189.
103. Arthur Crawford, Commissioner, Southern Division, to John Nugent, Secretary to Government, Poona dated 5 April 1886, MSA, R.D. Vol. No 118/1886, pp.209, 219 & 221.
104. *Ibid* p.22.
105. Native Opinion, Reporter Sathe, REPORT ON NATIVE PAPERS For the Week ending with 7 October 1891,New Secretariat Office, MSA, Bombay, p.13.
106. R.E.Candy, Collector of Ratnagiri, Ratnagiri Collector Office, Re: Exports of Forest Produce, dated 9 August 1886, MSA, R.D. Vol. No 23/1887, p.238.
107. R.E.Candy, Collector of Ratnagiri to N.Pratt the Commissioner, dated 27 October 1881, MSA, R.D.Vol No. 172/1889, p.34.
108. Rules to Regulate the Lopping of Reserved Trees on the Warkas Land and Cultivated Numbers in the Ratnagiri Collectorate, MSA, R.D. Vol. No. 9/188, pp. 99-0.
109. J. P. Brander, Collector of Ratnagiri to the Commissioner, Southern Division, dated 24 July 1911, Re: Forests of Ratnagiri, MSA, R.D File No. 415/1918, p.21.
110. *Ibid,* p.22.
111. *Ibid,* p.37.
112. J.P. Brander, Collector of Ratnagiri to the Commissioner,

Southern Division, dated 17 May 1917, MSA, R.D File No. 415/1918, p.85.

113. *Ibid*, p.22.
114. J.P.Brander, Collector of Ratnagiri, Re: Transfer of Forests, Revenue Department, Order No. 5205, dated 30 April 1918, Bombay Castle MSA, R.D. File No 415/1918, pp.12 and 24.
115. *Ibid*, p.47.
116. A.F.L.Brayne, Under Secretary to the Government to the Commissioner, Bombay Castle, Government of India, Order No.5205, dated 13 April 1918, MSA, R.D. File No 415/1918, p.79.
117. T.R. Bell, Conservator of Forests to Government of Bombay, Revenue Department, Order No.860, dated 16 June 1917, Bombay Castle MSA, R.D. File No 415/1918, p.91.
118. A.F.Maconochie, Collector of Ratnagiri to the Commissioner, Southern Division, Ratnagiri, dated 26 September 1907, MSA, R.D. Vol. No 30/1908, p.13.
119. Kenneth Ballhatchet, *op.cit.*, p.150.

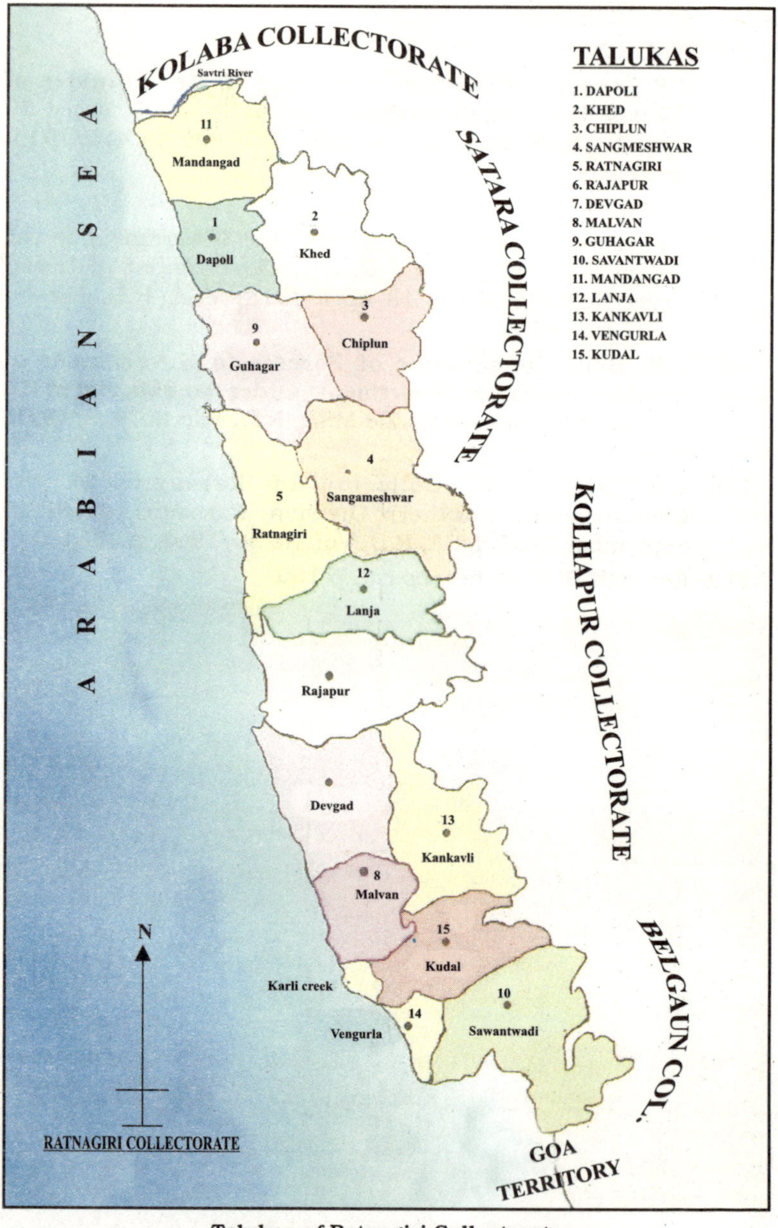

Talukas of Ratnagiri Collectorate

Source : Revenue Department, Vol. No. 30/1908

CHAPTER 3

THE ECONOMY OF THE SOUTH KONKAN IN THE FIRST FORTY YEARS OF ITS COLONIAL EXPERIENCE [1818-1860]

In 1818-20 the British divided the entire Konkan that lay below the ghats facing the Arabian Sea, into two administrative divisions-namely Northern and Southern Konkan. John Pelly was appointed as the first Collector.[1] South Konkan's headquarters was in Bankot at the time of its possession (1818) and was shifted to Ratnagiri in 1820 as Ratnagiri, the Company felt was centrally situated from the point of view of administration. Since then, South Konkan was called as Ratnagiri Zillah (district) or Ratnagiri Collectorate.

In these newly acquired territories, the East India Company had to establish its hold. The villages, their economy, the people, the new laws-all of them needed their share of attention. The new Government had to replace the old rules by new ones to suit its needs and requirements. Care had to be taken not to encroach upon the authority of hereditary village officers of the village. Various social classes of people had to be dealt with. These and many more such issues had to be taken care of. The Company had to be tactful while introducing new systems and laws, keeping in view, the customs and socio-political conditions of the newly acquired land. Various methods with thorough knowledge of the existing institutions, had to be implemented lest they result in failures. A cautious and pragmatic approach had to be adapted to each specific local problem.

The village communities in the ceded or conquered territories in the early nineteenth centuries consisted of several horizontal social layers with very different rights and claims.[2] South Konkan was not an exception to this rule that was prevalent in India. A number of survey assessments were done from the late eighteenth century in various talukas measuring most of the districts. Some survey assessments were done even before the Company established its full control. They were as follows:[3]

Table 3.1

Year	Survey Assessment done in South Konkan
1784-85	Vijayadurg Taluka
1784-85	Turuf of Guhaghar of Anjanvel Taluka
1788-89	Koondavi Mahal of Ratnagiri Taluka
1778-79	Raigad Taluka
1805-06	Suvarnadurg Taluka

Administrative Divisions under British Possession

The general appearance of the district was undulating and its height varying from 300 to 700 feet above the level of the sea towards the ghats, the hills being higher and woods thicker. On the coastal side the tableland was formed of the level red rocks running north to south. Below the foot of hills there were rice lands on the sea level. The district had thirteen talukas. There were innumerable mahals each containing a *Kasba* or town. The British for the sake of the Administrative convenience divided Konkan into two subdivisions.

The District of Thane also called as Northern Konkan further had subdivisions. They were *Dahanu, Mahim, Wada, Bassein, Bhiwandi, Sahapur, Sashti (salsette), Kalyan, Murbad, Panvel, and Karjat.*[4] The South Konkan rockier and rugged had the following talukas.

The term Collectorate was called as *District* in other parts of India. The revenue code introduced the term district in the general sense in which it was used in India, providing that the Collectorate or the Zillahs were to form districts.[5] The districts consisted of subdivisions called *'Talukas'*. They were locally further subdivided into *'petha'* or *'tarf''*, but the official designation under the code of a subdivision of *taluka*. It had an assistant to the taluka with an officer-in-charge and was called was *'mahal'*.[6]

The villages of the Southern Konkan were further divided into kasbao, *Mouje, Mujee, Waree, Peth, Gheras, Bunder, Konds (Hamlet), Bahadee villages, Gardens, Thikans, Islands, Forts.*[7] The Southern Konkan comprised mainly of *Ratnagiri, Kolaba, Malvan, Chiplun, Alibag, and Roha. Ratnagiri adjoined Kolaba* in the south. In the extreme south lay *Vengurla* (Vingorla). It contained *Dapoli, Khed, Chiplun, Sangamveshwar, Ratnagiri, Rajapur, Deogad, Malvan and Vengurla.* There was a great distance between inhabitations. The region was close to the ghat sections and the villages were small in size.

A list of Talukas in the British possession in the Southern Konkan was made when the Company took over the control of the region.[8] By the year 1818, the list of talukas in the British possession in the Southern Konkan were Anjanvel, Bankot, Kurnala, Malvan, Oondeeree, Ouchitghar, Rajapur, Raigad, Revadanda, Ratnagiri, Sanksi, Suvernadurg and Vijaydurg.[9] And the list of Mahals within the limits of the British possession was Ajgaon, Ashtàmee, Beerwaqdi, Bartow, Chiploon, Chitusu, Dewalin, Duoworukh, and Gramgaon wadia, Gherà, Ghonsallin. Some of the papers are missing and a complete list of the mahals cannot be compiled.[10]

Table 3.2

Sr No.	Talukas	Sr No.	Talukas
1	Anjanwel	8	Rygur
2	Bankot.	9	Redunda
3	Kurnalla	10	Rutnageery
4	Malvan	11	Sanksey
5	Oondaree	12	Sowarnadroog
6	Owchitgur	13	Viziadrroog
7	Razapoora		

The list of Mahals within the limits of the British possessions in the Southern Konkan were as follows:[11]

Table 3.3

Sr. No.	Mahal	Taluka	Sr. No.	Mahal	Taluka	Sr. No.	Mahal	Taluka
1	Ajgao	Malvan	24	Kelemazgao	Viziadroog	47	Penn	Sanksay
2	Astumee	Owchitgur	25	Khareepattun	Sovernadroog	48	Phoongoos	Rutnageeree
3	Beenwaree	Rygur	26	Kher	Rutnageeree	49	Praboulee	Rutnageeree
4	Beerwaree	Owchitghur	27	Kondewaren	Ryghur	50	Punchnudee	Soverndroog
5	Boretee	Kullian	28	Kondree	Rutnageeree	51	Puhoor	Oonderee
6	Chiploon	Anjunwel	29	Kuryat	Rutnageeree	52	Rajapoor	Viziadroog
7	Chiteesee	Kurnalla	30	Kuryat	Viziadroog	53	Reodanda	Owchitgur
8	Dewalay	Rutnageery	31	Lanjay	Rutnageree	54	Salsee	Malvan
9	Dewrookh	Rutnageery	32	Mahar	Rygur	55	Savurday	Anjanwel
10	Dhamunsay	Rutnageery	33	Mahalae	Oondaree	56	Shemahal	Owchitgur
11	Eman Gao Wadia	Owchitgur	34	Malund	Malvan	57	Sytowray	Rutnageeree
12	Ghera Preechetgur	Rutnageery	35	Malvan	Malvan	58	Sowndal	Viziadroog
13	Ghonsullin	Razapooree	36	Meradongur	Owchitgur	59	Sangameshwar	Rutnageeree
14	Gohagur	Anjanwel	37	Messoren	Malvan	60	Tulla	Razapooree
15	Goregaon	Ryegur	38	Nagotna	Owchitgur	61	Taoreel	Soverndroog
16	Govellee	Razpooree	39	Naten	Rygur	62	Vesvee	Soverndroog
17	Hathkhambay	Rutnageeree	40	Natoobunder	Sovernadroog	63	Velumb	Anjanwel
18	Hamrafwar	Kurnalla	41	Natoopalwan	Sovernadroog	64	Vingoorla	Malvan
19	Hurcheree	Rutnageeree	42	Nizampoor	Razapooree	65	Vinheron	Soverndroog
20	Hawelee Hamzabad	Anjanwel	43	Oonderee	Owchitgur	66	Vankheel	Kulian
21	Hawelee Jafrabad	Sovernadroog	44	Pait	Malvan	67	Varud	Malvan
22	Jalagaon	Sovernadroog	45	Pawees	Rutnareeree	68	Wasee	Sanksay
23	Kelsee	Rutnageeree	46	Pallee	Owchitgur	69	Garud	Oonderee

The following is the abstract of the number of Talukas and Mahals:[12]

Table 3.4

Sr.No	Taluka	Mahal	Sr.No	Taluka	Mahal
1	Sanksay	2	8	Bankot	4
2	Oonderee	3	9	Rygur	5
3	Reodanda	3	10	Sovernadroog	10
4	Owchitgur	9	11	Anjanwell	5
5	Kullian	2	12	Rutnageeree	15
6	Kurnalla	2	13	Viziadroog	4
7	Razapooree	4	14	Malvan	69

Mandangad taluka lay to the extreme north of the district. It had a seaboard of about five miles. Bankot lay in this taluka.[13] *Dapoli* was separated from the Sahyadri range by the Khed taluka. It had a seaboard of about twenty-five miles stretching from Kelsi to Dabhol. Khed was sandwiched between Dapoli and the Sahyadri range. It was in the interior part and rugged and hilly. The land of the region also was barren. To its right was the Satara Zillah. Between Vashisti River and Savitri River, lay the Guhaghar taluka from north to south. It had a seaboard of about eight miles. The climate of this region was unhealthy. Chiplun was situated between Guhaghar and Sahyadri watershed. The hill ranges crossed the region at two points. They were the Tivra and Kumbharli passes. Tivra, which was to the north, was a rough pass, while Kumbharli in the south was a cart road. Sangameshwar was away from the sea and lay in the interior part. The three passes were south Tivra, Mala and Kumbharli. The closest Zillah to Sangameshwar was Sangli.[14] Ratnagiri taluka stretched from Jaigad at the mouth of Shastri River in the north to the fort of Purangad, at the mouth of the Muchkundi River in the south. It adjoined the Sangameshwar taluka and Lanja taluka on the east. It had a triangular shape and had a seaboard of about thirty-seven miles. This was one of the most important talukas of the district.[15]

Rajapur taluka lay between Muchkundi River in the north and Vijaydurg creek in the south. On the west, it was bounded by the Arabian Sea and had a seaboard of about twenty miles. It extended from the sea to the watershed of the Sahyadri hill range. Its average breadth was about thirty-five miles. The passes of this region were Anaskura and Kajirda and they were cart roads. Deogad taluka, famous for its mango crop was situated in the southern part of the Ratnagiri district. It was one of the chief ports as it had a seaboard. It was connected to Phonda Ghat thus in return connecting it to the Kolhapur Zillah. Malvan seaboard was about eighteen miles in length from north to south. It was sixteen to eighteen miles from east to west. The historical Sindhudurg fort was situated in this taluka. The petha were Kankavli, Kudal Lanja and Vengurla. Amongst these Vengurla, although small in size enjoyed a longer sea board and was in close proximity to Sawantwadi to its east,

Goa to its south and Belgaum to its south-east. Lanja Mahal was situated in the inland and had no seaboard. It was close to Rajapur and Ratnagiri talukas.

Social Set-Up

Based on the surveys done in various parts, J.H.Pelly reported as to the census of the population of the Zillah of Southern Konkan taken in 1820 along with the number of houses occupied by each caste. When the acquisition of South Konkan was complete in 1818, South Konkan had about 10,50,70 houses with a population of 611,34,39.[16] There were at least 72 castes recorded out which most important were the Brahmins, Muslims who were found in administrative, military fields, Prabhus who were mainly cultivators, Marathas who were cultivators as well as soldiers, *sonars* or goldsmiths, *kasars* or coppersmiths, *shimpees* or tailors, *salees* or weavers, *telees* or oil makers, *bhandarees* or drawers of toddy, *guravs* or priests, *kumbhars* or potters, *dhangars* or cattle keepers, *malees* or gardeners, *dhangar kolis* or fishermen, *chambhar* or shoemakers, *sunghurs* or hemp prepares, *goojars* or shopkeepers from Gujarat, *dhurvids* or iron makers, *mahars* or the degraded class, *fakirs* or beggars, *kunbis* or husbandmen and others. Thus there was a group of cultivators & artisans in the making of a village.[18] Although South Konkan had generally a bad economy, it produced almost all that was required for its consumption. The land tax, a principal source of income during the Peshwa period was mostly made in kind and it was suitable to the farmers. Therefore the farmers although not really satisfied with the Peshwa rule preferred it to the new British rule that was foreign to them.[19] There was a mixed reaction to the coming of British. When James Grant visited South Konkan in 1819, he wrote privately to Mountstuart Elphinstone that the ryots appeared extremely dissatisfied and all their complaints were chiefly directed against the khots.[20] Mountstuart Elphinstone on his visit to the Konkan in 1823 found that the farmers in districts he visited did not have many complaints against the earlier rule.[21]

Establishment of Offices, Salaries and Allowances

Mountstuart Elphinstone demarcated the territorial

limits of the domains of the Peshwa into the districts of Nimar, Khandesh, Ahmednagar, Poona, Satara, Karnatak and the Konkan.[22] The collection of revenue, especially land revenue became a major function of the East India Company after it extended its political authority over Konkan. Additional receipts were raised in the form of *octroi, abwabs* and *mohturfa.*[23] Company Officers, some with only military or commercial experience could hardly be expected to be familiar with all the peculiarities of the land and complex relationships of the people to the land which so markedly varied from one locality to another.

Therefore, Collectors were appointed along with the Deputy and Assistant Collectors who were both Europeans and locals to collect information about the acquired territories.[24] Instructions from the Court of Directors were given to the Collectors appointed in the Ratnagiri Collectorate to put in efforts to enhance the revenue. Higher authorities made one consistent demand from their subordinates-Maximization of revenue.[25] Collecting the revenue or *dast* from each holder of land was not an easy job. The Collectors were to spend about four months in a year travelling in the district except in very large Collectorates. Assistant Collectors, assisted by the locals were appointed who were expected to travel for seven months of the year to study the existing system of revenue, win over people's confidence in the new government, avoid offending their feelings and yet collect the revenue for their treasury.[26]

The chief objects of these tours were:

- To supervise and test by personal inspection the work performed by the numerous subordinates, whose services were indispensable under their system of revenue administration.
- To gain acquaintance with subordinate government servants of all classes and influential local people to enable to achieve the objects.
- To give to the lower and poor class of people an opportunity to air their grievances by listening to them to gain their confidence.

The first thing for a Collector who was new to his work

on encamping in a village, was to send for the Patel and Kulkarni or Talati, and if they hesitated to come to him, then go there and simply talk to them about cultivation, roads and schools of the village and any other points that may occur to him on his journey to gain their support.[27] Thus a Collector who had the ability to collect a good amount of revenue without inviting resistance had a bright future.[28]

In the year 1818-19, new departments were established for the smooth working of the entire system. An accountant was appointed and paid Rs.7o, a clerk was paid a salary Rs.20.[29] The sea customs department at Malvan had a *jackutdar* who was given a salary of Rs.95, *karkuns* Rs.16, and peons Rs. 5. The tobacco department at Malvan had a Superintendent with a salary of Rs. 15 and 6 peons at Rs.5 each.[30] The appointment of *munims, ameens, karkuns* and chainmen and others was required for the survey work. The mode of paying the surveyors by the wages was altered to the more suitable one and efficient one of a contract. The new rules laid down for the *munims* in 1828 with regards to the survey are as shown below.[31]

Rules for Moonims or Examiners 1828

- When the survey of a village is completed, on receiving the survey books, the moonim is to proceed there to examine whether it has been properly surveyed. In the cultivated rice lands, he is to measure a fresh one-acre in every twenty. In the dry grain cultivation one acre in every twenty-five and in one village in every seven he receives, he is to measure a large piece of waste land, from 30 to 60 acres of trees bearing assessment he is to examine in every village one tree in fifty.

- Besides the measurements he is to notice that grazing jungle has not been entered as arable waste, that a due proportion has been allowed for rock, streams and roads where they exit both in waste and cultivated fields and that the names of the owners and tenants have not been incorrectly entered nor the name of the fields.

- He is to make written statement/ or nimtana/ of the error found in each village, and to write against each error what proportion in the acre, the survey ameen has measured incorrectly.

- He is to inspect the whole of the rice lands and to examines in each separate plot through out the village whether the survey the mean has correctly entered the sort of rice land in that plot by its proper name against every price that he finds correct he is to write 'examined' and those that he finds wrong he is to erase and enter by proper name and to make a list / or prutbundhee/ of the errors, stating the sorts originally entered and those he has to substituted.
- He is also to make extracts from the last mahratta survey of the quantity of rice land then contained in each field and to enter it against the same field in the present survey
- He is to inspect forty acres of rice land in a day including the extracts from the last survey completing his months duty partly re-measurements and partly by inspection of rice lands. The quantity he is to measure in a month is what has occupied 10 ameens to survey that is what has taken 300 days. But if the moonim is occupied 15 days in the rice land he will have to measure as much only as employed the ameens 150 days. Whatever deficient in this quantity of monthly day is to be deducted from the pay of the moonim.

The establishment of South Konkan had a Principal Collector, 1st Assistant Collector, 2nd Assistant Collector and 3rd Assistant Collector. The Collector was paid Rs.1800, 1st Assistant Rs.700, 2nd Assistant Rs.550 and 3rd Assistant Rs.400.[32]

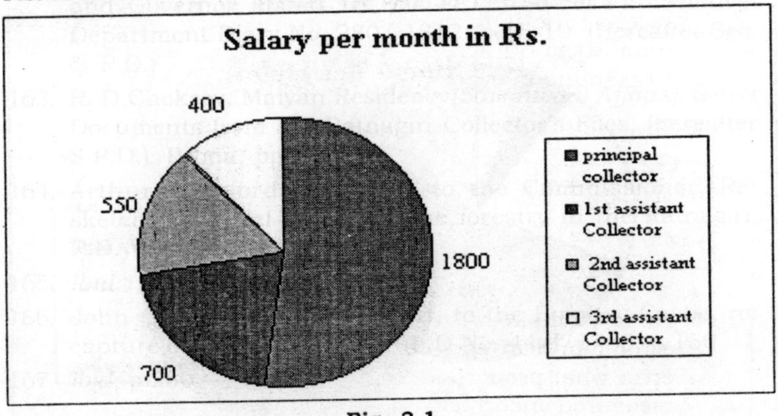

Fig. 3.1

There was a wide disparity in the salaries paid between the Collector's Office and smaller sub-divisions. The English Writers were paid Rs.675 per month in Collector's Office while they were paid only Rs.150 in smaller sub-divisions. In the Collector's Office the Treasury Department Officer received a salary of Rs.175, officers in the Native Daftar received a salary of Rs.69, and Peons were paid Rs.14, Petty Suppliers Rs.9 and Boat Establishment Men Rs.119.

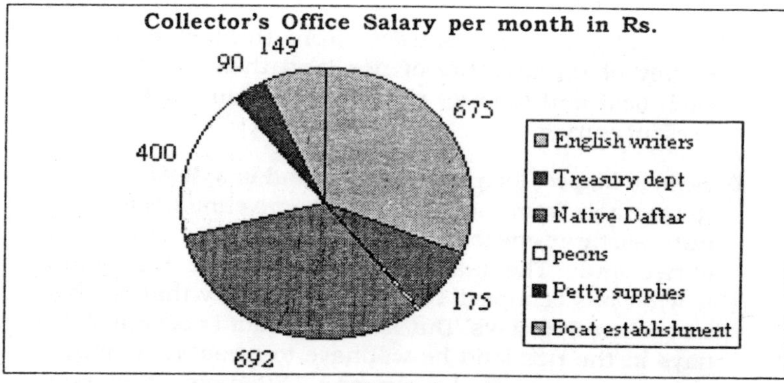

Fig. 3.2

The sub division office had the following establishment. The English writers were paid Rs.150, Treasury Department office received a salary of Rs.101, Officers in the Native Daftar received a salary of Rs. 388, Peons were paid Rs.192, Petty Suppliers (Englishmen) Rs.50 and Boat Establishment men Rs.47.

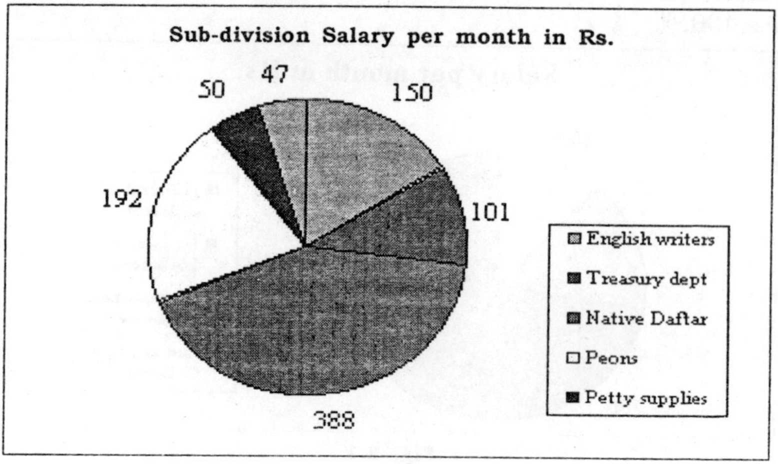

Fig. 3.3

The graphs shows total amount spent on salaries given to the various jobs done in the Collector's office.[33] The Judicial Department functioned with an Assistant Judge and Sectional Judge who were given compensation of 200 each per month. Allowances were given to all officers and clerks as and when the work demanded.[34]

Military officers were appointed in the Survey Departments as Supernumerary (Extra military persons appointed). He had to apply to the Private Secretary to the government as to the knowledge he possessed in the field of plane trigonometry, field surveying, and topographical drawing. If he was appointed for the post, he was to serve there till such time that the Superintendent reported as qualified for the next grade of assistant superintendent. He was not allowed to take up the next post until he passed an interpreter's examination either in Marathi or Gujarathi, and gained sufficient knowledge of the operations connected with the survey. A supernumerary assistant superintendent was to receive his net military pay and field allowances of his rank.

From the date of receiving charge of a native establishment until the expiration of two years of actual service in the department counted from the date of his promotion to the grade of Assistant Superintendent, he was to receive his net salary, salary as Assistant Superintendent-In-Charge of an establishment which was Rs. 375, along with allowance for office tent and carriage of Rs.75. A superintendent of survey was to receive per month, a net salary of Rs. 600, salary as Assistant Collector of Rs.100, district travelling allowance of Rs.300, allowance for office tent and carriage of Rs.75 along with his military pay.[35]

The Products of the South Konkan as a Source of Revenue: Some Observations on Surveys and Experiments:

J. H. Pelly in 1818-19, J.A.Dunlop in 1824, W. Dowell in 1829, J.J. Sparrow in 1821, T.B. Jervis, Henry Lindell in 1845-46, G. Coles in 1850, Alex Elphinstone, Acting Collector in 1838, J.A. Peter 1834, W.I. Turqand, Collector in 1856 were some of the officers who submitted various reports on the existing products, their relative prices, revenue collected from there either in cash or in kind. John Pelly the Collector of Ratnagiri Collectorate, reported that the district had about 6,32,000 inhabitants and 2,291 villages in 1818-19. But another report made by John Pelly after the assessment of 1818-20 also quoted that the Collectorate had 1336 villages, hamlets. Such disparities are bound to be inevitable in the initial years because of the lack of proper information.[36] He reported in 1820 that all the fertile lands of the Collectorate were found on the banks of the rivers or creeks or in the neighbourhood of the sea. The soil of the rest of the country was poor and consisted of ferruginous clay often mixed with gravel. Cultivation was of three types: Garden, rice and dry crops or warkas.

He said that the garden crops chiefly consisted of coconut plantations along with others like *supari* and such other articles. They were mainly watered from streams or wells although on finer kinds of sandy soils along the seacoast, the trees grew better with little or no water after attaining a certain height. On the *rice* lands grew sugar cane, rice, pulses, vegetables. Most of the rice lands were of inferior quality and yielded only one crop.[37]

The Warkas land was not so fertile and named according to its qualities. They were categorized as *dongur* or the steep part of the hill, *dagh* or the sloping ground at the brow and the base, *goorcheer* or the grazing jungle, kowulte and *siwur ran* or bushy land for manure or *bhurrad* or strong land. The warkas land on the level ground was called *bhatte* or level arable, *paistha* the gradual slope below the hill, *tambut* bearing chiefly grass. The common terms for rice land used were *laonee, ruhoo, rukhmee and thull.*[38]

Rice and other grains: with a rainfall of 75-100 inches, practically everywhere rice was a dominant crop. The sandy soil was locally known as *warkas.* It was found between the river belts and the high lands. The common sources of water supply were wells, water courses and *pats.* Malvan had few canals. The agricultural production was determined by the quality of soil and the availability of irrigational facilities.

The soil was also fit for the cultivation of paddy, ragi, vari millets and nachani grown on the hills. Nachani was grown on the higher ground and along the seacoast. Nachani or ragi was a rain crop and was generally sown on the land, which was too light for rice or too steep to be converted into terraced rice fields.[39] Ratnagiri Collectorate had a number of rivers. Although the rivers were not perennial and some of them having salt water were not too useful for the growth of rice, yet the river valleys were the

CAPTAIN THOMAS BEST JERVIS

Source: From an oil painting by Hopwood, Bombay, 1839, printed in Switzerland

scene of the rich cultivation of rice that occurred in the region. Thus the economy of the region was essentially centered on the cultivation of rice and other grains. The hilly warkas was manured.

Thomas Best Jervis was appointed as an Executive Engineer of the Southern Konkan in October 1819 to report on the existing conditions of Southern Konkan region after surveying the land.[40] The superintendence and reports of the yearly maintenance of the forts and buildings at Dapoli, Vengurla fell on him. A report of the things that had to be done in the newly conquered territories where there had been a European establishment or station earlier, was to be specified by him. He was also to provide information of the land and its products to the government. About the products, he forwarded a report to the government on 15 June 1822 that out of the aggregate produce of the land, at least 4/5 was rice. It was called *dhep* and was divided into 12 qualities or classes and the government share varied from 12/12 maunds per *beega* as shown below.[41]

Table 3.5 : Classification of the Rice Land called Dhep

	Maunds	**Paylee**
1st class	12	6
2nd class	10	-
3rd class	08	-
4th class	06	3
Land called		
5th Bawel	06	3
6th Khuwat	07	6
7th Rashoo	05	-
8th Kheree	06	3
Kuriat of two kinds.		
9th —	06	3
10th —	05	-
11th —	08	-
12th —	05	-

The cultivators during the survey said that the gross produce of rice land had decreased during the past half century. But he said that it was not possible as the former records showed a large increase of cultivation and decrease of land bearing grass, leaves and bushes which were the general manure. Thus, the report made by W. Dowell in 1829 showed an increase in the cultivated land. It also showed an increase in the growth of rice crop. In 1788, the produce of rice was 3,745 *khundis* and in the year it rose to 6,126 *khundis* in 1829 thereby there was an increase of 2,381 *khundis* or 64 % in a period of about forty years.[42] The table below also showed the increase of land in the Ratnagiri taluka.[43]

Table 3.6

	The Land of the Old Survey 1788	**The Land of the Present Survey 1829**	**Increase Formed in the Present Survey**
Rice land cultivated	17,408	20,746	3,338 or 19 %
Warkas or dry land cultivated	64,121	76,575	12,454 or 19 %
Arable wasteland.	2,69,881	3,59,618	39,737 or 33 %
Total arable land cultivated and waste.	3,51,410	4,56,939	1,05,529 or 30 %

The Brahmins normally ploughed their own rice land but the better-placed people employed *kunbis* for the hill land, which was dug with pick axes and were hard. Four bullocks ploughed the *warkas* land. The Brahmin villages were populated and were shaded with trees. Each house stood in a garden with a hedge around it and contained a few fruit trees commonly the jack, coconut, supari, undivi or oilnut and mango of which paid the revenue except the last. The Brahmins had the largest houses and nearest to the temples. The houses were usually built of mud walls and thatched roofs. The better ones with rice straw and the others with grass and yet the poorer ones with walls of reed.[44]

Despite the fact that the Brahmins were generally better off than the others in the village, they were assessed lightly and each new ryut who settled in the village was assessed by the khot for *ghurpattee* and *gaon kharch*.[45]

The study revealed to them that the salt rivers could not

be used for irrigation. Gujarat rice brought from Ahmedabad was tried in 1844, but the soil and the climate of the Collectorate were unfavorable for the cultivation of *teen paukalee* rice. About 24 maunds 9 pailees were sent from Gujarat to be distributed among the farmers. But of the seeds, only 16 *maunds* 2 *pailees* were used and others perished.[46] All grain was measured in the *khundi* and the *moora* was a measure exclusively used for measuring *bhat* or rice in the husk. The half *phura* measure and the *Phura* measures were called *sareteen seer* and *sawateen seer* in Ratnagiri.[47]

Table 3.7

	Total Grains as at Present Paid since A.D. 1788	Total Grains in Cultivation at the Present Survey, 1829	Increase of Grain on the Existing Payment found in the Present Survey
	Khundees	Khundees	Khundees
Rice	3745	6126	2381
Naglee, Nachni Ragee	1679	3087	1408
Waree	1051	2182	1131
Hurrick	1223	2874	1651
Teel Kala	47	268	221
Teel Gore	8	26	17 ½
Oored	33	66	33
Koolud	49	69	20
Teel Sala	1	3	2
Moong	¼	2	1 ¾
Seeras	½	1 ½	1
Tooree	2	2	½ Less
Kurvee	15	9	6 ½ Less
Warna Or Pavtta	16	67	50 ½ Less
Chuolya	2	3	1
Total	7873 ¾	14785 ½	6911 ¾ or 86 percent net increase.

The above table showed that there was an increase in the total grains in cultivation prepared from the survey of 1788 and the survey of 1829.It had almost increased from 7,883 khundees in the year 1788 to 14,785 khundees in the year 1829 showing a net increase of 86 %. By the year 1843-44 the quantity grown on batty showed a decrease to 7880 khundees, *naglee* to 2,553 khundees *waree* 1,651 khundees and hurrick to 18 khundees. The rate of the batty increased to Rs.19, *naglee* to Rs. 9, *Waree* to Rs. 11 and *hurrick* to Rs.14. Again the quantity of only batty increased to 8,319 candies in 1844-45 and its price rose to Rs. 27.These ups and downs were common in the district as the cultivation depended on the vagaries of nature.[48]

Dry grains of all sorts were ploughed as second crop. They were planted from November to March and were irrigated by two methods, by natural streams and by wells. The finest rice land however required no irrigation for the second crop.[49] The other kinds of produce besides rice measured by weight were called the *Wajnee.* They were the *hulud, hemp,* and sugar cane. *Hulud* was assessed at 5 maunds per *beega* after deducting 1/3rd of the ground cultivated, Hemp was assessed at 5 maunds but after deducting 1/4th of the ground cultivated.

Sugar cane was rated according to its class, the rate of the first quality being 6 maunds 10 seers to 3 maunds 5 seers and the other being goor.[50] Preference was shown in the Bombay market for the Mauritius sugar cane over the country cane and therefore the British Government showed interest in giving the farmers incentives to grow more of it. The price of the Mauritius sugar was twice or thrice more the country sugar.[51] The rate of the Mauritius sugar was from Rs.20 to 35 for thousand while the same quantity of country sugar was sold at Rs.10.[52]

Others

Udid, val (Indian beans) were also grown. Tamrind trees could be seen in large numbers in Ratnagiri. Cashew nut trees were found in Malvan taluka. Thus the crops of the coastal zone were divided into vari, kodra and millets.[53] Water melons, cucumbers, gourds, pumpkins were grown here. There was an abundant growth guava, plantains bamboos, and mulberries.[54]

Even the poorest people considered spices and ghee most essential. There was a cess on *toop* or ghee at the rate of two seers of ghee for every khundi of grain and was commuted for cash at the rate of Rs. 8 for every maund of 40 seers.[55] Normally the taxes collected for *'batty, nachni, waree, til, powte* were in the form of cash while the wajnee articles like the *supari, tel, gool, hulud, tag, toop, kath* were collected in kind.

J.A.Dunlop took charge from L.R.Reid of the Collectorship

of Southern Konkan on 21 Sep 1822.[56] Based on the records, he gave the following statement showing the items that had been added to the Ayen Dust under the Government of the Hubshee Angria and the Peshwa in 1824.[57]

He wrote that the government of Tulaji Angria began in the year 1145 and lasted till 1155 eleven years during which the following items were added to the revenue. They were the items of *nakat* revenue. Two annas were added for each rupee on the articles like pack bullocks, mohoturfa, jackfruits, oondine, wild coconuts, and toddy trees.[58]

Hemp: The British found hemp to be an important product of South Konkan. Hemp (tag) was mainly used for fishermen's nets and ropes. George Elliot, Assistant Collector recommended the growth of hemp in the Ratnagiri district. He stated that in a maritime Zillah like Ratnagiri the growth of hemp in the Ratnagiri district. He stated that in a maritime Zillah like Ratnagiri where ropes and nets were so extensively used and from where they could be profitably exported. The growth of hemp had to be encouraged among the cultivators and felt the necessity to bring to their notice its advantages. Although hemp growth was increasing, a proper check was not kept as to its yield in the first few years.[60] The rate per beega for hemp was 5 maunds and commuted at Rs.2 per maund and hemp was better in quality in Ratnagiri than in the Deccan.[61] 'The rent of hemp land', said M.V.Willoughby, the Revenue Commissioner, 'gives me an impression that it must partake the nature of a monopoly'.[62]

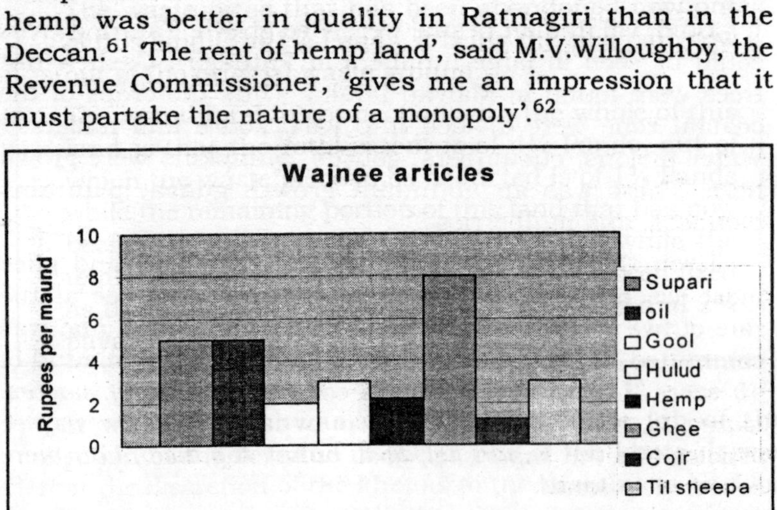

Fig. 3.4

Cocoanut: Cocoanut was one of the important *bagayat* produce. The Company took interest in its survey. The report given showed that it began to bear the first fruit in about eight or ten years and continued till thirty-five or more years and then declined after about forty-five years. Even after the rings of the bark disappeared, it continued to live ten to twenty years longer bearing fruits occasionally. A fine tree bore about ten fruit stems annually, each of which remained for four months and produced thirty to forty coconuts in succession. The trees bore through the year but most towards the end of rains.

The ordinary selling price of the fruit was Rs.3 per hundred. The best trees were selected to draw toddy. But such trees produced no coconuts. It then declined at about forty-five. A fine tree produced about 30 to 40 coconuts in succession. The ordinary selling price of the cocoanut was Rs.3 per hundred nuts. The best trees were selected for drawing toddy after they bore no fruits. The value of a tree was Rs.9.[63]

A cess was fixed and levied after assessing the kind of tree assessing its bearing capacity and nothing from the tree that gave toddy. It was called generally as the *bagayat soomaree* or things taken by number. The old method of assessing bagayat produce was to take as revenue half the annual produce of each tree. The Marathas had introduced a fixed money commutation rate to be paid for each tree. It was a lighter cess than the old one. The new rates were called as the *nugdee kaolee* and the British followed these after their acquisition. The *kowlee* rate was Rs.1 quarter and 6 reas for the coconut trees and 1 rupee and 6 reas for the toddy tree. The coconut trees seemed to have diminished in number as the *bagayat* assessment in the year 1829 which accounted for a deficiency of Rs. 5,000.[64] These assessments were very often not accurate in the initial years of the British rule. In 1851, a suggestion was made that instead of taking a fixed sum for each tree, assessment be made per beega and then the contribution per beega of land settled accordingly at a fixed rate per rupee, which would vary with the situation and quality of the ground. The advantage of this system would be simplicity in the management. Unproductive trees would be avoided. The number allowed at Bankot was 80 trees per beega and the revenue was fixed on these was twenty two Rupees, which was highly advantageous for the cultivator, when the trees were to mature, pawn leaves, plantains, pine apples were cultivated under the coconut trees, which by improving the soil and keeping it moist gave a large produce.[65] However, no steps seem to have been taken regarding the suggestions made by the Collector.

The other minor products of this Collectorate were tobacco, black pepper, jackfruit, oondoori oil, and supari. From the produce of the region, the Company was able to get a considerably good amount of revenue by mid- thirties of the nineteenth century. Here is a statement showing the collections on account of the land revenue in Malvan and Ratnagiri talukas for the years 1836-37 and 1837-38.[66]

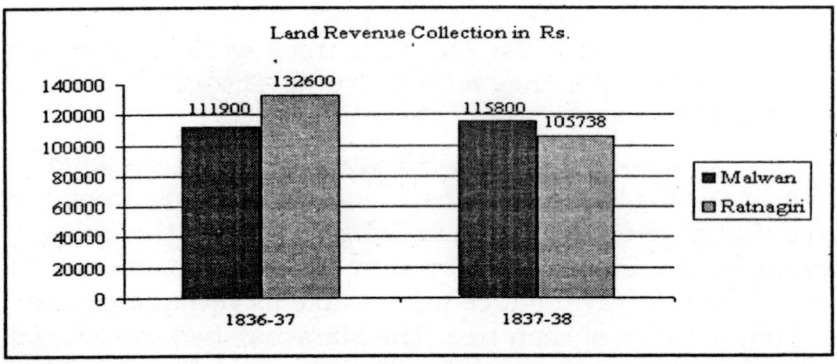

Fig. 3.5

Salt: The important saltpans were in Ratnagiri Mithbao, Achre, Malvan, Kochre and Shiroda. South Konkan being a coastal region had an income from salt making, fishing. There were salt bunders in almost all coastal parts. Salt was sold by the *phurra* measure. When a kowl was granted, the merchants took salt by bullock carts. This custom had been carried on from the time of Kanoji Angria in 1704. From the *pahanee* made, J.A.Dunlop found about 4,517 pans out of which 1,016 were not at that time used for manufacture of salt. There appeared to be three classes of salt in the *Kharepatan*, the *dosooree wanies*, the *muttoree purwal*, and the *juwar*. The wanes was sold @ of 3 ½ parras per bullock, Mutoree purwal charuns bullocks @ 3 ½, bookee and pattee @ 2 ½ and Jawadars @ 2 ½ parras.[67]

There were saltpans at Shiroda in Vengurla and many of them belonged to private individuals. In the initial years the Company often seized the saltpans but on request gave back to the private individuals. A letter from Atmaram Baba Ramdas who wrote to the Company and requested the government to return the produce of the saltpan as Ram Navami, a Hindoo festival was coming close by is attached in the index.[68]

The government in Malvan taluka in 1825 passed a regulation on salt and the introduction of the regulation resulted in the revenue increasing because traders were drawn to Malvan bunder from ports of Vijaydurg and Ratnagiri talukas where there were higher rates in force.[69] By the year 1836-37, the revenue from salt for the Company was Rs. 45,119 from the Collectorate.[70] There was a substantial increase in the produce of the salt by the late fifties and this hike was seen in the produce rising to 40,89,116.[71]

Fishing: sea fishing went on along the coast stretching about 250 miles. It was also done on the mouths of the creeks and rivers. A few miles away from the shore water creeks were there in which fishing was done. There were also small water creeks in which fishing was done.

Forests: Although Ratnagiri did not play an important role in the supply of timber, yet the fact cannot be denied that its forests also were put to maximum usage. The lands along the Savitri River and its tributary *Bav* were filled with thick forests. The Arab traders carried timber of best quality from here to Zanzibar along *Kajali* and *Muchkundi* rivers.

In 1756 when the British landed at Bankot they found thick forests.[72] The trees of Ratnagiri region were *teak (tectona grandis), Blackwood (Shisav), ain (Terminalia fomentosa), kinjal terminalia paniculata), khair, (acacia catechu), asa'na (briedelia retusa) bamboos and casurina.*[73] The wood of the jackfruit and tamarind was also extensively used as timber. From the scooped out trunks of the mango and *undi* serviceable canoes were made.[74] Such trees were used for furniture as well. The ribs and framework of fine ships were made from the wood brought from Bankot.[75]

The British obtained maximum use of the teak available in their venture of shipbuilding. The Ratnagiri wood was year after year carried to Bombay in their shipbuilding work. If trade had to prosper, if monopoly over sea had to be maintained, if more ships had to be built, if fortunes had to be made, they had to have a complete hold over the forests of the coast. Thus, although compared to the other western parts of India its forests were not thick and valuable, but still were a source of revenue.

To encourage the growth of teak and *sisoo*, John Andrew Dunlop, Collector of Southern Konkan, on 1 March 1824, issued, with the sanction of government, a Proclamation which declared that the people had the right to cut trees and that the government would not interfere in this matter. His intention in taking this step was to give an opportunity to the people to take more interest in forests and grow more trees which in turn would fetch good revenue. But the result of the proclamation had an adverse effect. Dunlop's Proclamation was not understood by local people and thus followed limitless hacking of trees for various uses. The people began felling trees recklessly and instead of growing more trees and preserving forests destroyed it further by carrying wood on flimsy grounds. This led to the devastation of forests.

Here is a translation by G.Coles Re: The Proclamation of 1823 by J.A.Dunlop as announced by him is subjoined here.[76]

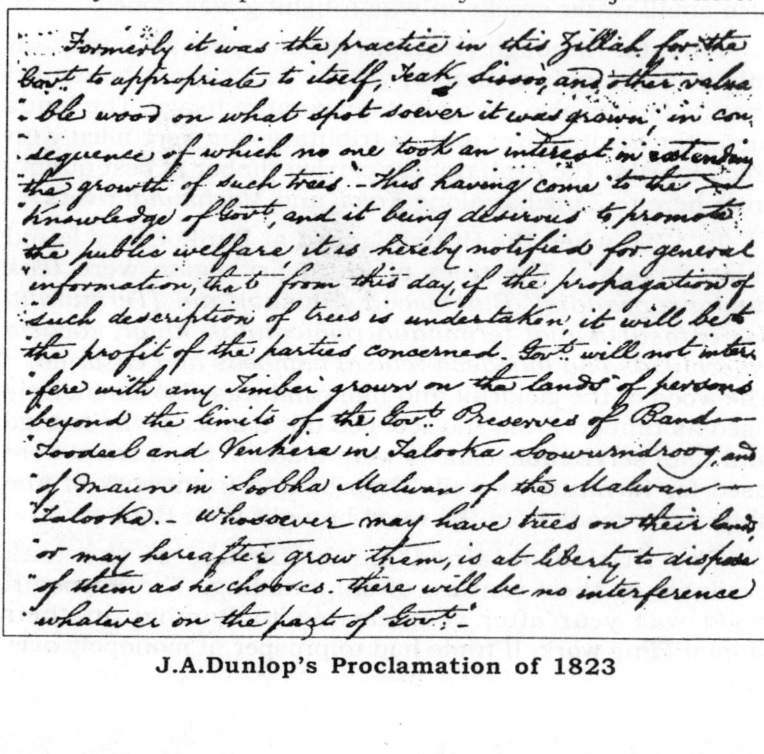

"Formerly it was the practice in this Zillah for the Govt. to appropriate to itself, Teak, Sissoo, and other valuable wood on what spot soever it was grown, in consequence of which no one took an interest in extending the growth of such trees - this having come to the knowledge of Govt., and it being desirous to promote the public welfare it is hereby notified for general information, that from this day, if the propagation of such description of trees is undertaken, it will be to the profit of the parties concerned. Govt. will not interfere with any Timber grown on the lands of persons beyond the limits of the Govt. Preserves of Band-Toodeel and Venkera in Talooka Soowurndroog, and of Maun in Soobha Malwan of the Malwan Talooka. - Whosoever may have trees on their lands or may hereafter grow them, is at liberty to dispose of them as he chooses. there will be no interference whatever on the part of Govt. -"

J.A.Dunlop's Proclamation of 1823

W.I. Turquand, Collector of Ratnagiri while reporting on the subject of conservation of forests said that useful timber such as *Aeen, kinpel, hussanee, nana, khayr, beola,* in addition to those (teak and sisoo already preserved) had to be taken care of.[77] Further, the khots in the khoti villages claimed that the lands belonged to them and they had full rights to not only to cultivate the lands by themselves or by their tenants but also claimed to fell timber therein.[78] He was of the opinion that forests had everywhere disappeared in consequence of the wrong use. He considered that well defined and strict plan of conservation was required, if the public were to have any wood at all for any purpose.

He stated that the bark of a prickly tree called *Shembee* was used for colouring fishing nets, the flowers of small plants called *dhatee* were used for medicinal purposes and they also furnished a red colour in colouring clothes. The fruits of *hurda* also were used for purpose and for dying clothes and as one of the materials of *chunam.*[79]

In handing up W.I.Turquand's suggestions, the Revenue Commissioner of Bombay Government observed that the individual property rights on occupied lands in Ratnagiri Collectorate would be sufficiently defined by the introduction of Revenue Survey as advocated by Capt. Wingate.

Capt.Wingate according to the instructions given by the Bombay Government resumed 'in regard to forests all seigniorial rights which it possessed previous to 1823 on 10 June 1851.'[80] Restrictions were put on felling of trees and new rules were laid down because the object of the said Proclamation was the extension of the growth of useful timber and on the contrary it had led to the annihilation of useful timber. At the same time it was understood that a few persons taking advantage of liberal offer made by the government in 1823 did attend to the teak and sisoo timber growing in their own grounds. The government was preferred to grant full benefit to such persons provided they satisfied the Collector and Conservator of forests that the woods in their lands had been attended to and nurtured since 1823. However, the forest preserves in Suvernadurg taluka and Malvan taluka remained exclusively Government Reserve.[81]

Amidst all this confusion, fire wood trade went on. Here is a statement showing the value of firewood that was sent to Bombay from the British and foreign ports in the Konkan in the following years.[82]

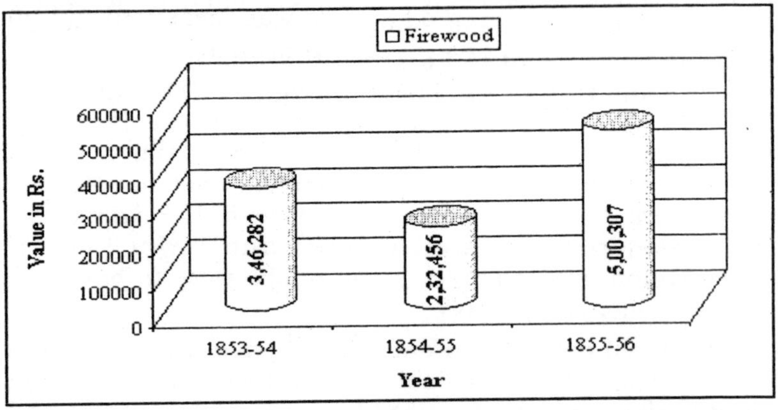

Fig. 3.6

A Report on the Prevailing Weights, Measures and Measurement of Surveys:

T.B.Jervis was called upon by the Government to furnish a report on the weights and measures of the Zillah in 1822.[83]

Table 3.8

Measures
2 tiprees =1 seer
8 ditto = 4 do = 1 pylee.
128 ditto = 64 do =16 ditto = 1 phura.
1024 ditto =512 do = 128 ditto = 8 do=1 khundee.
3200 ditto =1600 do = 400 ditto =25 do = 3 1/2 do =1 moora.

Table 3.9

The Table Measures of Grain in the Malvan Taluka
1 seer in weight equal to 30 surtee Rs..
4 seers =1 pylee.
8 ditto = 2 *pylee* 1 kooroo.
64 ditto = 16 ditto = 8 ditto = 1 phura or mun.
160 ditto =40 ditto= 20 ditto = 1 koondee khundee.
640 ditto = 160 ditto = 80 ditto = 4 ditto = 1 bhurra.
1280 ditto = 320 ditto = 160 ditto = 8 ditto = 2 bhurras = 1 khunee pylee.
2240ditto=560ditto=280ditto = 14 ditto= 3 1/3 ditto= 1 ¼ ditto = 1 koraj= 35 phurras.

T.B Jervis here observed that the Peshwa Government always received the revenue in grain by the *pylee* of 3 ½ *seers* and gave out to the retailers by the *pylee* of 3 ¼ *seers.* All grain disposed off by public sale was measured by the *sareteen seeree* measure or 3 ½ *seer* measure.

About the *pylee* measure he wrote thus

Vengurla pylee depth having 5.5 inches, diameter 6.3.5 inches contained 174,18110325 inches or 6,2794 lbs. *Malvan pylee* depth having 5.7 inches diameter 5.7 inches contained 145.4505822 in or 5.2436 lbs. The *mun* or *phurra* measures deduced from the *pylee* measures of 4 *seers* each, 16 of which were equal to a *mun* or *phurra* were as follows.[84]

Table 3.10

Place	Cubic Inches
Vengurla	2786. 897652
Malvan	2327. 2093152

Apart from the measures discussed about the grains, there was yet another measure used in the district which was exclusively for the sale of salt. The table of salt measure is given below.

Table 3.11

Measurement used for Salt
4 seers = 1 pylee.
6 seers =2 pylees = 1 kooroo.
6 ½ seers = 16 pylees = 8 kooroos = 1 phura or mun
1280 seers=320 pylees=160 kooroos=50 phura = 2 ½ khundee = 1 anna
51200 seers=12800 ditto=6400 ditto=80ditto= 40ditto=16 anna=1 ras or heap

It was customary to count 23 pands equal to one bheega. This system was said to have been first used by Malik Amber Raja about 400 hundred years ago and confirmed again by Cheemaji about 125 years ago.[85] His report was useful for the surveyors while they started their jobs of survey assessment of lands.

The *karkoon's* employments of lands consisted of 8 sets and occasionally10 sets, 1 set was composed of 1 *karkoon* at Rs. 20 a month, 1 *karkoon* at Rs. 15, 4 *kathi* or chain men at Rs.5 each and a sepoy from the Collector's Cutchery.

The person present at the measurements was the khot, *talati, mahar* and the owner of the field.

The baygat land was first measured and described as other fields, and then the trees separately entered with the owner for each. The survey for each village consisted of original books, maps, population records.[86]

Construction Works, Trade and Collection of Revenue

Reports about the location of the Konkan and the Deccan were addressed to the Chamber of Commerce in London which stated, 'The Deccan is separated from the Konkan by the mountain wall that rises above it and separates it from both the low country and the sea. In the konkan the road traverses a rich rice country. If the Konkan Coast and its products have to be made use of, it should be flanked by practicable passes and roads.'[87]

Keeping the physical features of the Collectorate of Ratnagiri in possession in view the surveyors made a study of the region and felt that a proper construction of bridges, roads, causeways through the ghats was necessary to link Ratnagiri Collectorate to the interior parts. They reported that various navigable rivers although rocky, hilly and rugged had a long coastline and a number of ports that intersected the land. Construction of bridges on the rivers would be less expensive. There were no regular roads in any part of the Zillah with the exception of a few paved causeways over the marshy ground. The officers suggested some routes to be constructed from some of the port towns like Ratnagiri, Malvan, Vengurla, Chiploon, Rajapur to the important places like Poona, Bombay, Goa, Satara, Kolhapur, Belgaum, Malabar and Gujarat. Some of them are given below:[88]

Table 3.12

Routes connecting Port Towns and Regions across the Ghats
From Ratnagiri through Sakarpa by the Amba ghat Mukhalpoor.
From Ratnagiri through Sangameshwar by the mullah ghat to Poona and Satara.
From Ratnagiri to Kolhapur.
From Chiploon by the Koomaurlee ghat to Satara and Poona.
From the port of Vengurla up the Ram ghat to Belgaum.
From the konkan through the Devamuny ghat to Kumta in Karwar. Kumta was a favourable point in the coast with a view to Bombay trade and connected to the cotton growing regions of Dharwar and Hubli.
From Suvernadurg through the military cantonments, Kheir and by the Pharghat or Purtaubgurh ghat to Satara.
From Malvan through Kudal and Amboli ghat to Kolhapur

Routes of Some of the prominent roads are given in detail.

Ratnagiri to Kolhapur*:* The length of the road from Ratnagiri was 82 miles. This road started from the Rama's temple in Ratnagiri town and ran more or less eastwards to Kolhapur and there it linked with Satara to Belgaum. The road was metalled, bridged and drained in its whole length. There was a main ghat called the Amba ghat from mile 34 and ended at mile 41. There were also rest houses at *Pali, Sakharpa, and Amba.*[89]

Malvan to Phonda: The length of the road was 38 miles. The road started from Malvan and was metalled throughout its length. But it crossed through many unbridged *nullas*, and two unbridged rivers and was therefore motorable in only good weather. The road ended in mile fifty near Phonda of the Nipani- Deogarh road.[90]

Vengurla to Belgaum: The length of the road was 78 miles. Starting from Belgaum, the road proceeded westwards crossing the Poona-Bangalore road at 21 miles. The entire road to Amboli was metalled. There were district bungalows at Tambulwadi, Amboli.[91]

Construction of Roads to facilitate Trade

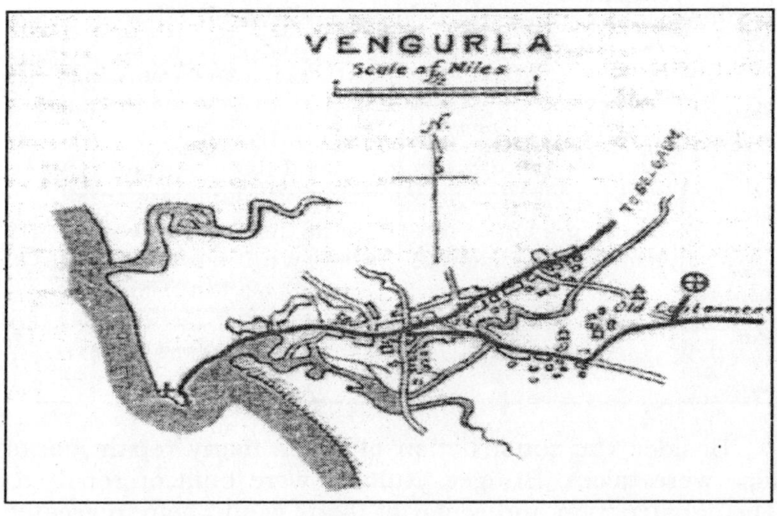

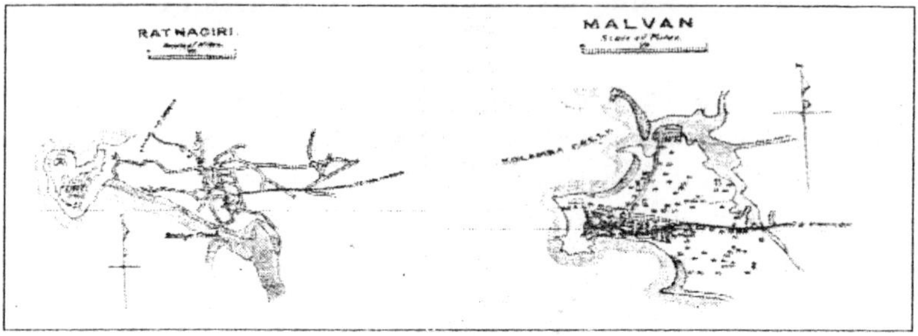

Source: E.M.Proes, 'Bombay Presidency Motor Guide', Government of Bombay, 1923.

Table 3.13

Village/ taluka	Description of work	Date of sanction	Amount sanctioned	Amount expended	Remarks	Villages Contribution
Mouje Malvan Malvan	Repairs to the road between Malvan and the ascent of the village Kopare	Govt Letter no4852 of 26 oct 1854 & rev commissioner's letter no 3958 of 20 Dec 1854	950 -0-0	-	Will be disbursed from then amt of gram khurch when the proposed work commenced & completed	
Bunder Vengurla Vengurla	Constructing an arch over nullah	Govt letter no,4852 of 26 oct 1854	49-6-9	31-0-0	Disbursed from ditto the work of progress of balance will as 18-6-9 will be paid	
Bunder Vengurla Vengurla	Repairs to a road leading to Sawantwadi	Ditto	226-2-7	138-8-0	Ditto—ditto—Rs.87-10-7 ditto	
Vengurla Vengurla	Constructing a road & making two arches on the nullah	Ditto	686-8-0	455-10-8	Ditto—ditto—Rs.227-13-14 ditto	
Ratnagiri Ratnagiri	Constructing a road from the Ratnagiri town to the bunder	9 may 1855	50-0-0	62-14-0	The work is in progress then balance will paid after completion of the work.	50-6-0
Ratnagiri pomendee to poonus Malvan	Repairs of a road	25 April 1856	100-0-0	-	The work is in progress the ryots have agreed to perform the work by personal labour	
Moyje Malvan Malvan	Repairs of tank	15 July 1855	-	29-4-3	Contribution by Villagers	29-4-3

Besides the construction of roads many repair works also were taken. Bridges, Nullahs were built or repaired. The construction and repair of roads would help in greater sale of merchandise and form better channels for the exportation and importation of the products. The road from Ratnagiri was recommended from the point of military importance also. The localities were also found to be favorable to the realization of duties at the entrance and frontier stations at the ghats or passes of the Sahyadri Mountains and at the ports. Thus there seemed every reason to put forth views that both land and sea custom duties would be more easily realized because of its natural advantages by appointing Nakadars at the nakas.

The two talukas namely Ratnagiri, Malvan and Petha Vengurla were centers of attractions for the Company since the early 18th century. Ratnagiri was the headquarters of the district and contained Head offices. It had its rivers, coast, ports and ghats leading to the trading centers across the ghats. Vengurla was a seaport and the Headquarters of Malvan taluka. It contained government offices, post and telegraph offices.[92] In a report W.Escombe, Secretary to Government sanctioned a staff for the post office at Vengurla because the Collector wrote to him thus, 'I would submit for your consideration the necessity which exists for permanently attaching a peon along with a good staff to the post office at Vengurla now that it is rising in commercial importance being situated on the ground line of communication between Bombay and the Southern Maratha Country.'[93] Malvan's chief fort Sindhudurg, Raje cote, forming the north point of the Bay of Malvan, along with cerji cote and Puddenghur did not go unnoticed by them as a place where its military could be stationed. The revenue collected from the produce, exports and imports of Malvan and Vengurla by the Kolhapur Raja and the Sawantwadi State encouraged it to acquire the territories.[94]

The three modes of transport of the three regions were road, creek and sea. Ratnagiri's principal ports were *Jaygad, Ratnagiri* and *Purangad.* The taluka had creeks namely the Bhatye creek, the Jaygad creek, the Muchkundi creek. Ratnagiri was close to Sangameshwar, Chiplun, Rajapur and other parts of Deccan across the ghats. The Malvan Taluka had *Malvan, Sarjekot* and *Achra* as its principal ports. The *Kalavali*, the *Karli* were the principal rivers. The Karli creek and Achra creek were navigable. The main places by road were Kankavli, Vengurla, Sawantwadi and also Deccan. The Vengurla petha's port of call was the Vengurla bunder. It was close to the Portuguese Goa, Belgaum and Sawantwadi. Attempts were made to build some *kucha* roads and some roads through passes for the bullock carts to go along with bridges over the rivers though they were not up to the mark.

The four *nakas* established at Malvan at various ghats yielded revenue of Rs.4,359.2.13. Compared to Malvan and Vengurla, Ratnagiri had more number of *nakas*. Vengurla's prime *naka* was at the Ram ghat. Out of the 18 *nakas* at Ratnagiri, 4 were constructed on the passes of the ghats between Ratnagiri and Sangameshwar. They yielded Rs.5,261.2.23, while the remaining *nakas* yielded only Rs.654.1.34.[95] By 1839, a number of *nakas* and the Company for the collection of duties from the traders erected chowkies. The Parpoli ghat had forty men guarding it under the leadership of Keshav Narain Ghorpady. Amrit Row Pant Pritividhee headed the Amboli ghat and fifty men safeguarded it. The Phonda ghat was under the control of Himmat Row Nimbalkar and was protected by fifty men. Smaller ghats had fewer men appointed.[96]

Some of the principal passes or ghats were significant because of their link with other places. And the Company tried to extract maximum revenue in the form of duties from them. This was often done without considering the inconvenience caused to the public. An appropriate example of this can be found cited about the Ram Ghat pass that linked Vengurla with Sholapur, Belgaum, Goa and Sawantwadi State. The Ram ghat had three prominent passes and three customhouses attached to them. They were *Bhersie, Kasarsaal,* and *Bande.* The Company took the right of collecting the transit duties on the road leading from Vengurla through the Sawantwadi Raja's territory to the Ram Ghat.[97] The Company constructed a new road also to facilitate the movement of the military stores from Vengurla to Belgaum and Shahapur.While the road was being made, the local people brought it to the notice of the company that a sum of Rs.1,200 had been spent by them to cut through a hill to obtain a stream of water for the cultivation of a place called *Panwal wadee* which had fruit tree plantations. For this they had already paid a customary tax to the Sawantwadi Raja. It was also told that an encroachment of their place for the construction of a road through this part would mean a loss of Rs.200 per annum to each ryot as their fields being deprived of water would suffer in the produce. Without giving heed to such requests, the Company constructed the road.[98]

The construction of a road strengthened the Company's trade with the nearby cotton producing regions. It brought more and more revenue to the Company. Vengurla became a port from where goods were taken to Bombay, Gujarat and to other parts on the Western Coast. Three traveller's bunglow's were built at Turkawadi, Baisti and Banda and the approximate amount spent for each bungalow was Rs.1,872. The existing bungalows were repaired one at Shahapoor the estimate of which was Rs.227 and one at Patna the estimate for which was Rs.370.[99] There were precautions taken to stop the frequent robberies as it caused inconvenience to travellers.[100] In the year 1832, about 342 bales of cotton were brought to Vengurla from Dharwar through the Karwar territory. The Ram Ghat became a busy road. Passes were granted to a number of persons. Land carriage tax was levied on the goods. The nakadars were supposed to maintain a register. However the duties were levied at rates fixed on the bullock loads that often were uncertain and disproportionate. Sometimes taxes were taken twice because of irregularity. Narayan Atmaram Usupkar complained that he incurred a loss, as he had to pay the land carriage tax on his goods second time although he had made the payment to the Jalmarg Co. & Sirkar once.[101] He also requested that the land carriage tax had to be decided on different articles that were being carried than the number of carts. In his petition he stated that the sum of 1,632 Rs. 2 quarter and 2 ½ annas were due to him.[102]

The complaint lodged by Narayan Usupkar was attended to. The Company by 1835 fixed the land customs according to the articles being carried in the bullock carts. The sea and land taxes at Ouchitghar taluka were as follows. However it must be mentioned here that they did not differ much from one taluka to the other.[103]

Table 3.14

Rates of Custom
Sea Custom
On Batty, Naglee and other Grains 1 Rupee per Candy.
On Oil, Ghee etc 5 % on the Estimated Value.
On Onions and Garlic 1 anna per Load.
On Fish 1 anna per Load.
Land Customs
Batty at 2 annas per Bullock Load.
Waree ,, 2 ,, ,, ,,
Naglee ,, 3 ,, ,, ,,
All other Grains at ¼ per Bullock Load.
On all other Articles:
Ghee and Oil at 1 Rupee per Bullock Load.
Keerana (Sundries) at ¾ of a Rupee per Bullock Load.
Tobacco at 2 Qrs. of a Rupee per Bullock Load.
Cumblies,, 2 Qrs. ,, ,, ,,
Piece Goods at 1¼ of a Rupee per Bullock Load.
Mohfool (Flowers of Moh Tree from which Arrack is extracted.) at 2 Qrs of a Rupee per Bullock Load.
Garlic, Chillies etc. at 2 Qrs. of a Rupee per Bullock Load.
Cocoanuts at 2 Qrs. of a rupee per Bullock Load.

Despite so much care taken, the state of roads in the Collectorate were bad and James Erksine, commented after a survey in 1851 thus ' The state of roads in the Zillah cannot fail to strike a stranger with wonder and regret as absolutely nothing seems to have been done for the country in this respect since the introduction of British power and bad though they lie those parts of the road which were constructed during Peshwa rule and which to this day bear his name, are decidedly more passable and useful I have seen.'[104]

Introduction of New currency

The people found it difficult in the first quarter of the British rule to pay the taxes in the new currency introduced by them. The inhabitants could not understand the new currency introduced and it also caused inconvenience to the government. The new coins circulated in the Southern Konkan were Bombay or *Surat rupee, Chinchori, Bagulkotee, Poona sicca* rupee. The weight of the Bombay rupee or gold *mohur* as it was called (179 grains troy)divided by 11.5 the number of masses contained 15,5652 grains. The weight of the Surat rupee (178.314 grains troy) divided by 11.5, the number of masses contained was 15.5055 grains. And those obtained from the district of Ratnagiri and Malvan were as follows.

Ratnagiri ————186.25 divided by 12 = 15.5208.

Malvan —————186.064 ditto by 12 = 15.5053.

The large weights were founded on the weights of a tola, which formed the medium of trade. On the western shores of the Bombay Presidency it was the Surat rupee which was common while in the Deccan the unkoosee *chinchoree* rupee was common. In Ratnagiri and Malvan weights of tolas were 28 each while in vengurla it was 26. The grains troy were 5,260 and 5,238 respectively, while the grain troy was 47,165. The large weights were as follows in the three talukas.

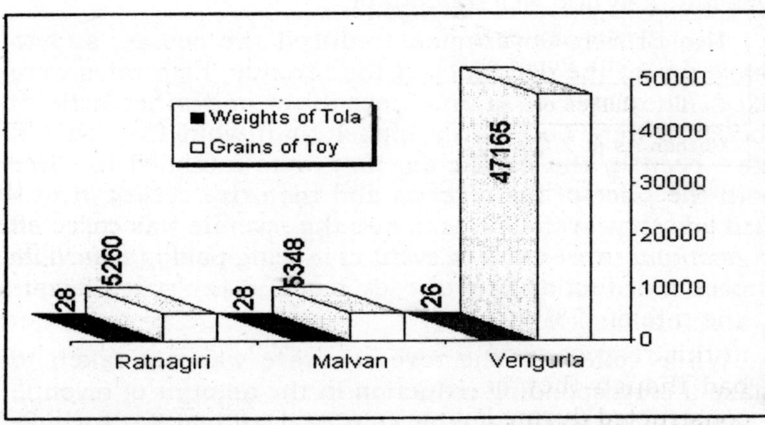

Fig. 3.7

This coinage thus used was replaced by the *hullee sicca, furshee, waee sicca, peerkanee, sambo peerkanee, timbornee, foolsheree, colaba rupee, bellaporee rupee.* The distinguishing marks of the coins were so indistinct that the most experienced shroffs were deceived. The cultivators could not know the value of the rupees they received and often rejected them. The substitution of the *chinchori* or *Poona sicca rupee* for the very inferior coin the peerkani in which the revenues was assessed and paid bore heavily upon the payers because the difference between the two coins was about 13%.

The ryuts of the Sindhudurg Zillah, Raghunath Vitey and Prabhoo Kocharkar appealed to the government to take the taxes in the common village currency or to take the gross produce. Moreover, they complained that the new taxes on produce were high and it was beyond the capacity of common ryuts to pay such high taxes. The new form of currency and high taxes they further grumbled was making them miserably poor.[106]

But in his reply the Collector refused to give any such concession and elucidated that according to the Government Proclamation of the October 1822, the *chinchore* rupee had been made the general currency in South Konkan and since then no exchange was allowed. Moreover, the former governments imposed several cesses besides the original tax. Therefore he said that the system introduced was fair, just and well thought of.

The British Government reduced the cesses, and to make up for the deficiency of the revenue, high rates were fixed. The rates of grains, cocoanuts and other articles therefore were necessarily higher than what they should have been in the bazaar as, they were intended to cover both the price of the revenue and the extra cesses. It was also told that in the former years the revenue was collected in *peerkani* rupees and in event of it being paid in *chinchore* rupees a deduction was already made in the ryut's favour at the rate of 17%.[107]

While collecting the revenue, care was not taken to make a corresponding reduction in the amount of revenue if rated in the more valuable coin. Malvan had Surat rupee in circulation and the company found it more convenient to circulate it in the neighboring parts of Konkan.[108]

Imports, Exports and Revenue collection-Some observations

It is an established fact that India's trade developed as part of an International Network of world trade centering on the British economy. India's trade was one of the important parts of this worldwide trade network.[109] The Southern Konkan economy being solely agricultural depended on imports for many of its requirements. Its main exports comprised mainly of rice, cocoanuts, and supari. A general idea can be had from the list of imports into Konkan. A duty of 3½ % was levied on the import of these articles.

Table 3.15 : Imports into Panvell and Konkan.[110]

Imports	Amount	Imports	Amount
Alum	25,268	Brimstone	7,778
Arrach	18,321	Broad cloth	72,584
Apparel wearing	44,694	Camphire	19,077
Beads	12,353	Canes and Rattans	10,892
Beer	1,74,164	Cardamoms	5,172
Beetlennut	55,971	Cassia	9,271
Benjamin (?)	12,682	Cloves	1,20,020
Brandy	55,796	Cooa Red	7,100
Brassleaf & Orsidue (?)	6,325	Cochineal	13,746
Copper	1,75,532	Cocoanuts	62,616
Copper Old	17,749	Pearls	1,07,181
Copra	1,29,230	Pepper	59,264
Coral	15,460	Salt	13,587
Dates	96,534	Piece goods	5,04,114
Drugs	5,900	Plate and plated ware	11,448
Earthenware	6,425	Printed Cotton, Calicoes	11,302
Eatables	8,999	Raw silk	11,74,113
Empty bottles	5,671	Red and white lead	11,254
Fire works	6,691	Saddlery	12,816
Furniture	10,990	Ivory sorts	20,845
Ghee	12,780	Shawls	17,458
Gin	11,905	Stationary & books	28,842
Glassware	44,552	Steel	9,967
Grain	25,017	Sugar	3,43,001
Hing	27,050	Summerheads (?)	5,074
Jagree	7,082	Tea	18,880
Jewelry country	5,174	Tents	6,245
Iron	3,169	Tin	19,046
Lakh	7,252	Tobacco and Snuff	5,833
Mace	5,295	Tutanag (?)	34,286
Nankeen (?)	74,224	Sundries	6,814
Nutmeg	19,208	Horses	44,700
Oil of sorts	25,857	Wine	1,63,408
Turmeric	8,295	Treasures	1,13,161

When the Company took control of Malvan it had a prosperous trade. Its total imports were almost Rs.2,32,960. Its total exports amounted to Rs.52, 830 and the total value of trade was Rs.2, 85,790.[111] The figures given below are from Hale's diary, which was submitted in 1819.The trade being under control of the British the figures are shown in terms of British sterling.[112] The exchange rate was approximately Rs.10 per sterling. The items of export and import of Malvan and Vengurla show the trade that went on as early as 1819.

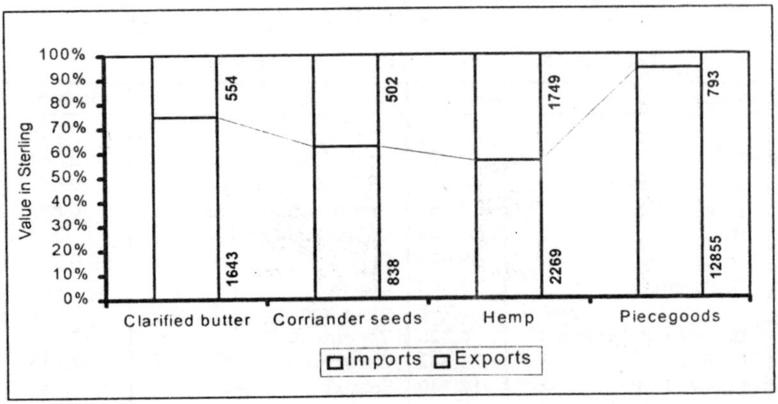

Fig. 3.8

The above figure shows that despite being a rice-growing region, the import of rice was the highest. Hemp was exported in large quantity. Similarly, some of the commodities of South Konkan discussed hereafter show the variations in growth, which resulted in constant insecurity among the people who preferred to go to the nearby cities for a living.

Rice: Rice was also imported from Penn in the Northern Taluka. Selling the grain by public auction collected from the Ratnagiri taluka was in *chinchore* currency. The amount was 1,049.0.44 for sweet batty, 531.3.0 for *naglee* and 239.1.63 for *vuree* in the year 1822-23. The revenue collected from grain, timber that was exported from Malvan to the Island of Bombay in the year 1832 was Rs. 9,636.2.76.[113] Rice was a principal commodity carried on in the coastal trade. At least in terms of volume the types of rice differed depending upon the port of export. Although

Konkan itself was a rice growing area yet it imported rice from the ports of Bhatkal, Basrur, Barkur, Mangalore.[114] It is evident that the grain trade although less spectacular, showed a good amount of business although it was tiny compared to the mammoth business of Kanara. Henry Lindell in 1847 therefore wrote, ' I may observe that the staple product in this zillah is rice together with other grains is what is chiefly attended to and the population being abundant the quantity produced is barely sufficient for the internal consumption.'[115]

The Brahmin settlements along the coast dominated the trade and their lands were cultivated by the kunbis that was the labour class. Henry Lindell further commented based on his observation that the khots sometimes were apathetic and selfish and being generally Brahmins took no interest whatsoever in the introduction of new and valuable production.[116]

Hemp: was brought from Deccan although, hemp of this region was better in quality. Along with the Hemp, Cocoanuts were imported from Goa and Malvan to the Ratnagiri.[117] The cultivation of hemp showed great variations from one taluka to another. In the 1830s there was an increase in the cultivation of hemp in Malvan and Suvarnadurg taluka and in later years it showed a decline. In the Ratnagiri taluka the cultivation hemp cultivation was extended from 26 beegas of land in 1840 to 50 ¼ beegas in 1841[118] but it reduced to 19 beegas of land in 1945. It showed an increase to 25 beegas in 1846. It was 27 beegas in 1850 while showed an increase to 35 beegas in 1856. What was seen was that there was no consistency in growth of hemp.[119]

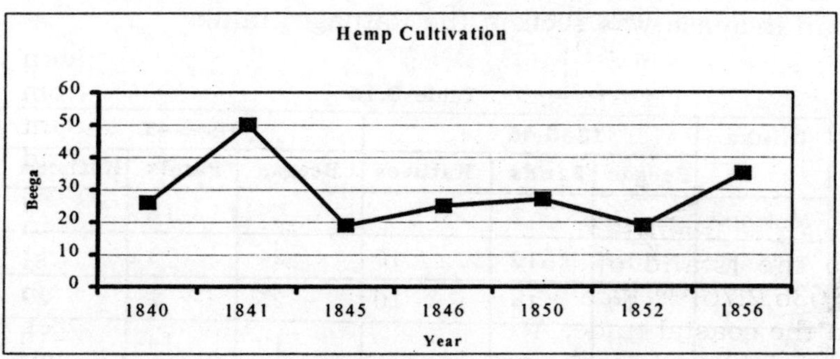

Fig. 3.9

One reason given for the decrease in the demand for hemp in the Collectorate in 1845 was ascribed to the reduced local demand for that article among fishermen of the Muslim population to whom the cultivation of the article was chiefly confined. Many of them, owing to the enhanced price of salt abandoned their occupation as fishermen to serve as sailors on board of boats and coasting vessels for which service they were well qualified.[120] Another reason was as follows. Hemp was in demand in Europe and if the ryuts took a little more interest in its growth it would fetch them good income. But since rice was not sufficient for their own local use they preferred the growth of rice to hemp.

Henry Lindell therefore felt that the ryuts should be encouraged to grow more articles of commerce. He was of the opinion that lending easy money with lower rates of interest and providing banking services would encourage them and in turn would facilitate them to experiment on the commercial goods.[121] Henry Lindell wrote *'I observe that one great inducement to overcome the indifference of the natives to produce superior articles would be the certainty of market. If therefore any of the merchants or agents would go into the districts with samples of the different products required like cotton, hemp and tell the natives that they would give them a good price for superior articles not only now but promise a steady demand hereafter, I am confident that the native would produce superior article'.*[122] Although such amenities did not benefit the ryuts on a large scale, yet in certain parts showed some advantages taken by them. The following table shows that there was an increase in the cultivation of hemp in the Malvan taluka in the 1830s but by 1840s an increase was seen in the Ratnagiri taluka.

Table 3.16

Taluka	1845-46			1846-47		
	Beegas	Pands	Kathees	Beegas	Pands	Kathees
Malvan	1	2	-	-	18	18
Ratnagiri	18	12	10	24	3	11
	19	14	10	25	2	29
				19	14	10
Increase	5	7	19			

The experiments done by the Company in the cultivation of hemp, by and large, seemed to be on the decline in the 1850s and it was reported that hemp seemed to be grown in the Collectorate among the fishermen and boatmen for their local use than for export.[123] It was seen that the area of cultivation increased in some talukas while decreased in others. Such cynical variations were observed not only in the cultivation of hemp but also in many other products. The following graph shows an increase of Beegas under cultivation increasing in Malvan while decreasing in Ratnagiri.

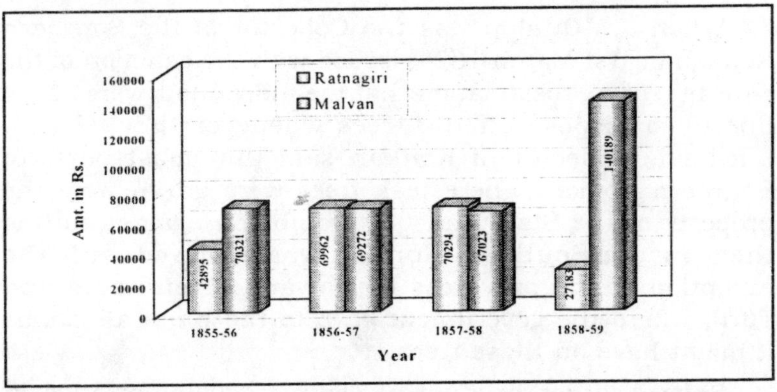

Fig. 3.10

Forests: Early in the nineteenth century the requirements of the Royal Navy Dockyard in Bombay drew the attention of the government to the forests of Ratnagiri. The South Konkan forests had a good number of trees used for different parts of ship building. Teak (tectonic Grandis), blackwood (shisav), *ain* (terminalia tomentosa), *kinjal* (Terminaliaculata), *khair* (acaciacatechu), *asana* (briedelia retusa), bamboos, *and casurina* were some of the trees, which grew well in the Southern Konkan.[124]

As early as 1825 it was brought to light that slopes of hills below 400 contour could be used for different kinds of fruit trees like mango, jack fruit, *undi* (calophyllum), Indianmangosteen-*ratambi* (carcinia purpurea) cashewnut tree (anarcadium Occidentale), tamarind, *jambhul* (eugenia jambolana) Wood apple (kanvathi), *behaeda, bibla, avle,* grew well. The wood of jackfruit tree was used for timber, the scooped out trunks of mango and *undi* trees were used extensively for canoes.[125]

A survey report on the Ratnagiri taluka by W.Dowell in 1829 stated that small boats loaded on their banks with firewood sailed to Bombay and the revenue amounted to about 6000-8000 Rs.[126] The People did not in fact take excessive interest in this product as it was found too bulky for carriage from a distance. This resulted in firewood becoming a local product and was collected in the immediate neighbourhood of creeks and from the places that afforded easy means of production.[127]

When J.A.Dunlop was the Collector of the Southern Konkan on 1st March 1824, issued with the sanction of the government a Proclamation that the individuals were at the liberty to dispose off the trees whenever they wished. L.R.Reid, Collector of Konkan said that most parts of Southern Konkan where teak trees were grown were the property of the State and the prohibition against cutting them in the Southern Konkan was removed with the exception of the provinces of Malvan, Suvernadurg and Turil, where the government gave to the ryuts all claims it might have on those trees.[128]

Salt: Another product of commercial importance in South Konkan was salt. Saltpans mostly belonged to private individuals, but there were also pans owned by the government. Whenever the saltpans belonged to the private individuals, there was a contract signed between them and the private individuals. The contract would be of different types. One practice was that the owners of the saltpans sold to the Company's shop with all the salt that was required for it at the reduced rates. And the highest that was paid in 1830 was Rs. 80 per *ras.* Another method was a contract made between the government and the owner in which the contractor had to pay an annual sum fixed between them by monthly installments.[129]

Salt was imported from Penn, Salsette and Caranjah.[130] The price of the salt coming from Bombay was about 2 to 3 ½ rupees per candy. In the Malvan taluka it was 4 ½ rupees per maund per rupee if taken from the pans and 3 ½ rupees if taken from the shopkeeper in the interior. Most of the salt trade went on by land through the ghats as far as

Khandesh, Buglana, Murar and the neighbouring countries of Deccan were concerned. The price of salt at the place of manufacture was from Rs. 2 to 3 per candy at Malvan and Rs. 4 ½ per rupee at Ratnagiri. Statement of the revenue derived from salt during the years 1825-1826 was as follows.[131]

Table 3.17

Station	Quantity Sold	
	Phuras	Amt. of Revenue
Malvan	76,068	6,822.2.91
Rutnagery	83,382	15,969.1.06
Estimated	159,450	22,790.3.97

Below is given a statement of the sale of salt bundars on the 19th January 1833.

Table 3.18

	Amount realized last year from Feb- Sep 1832	Amount bid for each bundar	Amount bid for each taluka
Malvan	3,231.2.43	501.0.0	3,500.0.0
Vengurla	503.3.13	1900.0.0	Nil
Ratnagiri	1059.3.89	725.0.0	6,500.0.0

This increase of trade in salt was due to the removal of all former restrictions, which brought additional revenue to the government. At the same time it induced competition among the importers of salt. Among the dealers the Banjari Community was and other dealers.

The salt would be carried to the other parts by the bullock carts and it was sold to the retailers from 12 ½ to 25 percent of the manufacturing cost. The rate differed from one taluka to the other. At Malvan the revenue yielded was Rs. 1,858.8.99 and at Ratnagiri it was Rs.1,054.1.51. Considering the entire Southern Konkan, the meetbunder under the Collector of sea bunder would yield the government about Rs.23, 000 per annum in the first few years of its rule. By 1827-28, the net revenue for the government from salt trade was about Rs. 16,000. This resulted in the deficiency of Rs. 18,000 showing a decrease in salt trade.[133] But by 1833-34 there was a net increase in the revenue by 4,901.3.48.[134] The variation in the salt revenue was probably because salt manufacturing was an extra for occupation upon which they were not dependent their subsistence.

The working in the saltpans being a laborious task needed a lot of stimulation was called for. The *Augrees* and the other locals who belonged to the lesser strata of society worked in the pans and indulged themselves in the use of strong drinking habits. They were compelled probably to do so because of the exposure to weather at the saltpans and the hard work that was necessary. This again led to absenteeism. To restrict such malpractices, steps were taken by the company to monopolize the salt pans but they could not succeed in it. Thus it is evident that there was continual pressure to raise the revenue. However, it is seen that the overall trade that went on after 1840s in Malvan showed an upward trend between 1840 and 1850. The overall trade in Malvan in 1840 was Rs. 10,775 in 1850 it was Rs.13,274.[135]

In 1854 there was a slight decrease of rupees 60 in the Malvan taluka and Vijaydurg taluka. This was because of the early rains that set in washing away the salt on the shores. In the same year there was a large amount of importation at one instance. This led to a deficiency of Rs.1,466-3-4 in the first case and Rs. 8,307-8-9 in the second case. Thus there was erratic behavior in the case of prices in salt also.[136]

Cocoanut: Cocoanut trees were another product of attraction in import export business. Cocoanut trees inspected in 1825 gave between five and ninety-five nuts and those trees not producing below five were considered unproductive. Half the produce belonged to the farmer and half to the *Sircar* or the government. Cadjans were assessed on the cocoanut trees according to the following rules and assessed at the rate of Rs.1. 2. per hundred cadjans:[137]

Table 3.19

Young trees not considered	
Trees about to bear	3
Toddy trees	3
Fruitful trees	4
Trees that do not yield fruit	4
Barren trees	1

Cocoanuts trees, from which toddy was extracted, gave a good income. The ordinary selling price of the cocoanut was Rs.3 per hundred. The best trees were selected to draw toddy during which time the tree bears no fruits.[138]

Sometimes the cocoanut trees would be blown down during storms. For example a storm in Malvan taluka in May 1820 blew down as many as 519 trees in Vengurla, 600 trees in turf Paut, 493 trees in turf Auzgaon sustaining a loss to the government property.[139] Access was laid on each tree without referring to the produce and differed from one place to another. Malvan coconuts were exported to Europe. Coconuts were imported from Goa and Malvan to be proceeded to the Ratnagiri.[140]

Despite the trade that went on, the talukas of Ratnagiri Collectorate did not have much yield, the prices were already low and sometimes natural calamities like the famines, storms sometimes would add to the woes of the farmers. An example of the calamity that befell shows the problems that the people faced. The storm at Malvan taluka in 1820 affected the produce of the region. This meant loss to the Government property but it was even worse for the people who faced the storm. The following table shows the effects of the low prices aggravated by heavy taxation.[141]

When it was informed to the Government remissions were sanctioned to the people. In this case of the storm a remission of Rs.3,187.1.91 was granted.[142]

Sugar Cane: Another produce worth mentioning was sugar cane. The article, the Company felt, had to be encouraged was Mauritius sugar. Henry Lindell reported that there was an increase in its cultivation but it was not up to the mark. Although the production of Mauritius sugar

Table 3.20

Vengurla	
519 cocoanut trees blown down the government share of which 8996 cocoanuts at rs.20 per mill. 318 bhurah measure of salt washed away from 7	1743.3.68
salt pans the government share thereof being 212 burah @2 rupees per burah.	424. 0.0
Proportion of loss sustained by the farmer of government land.	84. 0.0
Total	2251.3.68

Table 3.21

Malvan	
The government share of the loss of the cocoanuts being 838 cocoanuts @ 20 rupees per mill	16.3.04
Ditto——ditto———2.2.5 1 betlenuts @ 3 rupees per month.	7.3.65
Ditto———ditto———13.3.151.1 grain at variation rates.	150.3.72
The proportion of the loss sustained by the farmer of the salt pans.	4323.0.0
Ditto——ditto——of the government lands.	31.07.4
Total	1668.6.8

cane was not very high yet an increase in the land cultivated was seen. The following table shows slight increase in the cultivation of Mauritius sugar:[143]

Table 3.22

Taluka	1844-45			1845-46		
	Beegas	Pands	Kathees	Beegas	Pands	Kathees
Ratnagiri	16	4	17	18	12	10
Malvan	2	10	13	1	2	0
	18	15	10	19	14	10
				18	15	10
Increase in 1845-46	,,	9	,,			

An introduction of Mauritius sugar cane was experimented in Ratnagiri and it was sent to Bombay and sold there at the rate of Rs. 20 to Rs. 35 for thousand canes while the same quantity of local sugar from the same place was sold at 10 Rs.[144] M.V. Willoughby, in 1838 in his report stated that there was so much preference shown in the

Bombay market for the Mauritius sugar over the local cane that the price quoted was twice or three times more.[145] The sugar thus taken to Bombay market was also used for making sweet meats.

Fruit trees were grown in the bagayat lands and also in the Ratnagiri taluka. The chief bagayat productions were mango, supari, jack, oondanee or oil nut that paid revenue to the government. There were other products like the salt fishing nets, gunny bags that were also a good source of revenue for the Company.[146] Fishing was carried on at almost all coastal parts. Fish curing, drying and exporting was another industry of South Konkan.

N.B. Erksine, the Collector visited several parts of the district and during his visit spent 26 days in Malvan taluka and 47 days in Ratnagiri taluka. He reported that a road from Vengurla and Karli creek had been cleared and a tolerably good road had been constructed from Malvan and Dhamapoor thus facilitating the merchants to carry goods. A road was constructed via Ramghat road from Belgaum to Vengurla.[147]

Other Articles: An increase in the import was seen in the import of cotton at Vijaydurg for experimentation. It came from above the ghats and an increase of 50% was seen. Turmeric and hemp import increased by 25%, whereas in the Malvan taluka, the increase in the import of cotton was 7½ times more than Vijaydurg and hemp was 20% more. This facility was enjoyed because of the improved mode of transport via Ramghat road from Belgaum to Vengurla. A number of Parsee traders and other merchants brought down their purchases from the upper country and exported them to Bombay. The abolition of the inland duties or land customs was considered generally to have operated favourably to the extension of commerce.[148] The other exports were coriander seeds, clarified butter, piece goods, despite being areas, which grew rice and coconuts, there was an import of goods.

The under mentioned increase of customs realized at the port of Vengurla will show the advantages got from the road which had been made from that port to the upper country over the Ramghat.

Table 3.23

	1839-40	1840-41	Increase
Salt	6079	6698	619
Cotton	3380	16820	13440

Thus although a substantial amount of export import took place in this region yet it was not consistent. The reports of the trade of Ratnagiri zillah given from time to time showed doubtful behaviour. An example of this can be seen in the reports of 1842 to 1847. The value of importations by sea and land and also of the produce of the Collectorate are shown below:[149]

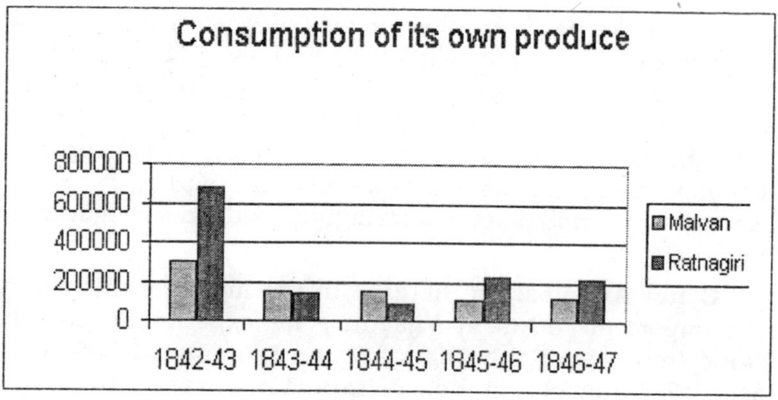

Fig. 3.11

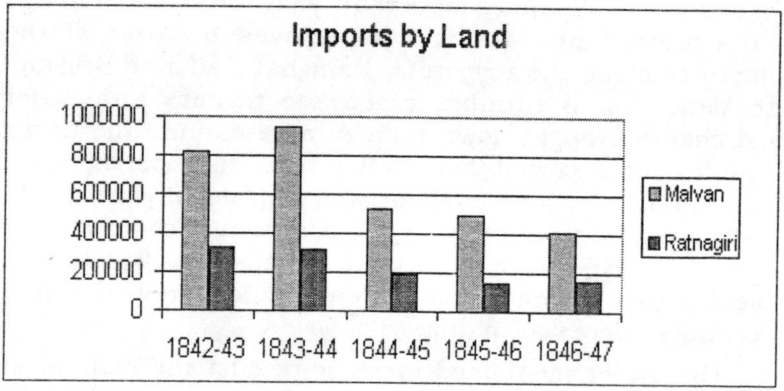

Fig. 3.12

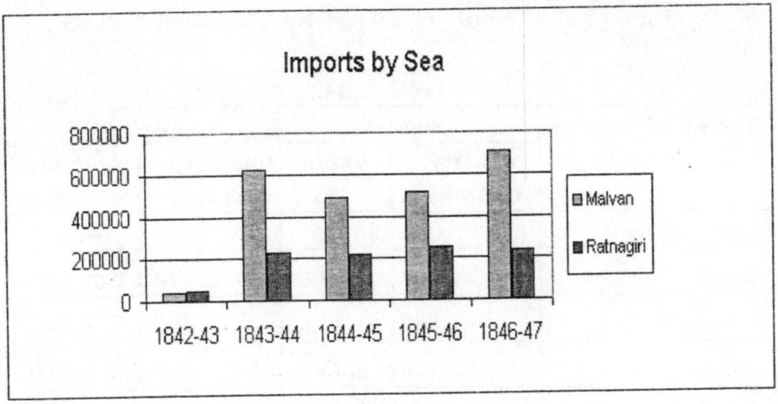

Fig. 3.13

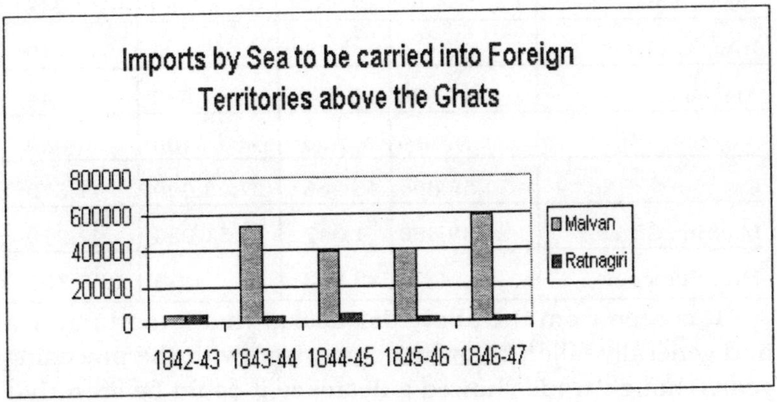

Fig. 3.14

Duty was levied on the goods that were passed under the Act XVI of 1844 and this gave a good income for the Company. The Ratnagiri Collectorate's collections from 1st February to 30th April 1853, on the excise duty levied amounted to Rs. 30,344 and it showed a nominal increase to Rs. 34,402 from the collections made from 1st February to 30th April 1854.[150] Thus the Company collected a considerable amount by the way of excise duties.

Produce of the Zillah exported by land and Sea was as follows:[151]

Table 3.24

Names Of Articles	1844-45		1845-46	
	Quantity Candies	Value Rs.	Quantity Candies	Value Rs.
Grain Of Sorts	2,046	29,688	3,769	78,283
Salt	2,787	48,978	3,970	7,02,207
Turmeric	107	1,872	206	6,284
Hemp	369	8,480	260	6,750
Betelnuts	1,152	58,425	855	45,200
Chillies	170	8,500	200	8,200
Oil Of Fats	62	2,650	59	3,248
Iron	0	0	0	0
Ambsol	996	10,961	943	11,144
Jagree	0	0	100	3,000
Coconuts(in No.)	30,58,800	45,966	27,63,000	41,570
Maurius Sugar	89,850	1,347	1,51,250	2,270
Miscellaneous	0	82,983	0	1,75,751

It is seen from the above discussion that imports by sea had generally fallen below in comparison with the preceding year. Though trade showed a decrease it could be seen that by 1840-45 the movement of commodities increased. Yet Custom duties on land and sea became indispensable for the raising of the revenue. The work was done scrupulously and therefore demanded proper policing at the collection stations. Very often, there were attacks on the customhouses from nearby regions. Besides the British army, there were also the Native Regiments stationed to protect the treasury. Malvan custom houses used to be attacked by plunderers from Kolhapur. An example of an attempt of robbery can be seen from the Company's treasury at Malvan being attacked in 1839 in which a sepoy of the Mamlatdar's regiment was killed and some of the

Konkan Rangers wounded. Vengurla also had a busy trade route attracting the robbers. The *havaldar, naique* were appointed in Malvan along with private police. A list of the party of the 18th Regiment of Native Infantry who were present at the time of Malvan attack as given by M.Elphinstone is given below. He in his letter said that if the local police also had supported at the time the treasury could have been saved. However, such cases were frequent showing the poverty of the people of the region.

Table 3.25

General No.	Rank and Names	2nd class-16 years service
142	Havildar	Mohomed
223	Naique	Mohomed saib
264	Private	Ramaswamy
386	,,	Parmaloo
642	,,	Venkatachalam
649	,,	Paramoloo
658	,,	Pariah
666	,,	Narrainswamy
689	,,	Chesinaih
690	,,	Shaikh Kureem
607	,,	Indur amootoo
618	,,	Inidai Badshah
642	,,	Muee Joothla Ullee
647	,,	Ulee khan

Similarly, a Joint Police Amildar was appointed on request at Vengurla as large amount of trade was carried on there. The person had to be present at his post to enable the *kotwal* to devote his attention to the other requirements of Vengurla.[153]

It is to be noted here that there was no relation between the agricultural output, agricultural income and the benefits given to the poor farmers. Why other wise so many were forced to abscond for not paying the debts. Statement of the outstanding balances in the Zillah Southern Konkan with the reasons why they have not been recovered and which should be written off:[154]

Table 3.26

Names of Villages	Names of Mahals	Names of Persons by whom the balances are due	Amount Irreco-verable	Reasons why the Balance cannot be recovered
Malvan	Malvan	Ebrahim Khan Nazir & Others	143,,1,,57	This balance on a/c of 1815/16 is due by a variety of person who have absconded and whose debts are irrecoverable and were reported as such by the resident Mr. Hale in 1818 they should be struck off.
Banda	Vengoorlay	Lowrence Portuguese & Others	149,,3,,19	The balance amounting to tobacco farmer of 1815/16 is due by a variety of persons who have absconded
Vingoorlay	Vingoorlay	Ryots	155,,2,,78	The balance is of 1815/16. The sum was allotted to the ryots of vengoorlay in consequence to the injury sustained to their crops but not submitted to govt. So that it appears as a balance against the ryots.
Vingoorlay	Malvan	Farmers of Arrack Shops	159,,2,,	The balance is of 1817/18 the farmers have either deserted or died and therefore irrecoverable.
Malvan	Vingoorlay	Kutee Koomuree Or Drawers of Toddy	24,,3,,46	The balance is of 1817/18 the farmers have either deserted or died and therefore irrecoverable.
Vingoorlay	Vingoorlay	Narrain Shetty Senoy	311,2,,63	This balance of 1818/19 is due by NSS who has absconded the resident of Malvan filed a suit against him, realized some part but remaining balance is irrecoverable.
Vingoorlay	Vingoorlay	Harry Narrain Wagley	38,,3,94	The management of the estate of the person was taken into the hands of govt. And a net loss incurred on the fixed Jumma, which loss stands against Wagley but may not be recovered by him.
Vingoorlay	Malvan	Shree Sirkar Gayr Dongiri	28,11,75 21,2,57	These balances 1820/21are irrecoverable being due by person emigrated & become insolvent.
Malvan	Malvan	Ladoo Withal Gunesham Luxuman	49,3, 2,1,16	The balance of 1820/21 were allowed to cultivators according to the terms of their cowls in consequence of their coconut trees having become unproductive but not submitted to govt.
Malvan	Vingoorlay	Mahadojee Pandoorang	7,,1,,10	The balance of 1821-22 was allowed to the person in consequence of some of his coconut trees being destroyed and rendered unproductive by lightening which cannot be recovered.
Vingoorlay	Vingoorlay	Ramdass Bawa	12,,	This portion of the farm of saltpan in vingoorlay, which was brought in the account and the pan afterwards being proved to private property.

Remissions, concessions, were given to the people on occasion of famines, failure of crops, storms and such other calamities. But these remissions were often found to be far from satisfactory. When the monsoon of 1823 was light, J.A.Dunlop wrote that there was considerable loss in the dry land resulting in the failure in crops. He asked the government to grant remissions. Malvan was given a remission of Rs.2,273 Ratnagiri Rs.12,441 and Vengurla Rs.1,190.[155]

While the revenue was to be fixed little weight age was given to scanty rainfall, famines or any other natural calamity that would befall. To add to their problems cholera epidemics took toll of many lives. Few who survived left the villages.[156] It is said that those who left the houses had no roofs left when the Collector of Ahmednagar paid a visit to the areas he found only four walls with no roofs.[157]

By the mid nineteenth century, attempts were made and efforts taken to provide irrigational facilities in the various talukas in the Ratnagiri. But it did not help the farmers greatly. An example of an irrigational facility given in the Malvan taluka shall explain the loopholes in the system. Lieut T.B.Jervis, the Chief Engineer on 15 January 1851 wrote a letter regarding public work done in Malvan. He submitted a bill amounting to Rupees one thousand five hundred and two four annas and five pice (Rs.1502.4.5) for strengthening the earthern embankment of the tank at Pendoor in the Malvan taluka of the Ratnagiri Collectorate. This work was felt necessary because the earthern bund was not substantial enough to retain the water permanently in the tank and therefore the bund required the strengthening.[158]

Nonetheless, such strengthening of bunds often, were failures. This is seen from another letter written on 8 May 1851. In the letter the Officer stated that it was a practice to give a sum of Rs. 25 towards *gram khurch* or village expenses annually to close the outlet of the Pendoor tank after the rains and the job was done by the Mamlatdar.[159]

But the embankment burst in a short time. The Mamlatdar declared that the embankment was well constructed with stones, mud, and branches of trees. The extent of the said embankment was 66 cubits in length, 16 in breadth and 7 in height.[160] He protested by indicating that the work was done in the month of October but the earth thrown in for the purpose gave way owing to the roots of trees having found their way to the water's edge must have let the water into the embankment and this may have caused it to burst. The Mamlatdar also brought to the notice of the company that the mishap that took place in December was not due to the neglect on the part of the villagers who annually closed the outlets.

Similarly an aqueduct (bridge) consisting of three arches over the rivulet at Mouje, Kalse turf, and Wurrad in the Malvan taluka was in a dilapidated state. This aqueduct required thorough repairs. It was important because, it was useful for cultivation. The masonary work for this job amounted to 3,240 cubic feet for the execution of which the following sum was agreed.[161]

Table 3.27

	Rs.a.p
3056cubic feet of plain work at Rs.12 per % feet	366.11.4
184 cubic feet work of a more difficult nature immediately over the arches	27.9.7
Deduct	
Estimated value of cut stones in the present old arches	162.0.0
Amount to be Sanctioned.	232.5.1

Here is a statement the construction of a new work sanctioned in June 1851.[162]

Table 3.28

No	Collec-torate	Description of Work	Amount	Remarks	Date of Construction	Vouc-hers
54	Ratnagiri	Reconstructing an aqueduct over a rivulet at mouje kalsee turf wurrad in the Malvan taluka	232.5.1	Sanctioned at the reconstruction of the rivulet	28th April 1851.	67103 C1249

But such improvements in constructing the embankments or repairing the bridges were far from satisfactory compared to the needs of the people.

Changing Social Scene under the Company Rule

To add the already existing woes, the new administration of the foreigners was not understood by the people in the initial years. It indeed took sometime for them follow measures adopted by them. The introduction of *Tulatis, Desais, Munims, Ameens* as local agents between the Government and the ryots in revenue transactions, was at first supposed to merely increase the revenue and therefore, opposed in consequence. The establishment of offices like *Akbarees, Awadalat* were looked upon with suspicion.[163] The Brahmanas had suffered from the change of government. The Peshwas themselves were Brahmanas and therefore a lot of patronage and charities had gone to the Brahmanas of the times. This was highlighted by the reports made by Marriot who had taken charge of the Ratnagiri Collectorate in 1817. At that time he found a general impression among the people that the new government would not survive for long. It was difficult for Marriot to find out who would be loyal to the newly established government. Therefore, when he appointed *kamvisdars* or district officers, he made sure that they had served in the Company for almost twenty years either as *karkuns* or clerks. He, indeed, had to appoint majority of his clerks from those who had served the Peshwa. As a result he nursed a grudge against the Brahmanas who were brought from the Peshwa Government.[164] Although his first impressions changed by 1820-21 yet, he was unsure about his views on them. This is seen from the following argument put forward by him.

On the one hand he wrote *'if we give encouragement to Brahmins, shall we not make the Mussalmans and Lower castes of Hindoos our enemies?'* and on the other hand he said, *'Brahmanas were of all the social groups the best informed and the most respectable, that if they were not conciliated by office, they might try to thwart all the new governments' plans and that to impoverish them would be eventually to destroy the only learned in the country.'*[165]

J.A. Dunlop, in twenties, took greater care in selecting persons, who had held responsible positions under the former government, but very often-found difficulty as a result of the lack of requisite qualifications and partly on the part of the government, which did not wish to give responsible positions. He wrote thus, *'It is regretted that the most respectable natives avoided our service at first but those who entered it, have since qualifications and claims, which neither it would be advisable to neglect, so that future promotions be confined to our own government'.*[166]

A passage written in 1824 and reproduced in the old Gazetteer of the Ratnagiri district says that the chitapavans were a discontented class for some years after the transfer of Ratnagiri to the British. But the Gazetteer in the 1880 noted that their scruples about serving under the British had passed away and their favourite occupation thus was government service in which they held places from the humblest village accountant, schoolmaster, and clerk to very high and responsible posts.[167]

It was also a general tendency of the British officers not to give the Indians substantial salaries. According to them it was needless extravagance. It is seen from the recommendation given by J.H.Pelly to the Government to stop the practice of an extra cess for certain class of people in the district, which in return given to the local Brahmanas. But Mountstuart Elphinstone discouraged Pelly's stand. In the minutes of the Council indicated that it was desirable that J.H. Pelly was cautious in recommending the abolition of any type of taxes or cesses merely because, they seem irregular since the whole system in the native place was irregular and one part of it would make up for the other.[168]

But it was not easy to run the government without the help of the local people and the company could not have gone ahead in any field without the their help. Without education to the people, it would have been difficult to run the administration. Therefore, T.B. Jervis, an officer employed by the government of Bombay for a Statistical Survey of Southern Konkan, took interest in the education of the district. He started collecting statistics of the schools and scholars of the district in 1820. Schools were started with the object of teaching Western science and literature. However, the beginning was made with vernacular schools. The first Government School was started at Ratnagiri in 1826 under the supervision of T.B. Jervis.[169]

Between 1826 and 1840 seven schools were opened at government expense. From 1840 to 1855 from the commencement of the Board of Education 11 more schools were established at Ratnagiri. The first of these was opened at Malvan in 1841 and one more school opened at Vengurla in the following year. The best schools in the division at Ratnagiri were found in Vengurla, Chiplun, and Malvan in the Ratnagiri Collectorate.[170] The Ratnagiri school No. 1 was continued under the able management of Gangadhar

Ramchandra who also was an excellent teacher, well-informed and industrious.[171] The contribution of the locals towards education was common as they were aware of its benefits. This is seen in the contribution of the inhabitants of Rs. 661 for the completion of a building of Ratnagherry English school in 1846.[172]

Although most students belonged to the Brahmin caste yet there were students coming from varied communities. This is seen from the following tables:

Table 3.29 : Castes and Number of Scholars[173]

Sr. No.	Scholars	Scholars	Sr. No.	Scholars	Scholars
1	Brahmins	1029	19	Jingar	1
2	Purohoo	26	20	Tellee	20
3	Shenvee	243	21	Purit	37
4	Wanee	217	22	Goorow	4
5	Koonbee	17	23	Goorzur	9
6	Christian	4	24	Hajjam	15
7	Mussalman	952	25	Kassar	20
8	Maratha	550	26	Jangam Lingayat	10
9	Sonar	117	27.	Kostee	8
10	Sootar	10	28	Sinde	9
11	Koombhar	6	29	Chumar	—
12	Gabeet	29	30	Tambat	6
13	Njamdaree	419	31	Gosavee	5
14	Jyne	15	32	Mahar	2
15	Gaode	35	33	Juwul	24
16	Deolee	1	34	Kolee	8
17	Lingayat Wani	10	35	Gondhalee	1
18	Shimpee	10	36	Caste Uncertain	—
	Total	**3690**		**Total**	**179**

The benefits of education resulted in the locals getting jobs in the Company's offices. Ratnagiri was dominated by the Brahmins who already well read from the time of the Peshwas did not lose the opportunity to sharpen their intellects. So, for the first decades of the British rule in South Konkan the clerical, bureaucratic and government were by and large monopolized by the people from South Konkan, the highest posts being of course in the hands of the British officers. But throughout this period, the people were aware that for their own economic existence and survival, they must adapt to the new conditions.

References

1. Kenneth Ballhachet, *Social Policy and Social Change in Western India*, London, Oxford University Press, 1961, p.142.
2. H.S.Maine, *Village Communities in the East and the West*, London, 1895, pp.123 and 176.
3. J.J.Sparrow, Collector, Ratnagiri Collectorate, to Francis Warden, Secretary to Government, Bombay, dated 5 August 1823,MSA, Revenue Department Vol. No. 24 of 1824(hereafter R.D.), pp. 501-06.
4. Alexander Rogers, *The Land Revenue of Bombay- A History of its Administration, Rise and Progress*, Vol- I, Low Price Publications, New Delhi, 1982, p.4.
5. B.H.Baden Powell, *Administration of the Land Systems of British India*, Vol. III, Oxford Press, London, 1974, Printed in India, p.308.
6. George Coles, Collector, Ratnagiri Collector Office, to Capt. Wingate, Superintendent, Revenue Survey and Assessment, MSA, R.D. Vol No.225 of 1851, p.397.
7. George Coles, Collector, Ratnagiri Collector Office, to Capt. Wingate, Superintendent, Revenue Survey and Assessment, MSA, R.D. Vol No. 225 of 1851, p.397.
8. J.H.Pelly, Collector, Southern Konkan's Office, to John Dunlop, Bombay, dated 20 December 1820, MSA, R.D.Vol No.11/12/1825, pp 461-62; also Selections Vol No.58/ 1819@1821, List of villages under the British Possessions.
9. Selections, Vol No.58/1819 @ 1821, List of villages under British possession, MSA, p.158.

9. *Ibid*, p.159.

10. *Ibid*, pp.462-66.

11. *Ibid*, p. 466.

12. M.S.Rege, 'History and Survey of Education, Ratnagiri District', Unpublished Ph.D. Thesis, University of Bombay, 1961, pp.11-16.

14. *Ibid*.

15. C.B. Joshi, 'The Ratnagiri Taluka, Land Use and Settlements', *Bombay Geographical Magazine,* Vol. No.9, Mumbai, p.5.
16. J.H.Pelly, Collector, Ratnagiri Collectorate, to Francis Warden, Secretary to Government, Bombay, dated 4 October 1820,MSA, R.D.Vol No. 16/16/1821, p.471.
17. *Ibid,* pp.458-71.
18. *op.cit,* p.176.
19. D. G. Gadgil, *Hindusthancha Arthik Itihas* (Marathi), Jambhekar G, Lokshikshan Laghu Grantha Mala, Poona, 1932, p.44.
20. Kenneth Ballhachet, *op.cit,* 1961, p.142.
21. *Ibid,* p.142.
22. Indu Banga, *Ports and their Hinterlands in India,* (1700-1950), Manohar Publications, 1992, p.156; Also J.C. Srivastava, *Territories Conquered from the Peshwa: A report by Mountstuart Elphinstone,* ed, Orient Publishers, New Delhi, 1973, (reprint), p.78.
23. *Ibid*; Also Home Miscellaneous No. 329: Some Observations on the English Possessions in India, their Government, Population, Cultivation, Produce and Commerce, in the Asiatic Annual Register, 1803.
24. B.H.Baden Powell, *op.cit,* p.31.
25. A.K.Nairne, *A Handbook for Revenue Officers in the Presidency of Bombay,* Bombay, 1884, p.74. (A.S.B.)
26. *Ibid,* p.79.
27. A.K.Nairne, *History of Konkan,* Vol No. I, part II, Bombay, 1894, pp.74-75.
28. N.Rabitoy,'System vs. Expediency' The Reality of Land Revenue Administration in the Bombay Presidency g1812-1820, MSA, *Modern Asian Studies,* Vol No. 9, 4, 1975, pp.544-45.
29. General Smith to Newsham Letter No 41, Ratnagiri Collector's Office, List No.15, Ratnagiri, Malvan ffResidency Correspondence for 1818, MSA, Malvan Political Secret (hereafter MPS).
30. *Ibid.*
31. W.Dowell, Assistant, 2nd Class Survey Department, Ratnagiri, dated 1 November 1829, MSA, R.D. Vol No. ff225/1851, pp.303 and 330-32.
32. Civil Auditor, Bombay Castle to John Bax, Secretary to Government, dated 29 August 1832, MSA, fffR.D.Vol No.4/ 408/1832, pp.114-15 and 295.

33. *Ibid*, pp.114-15.
34. *Ibid*, p.83.
35. H.E.Goldsmid, Secretary to Government, Bombay Castle, dated 10 October 1853, Published by Order of the Hon. the Governor in Council, MSA, R.D.Vol No. 138/1854, pp.143-44.
36. J.J.Sparrow, Southern Konkan, A Report to Francis Warden, Chief Secretary to Government, dated 23 July 1821, MSA, R.D.Vol No.30/1821, p.486.
37. Extract from the Revenue Report of 1819 as given by Collector J.H.Pelly dated 18 December, 1820, MSA, R.D.Vol No. 225/ 1851, p.24.
38. W.Dowell, Lieut and Assistant, 2nd Class Survey Department, Ratnagiri, dated 1 November 1829, Re: Report of the Survey of Ratnagiri taluka, MSA, R.D.Vol No 225/ 1851, pp.252-53.
39. G.R. Ambedkar, *The Crops of the Bombay Presidency*, Part-IX, Government Central Press, Bombay, p.14.
40. W. Jervis, *Thomas Best Jervis*, (A Centenary Tribute), London, 1898, p.10.
41. Extract of the Jummabundi Report for 1823-24 by J.A.Dunlop, dated 15 August 1824, No.53, MSA, R.D. fVol No. 225/1851, p.160.
42. W. Dowell, *op.cit.*, p.276.
43. W.Dowell, *op.cit.*, p.275.
44. W.Dowell, Assistant 2nd Class Survey Department, Ratnagiri, dated 1 November 1829, Re: report of the Ratnagiri taluka, MSA, R.D.Vol No.275/1851, pp.261 and 273.
45. *Ibid.*
46. Henry Lindell, Collector, Ratnagiri Collector's Office, Re: A Report on Land Revenues of the Ratnagiri Collectorate for the year 1845-46, MSA, R.D.Vol. No. 16/1848, p.75.
47. T.B.Jervis, *A Report of the Weights and Measures of the Konkan Province*, Bombay, American Mission jPress, 1929, p.24. Fort Library, Bombay. (hereafter FL)
48. G.Coles, Collector, Ratnagiri Collector's Office to Francis Warden, Secretary to Government, 31 March 1849, MSA, R.D.Vol No. 17/1850, pp.132-33.
49. W.Dowell, Assistant 2nd Class Survey Department, Ratnagiri, dated 1 November 1829, Re: report of the Ratnagiri taluka, MSA, R.D.Vol No 275/1851, p.276.
50. *Ibid.*

51. Thomas Williamson, Revenue Commissioner to L.R.Reid, Acting Chief Secretary, Bombay, dated 13 November 1838 and 11 February 1839, MSA, R.D.Vol No. 159/1839, p.2.
52. Alex Elphinstone, Acting Collector to Thomas Williamson, Revenue Commissioner, Bombay, dated 13 November 1838 and 11 February 1839, MSA, R.D.Vol No. 159/1839, p.17.
53. The Bombay Provincial Banking Enquiry Committee, Government of India, A Report, 1949, p.10.
54. James Forbes, *Oriental Memories: A Narrative of Seventeen Years of Residence in India,* Vol No.I, London, p.208.
55. *Ibid.*
56. J.A.Dunlop, Collector, Southern Konkan Collector's Office, dated 21 September 1822 to James Farish, Secretary to Government, Bombay, MSA, R.D.Vol. No 8/32/ 1822, p.243.
57. J.A.Dunlop, Collector, Southern Konkan Collector's Office, Re: Statement showing the articles added to the Ayen Dust under the New Government, dated 13 August 1824, MSA, R.D.Vol No.17/1825, p.103.
58. *Ibid,* p.75.
59. M.V.Willoughby, Revenue Commissioner, Poona Revenue Commissioner's Office to L.R.Reid Secretary to Government, Bombay, dated 9 October 1834, MSA, R.D.Vol No. 6/550/1834, p.141.
60. Alex Elphinstone, Acting Collector, Ratnagiri Collector Office to L.R.Reid, Acting Chief Secretary, Bombay, dated 20 September 1838, MSA, R.D.Vol No.159/1839, p.17.
61. W.Dowell, Lieut & Assistant Surveyor, 2nd Class, Ratnagiri, 1 November 1829, Re: Report on the Survey of Ratnagiri taluka, MSA, R.D. Vol No. 225/1851, p.322.
62. M.V.Willoughby, Revenue commissioner, Revenue Commissioner's Office to L.R.Reid, Acting Chief Secretary, Bombay, 13 November 1838, MSA, R.D.Vol No. 159/1839, p.3.
63. W.Dowell, Assistant 2nd Class Survey Department, Ratnagiri, dated 1 November 1829, Re: Report of the Ratnagiri taluka, MSA, R.D.Vol No.225/1851, pp.292-93.
64. W.Dowell, Signed on the table showing the General Results of the Survey of the Ratnagiri, MSA, R.D.Vol No. 225/1851, p. 499.
65. D.Blane, to H.E.Goldsmith, Secretary to Government, dated 12 March 1851, MSA, R.D.Vol No. 7/1851, pp.67-69.

66. Alex Elphinstone, Acting Collector, Ratnagiri Collector's Office, to L.R.Reid, Acting Chief Secretary, Bombay, dated 20 September 1838, MSA, R.D.Vol No.159/1839, p.27.
67. H.A.Harrison, 2nd Assistant Collector to J.A.Dunlop, Ratnagiri Collector's Office, MSA, R.D.Vol No. 12/64/1823, p.407.
68. Atmaram Baba Ramdas of Southern Konkan, to Mountstuart Elphinstone, President and Governor in Council, dated 17 October 1825, MSA, R.D.Vol No. 11/1825, pp.449-51.
69. J.A.Porter, Collector, Southern Konkan Collector's Office, Ratnagiri, to Thomas Williamson, Revenue Commissioner, Poona, dated 26 September 1833, MSA, R.D.Vol. No. 6/550/1834, p.127.
70. Alex Elphinstone, Acting Collector, to the Secretary to Government, Re: Revenue statement of the Ratnagiri Collectorate, dated 20 September 1838, MSA, R.D.Vol No. 159/1839, p.21.
71. H.Young, Commissioner of Customs, Salt and Opium, Appendix A, Statements showing the salt works, MSA, R.D.Vol No. 143/1854, p.73.
72. C.B.Joshi, *op.cit.*, p.10; also R.D.Choksey, *Economic Life in the Bombay Deccan and Karnatak*, Asia hPublishing House, Bombay, 1960, p.138.
73. C.B.Joshi, *op.cit.*, pp.10-11.
74. *Ibid.*
75. R.D.Choksey, *op.cit.*, p.138.
76. George Scott, 1st Assistant Collector to H.W.Reeves, Revenue Commissioner, Camp Wagotna, dated 25 August 1856, Collector, True Translation by G.Coles, Collector, Re: Translation of the Proclamation issued by J.A.Dunlop, MSA, R.D. Vol. No 89/1856, p.183.
77. W.I.Turqand, Officiating Collector of Ratnagiri to H.Young, Chief Secretary to Government, Bombay, Ratnagiri district, dated 9 February 1856, MSA, R.D.Vol No. 89/1856, p.70.
78. *Ibid*, p.69.
79. W.I.Turqand, Officiating Collector of Ratnagiri to H.Young, Chief Secretary to Government, Bombay, Ratnagiri District, dated 9 February 1856, MSA, R.D.Vol No. 89/1856, p.76.
80. George Scott, 1st Assistant Collector in charge of Ratnagiri, to H.W.Reeves, Revenue Commissioner, camp Wagotne, dated 25 August 1856, MSA, R.D.Vol No. 89/1856, p.174.

81. George Scott, 1st Assistant Collector to H.W.Reeves, Revenue Commissioner, Camp Wagotna, dated 25 August 1856, Collector, True Translation by G.Coles, Collector, Re: Translation of the Proclamation Issued by J.A.Dunlop, MSA, R.D. Vol. No 89/1856, pp.198-202.
82. Rutrand Scooner, Officiating Commissioner of Customs, Salt and Opium, to the Territorial Department, dated 11 August 1836, MSA, R.D.Vol. No. 89/1856, p.147.
83. J.J.Sparrow, Collector, South Konkan Collector's Office to T.B.Jervis, Executive Engineer, South Konkan, Ratnagiri, MSA, General Department (hereafter G.D.) Vol No. 47/ 52/1821-23, p.87.
84. T.B.Jervis, *op.cit.*, FL, pp.24-32.
85. *Ibid*; also MSA, G.D.Vol No.47/52/1821-23, p.128.
86. W.W.Dowell, Lieuteant, Superintendent, Survey, Re: Account of the Mode of Survey in Ratnagiri Taluka Completed in May 1827, Capt. Dowell's Notes on Survey of Ratnagiri Taluka, MSA, BGS, CXCVII-New Series, Bombay Government Central Press, 1912, pp.6,7 and 9.
87. James Roberts, Ed.,(DCP) *Western Indian Reports Addressed to the Chambers of the Commerce of Manchester, Liverpool, Blackburn and Glasgow by their Commissioner Late,* Alexander MacKay, London, Nathanial Cooke, Milford House, London, 1953, pp.369-70.
88. *Ibid.*
89. E.M.Proes, Chief Engineer & Secretary to Government, PWD, Bombay, *Bombay Presidency Motor Guide*, Government of Bombay, September1923, p.99. Jawaharlal Nehru Library, Rare book section Mumbai (hereafter JNL).
90. W.J. Turquand Officiating Collector of Ratnagiri, dated 31 December 1856 R.D.Vol No.16/1860, pp.136-145.
91. *Ibid*, pp.101 & 131.
92. *Ibid*, pp.103 and131.
93. H.Lindell, Ratnagiri post office, to the Post Master General, Bombay, dated 1 July 1845, MSA,G.D.Vol No. 70/ 976/1845, p.194.
94. MSA, L. Smith, Re: Remarks on Military Importance of Malwan and Vengurla and the General Conditions of the District, Bombay, 4 December 1812 in R.D.Choksey, *Malwan Residency, op.cit.*, pp.1-11.
95. R. D. Choksey, Ratnagiri Collectorate, *op.cit.*, p.123.
96. A.Elphinstone, Magistrate, Ratnagiri, to J.Willoughby, Secretary to Government, Bombay, Re: Statement showing

the guarded chowkies on the way to Kolhapur, MSA, Political Department Vol No.51/1046/1839(hereafter P.D.), p.55.

97. H. Hebbert, Deputy Secretary, Bombay Castle, Re: Substance of a Letter from Khem Sawant, to the Right Hon. Governor-in-Council, dated 5th Zilkaad-5 March received 17 March 1835, 20 March 1835, p.281, MSA, R.D.Vol. No. 20/642/1835, p.281.

98. Substance of a petition from Narayan Bhat Patwardhan Kharam Bhut Tunsekar, Pitre, and Deooskar of the port of Vingoorley Ziyera / Sindoodurg / Southern Conkan to the Honorable Mountstuart Elphinstone, Governor of Bombay, dated 20 April 1825, MSA, R.D.Vol No. 11/121/1825, p.331.

99. John Anderson, Acting Principal Collector, to J.Bax, Secretary to Government Office, dated 19 November 1832, MSA, G.D.Vol No. 25/270/1832, p.303.

100. Alex Elphinstone, Collector Ratnagiri, to the Executive Engineer's office, B.D.Camp, MSA, Territorial Department, Vengurla, dated 28 March 1843, G.D.Vol No. 70/1845, pp.75-76.

101. H. Hebbert, Deputy Secretary, Persian Department, dated 20 March 1835, MSA, R.D.Vol No. 20/642, 1835, p.281.

102. *Ibid.*

103. H. A. Harrison, Assistant Collector, re: Revenue Report of the Owcthitghar Taluka, MSA, R.D.Vol No.18/ 1840, p.182.

104. James. M. Erskine, 2nd Assistant Collector of Ratnagiri, to G Coles, Collector of Ratnagiri, Camp Hurnee, dated 29 November 1851, MSA, R.D.Vol. No 19/1852, p. 323.

105. R.D.Choksey, *op.cit.*, pp.164-65.

106. N. Laud, to H.E, Goldsmith, Secretary to Government, Re: Substance of the Petition from the Ryots, dated 23 September 1834, MSA, R.D.Vol No.7/551, p.275.

107. George Elliot, Collector, Southern Konkan Collector Office, dated 17 May 1834, to the Revenue Commissioner, Territorial Department, MSA, R.D.Vol No. 3497/1834, pp.295-300.

108. George Elliot, Collector, Southern Konkan Collector's Office, dated 20 December 1834, to the Revenue Commissioner, MSA, *Ibid*, pp.297-98.

109. Haruka Yanagisawa, Indira Gandhi Institute of Development and Research (hereafter IGIDR), *A century*

of Change- Caste and Irrigated Land in Tamilnadu, Manohar Publications, 1996, New Delhi, p.67.

110. R.D.Choksey, *op.cit.*, pp.113-114.
111. A.R.Kulkarni, *op.cit.*, p.201.
112. Bombay Gazetteer, Ratnagiri and Sawantwadi, Vol No. X, *op.cit.*, p.377.
113. H.Richardson, 2nd Assistant Collector, Ratnagiri, dated 21 October 1822, Revenue Commissioner, MSA, R.D.Vol No. 499, 11/H/1833,*op.cit.*, p. 27.
114. Sanjay Subramanyam, 'The Portuguese, the Port of Basrur, and the Rice Trade, 1600-50', *Indian Economic Social and Historical Review* (hereafter *IESHR*), No.21, 4, 1984, p.438.
115. J.Lindell Collector, Ratnagiri Collector Office to H.E.Goldsmith, Secretary to Government, MSA,Territorial Department, Bombay, dated 13 December 1847, MSA, R.D.Vol No. 24/1849, p.96.
116. *Ibid,* p.97.
117. W.Dowell, Ratnagiri, dated 1 November 1829, Re: Report on the Survey of Ratnagiri taluka, MSA, R.D.Vol No 251/ 1851, p.293.
118. Alex Elphinstone, Ratnagiri Collector's Office, to John Vibart, Revenue Commissioner, Poona, dated 21 fNovember 1841, MSA, R.D.Vol. No. 12/1345/1842, p.43.
119. J.Turqand, Collector of Ratnagiri to J.D.Inverarity, Revenue Commissioner, dated 31 December 1857, fMSA, R.D.Vol No 16/1860, p.227.
120. H.Lindell Collector, Ratnagiri Collector Office to H.E.Goldsmith, Secretary to Government, Territorial fDepartment, Bombay, dated 13 December 1847, MSA, R.D.Vol No. 24/1849. p.43.
121. *Ibid* pp.41-42.
122. *Ibid,* p.43.
123. William Courtney, Revenue Commissioner, to H.E.Goldsmid, Secretary to Government, Belgaum District, dated 16 February 1852, MSA, R.D.Vol. No. 19/1852, p.20.
124. C. B. Joshi, *op.cit.*, p.10.
125. W.E.Copleston, *The Bombay Forests*, Government Central Press, Bombay, 1925, p.4.
126. W.Dowell, Ratnagiri, dated 1 November 1829, Re: Report to the Ratnagiri Collectorate, MSA, R.D.Vol No 225/1851, p.247.
127. R. D. Choksey, *Ratnagiri Collectorate, op.cit.*, p.156.

128. L.R.Reid, Principal Collector, Konkan, to Thomas Williamson, Secretary to Government, Bombay, dated 30 October 1831, MSA, G.D.Vol. No 23/242/1831, p.205.
129. P.R.Doucton, Collector of Land Revenue, to Charles Norris, Chief Secretary to Government, Territorial Department, dated 3 February 1830, MSA, R.D.Vol.No.4/284/1830, pp.17-19.
130. R. D. Choksey, *op.cit.*, p.45.
131. R. D. Choksey, *op.cit.*, p.162.
132. George Elliot, Collector, Southern Konkan Collector's Office, dated 20 March 1834, to the Revenue Commissioner, MSA, R.D.Vol No. 499, 11/H, 1835, p.231.
133. L.R.Reid, Collector, Southern Konkan Collectors Office, dated 31 July 1829, to the Territorial Department, MSA, R.D.Vol No.225/1851, p.239.
134. Collector, Territorial Department, to Thomas Williamson, Revenue Commissioner, Poona, MSA, R.D.Vol No. 498/1834, p.145.
135. G. S. Hardy Assistant Settlement Officer Ratnagiri, to the Collector of Ratnagiri, Camp Dapoli, dated 3 February 1913, MSA, BGS, No. DXXVIII -New Series, Papers relating to the Revision Survey Settlement of the Malwan Taluka of the Ratnagiri Collectorate, Bombay, Government Central Press, No.2-A of 1913, 1915, p.22.
136. J.W.Robertson, Deputy Commissioner, Konkan division, to H.Young, Commissioner of Customs, Salt and Opium, dated 31 August 1854, MSA, pp.135-141.
137. J.A Dunlop, Collector, Ratnagiri, Re: Extracts from the Revenue Report of 1823-24, MSA, R.D.Vol No. 225/1851, p.162.
138. William Courtny, Revenue Commissioner to H.E.Goldsmith, Secretary to Government, Belgaum District, dated 16 February 1852, MSA, R.D.Vol No.19/1853, p.20.
139. J.J.Sparrow, Southern Konkan Collector's Office, to Francis Warden, Chief Secretary to Government, Bombay, dated 12 November 1821, MSA, R.D.Vol No. 16/1821, pp.695-96.
140. W.Dowell, Assistant 2nd Class Survey Department, Ratnagiri, dated 1 November 1829, Re: Report of the Ratnagiri taluka, MSA, R.D.Vol No. 225/1851, pp.292-93.
141. J.J.Sparrow, Southern Konkan Collector's Office, to the James Farish, Secretary to Government, dated 12 November 1821, Bombay, MSA, R.D.Vol No.1689 of 1821, pp.531,673, 695-697.

142. James Warden, Chief Secretary, Bombay Castle, to the Collector in the South Konkan, dated 23 November 1821, MSA, R.D.Vol No.1627 of 1821, p.699.
143. Henry Lindell, Collector, Ratnagiri, Re: A report on Land Revenue of Ratnagiri Collectorate for 1845-46, MSA, R.D.Vol. No. 16/1848, p. 49.
144. Alex Elphinstone Acting Collector, Ratnagiri Collector's Office, to L.R.Reid, Acting Secretary, Bombay, MSA, R.D.Vol No. 159/1839, p.17.
145. M.V.Willoughby, Revenue Commissioner, Revenue Commissioner's Office, to L.R.Reid, Acting Chief Secretary, Bombay, dated 13 November 1838, dated 10 July 1823, pp.505&507, MSA, R.D.Vol No. 159/1839, p.2.
146. *Ibid*
147. William Courtney, Revenue Commissioner, to H.E.Goldsmith, Secretary to Government, Belgaum district, dated 16 February 1852, MSA, R.D.Vol. No.19/ 1852, pp.21-22.
148. Alex Elphinstone, Acting Collector, Ratnagiri to the Chief Secretary, Bombay, dated 6 November 1841, MSA, R.D.Vol No. 12/1842, p.154.
149. H.Lindell, Collector, Ratnagiri Collectors Office, to Territorial Department, Re:Trade Reports, 1 December 1846, R.D.Vol No. 16/1848 & 13/1844, pp.101,152&153; also R.D. Vol No. 24/1849, dated 13 December 1847, pp.217-218.
150. MSA, R.D.Vol No.144/1854, p.194.
151. H.Lindell, Collector of Ratnagiri, to the Territorial Department, Re: Trade Reports 1846, MSA, R.D.Vol jNo.16/1848, p.152.
152. B.C, to the Magistrate of Ratnagiri, Secret Department, MSA, Public Department (hereafter Pub.D.) Vol No.51/ 1046/1839, pp.181-82.
153. George Coles, Ratnagiri Magistrate Office, to Capt. A.M.Haselwood, Superintendent of Police, Re:Outpost at Vengurla, dated 22 February 1853, MSA, Judicial Department(hereafter J.D.),Vol No.48/1853, pp.17-19.
154. MSA, R.D.Vol No.11/121/1825,Re: Statement of the Outstanding Balances of Southern Konkan, p.508.
155. Territorial Department, Ratnagiri Collector's office, dated 10 December 1825, MSA, R.D.Vol No. 11/12/1825, pp.508-09.
156. V. G. Khobrekar, *Maharashrache Arthik VA Samajik Khacchikaran* (Marathi), Maharashtratil Sahastra jUtsav, Bombay, 1958, p.10.

157. Deccan Commissioner's Records Inward Letter 2111 of 29 October 1824; 2035 of 19 August 1824; 2208 of 8 February 1825.
158. T.B.Jervis, Colonel, Chief Engineer, Military Board Office, to Lord Viscount Falkland, Governor and President in Council, dated 15 January 1851,MSA, R.D.Vol No. 249/ 1851, pp.171-72.
159. G.S.Hardy Assistant Settlement Officer Ratnagiri, to the Collector of Ratnagiri, Camp Dapoli, dated 3 February 1913, MSA, BGS, No. DXXVIII -New Series, *op.cit.*, pp. 2-3.
160. Collector, Ratnagiri Collectorate office, Camp Malvan, dated 8 May 1851, to the Secretary to Government Office Bombay, MSA, R.D.Vol No.249/1851, pp.177-79.
161. BGS, No. DXXVIII -New Series, Malvan taluka, *op.cit.*, Report, given on 19 April 1851, Bombay Castle, MSA, R.D. Vol No.211/1851, p.217.
162. A Report, Re: Irrigation, Malwan taluka, p.11, MSA, Revenue Department under the Government of Bombay forwarded to the Hon. Court of Justice with Letter No. 1260/23, August 1851, R.D.Vol No. 211/1851, p.533.
163. R. D. Choksey, *op.cit.*, pp.53-55.
164. Kenneth Ballhatchet, op cit., p.43; also Marriot to Mountstuart Elphinstone, Bombay Government, dated 17 April, 1824, p.129.
165. G.Guriyale, Superintendent, Revenue Survey to E.H.Townsend, Revenue commissioner, Extracts from the Revenue Report for 1819-20 by the Collector J.H.Pelly dated 18 December 1820, MSA, R.D.Vol No. 225/1851, pp.34-35.
166. J.A.Dunlop, Collector Southern Konkan to G.More, Acting Secretary to Bombay Government, dated 15 August 1824, MSA, R.D.Vol No.11/1824, part III , pp.77-78; also J.Dunlop to the Government ,1824, Para 169f Bombay Revenue Collectors Office,12 January 44.
167. Gazetteer of the Bombay Presidency, Vol X, p.113; also John Wilson, *Indian Caste*, Vol No.I, Deep Publication, New Delhi, 1976, p.44.
168. Minutes, dated 9 August 1820,MSA, R.D.Vol No.14/1821, pp.26-27. (This declaration was qualified by the suggestion that if Pelly found that the cess was really oppressive the Government would sanction its abolition.)
169. R.V.Parulekar and C.L.Bakshi, MSA, Selections from

Educational Records, Bombay, part II (1815-1840), published by Indian Institute of Education, Bombay, 1955, p.88.

170. Report of the Board of Education, 1853, p.78.
171. Report of the Board of Education, 1852, pp.74-75,(He was the father of Lokmanya Balgangadhar Tilak.)
172. Stowell, Secretary, Board of Education, Ratnagiri Collector's Office, to J.G.Lumsden, Secretary to Government, General Department, Board of Education, Bombay, dated 6 May 1850, MSA, R.D.Vol. fNo.30/274/ 1850, p.7.
173. Information was found in Unpublished old Record of the Education Department and was obtained through the Courtesy of Indian Institute of Education, Bombay Selections from Educational Records, Bombay,(1815-1840).

[illegible] Khoti in the [illegible] Kolaba districts and Thana district [illegible]

3. The Khoti and [illegible] tenures in the ex-states of [illegible] and Sawantwadi and Kolhapur merged in the [illegible] and Kolhapur districts.

[illegible] in the [illegible] and Bhor states merged [illegible] in the Kolaba district.

[illegible] the khoti system differed in the coastal parts of Maharashtra. After the acquisition of Salsette by the British [illegible] the khoti tenure was extended to about 51 villages because the island was depopulated and scantily cultivated. With a view to attract population and introduce cultivation the British Government gave the right of absolute ownership [illegible] on lease perpetual or periodical. However the leases differed according to the exigencies of administration. Powai, Goregaon, Deonar, Bhandup, Chincavli, Marol, Mahul, Kanjur and Vikroli had estates which were leased for revenue farming. While the leases in the case of Vile Parle and Juhu were hereditary inams. The motive behind the leases of Ghodbunder, Bhavandar and Mira estates was maintenance of embankments. Kurla and Malad estates were leased for exchange of lands.[16] The lessees paid remuneration to village *Patels* or *Madhvis*. It was also found that many villages were granted to the Parsis as they ventured to develop the village.

In Kolaba, the khots had to execute the *kabulayats* which defined their rights and responsibilities. Accordingly, they had to pay local fund cess to government and recover the dues from the cultivators. The dues could be survey assessment from the dhara lands. They could be customary *khoti faida* in kind or in cash.[18] There were 454 villages in Kolaba district. There were two types of ownership granted to the khots in Kolaba. They were *khoti khasgi* and *khoti nisbat*. The *khoti khasgi* was a private property of the khots, the *khoti nisbat* land was vested in the government. As far as the forest rights were concerned the khots in kolaba were entitled to one third of the net proceeds after deducting all the felling expenses incurred by the

CHAPTER 4

THE SECOND PHASE OF BRITISH RULE IN THE RATNAGIRI COLLECTORATE [1860-1920]

The Ratnagiri Collectorate had become a part of British India in 1818 but it was not until 1840s that the direct British administration was introduced uniformly in all the talukas of the Collectorate. By 1858 British rule was established and the main impact of the rule in the processes of socio-economic development of the Ratnagiri Collectorate was witnessed. Though the rules laid down were uniform throughout the territories acquired, the impact varied though not greatly but some extent, from place to place depending on its social, geographical and economic conditions. The study of the three talukas namely, Ratnagiri, Malvan and Vengurla have been dealt separately for a better understanding of the impact of British rule in each of the talukas.

Ratnagiri Taluka of the Ratnagiri Collectorate

Ratnagiri taluka was bounded in the north by the Guhaghar petha of the Chiplun Taluka, which was divided by the Shastri River. It was bounded on the east by Sangameshwar Taluka and on the South by Rajapur taluka. Steep ravines, deep waterfalls intersected the hills. The coastline had many bays, creeks and backwaters. To the northern most taluka was situated the Saitwada petha. Jaygad, Purangad and Achre were ports with Custom offices.

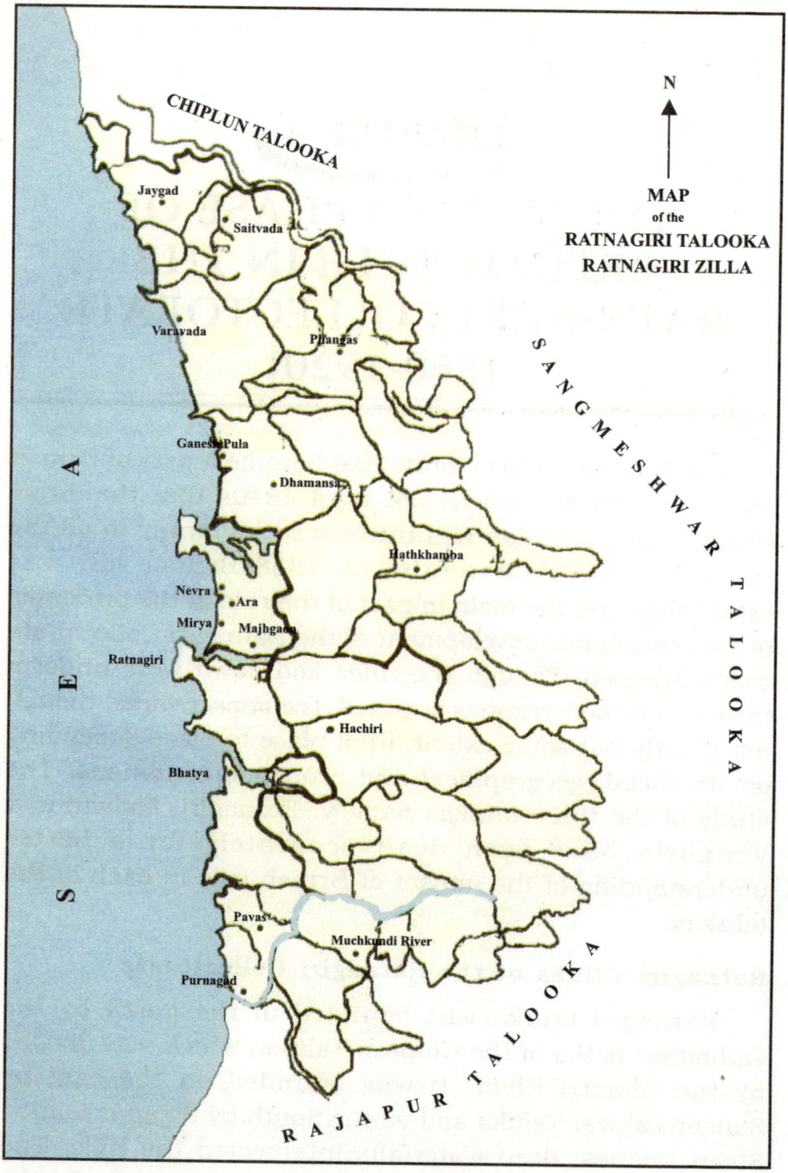

Ratnagiri Taluka

Source : MSA, Revenue Department, Vol. No. 194/1898.

Ratnagiri town was the headquarters of the Ratnagiri Collectorate. It consisted of high hills with deep valleys. The sides of the hills were steep producing the usual rotation of warkas crops. At the lower levels grew a second crop which ripened towards the end of the hot season.

The areas actually cultivated often were more or less than the figures recorded. A number of adjustments were necessary before the figures could be compared. Calculations were often inaccurate because of the encroachments on roads, paths, and common grounds, the unusable lands and the existing khoti tenures. Addition to government lands after acquisition also often led to confusion. The *Inam* lands usually were deducted wherever statistics were available.

An example of the inaccuracy of the records can be observed from the two surveys done in the Saitwada taluka of the Ratnagiri taluka. The first one was undertaken under the supervision of Lieutenant Dowell from 1827 to 1833 and the second one undertaken by Lieutenant Kemball first and later by Mr.Doyly from 1852 to 1857. The survey prosecuted by Lieutenant. Dowell was done with a *kathi* or staff. The length of which to accommodate it to the English measure of the acre was fixed at 10 feet 5.222 inches.[1] No boundary marks were erected. Collector C. Coles failed to identify the rice plots. Nearly half of the entire area was rocky. The assessment was an approximate measurement as the rocks and streams were not measured. The object of the surveys was to ascertain the quantity of land under cultivation and compare it with the one inserted in the account of the last survey. However, Lieutenant Dowell's information around 1829 was of little value yet, the information he had collected regarding the customs and conditions of the people and the khoti system in general, was of a great value. A survey settlement was introduced under the Provisions Act No.I of 1865 into the below mentioned villages belonging to the Ratnagiri taluka of the Ratnagiri Collectorate.[2]

Table 4.1

Villages				
Kalbadevi	Phansap	Hatis	Phansole	Niwsar
Wada Are	Someshwar	Sonde	Adomb Dande	Chindroli
Wada Juwe	Majgaon	Adomb Bhawe	Napare	Agwe
Peth Shiwapur	Kale	Sewar Ambere	Khedshi	Karbunde
Ratnagiri	Mamurwadi	Tikan Natondi	Thike	Shirbawli
Pordavne	Jambulada	Kolambe	Hath Khambe	Pathrat
Kasarvel	Madbundgule	Dabil Ambere	Pomendi Budruk	Walke
Wada Jun	Gawdegule	Kasba Pawas	Kurtudi	Satre
Wada Sdge	Merwi	Mahalugi	Wasurle	Nandawli
Newre	Tikan Sowan	Dorle	Chandori	Asondi
Dhokambe	Tikan Behre	Mirjole	Bhoke	Welwand
Rahtagar	Agargule	Tembeye	Niwli	Kasheli
Karle	Ghera Purngad	Shil	Vetoshi	Math
Naghne	Waigani	Pomendi Khurd	Jambrun	Nanej
Wada Miria	Wada Phadke	Kond Kankur	Kolwan	Ajnari
Jhadgaon	Gavde Ambere	Nirole	Pali	
Wada Basni	Golap	Harchiri	Panwal	
Shirgaon	Wada Ranpar	Dugwe	Khanu	
Kotowde	Tikan Bag Agashi	Bag Patole	Cheroli	
Bhati	Tikan Chakradev	Kharote	Umbre	

A Settlement was done for the Ratnagiri Taluka in 1866-67 from 5th March 1866 to 5th March 1867. A.K.Nairne, 1st Assistant and collector-in-Charge surveyed the lands.[3] The amount collected from the Ratnagiri Collectorate during these two years was Rs. 1,30,420-11-11 in 1866-67 and Rs. 1,33,643-8-5 in 1867-68.showing an increase of Rs. 3,222-12-6.[4]

In 1869, there were five tarafs recorded namely Hacheri, Majgaon, Hatkhambe and Pawas. They contained 99 villages of which 33 were Khalsa, 161/2 were *dharekari*, 3 *khichari*, 42 *nival khoti*, and 4 *Inam* . In the year 1879, under section 102 of Bombay Act Volume of 1879, it was declared that all assessments, imposed under the said settlement, were fixed for a period of 28 years commencing with the revenue year 1869-70 and ending with 1896-97.[5]

A report of the Revision of the Survey Settlement of 131 villages was made of the taluka in 1897. According to the Revenue Settlement Report of 1897, the area was approximately 2,64,284 acres or 357 square miles. There were six *Inam* villages. (rent free lands) They were Ch*akradeo, Kasari, Bondye, Kaodgaon, Tikan Datye, Chandroli.*

There were different tenures followed in several villages of the Ratnagiri taluka. Twenty six of the villages belonged to government. There were as many as fifty one khoti villages. This shows the domination of the khots in this taluka. There existed villages like the khichadi, *dharekari*, quasi *dharekari* and these kind of villages belonged to both government, khots or private people. These kind of varied tenures made it all the more difficult for the British to assess lands. The khots of Ratnagiri had been so powerful that the British could neither neglect them nor entertain them thus making the revenue collection all the more complicated. The village tenures are as given below[6] :

Table 4.2 : Villages with different tenures

26 Government Villages.
51 Khoti Villages.
16 Khichdi Villages.
23 Dharekari.
3 Part Khoti and Part Government.
3 Part Government, Part Khoti.
1 Part Government, Part Dharekari.

Once the tenures were known the first thing that the British did was to begin survey the villages systematically and make settlements. A survey settlement was introduced under the Provisions of the Bombay Act of 1879 into the below mentioned villages, belonging to the government in the Ratnagiri taluka of the Ratnagiri Collectorate. It was declared that the assessments imposed under the said settlement fixed for a period of thirty years commencing with the revenue year 1885-86 and ending with the revenue year 1914-15.[7]

Table 4.3

Ratnagiri taluka, Government villages		
Villages		
Bhode	Uple	Koldhe
Lawgan Khanoli	Punas	Kanti
Wada Nimbuchi	Chafet	Javde
Waghrat	Kurne	Werul
Kot	Gawane	Japde

The government occupied area was divided into cultivable and uncultivable areas. The cultivated area was 1,36,689 acres and the *Inam* acres were lands measured 2,046 acres. The rice lands occupied 13,166 acres, the garden lands occupied 1,492 acres, Rabi occupied 15, and the Warkas land was 1,22,016. The land belonging to *Inamdars* was 2,048 acres, out of which 262 acres was waste land. The uncultivated area divided into pot khrab in warkas and included lands not given out for cultivation, roads, rivers, nalas, village sites. The pot khrab area was 78,628 acres and the other uncultivated land included 10,913 acres.

The total area of the Ratnagiri Collectorate had increased from 3789 square miles to 3989 square miles by the year 1901-02. But Ratnagiri taluka showed a decrease of 15 acres according to the measurement taken at that time. The irrigational facilities were provided by 1901-02 and the cultivated acreage was 86,204.[8] Despite the irrigational facilities provided, the cultivated land decreased to 51,526 by 1910-11.[9]

The Second proposal of the Revision Settlement of the Ratnagiri taluka was submitted in 1914. The taluka at that time consisted of 152 villages of which six were *Inam*. 37 villages belonged earlier to the Saitwada petha, 94 formed the old Ratnagiri taluka and 15 belonged to the Lanje Petha. It is noted earlier that the Saitwada Petha had its settlement done in 1867-68 and the villages of the Ratnagiri taluka had its settlement done in 1869-70. The period of guarantee had expired for both and an inquiry of revision was undertaken and orders were sent that the existing rates were to continue until 1914-15. The 15 villages of Lanje Petha whose work was done in 1875 were to come under the Revenue Settlement.

A new proposal was placed to start with surveys. Despite the efforts put in by the British it is witnessed that the importance of the khots had not reduced a bit. On the other hand, the number of khoti villages had increased from fifty one in 1868 to sixty in 1914. However, the villages belonging to government also showed an increase from twenty six to forty seven in 1914. At the time of the proposal in 1914 the following were the land tenures that existed in the Ratnagiri Taluka.[10]

Table 4.4

Villages with different tenures(1914)
47 Government Villages.
60 Khoti.
18 Khichadi.
6 Dharekari.
11 Sharakati.
3 Part Government, Part Khoti.
1 Part Government, Part Dharekari.

This information is indicative of the strength of the khots in the Taluka. Almost a century had passed since the British acquired the South Konkan. Many reports had been prepared and submitted, and so many Acts passed but the khoti problem still persisted and hampered the collection of revenue for the British. The taluka in 1914 constituted three groups settled at three different times. Amalgamating the villages of the three groups, the following summary of the grouping and rates under the current settlement was done:[11]

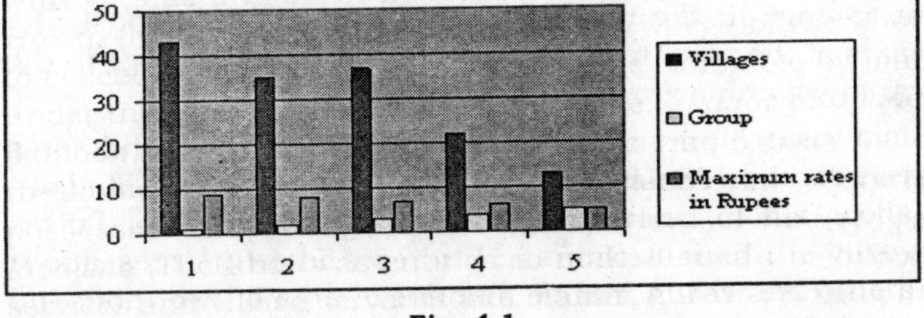

Fig. 4.1

An overall picture that was seen was that there was no change in the conditions. Much of the newly tilled land was of a poor quality. The land converted from pasture to arable was achieved at the cost of a reduction in the cattle power and manure available per unit of tilled land. The output of the land was not in proportion to the cultivated acres. On the other hand, the population increased rapidly than the output.

But the general picture that evolved was that there was an increase in the cultivated land with a provision of irrigational facilities. An increase in the cultivable land gives an impression that there must have been a notable increase and upward trend in the production of agricultural products and in the volume of trade giving Ratnagiri a steady position. It may be accepted that this was a period of expansion. Then why did this once famous port town and the taluka witness the downward trend ? It could be for several reasons- Perhaps the areas cultivated were over estimated by the government or the prices of the articles were not keeping with the rate they should have been in markets or the population was drifting away from agriculture or perhaps migrating.

Agrarian Changes

Ratnagiri taluka's best soils were found in the low lying areas at the foot of the hills, in the valleys or on the banks of the rivers. The sandy strip of land along the coast, was largely occupied with coconut plantations. The soil on the plateaus and hills consisted almost entirely of laterite, which cropped to the surface of the boulders and flat sheets of the rocks. A sizable part of the land produced crops like rice, coarse grains, pulses, fruits, chillies. There was practically no change in the methods of cultivation for the past fifty years of the new British rule. Nor was there a change in the variety of crops grown.

A sizable part of seventeen to eighteen thousand acres cropped, was consistently under rice. A large area of about eighty-nine to ninety acres was under coarse grains. Pulses occupied about a thousand acres and fruit trees about thousand acres. A sizable amount of area of two thousand seven hundred acres was occupied by oil-seeds.

The table given below shows the area in acres occupied and variety of crops grown after the rains in the Ratnagiri Taluka. The crops grown as shown in the table below it seems to reveal that little care was taken to use land to the maximum. The area under usage after the rains was just about 3000 acres which shows the percentage of land used for half the year was only.[12]

Table 4.5

Crops	Acres
Cereals-Rice	17,932
Coarse Grains	39,383
Pulses	1,628
Fruit Trees	1,230
Condiment and Spices	355
Oil-Seeds	2,771
Fibres	250
After Rains (3000 acres Used)	
Rice	1,624
Patwa Or Varna	652
Kulith	314
Chillies	133
Miscellaneous	255

Rice: Taking rice first, the commonest varieties grown were *Kudal patni, panwel, halva* or early rice and the latter *mahan.* It was sown on the commencement of the rains and transplanted after a month. Class one rice was grown in about forty villages of the taluka in 1867-68 and yielded a revenue of Rs. 21, 993. On the bagayat land, it yielded Rs. 9027 and on warkas land it was Rs. 5,240. However there were other kinds of rice divided according to quality yielding a revenue from Rs. 3000 to 7000.[13] Cleaned rice fetched a higher price as compared to the uncleaned one. There was a nominal increase in some of the principal commodities. It can be noticed in the following table that the increase in price is much higher for uncleaned rice, than in the case of cleaned rice.

Table 4.6

Years	Average rate per rupee for			
	Rice in husk		Cleaned rice	
	Seers	Chataks	Seers	Chataks
1888-1892	19	7	11	6
1893-1897	17	12	10	14
1893-1902	17	4	101	4
1903-1907	16	10	9	15
1908-1912	14	2	8	7

Nachni,Vari: The other principal products were harik, nagli and wari. Harik and nachni was kept by the cultivators for home consumption. W.Doderet, Assistant Collector experimented on two crops, one on nagli and the other on rice, both in rabed plots and with fish manure in 1886-87. However, the results of the experiment were ambiguous. W.C.Rand, Assistant Collector experimented on rice mixed with an equal quantity of *pavta* (Dolichos lablab) and the other on vari. The grain and straw were weighed when wet, and a reasonable deduction was made for drying. But whether the proportion was fixed on actual test or mere guess was not stated and therefore whether the tests were successful or not was doubtful. The experimenter said that heavy rains prevented him from weighing them when they were dry. But it was reported that the weight of 1 *seer* measure of rice was 40 ½ *tolas* and of vari 47 *tolas.*

Two tests by A.T.M. Jackson, Assistant Collector who furnished information about the experiments done on two nagli crops, one grown from the transplanted seedlings and the other from seed cast in the field. The results proved that the rabed seed bed was more advantageous in nagli cultivation than rice.

An experiment was done in June 1892 to improve the crop of nachni. It was manured with goat dropping and cowdung. Seed at the rate of 2 ½ per acre was sown. The return was 10 annas per *seer* and amounted to 524 Pounds grain and 637 straw per acre. It was found that the field was able to grow nagli followed by harik after keeping it fallow for five years. After two years cropping, it had to be again fallowed. The field had to be ploughed three times before the seed was sown.

The second test was taken on land assessed slightly higher and cultivated by a tenant. The seed bed was rabbed with cowdung, tree loppings and grass. The proportional area of seedbed of transplantation was 8¾ gunthas to an acre. Seed at the rate of 3 pounds was sown after once ploughing the seed bed. Six weeks after sowing, the seedlings were transplanted into holes made at regular intervals presumably in the ordinary way with a pointed stick. A piece of dried fish *kuta* was filled in each hole. The crop harvested produced 1,348 pounds grain and 2,092 pounds straw per acre. Experiments were also done on millets and harik on the same lines. Yield was excellent when dried fish was added.[14] Though the experiments were done to increase the yield in the lands of the taluka they were not consistent. Moreover these experiments then adopted did not cover large areas.

Sugar Cane: In 1874-75, The British experimented on sugar cane in Ratnagiri along with other parts of the Presidency. Ratnagiri had cane growing talukas but compared to other districts in Bombay Presidency, their yield was almost negligible. The information was collected about the variety of canes available. One was, the large white cane that was soft, juicy and thick. Because of its softness, it was more liable to damage by the cattle and jackals. The most common name for it was *pundia or phundia.* The word probably meant white colour, though colloquially it was used for a fat dumpy child. It was also supposed to be two varieties, one indigenous and the other imported from Mauritius. This type of a sugar in Ratnagiri was called *morisas or moris-* a corrupted name for Mauritius. It was also called as *vilayati* meaning foreign.

The second variety was the red or black cane. Although it was sweeter but the colour of the *gool* being darker, its commercial value was lowered. The red cane was called *kala, tambda, nila* and *jambhala* depending on the colour of the cane.

There were the other varieties, namely, the striped cane and the straw cane. The striped cane was known as *bangdiya* derived from the shape of a bangle. The straw cane was a harder variety. It could grow in areas with scanty supply of water. *Bhonsa* was kind of reed grown in Ratnagiri.[15]

The dung of cattle mixed with house sweepings and all refuse by-products of crops was the chief manure for cane. Salt and *hing* were used in large quantity in the Deccan but also in Ratnagiri. The British experimented by sowing the seeds of Mauritius sugar in the Ratnagiri district. The Mauritius sugar fetched a better price than the local one. Yet the efforts of the British did not give many results because the local people took little interest to grow that variety for reasons unknown. Moreover, the Deccan grew more varieties of sugarcane and covered a substantially a larger area. There were 37,774 acres in the Deccan, while the Konkan at large had 16,977 acres. The following statement shows the area under cane in the Konkan in 1887.[16]

Table 4.7

Konkan	Total area of sugar cane grown		Percentage on net cultivated area
	Average	1885-86	
Thana	1531	1541	.29
Kolaba	—	79	.002
Ratnagiri	7564	12095	1.22
Kanara	3552	3262	1.56
	12,657	16,977	.81

The agricultural population was dependent on the vagaries of nature. Five years from 1904 showed a fall in rainfall. At such time, the Collectorate had to depend on outside help for supply of foodgrain. It is seen from the following table that the rainfall from 1904 to 1909 was varied between 96 inches to 85 inches only.[17]

Table 4.8

Year	Ratnagiri taluka	
	Inches	Cents
1904-05	96	36
1905-06	56	63
1906-07	91	70
1907-08	80	74
1908-09	**85**	**44**

If the rains suddenly stopped and disappeared before October, it would badly affect the late crops of nagli which also was one of the principal crops. At such times the prices of some crops fell low while the prices of others soared abnormally high. The British Government tried to improve irrigational facility. And its claim that widespread irrigational facilities were provided did not hold true. Rice was irrigated either from the pats or wells. Patwa and kulith usually required no irrigation. But there were small areas that grew three crops a year. Such lands that grew crops rice, pawata, nachni on the same land a year needed good irrigational facilities. But there was an overall decrease in the irrigational facilities provided for the agricultural purposes from 1897 to 1915 which is seen in the table below:[18]

Table 4.9

Description	Figures for 131 Villages (1897)	Figures for 131 (15) Villages (1913)	Increase for 131 Villages
For irrigation			
Wells	1,417	1,312 (116)	-105
Tanks	8	8	
For drinking supply of Human beings			
Wells bunds	2,202	2,930 (94)	737
Tanks	57	93 (4)	36
For cattle	112	445 (16)	333
Wells, bundies Tanks	113	117 (16)	4

Work Done by Co-operative Credit Societies

The Act to establish Co-operative Credit Societies was passed in 1904 with Dr. H. H. Mann as the Director of Agriculture. R.C.Mainkar, Senior Organiser in the Ratnagiri District, was co-opted member for the whole district. Rao Saheb Parulekar was co-opted as a member of the committee during its session at Ratnagiri.[19]

The main aims of the Co-operative Committees was to ascertain the extent of indebtedness, to enquire into the economic condition of the agriculturists, to enquire into the nature, organization of the subsidiary industries of the agriculturists and to make recommendations for the rapid growth of co-operation among the people. The first few years after the establishment showed a downward trend in Ratnagiri. An investigation into the causes for its slow progress showed that among the various problems that prevailed, the following were more conspicuous.

1. The rates of interest were very low and therefore the scope for the expansion of credit societies was bleak.
2. Ratnagiri was a land of the khots and unless the khots were brought to the forefront and made to lead the co-operative societies, the chances of improvement of the societies was not possible.

As a result of the varied problems Ratnagiri district had only ten co-operative societies. Although in the initial years the existing societies were unaffected by 1917, almost all societies felt its impact and almost came to a standstill. This did not mean that no efforts were taken to improve the methods of cultivation. There were experiments done for various crops but the pace had slowed down. For example Chilies were grown in almost every village in Ratnagiri. An experiment was done in 1914 and 1915 on the fields where chillies were grown by using manure. Ratnagiri consisting of laterite soil and being close to the sea, a fairly heavy dressing of fish as well as farm yard manure was required. It was as follows:[20]

Table 4.10

	1914-15 per acre	1915-16 per acre
Fish	2000 Lbs	1000 Lbs
Farm Yard Manure	20 Cartloads	40 Cartloads
Sulphate of Potash	120 Lbs	120 Lbs

The lands on which fish and farm yard manure was used, the yield per acre was 1040 lbs and the cost of the manure was Rs. 90. The land where fish, farm yard manure and Sulphate of potash were used together the yield per acre was 1,100 lbs and the cost per acre was almost Rs. 100. This was in 1914. In the year 1915 in the first case the yield per acre was 1,400 lbs and the cost of manure was Rs. 87 and in the second case the yield was 2,040 lbs and the cost of manure was Rs. 104. This shows that in both the cases the use of potash had yielded good result and in 1915-16 output increased substantially.[21] There was a great demand for manure in order to carry out experiments in different crops. Ammonium Sulphate was also used extensively by the 1920s.[22]

Onions: Another important crop was onion. It being a commodity, essential to the everyday diet of both poor, and the rich, it found a ready market and proved a profitable crop. In the Konkan it was a rabi crop to be grown in the rice lands after the harvest of the latter. What was most important for its growth was the requirement of irrigational facility till the end of March. Onions were grown on a large scale in North Konkan.[23] An experiment was conducted to increase the output on Ratnagiri farms by using fish and farmyard manure. Fish used was 1,120 lbs and farm yard manure was 30 cartloads. The out turn per acre was 14,000 lbs. After deducting the cost of cultivation that amounted to Rs. 242.8.0 and value per yield was Rs. 313.5.4 the net profit per acre amounted to Rs. 68.13.4.[24]

The First World War followed by the Non-Co-Operation Movement brought Ratnagiri societies almost to a standstill. The political disturbances in the country at large had their impact on the smaller towns as well. During the First World War many agriculturists joined the British army to earn more money. Followed by this was Non-Co-Operation Movement. An important thing to note that, during this time most of the population was in no mood to go ahead with new or innovative measures.

In 1923 a Committee was formed by the government with he help of the local people to ascertain the extent of indebtedness, the availability of funds, the availability of obtaining manures, seeds and to learn more about the small industries. The Committee consisted of Prof. R.M.Joshi, Sydnam College, Bombay, Rao Bahadur D.A.Vichare, M.L.C., S.K.Bole, L.M.C. The Committee visited the entire district and was at Ratnagiri town in mid April. In its report, it stated that every acre of rice land in Ratnagiri required four to five acres of Warkas land to go with it so that it could supply raw materials, fodder. The size of the actual holding was small and because there was no Warkas land to work on to grow inferior grains, the income of the family would not suffice for the entire year. This compelled the stronger members of the family to migrate to earn their own living.[25] The list of persons who gave oral or written evidences based on which the reports was written were :

Table 4.11

List of Persons
The Mamlatdar
Rao Saheb L.V.Parulekar, M.L.C.
A.S. Phadke, Pleader, Landlord And Merchant
B.K.Sohoni, Pensioner, Someshwar
S.V.Tikekar, Khot, Tike
V.G.Gokhale, Deputy Director Of Agriculture
H.A.Salvi, Pensioner, Phansop
D.K.Kamat , Malgund
N.B.Rajwade, Honorary Organizer
S.N.Surve, Machva Builder

But the attempts of the British Government to amend land rules for the benefit of the farmers had not given satisfactory results. The Efforts to curb the powers of the khot also had not proved successful. The actual cultivators yet were not the owners of the land holdings. Many of the holdings were leased to the cultivators for a period of one year even at the beginning of the twentieth century. The terms in the early twentieth century amounted to half the share of the produce to be paid to the land lord. After a century of British rule in Ratnagiri, rents were still fixed in kind. If one good thing happened in favor of the farmers it was fixing of the rents under the Khoti Act passed in 1880. The Report of the Registrar of the Co-operatives, Bombay Presidency for the year 1928-29 was a hopeful document giving details about the progress of the societies all over.[26] The freedom struggle had an impact on the economic front. Not only the middle class but the common farmer became a part of the Indian National movement.

Mangoes: Ratnagiri was and is well known for its excellent mangoes. The red laterite soil containing a sufficient quantity of lime was found suitable for the development of mango grafts. Alphonso was the best variety of fruit grown in the taluka. The seedlings were raised in small earthern pots and when they were a year or two old were grafted. In three or six months the grafts were ready for planting. On an acre of land about 40 grafts could be planted. Normally the life of a tree was hundred years and it bore fruits during this period.[27]

Canning Appartus : Method of putting in or taking out Mango Pulp of the Cans when the Appartus is hot

Source: W.Burns, *'The Book of the Mango'*, Department of Agriculture, Bombay, Bulletin No. 103 of 1920.

Government Central Press, 1921

Canning was experimented in Ratnagiri as early as 1913. Experiments were carried out in canning of mango fruits in places like Ganesh khind Botanical gardens in Poona. An imported apparatus from U.S.A. contributed to the better canning methods. The apparatus used was a steam pressure canning apparatus (hotel outfit No 1), made by the Northwestern Ironworks, Eau Claire, Wisconsin, United States of America. The net price paid for the apparatus was 50 Dollars (Rs. 156.4.0). This particular type of apparatus was chosen because the steam pressure in it was a much more effective sterilizer than simply boiling water.[28]

There were other uses of mango which gave rise to various industries. When not ripened and green, the fruit was cut into halves or slices and made into pickles with salt, sweet oil, chillies, and other ingredients, or made into preserves known as *'moramba'* by being boiled and cooked in sugar syrup, or dried and made into native *'amboshi'* to be used in certain curries, for making *'chutney'*, or to make a thin cake known as *'Amba -poli'* by squeezing the juice of the mango and spreading it on plates and drying it. All these gave rise to subsidiary industries in the taluka.[29] There were varieties of mangoes namely *Mothi payari, Payari, Khoont, Popoatya, Cowasji-Patel, Batli, Borsha, Alphonso, Mulgoba.*[30] The co-operatives in mango production in Ratnagiri took great interest. *Alphonso* and *Payari* and almost the whole crop of mangoes were annually sent to Bombay. Ratnagiri, Vengurla, Malvan, Devgad, Jaitpur and Jaigad were the most important ports from where mangoes were shipped to Bombay.

N.D.S. Suryavanshi suggested that Co-operatives through the Co-operative federation ought to negotiate with Steam-Shipping Companies. This would result in the reduction in freight charges. He further said that all the taluka towns in the Ratnagiri district had urban co-operative banks, which were linked, to the Bombay Provincial Co-operative Banks in Bombay. Arrangements of remitting money for loan purposes could be made through the urban banks and the Bombay provincial banks. Discounts also could be given to trade bills relating to mango sale. He requested the people who grew mangoes to unite for the purpose.[31]

Fodder : The growing of crops for the sake of fodder value was in itself a novel idea in India. As it was not given importance. There was a demand for fodder in larger cities. This led to the extensive growth of such crops as Lucerne. If an animal was expected to do work or produce more milk, it had to have good food.[32] Lucrene growing as a mixed crop was experimented in South Konkan in the 1920s because konkan cattle was poor. Fodder was insufficient in many parts. Particularly in South Konkan it was suggested that there was a considerable need for cultivation of Lucerne. Experiments made at Ratnagiri revealed that the crop grew luxuriantly and well wherever irrigational facilities were available.[33] Moreover attempts were continuously made from 1915 to 1919 to establish a permanent pasture of Andropogon Caricosus Var - mollicomus on high porous land (warkas land) in the tracts where rainfall was heavy. As a result of this, the grass grew fairly well the first two years but after that showed no signs of progress.[34] It may be noted that the experiments done were not adequate.

Fish: Next to agriculture and gardening the most important economic activity was fishing. The fishermen were Kolis, Marathas, Muslims, Christians, Govits. They could carry on their business very well during the fair season but during the monsoon they were handicapped owing to the roughness of the sea, creeks and rivers and on the Arabian coasts and they were helpless. They normally constructed or hired a boat worth about Rs. 1000, manufactured common nets called *'rapin'* worth about Rs. 500. Nearly 20 to 25 persons went on fishing everyday.

The most valuable products that the fishermen got out of some fish were pok (shark fins) and the *pok* that is fish '*maws*'. The pok trade was mostly in the hands of the khoja Mohammedans and these traders had their agents all over the Malabar and the Konkan coasts. The pok sailed first to Bombay, from where they were sent to Japan and China. One Christian trader told the writer that he disposed of the pok-pok from 80 to 90 Rs. in Bombay. These fishermen generally had no agricultural lands.[35]

Salt: Besides the agricultural commodities, the product, which was in demand in the Ratnagiri taluka, was salt. The Ratnagiri taluka had a balance of about 18,629 Indian maunds salt in store in 1863.[36] An increase in the manufacture of salt was seen in the Ratnagiri taluka in 1869-70 as compared to the earlier year. In 1868-69 the stock was 23,407 Indian maunds while it increased to 25,410

Indian maunds in 1869-70 showing an increase of about 2,002 Indian Maunds.[37] The next few years witness fluctuations in prices. State-aid efforts until the beginning of the twentieth century attempted to the improvement of salt trade. But adverse prices and rates of interest in the inter-war years led to the reduced output and investment and ultimately to the decline of salt produce in the nineteen twenties and thirties. Moreover in comparison with the Shiroda works in Vengurla the salt production was negligible.

Water improvement: Government sanctioned a grant of Rs 800 for experiments for the improvement of water supply (vide Government Resolution Revenue department no 2780 dated 17 March 1909). The necessary tools were received but later no prominent results were found.[38]

The British Government consulted the provincial Rural Development Board regarding the development of Co-operative farming to give considerable scope for experiments which would prove beneficial to agriculture. To achieve this goal, meetings were conducted with the co-operators, cultivators, landlord's officials and non- officials in Southern Divisions like Belgaum, Dharwar and Ratnagiri.

Besides the efforts for the development of farming in the district, ex-servicemen who were found in large numbers in Ratnagiri taluka and who had served the British in First World War also were given lands. Before they enlisted in the armed forces, they were either agriculturists or agricultural labourers. The government waste lands and forest lands were given for cultivation to the co-operative societies whose membership included both ex-servicemen and agriculturists. The Services Post War Reconstruction Fund Committee had an amount of Rs. 48 lakhs plus the interest in 25 to 30 years that was used for this purpose.[39]

There were nearly 9000 military pensioners in Ratnagiri district. Most of them lived in debt. These men were given lands to work on.[40] Liberal grants out of the service of the Services Post War Reconstruction Fund were made available to them. This was done to develop uncultivated lands, purchase agricultural equipments, manure and seeds.[41] Thus Ex-servicemen were encouraged to join freely with their fellow villagers in all social and economic enterprises.

Bamboos, betel nuts, charcoal, chunah, coconut, firewood, ghee, bajri, dal, castor, til, timber, tobacco and such other articles were sold in the markets of Ratnagiri town. The price of 100 bamboos was Rs. 10. Ghee was sold for Rs. 44 per maund, while castor cost Rs. 44 per maund. Timber was measured in cubic foot. The price of other commodities like barley, grain, jowari, moong, dal, nachni were measured in maunds and their prices were between Rs. 2 to 6 in the year 1873. The weights entered were of the Indian Standard and the linear measurements were the English weight 180 grains.[42] The Superintendent was requested to publish it in the Government Central Press.

Weights In Indian Std	Measures
Troy = 1 Tola.	12 inches= 1 foot
1 Chatak=5 Tolas.	3 feet= 1 yard.
80 Tolas=1 Seer.	
40 Seers = 1 Maund.	.

The following table shows the prevalent prices in rupees Ratnagiri Taluka from 1888-66 and from 1912.[43]

Table 4.12

Year	Rice		Nagli		Vari	
	S.	Ca.	S.	Ch.	S.	Ch.
1888-89	11	12	16	13	13	3
1889-90	12	9	19	6	18	12
1890-91	11	3	18	13	19	14
1891-92	10	14	18	11	19	15
1892-93	10	9	16	0	17	12
1893-94	10	6	14	0	16	1
1894-95	11	10	14	12	14	10
1895	11	14	16	11	16	7
1896	11	10	16	9	16	15
1897	8	14	10	3	9	13
1898	10	14	13	5	13	2
1899	10	14	13	9	13	1
1900	9	15	10	9	10	11
1901	11	1	11	14	12	4
1902	11	8	..	..	14	0
1903	10	6	14	8	14	8
1904	10	15	15	7	14	8
1905	10	11	14	6	14	2
1906	8	15	11	8	10	13
1907	8	11	11	6	10	12
1908	8	0	11	9	10	5
1909	9	8	12	9	11	15
1910	8	10	13	5	11	14
1911	8	1	13	3	11	11
1912	7	14	10	13	9	8

Decline in Agricultural Output

Scarcely any improvements were made in the grain crops despite the pains taken by the government and the people. The increased yields in any crop seemed to have been achieved through new practices evolved by the cultivators themselves. Notwithstanding the acclimatization of and propagation of foreign early maturing varieties and improved methods the crops were susceptible to fungus diseases. For example, the rice crop of Ratnagiri suffered from *karpa* disease and *kanne* pest. (Black smut) and also from a severe attack of Leptispa beetles in some areas. Swarming caterpillars damaged the crop in many places.[44] Onion was vulnerable to an attack from an insect pest called thrips locally known as *veet.* A fungus disease also made its appearance sometimes in the early years of twentieth century.[45]

One of the most easily propagated schemes for a population that is illiterate, impoverished and has smallholdings is the introduction of improved seeds at low cost. As against it the propagation of a difficult scheme of land and crop management practice, especially when it includes large cash interactions in most cases proved to be a failure. The Agricultural Department adopted the more complex method of package, which was not understood by the illiterate population.

Nor was the record much better with regard to the prices. There was lot of fluctuation in prices of principal crops. The price of jowar was cheaper by nearly one tenth of a *seer* per rupee, while wheat was dearer by nearly one half *seer* to one-fifth *seer* per rupee. The price of rice and gool remained stationary.[46] There was cynical change in the price of commodities.

The cultivators required advances for the purchase of seeds. Wages did not rise along with the prices. In 1904-05, in the particular case of rice, the rise may have been due to the political distress in Bengal, which drew off much of the Burma rice usually available for export to those parts. But the general rise of prices was harder to explain, being caused by the operation of vast economic forces, which were beyond the hands of the government. This serious increase in the cost of living pressed hard upon the masses, gave rise to great discontent and called for investigation and remedy at the hands of the government.[47] But the general trend of prices was that they were fluctuating from 1870 onwards almost up to 1920 were of little or no significance.[48]

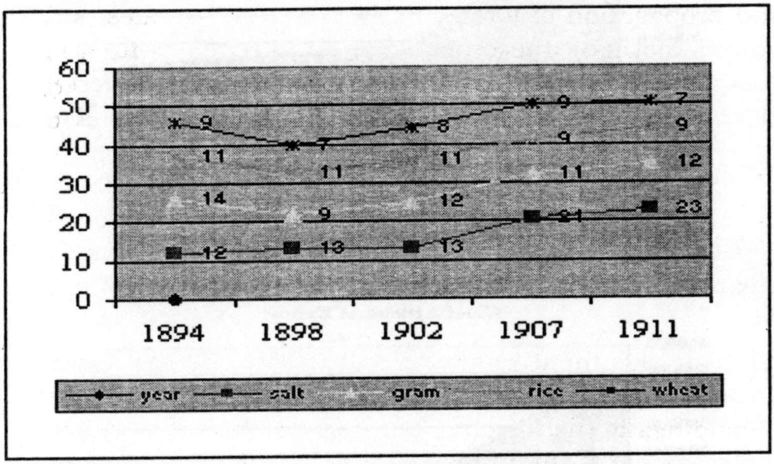

Fig. 4.2

Transport, Manufacture and Trade

There was daily bazaar held in Ratnagiri town for the sale of grains. Perishable articles such as fish, vegetables also were sold along with the grains. A weekly bazaar was held at Hachiri, which was about 12 miles from Ratnagiri by creek. Almost about seventy-five boats came to this bazaar with salt fish worth Rs. 500. These boats returned with wood and grain especially rice and coarse rice to the value of about Rs. 800.[49]

Ratnagiri was also famous for furniture at its school of Industry. Although the products were sold, commercially it was by no means in a flourishing condition. The articles were priced too high, to obtain a large sale among the local public. In 1896, two new soda bottle factories were also established, one managed by a Brahmin and the other by a bania. They were however, conducted on a small scale but were in a prosperous condition.

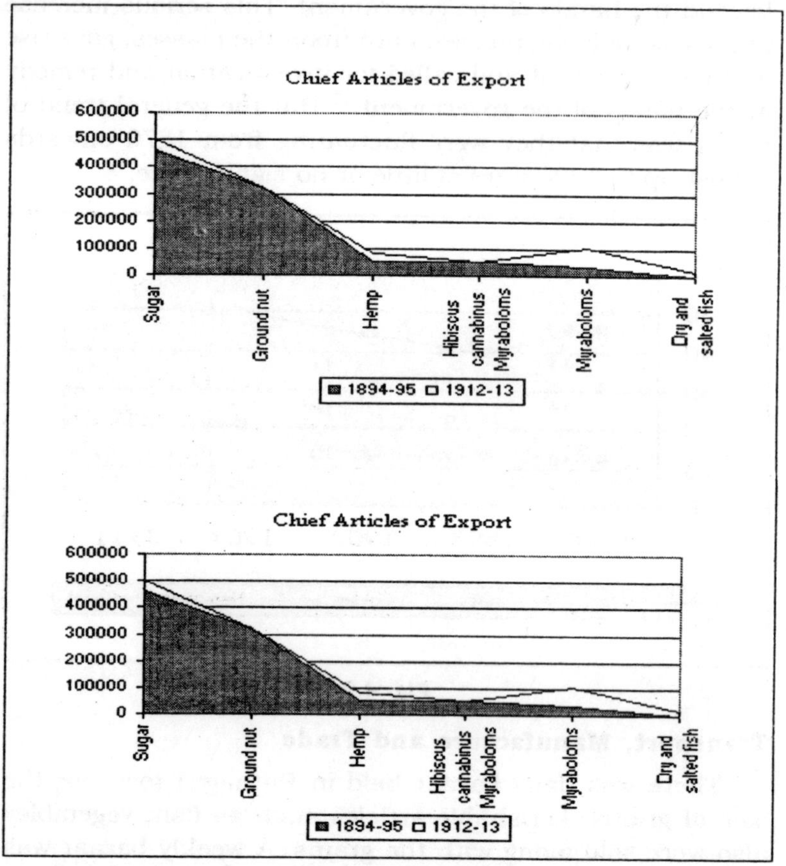

Fig. 4.3

An observation of the general trend shows that in spite of growing articles of daily need, Ratnagiri chiefly imported foodstuffs. During the period from 1894 to 1912-13 the amount of imports exceeded the exports. It will be seen from the following figure that husked rice worth Rs. 1,87,610 was imported into Ratnagiri in 1912-13 and the demand remained almost the same even after a decade. The imports of other articles like kerosene oil, coconut, sugar, salt decreased in demand from 1894-95 to 1912-13. The export of sugar was Rs. 4,60,873 in 1894-95 and it increased to 5,00,000 in 1912-13. The demand for groundnut almost remained the same during the same period. The exports of other articles like hemp, myabolans, dried and salted fish also decreased. The value of the mango exported during 1913-14 was Rs. 1,29,542.[50] The considerable decrease in exports since 1894-95 was probably due to the diversion of commodities earlier sent by road were sent by rail. More over figures shown to be passing through the four ports of the taluka may not have represented the trade of that taluka alone because the ports also served the different neighboring talukas of Chiplun, Sangameshwar and Rajapur.

At the same time, experiments done in the agricultural field were not giving expected results. The yields of Ratnagiri taluka had almost stagnated. If there were any industries, they were running on small scale. A good deal of over-ghat traffic, which formerly used to pass through the port of Jaygad, was diverted by the Southern Maratha Railway. This diversion affected the traders and middlemen rather than agriculturists. The trade that went on seemed to mostly the imports, which the local people needed for their daily consumption.

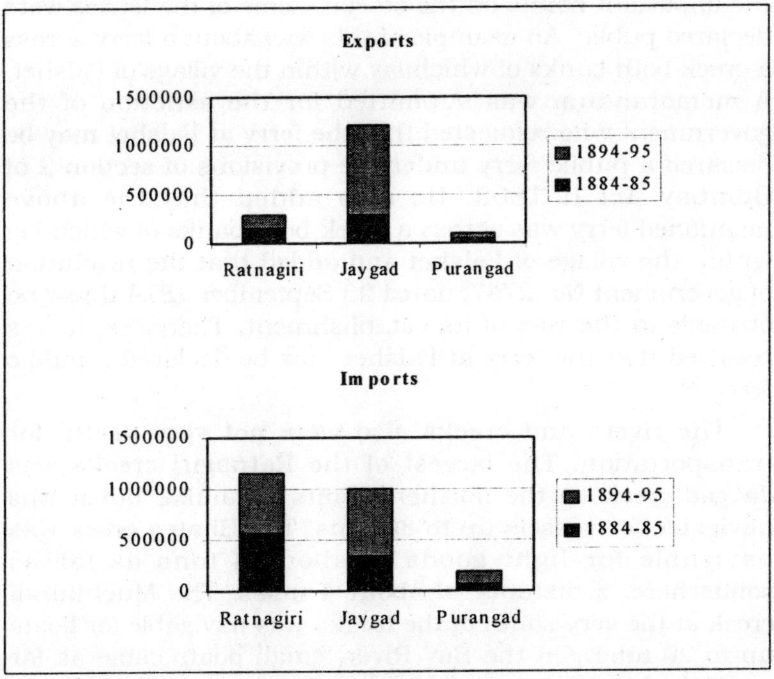

Fig.4.4

The chief imports and exports of Ratnagiri from the ports of Ratnagiri, Jaygad, and Purangad for the years 1884-85 and 1894-95 show that the imports were on the increase and the exports were on the decrease. The Indian Ports Act was passed so as to extend the provisions of the ports. Duties were levied and the port due was fixed at 2 annas a ton.[51]

Transportation: Ratnagiri taluka's trade was chiefly carried on by three modes of transport road, creek and sea. The most important road was the Ratnagiri-Kolhapur road. The others were the Bhatye-Purangad road, Ratnagiri-Jaygad road via Shirgaon, Ratnagiri-Meria road, Ratnagiri-Lanje road via Hacheri, Ratnagiri Mirjole road. Roads were connected through the ghats and the goods were carried to Deccan. Most trade to Bombay or to the ports was carried on through the waterways.[52]

The three principal creeks were the Jaygad creek, the Bhatye creek and the Muchkundi creek. The ferries joined the important points on the creeks. Some of the ferries were declared public. An example of this was about a ferry across a creek both banks of which lay within the village of Palshet. A memorandum was submitted for the sanction of the government who requested that the ferry at Palshet may be declared a public ferry under the provisions of section 2 of Bombay Act II 1868. He also added that the above mentioned ferry was across a creek both banks of which lay within the village of Palshet and added that the resolution of government No. 2747, dated 23 September 1874 threw no obstacle in the way of its establishment. Therefore, it was resolved that the ferry at Palshet may be declared a public ferry.[53]

The rivers and creeks also were not very useful for transportation. The largest of the Ratnagiri creeks was Jaygad creek on the northern limits of taluka, but it was navigable for vessels up to 80 tons. The Bhatya creek was navigable for light goods of about 8 tons as far as somewhere, a distance of about 4 miles. The Muchkundi creek at the very south of the taluka was navigable for boats up to 20 tons. On the Bav River, small boats came as far as Ukshi from the north but these creeks were all gradually silting up. For example, in case Bhatya creek, bigger boats could now go to Hachiri only at high tide and even then, they had to stop at a distance of a mile from the village.

The taluka had a sea board of 35 miles. It had four principal ports, *Jaygad, Warawde, Purangad* and *Ratnagiri*. Besides the usual *patimars* that were plying up and down the coast smaller steamers travelled both between the north and the south. The Shephard Company's large steamers carried both cargo and passengers. These ports were declared to be in the list of British Indian ports.[54] The list of British Indian Ports declared in 1882 is given in the index.

The taluka was served with steamers of the Bombay Steam Navigation Company and the Indian Co-operative Navigation and Trading Company. The former had a daily service from October to May, touching Jaygad, Warawade, and Ratnagiri. Except in rainy season, each of the two companies ran two boats four times weekly between Bombay and Goa, touching Ratnagiri and the other ports. The cargo boats of the Bombay Steam Navigation Company put into the ports of Jaygad and Ratnagiri twice weekly during the rainy season.[55] In 1863 that a steamer of Burmah India Steam Navigation Company entered the Meria Donghur Bay, a few miles north of Ratnagiri and found a good anchorage there in the rains in the middle of the night. The British wished to know how safe was the bay for the anchorage of larger ships. A letter was given by J.W.Young, Superintendent of Marine with the sketch of the coast and its neighborhood of the taluka. A resolution was passed to get information on the following points.

1. Whether the advantages offered by the Meria Donghur Bay as a harbour of refuge, called for artificial improvements of that harbour.
2. Whether a lighthouse had to be placed at Ratnagiri.[56]

D.J. Kennelly, Assistant Dock Master, inspected the Meria Donghur bay by entering the bay, anchoring the Goolanar in 3 fathoms, close to the southern shore. He reported that the bay did not possess the natural capabilities, which were necessary for an unaided ship to take refuge. He gave several reasons for it and one important among them was that at about half a mile from

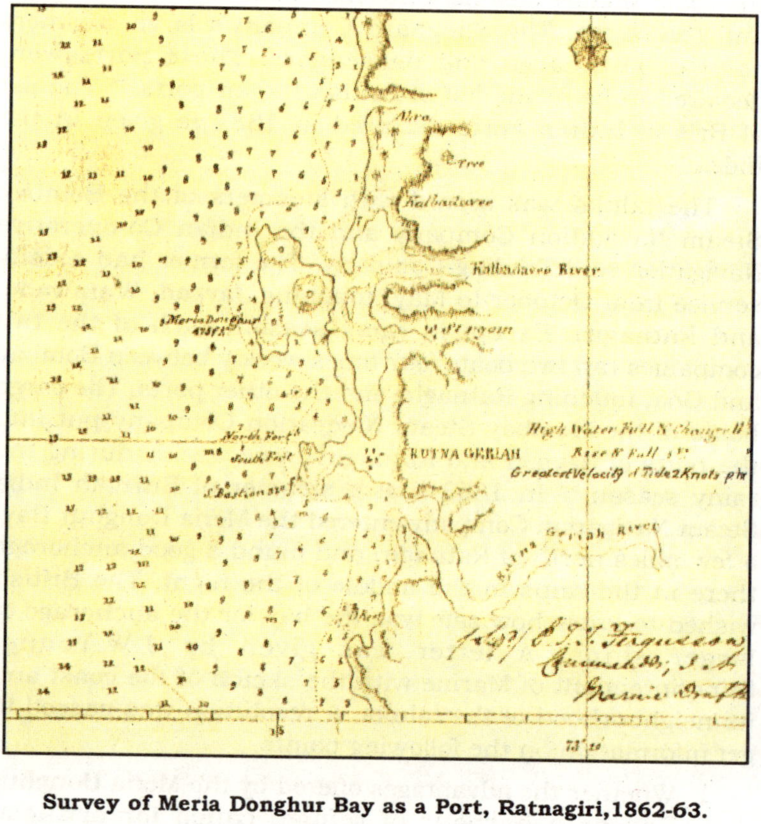

Survey of Meria Donghur Bay as a Port, Ratnagiri, 1862-63.

Source: Revenue Department Volume No. 121/1862 & 64.

the extreme north west of the bay and a depth of 18 feet was found and the depth increased to 30 feet with a bottom composed of sand. He opined that the anchorage in bay would be a dangerous one except in good weather. He further mentioned that for general purposes of trade it would be practicable for coasting steamers of a moderate draught from 10-12 feet so that they would had to anchor far from the shore to find a secure position. Also Lieut. Taylor's survey showed that Meria Donghur bay leading to the Kalbadevi River was quite useless as harbour or refuge, or even a port to touch at, during the S.W.Monsoon.

However, as to the construction of a light House, the Southern bastion of the fort of Ratnagiri was selected because it had a solid foundation faced with a cut stone (Latrterite) and could be erected with minimum cost.[57]

A downward trend was seen in this industry after 1910. The forests of the region were already devastated and few efforts were taken to grow more trees. The quantity of wood available was carried to Bombay. This again worsened the conditions of ship building industry in Ratnagiri. However, more importance was given to the building of small vessels, which normally weighed from 10 to 25 tons.[58]

Declining Trend of Ship Building Industry at Ratnagiri Port

Table 4.13

Year	Vessels	10-100 Tons	Vessels	100-300 Tons
1909-10 1913-14	-	--	-	--
1914-15 1918-19	1	10	3	347
1919-20 1923-24	6	113	2	217
1924-25 1928-29	4	98	-	--
1929-30 1933-34	4	98	-	--

In 1909 there was only one vessel constructed weighing 10 tons, while there were three vessels built weighing 347 tons. By the year 1925, there were 4 vessels built of 98 tons while there were no vessels built between 100-300 tons showing decline in shipbuilding.[59]

Cost of Thane-Ratnagiri type 65-ton sailing vessel (decked)

Table 4.14

Materials used for Ship Building 1890-1935	1890 to 1935
Timber	3,750
Nails	800
Ropes	700
Sail Cloth	550
Pulleys	150
Anchors	600
Chains	250
Wet Paints	30
Lime	15
Varnish	15
Fat	30
Ground Nut Oil	30
Fish Oil or Varnish	15
Cotton	50
Compass	30
Lights	50
Cooking Utensils	30
Lead Line	20
Labour Charges	2000
Supervision	500

By the year 1920, the cost had more than doubled. The cost of a 50-ton vessel was approximately Rs. 18,000 in 1924 and it almost doubled and was between 30,000 and 35,000.[60] As a result the employer had a very thin margin for profit between the cost of construction and the rise in prices.

Secondly, due to a decline in the cargo shipping business the demand for sailing vessels also decreased.[61] The various types of cargo vessels were *shibadis, kothis, balaos, galbats, mhangiris, phatemaris, and machavas.* These vessels were busy mainly during the month of January.[62] They carried mangoes, mango products, jackfruits and other grains in January to Bombay. They brought back salt, foodgrain, and piece goods from Bombay, coconut, timber from Cochin and Calicut, tiles from Mangalore, timber, grains from Thane district.[63]

Despite the statistics available, it is difficult to give an exact picture of the volume of trade that was carried from the port of Ratnagiri. In January 1909-10 the extent of trade at the port of Ratnagiri showed an inflow of Rs. 24-34 lakhs. It was Rs. 38.62 annas in 1918-19. In the year 1947-48, the amount received by the Ratnagiri port was Rs. 92-2 annas 7 paise. However it is not possible to gauge accurately the extent of rise in prices.[64]

The other means of transportation other than the ports were the roads. Although attempts were made by the Government from time to time to improve transport facilities, they were definitely hindered by the topography of the region. Ratnagiri was a difficult country to travel, for in addition to the small rivers and creeks there were a number of isolated peaks and detatched range of hills and most of the area was isolated.[65]

The Amba ghat road was completed by the joint expenses of the British Government and the Ratnagiri local funds in 1877-78. Another road from the Ratnagiri town to the new port in Kalbadevi Bay (sometimes called as Meria) was also taken and completed at the same time.[66] Fifteen village maps of the Ratnagiri taluka, which were copied by lithography so as to help in the construction of roads were drawn.[67]

In Ratnagiri, there were tracks, which were scarcely considered as roads that resulted in the interior villages not having any contact with neighbouring towns and cities. The available roads were not really attended to. This is evident from a report in the newspaper, in which a complaint was made that a wooden bridge on the nullah of the public road leading from Ratnagiri and Kolhapur frequently needed repairs. Since a portion of the bridge had decayed, it ran the risk of meeting with serious accidents.[68] Moreover as the railways developed the trade which came down the Amba Ghat to Ratnagiri started decreasing and therefore the export of merchandise started decreasing. An overall decline in the volume of trade took place by the early twentieth century but the decline was rapid by mid twentieth century as shown in the following table :[69]

Table 4.15

Year	1909-10	1910-11	1920-21	1930-31	1940-41	1945-46	1947-48
	Rs.	Rs.	Rs.	Rs	Rs.	Rs.	Rs.
Inward	16,75,637	18,99,768	38,71,566	28,35,783	...	...	...
Outward	4,26,033	18,99,768	3,28,319	2,96,125	...	...	...

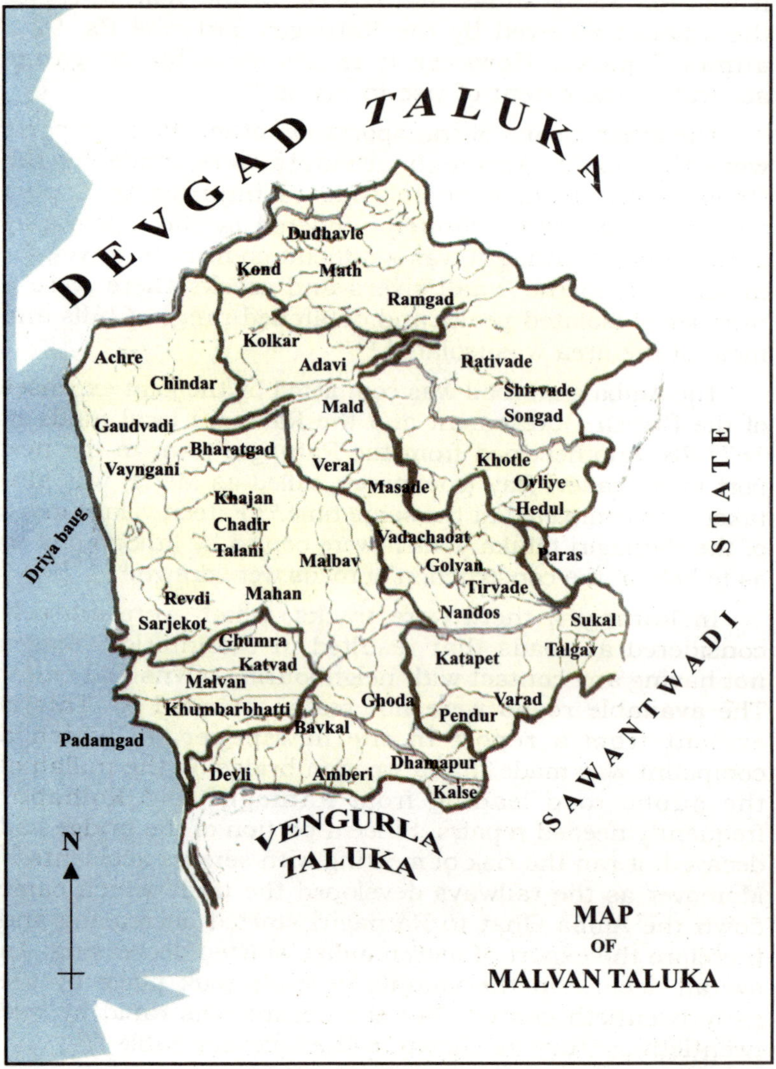

Source : MSA, Revenue Department, Vol. No. 240/1893.

Malvan Taluka of the Ratnagiri Collectorate

Malvan taluka was bounded by the Devgad taluka in the north and Karli River in the south, to the west was the Arabian Sea and to the east was the Sawantwadi State. The Karli River in the south separated it from Vengurla petha and the Sawantwadi state. The taluka was square in shape. The average length of the taluka was about 18 miles from north to south and the breadth was about 16 miles from east to west.

The general appearance of the taluka was a narrow strip of low- lying sandy land from1-2 miles broad extending along nearly the whole coastline of the taluka and protected from the sea by a line of sand hills or sand dunes. On the eastern edge of this strip of land, the hills rose abruptly to the height of about 200 feet and from their western crests an undulating plateau extended inland for about 4-5 miles. The plateau gradually sloped upwards towards the east until it reached the elevation of about 400 feet above the sea level. The surface was capped with laterite rock cut through the numerous deep and narrow ravines and had a black and barren appearance.[70] This historic port town had a well-fortified harbour with forts like Sindhudurg, Sarjekot, Rajkot and Padamgad. The northern and the eastern portion of the taluka were fairly well wooded. The three principal rivers of the taluka were the Achra, the Karli and the Kalavali and the best soils were found in the low-lying lands on the banks of these rivers. In about 1870, the taluka was divided into five turufs and had 69 villages.[71]

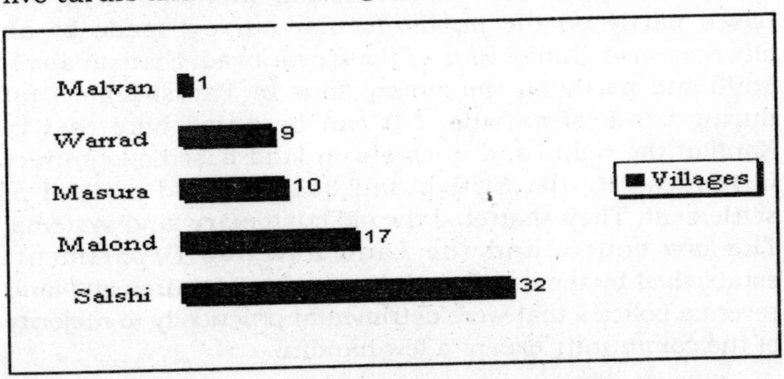

Fig. 4.5

The British Government started assessing the lands in mid nineties. In the Southern Konkan in general and Malvan in particular, survey was delayed almost up to 1880 due to the administrative problems faced by the British.

The Kolhapur Raja ceded the villages of Salshi tarf and half share in the villages of the Masur tarf together with the town and fort of Malvan to the East India Company in the year 1812-13. The Warrad tarf with its 8 villages were ceded to the Company in 1815. However, the Pat and Haveli tarf of the Wadi State were given to the Company for collection of revenue and in return the Company handed over the villages of Malond taraf. The other 9 villages of the Malond tarf belonged to the Peshwas who had a two third share in the revenue and the Raja of Kolhapur whose share was one third. All these villages finally came under the control of the Company in the year 1817-18. Half of the Masur tarf was the property of Dinkar Rao Gaikwad. There were constant rivalries between the Gaikwad and the Sawantwadi rulers and at last the revenue of the territories was attached to the East India Company in the year 1845. These villages were declared Khalsa finally in 1858-59 when the British Crown took over. During the mutiny of 1857, one of the insurgent leaders attempted to raise the people of Malvan against the British Government. In such disturbed circumstances, assessments had to be undertaken at slow pace and with care.[72]

The first assessment that began in 1860s of the Malvan Taluka was completed in 1880s, and the Settlement was based partly on the *pahani* (ocular survey) made by an officer named Gunaji Ram of the Sawantwadi State in about 1690 and partly on the survey done by Parashuram Pant during the Peshwa rule.[73] It can be noted here that in Konkan the rights and interests on land based on contract introduced by the British and based on old method of settlement. They shattered the old customary land systems. The law courts and the Land Revenue Department, established by them enforced the new land tenures and land revenue policies that were detrimental practically to majority of the community except a few handful.

A measuring establishment was kept in 1869 at Ratnagiri to complete the survey of the Malvan Taluka. The officers C. Hexton, E. Hearn and J.Young who were employed for the job worked throughout the season in 1869, examined the disputes and measured a total area of 1,23,751 arable lands. The unarable land was approximately 4,874. The total area of the taluka as reported by the officers was about 1,23,752 acres. It was as follows:[74]

Table 4.16

Names of the officer	Arable	Unarable	Total
C.Hexton	51,616	1	51,617
E.Hearn	64,884	1,713	64,884
J.Young	7,251	4,92,211	7,251
Total	1,23,751	4,93,925	1,23,752

The Settlement report done in 1880 showed the area of the taluka to be 238 Square miles. The total cultivable area belonging to the government was 1,00,224 acres and uncultivable area was 44,259 acres. The total area of the taluka as reported in 1880 showed an increase from 1,28,625 to 1,52,243 acres in a decade. According to the report, the land was classified as follows:[75]

Table 4.17

	Government		Alienated		Total	
	No of Fields	Area	No of Fields	Area	No of Fields	Area
Cultivable						
Rice	38,046	18,837	21,156	1,145	40,202	19,982
Garden	7,457	3,173	356	78	7,183	3,251
Rabi	150	78	-	-	150	78
Warkas	55,235	78,136	2,928	6,197	58,163	84,333
Total	1,00,888	1,00,224	5,440	7,420	1,06,328	1,07,644
Uncultivable						
Land Divided Into Survey	-	38,842	-	167	-	39,009
No Village Sites Roads, Rivers,	-	211	-	11	-	222
Tanks	-	5,206	-	162	-	5,368
Total	-	44,259	-	340	-	44,599
Grand Total	1,00,888	1,44,483	5,440	7,760	1,06,328	1,52,243

There were three full *Inam* villages in the taluka, two *sharkati* villages in which the land revenue was shared by government and the *Inamdar.* Eleven villages in the taluka held the khoti tenure. There were the *Sheri* lands also. The *Inamdars* were not hereditary officials, but they probably held larger part of the tax-exempt lands. Even though their position in practice was unchallenged, the *Inam* land could be directly taxed. Another practice although not too common was that the cultivators of the *Inam* had to till heavily assessed government land. These practices, however, became less frequent by 1850s and the government made sure according to the settlements that the *Inamdars* surrendered a part of their claims and kept the remaining with them. The government also decided that the leases of the Sheri lands or the Crown lands were to be renewed for a period of 30 years from 21 July 1879.

Large increases were seen in the revenue in occupied area in 1884-85 and 1885-86. In 1884-85 the land occupied and paying assessment to government was Rs. 83,878 while in 1885-86 it was Rs.83,514. The arable area still available was 3,978 acres.[76] This was probably because of the inclusion of the kauli and the sheri lands. As no change was to be made on the rent levied on these lands assessments according to the survey rates was not done on them. Subsequently they were calculated in 1893 and included in the totals of the occupied lands. In 1893-94, the revenue was decreased to 70,843 and in 1894-95 to 70,819.[77] These decreases were due to certain forest areas being appropriated and treated as unoccupied waste. Thus the increase and decrease in the amount of revenue from occupied government assessable land changed from time to time depending upon the type of land, remissions and suspensions resulting from natural calamities. For example revenue amounting to Rs. 11,000 on lands, which suffered from locust visitation.[78] Under British rule there was a conspicuous disappearance of the hereditary offices as a secure and transferable form of property. Lands, gifts, public offices, tax liabilities were no longer for sale.[79] Some of them were acquired individually. All lands directly or indirectly became a source of earning revenue for the British Government.

On the other hand there was an imbalance between the lands available for cultivation, the revenue to be paid to the government and the population that was increasing rapidly. There was always arable land available. For example the population of Malvan, according to the census of 1872 was 88,185.[80] There were 35,074 who were engaged in only agriculture, about 7,547 partly engaged in agriculture while there were about 45,564 who were non agricultural. The total area was 238 square miles and the area that was actually useful for agriculture was 163.10 square miles.[81] In comparison with that the population per square mile was about 373.67. The grain produced was not sufficient for the dense population.

Having taken all the reports and assessments of record, a revised Survey Settlement was introduced under the Provisions of Bombay Act of 1879 into the villages belonging to the taluka. The assessments were imposed under the said Settlement fixed for a period of 30 years commencing with the revenue year 1883-84 and ending with the revenue year 1912-13.

Table 4.18

Villages of Malvan

Malvan	**Dhamapur**	**Trimbak**	**Hendal**
Masura	Malgaon	Bandiwde Khurd	Chunowre
Kandalgaon	Salel	Kumame	Poip
Kalse	Juwa Dhanji	Nandos	Hiwali
Hadi	Verul	Pendur	Shrawan
Rewdi	Waingowde	Adowli	Beli Budruk
Dewli	Parade	Warad	Asgani
Amberi	Tirowde	Talgaon	Rahatiwad
Achra	Musde	Golwan	Kirlos
Chinder	Dangmode	Malad	Mut Budruk
Peit Bhagwantgad	Wadachapat	Budhawli	Gotne
Juwa Anjanacha	Koil	Kudopi	Shirowde
Wadi Tondowli	Juwa Koil	Pulsambe	Asrondi
Waingani	Maldi	Khotal	
Ambdos	Bandiwde Budruk	Waliye	

Agriculture and prices- cynical trends: The soil of the Taluka was varied. The best soil was found in the low lying lands of the Karli, Kalowli and Achre rivers. The upland soil was not deep and had gravel in large quantities. In the villages to the east of Dhamapur, the soil was yellowish white in colour and contained large quantity of sand and quartz. The warkas soil was poor and was a mixture of about 3/4 of gravel and 1/4 of soil. It was derived from sand-stones. It was of a light colour and was mixed with pieces of sand, pieces of quartz and gravel. On this soil even grass was difficult to grow. The coast was composed of white sand and a mixture of vegetable matter. The hills of the taluka composed of sand stone or quartzite and this was the main reason why the soil of the land had an abundance of these two mixtures.[82]

The following was the figure, which shows that crops grown in the Taluka in 1867 along with the percentage of growth.[83]

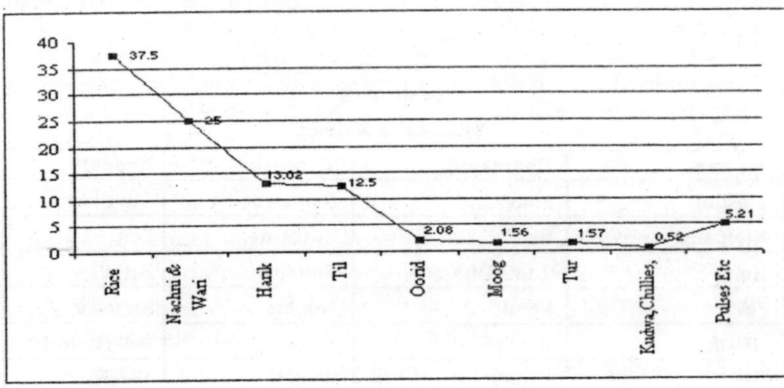

Fig. 4.6

Rice: From the above graph it can be observed that the most important grain crop in the taluka was rice. The percentage of rice grown in the taluka was 37.50% of the total production of grain. A large number of different varieties were grown which may be grouped under two classes namely halva (early rice) and garva (broken rice). Rice was grown both in the rainy and the dry weather. Malvan, in spite of being a grain growing area, was faced with problems of competition as far as rice business was concerned. The local farmer faced competition of cheap imported food grains mainly from interior parts of Deccan. The cause of this was of course, increase of a large import trade in cleaned rice, coupled with a much smaller import trade in uncleaned rice. The flooding of the local markets with cheap cleaned rice specially Burmese or Rangoon as it was called, had kept down the price of the local product to such an extent that rice was relatively cheap compared to the other crops of the taluka, not so valuable a crop as it was in the beginning of the British rule.

The principal imports into the ports in 1910-1911 were husked rice 5,79,731 rice in the husk 1,56,249.[84] A visible change that was seen in this time of the colonial era was its deviation in its traditional trade with others. The ships that came to the west coast before Colonial rule went up to Bengal and other East Coasts. This enabled the Europeans and Arabs to extend their commerce as far as the east; they began importing from east, articles which they had previously looked for only in the West Asia. Thus by the nineteenth century the Arabs for example had found alternative supply of cheap rice.

Malvan had shortage of food grains especially rice or at least it was reported so by the British officials. A. R. Bonus, Collector of Ratnagiri in his letter to the Settlement Commissioner and Director of Land Records on 10th April 1913 wrote that "The Taluka does not provide enough food grains for its own maintenance but imports over 7 lakhs worth of rice in a year to say nothing of other grains."[85] Therefore the local ryut had to face the competition of cheap imported goods. With an increasing population, the demand of food products increased. But the common man could not profit by this trade. The chief reason for this was lack of land and the plough cattle.

The influence of the imported rice on the prices was further affected by the prices relating to nachni, the principal coarse grain and kulith, the principal pulse. The price of the nachni had gone up about 50% and the price of the kulith had nearly doubled. Experiments were done by sowing the special seeds in the Malvan Taluka but the yield per acre of a given quantity of that rice was almost the same as that of any other quality.[86]

The following table shows the general trend that cleaned rice had not shared in the general rise as that of uncleaned rice.[87]

Table 4.19

	Rice in the Husk		Cleaned Rice	
	Seers	Chataks	Seers	Chataks
1887-1891	20	12	10	10
1892-1896	19	13	09	15
1897-1901	16	09	10	05
1902-1906	17	04	10	10
1906-1911	14	13	09	03

The government tried to give irrigational facilities wherever required. In 1878, a dam was strengthened at Pednur and the cost of it as reported by the Public Works Department was Rs. 6033.10.10.[88] *Ardhilee* Bridge at Malvan was constructed. Similarly, cart roads were repaired. Yet much of the rice of the Malvan taluka was a have an inferior quality and large amount of manuring was necessary to enable it to grow two good crops.

Other crops: The principal crop grown on the warkas land was nachni. It was followed by other coarse grains of which harik and vari were the principal varieties. It was occasionally followed by pulse crop, the favorite being kulith. But wari and harik were grown in the monsoon on the warkas land and followed Nachni in rotation. A.R.Bonus, collector of Ratnagiri, expressed his dissatisfaction regarding other agricultural products namely pulse (kulith), hemp also as they were not of good quality. According to him, although the area covered for the growth of kulith in 1910 -11 was more than the area covered in 1902 but it was negligible as it was only 830 acres. In 1911-12 was only 268 acres and had dwindled from 570 acres in 1902. The price of the hemp although not increased, yet it remained a paying crop to grow and did pay revenue to the taluka along with the coconuts and dried fish. F.G. Pratt said that hemp or kulith were such minor products that they were hardly worth discussing.

Sugar cane was also grown in some of the better rice lands with the help of irrigation from streams and wells.

Hemp was also cultivated as a monsoon crop. The principal oil seed was Sesamum. The experiments tried by the government to grow better quality sugarcane although showed good signs in the initial years of British rule soon showed a declining trend. Sugar cane and chillies, were cultivated as a dry crop wherever irrigation was available. Onions grew in the sandy soils near the seacoast.[89]

Coconut: The product of the garden lands in Malvan was coconut. Coconuts were a handy crop little affected by the uncertainty of the rainfall, provided that the total fall was sufficient. Almost every part of the tree was put to economic use. The trunk was used for rafters, lath, and firewood. The leaves for roofing, for mats, baskets, brooms, fodder and manure. The stems of the leaf for fences, fishing rods and domestic utensils; the leaves and nuts for pickle and chuttny; the sap for toddy, for distilling and for making vinegar and sugar; the riped fruit for eating for its milk and cooking; the dried flesh (copra) for margarine; oil for soaps and candles, for treatment of rheumatism, for the hair and as an illuminant; the residue of the flesh after extracting the oil, for cattle food and poultry cake; the shell for drinking cups, bottles, charcoal, tooth powder and linoleum; the coir fiber from the husk for mattresses, rope, canvas, fuel, brush doormat and floor matting. The coconut palm flourished best on flat agri-bagayat lands on the coast and riverbanks. In the dongri or hillside garden, jackfruit trees, mangoes, both coarse and grafted betel nut palms were grown in addition to the coconut.[90]

Yet A.R.Bonus, Collector of Ratnagiri was unhappy about the Malvan taluka coconuts and said *'As to the coconuts it is to be noted that the area under 'fruit trees' shows hardly any increase over the figures for 1904-05. I had the occasion to look into this very matter some months ago; and knowing that 'Malabar copra commanded a high price in London, I expected to find a considerable trade in that commodity from Bombay. Much to my surprise the figures I obtained showed trade to be insignificant- almost negligible. I doubt, therefore whether Malvan coconuts do found their way to Europe.'* A Malvan merchant made some experiments in extracting coconut fibre from machinery but nothing more was heard whether he was successful or not.[91]

But the statement made by A.R.Bonus seemed exaggerated. Cocoanuts or coconut products exported from the taluka definitely showed a considerable rise in prices. (Nearly 50% since 1903) There was a good reason to believe that it was a permanent rise. This was partly because of the visits of the vessels from foreign countries to get first hand knowledge about the product and partly because of the demand of the coconut products all over the world. The import of coconut into Great Britain between 1906 and 1910 doubled in quantity and nearly trebled in value. The imports of copra into Germany rose from 1½ to nearly 4 ¼ million sterling between 1908 and 1910.The rise of price in Malvan was not a mere local fluctuation but, a result of trade beyond the reach of local condition. Whenever the demand increased the prices rose and whenever they decreased the prices fell. A very notable rise in prices occurred in 1906-07. Prices again relaxed a little in 1908 and 1909 but recovered in 1910 and in 1911 and 1912 the demand went up so much that the best types of coconuts could not be bought retail for less than an anna and they reached the wholesale price of Rs. 50 per thousand. But according G.S. Hatch, Assistant Settlement Officer the question whether the Malvan products did or did not find their way to the European markets did not appear to be of much relevance. He stated that 80 trees per acre bore 60 nuts per tree per annum. Over 3,000 trees were also licensed to be tapped for toddy. The rise in prices was reflected in a considerable rise in rents. In coconut plantations, the tenant often paid at a fixed rate per bearing tree. In the lease fixed in the early 19th century, the rate was generally from 4 ½ to 6 annas. In 1910-11 the rate varied from 12 annas to a rupee.[92]

The Co-operative society for the development of agriculture and for helping the farmers with new techniques was started in the Malvan taluka in 1904. An Enquiry Committee visited Ratnagiri and toured almost all parts of the district and gave its report in December 1923.There were people from various fields who gave oral or written evidence before the Committee about the existing economy conditions. Besides the tours, these evidences also helped them to assess the conditions of the taluka. The list of persons who gave the evidences was as follows.[93]

Table 4.20

List of Persons	
The Sarkarkun. (Customs)	Vaze Ganpatrao, Tutor.
M. P. Pawaskar of Sukalwadi, Cultivator.	R. W. Ajgaonkar, Medical Practitioner.
W. A. Samant,, ,,	G. R. Prabhushirodkar, Cultivator of Katta.
R. M. Musale. ,, ,,	S. D. Kharade, T.H.O.
T. N. Amberkar, Potter of Kumbharmath.	V. G. Prabhugaokar of Masure.
P.N.Misal, School Master & Secretary of Kumbharmath.	S. V. Gaokar of Vairi.
G. R. Varadkar, Cultivator.	T. G. Bhalekar of Devbag.
D. N. Vairikar, Cultivator.	J. M. Karande, of Achre.
G. S. Bandivadekar, Cultivator.	Vaze Govindrao, Pleader.

It was reported by the Committee members that although the khoti system existed in certain parts yet, it was rayatwari that was dominant. In the rayatwari tracts the rent paid by the tenant to the landlord amounted to half the crop, but was fixed before hand annually. The report also threw light on the slow progress of co-operative movement because the farmers were reluctant to take loans for agricultural seeds and implements. Some of them regarded agriculture as subsidiary rather than as their main occupation as they went in search of jobs in Bombay. It was also because their need for loans for agricultural purposes was not usually so urgent as they had to pay exhorbitant interest on the loans taken from the co-operative society. This did not mean that there was no field for co-operative credit societies in the villages of Malvan. At this time, there were 12 co-operative credit societies, out of which 7 were in good working condition and the remaining 5 societies existed showing losses. This was possible because of the efforts of the honorary organizers and energetic gentlemen like V.V. Athalye and R.G.Mainkar who nursed the societies.[94]

Trade-Internal & External

The weekly bazars were held at Sukalvadi (Talegaon) Masde and Achra. There were smaller trading and marketing centres at places like Chindar, Maldi, and Nandos Katta. However, the principal trade went on from Malvan. For the most part, they were sold either in Kankavli bazaar in Devgad taluka or in one of the bazaars of the Savantwadi

State. However, there was no special market day in Malvan. Although it is difficult to make reliable estimate of the sales yet some details may be given based on the details supplied by the *Mamlatdars.*[95]

Table 4.21

Weekly sale in Masde	Amt. in	Weekly sale in Sukalwadi (Talegaon)	Amt. in	Weekly sale in Achre	Amt. in
	Rs. A. P		Rs. A. P.		Rs. A. P.
Rice	415. 0.0.	Rice	80.0.0.	Rice	24.0.0.
Other Grains	23.0.0.	Other Grains	—	Other Grains	1.0.0.
Pulses	15.0.0.	Pulses	36.0.00.	Pulses	8.8.0.
Coconuts	12.0.0.	Coconuts	51.0.0.	Coconuts	2.0.0.
Fish	75.0.0.	Fish	150.0.0.	Fish	5.0.0.
Salt	20.0.0.	Salt	52.0.0.	Salt	25.0.0.
Cloth	26.0.0.	Cloth	100.0.0.	Cloth	36.0.0.
Miscellaneous	271.0.0.	Miscellaneous	295.0.0.	Miscellaneous	183.0.0.
Total	857.0.0.	**Total**	684.0.0.	**Total**	284.8.0

The government reported statistics of the output of the principal crops and their prices from 1884 onwards. The calculations were generally based on a certain number of lbs per acre, maunds, *seers* and *chataks, tolas* and number of items as a standard yield in a given segment. This standard yield was then multiplied by a condition factor that showed the proportion of crops grown normally in the region. When the condition factor was given it showed the varying number of annas. Therefore it was called as *annewari* system.[96] The chief reporting agents of the yield and the prices were the *Mamlatdars* who were in charge of the talukas. After getting the figures they would be sent to the government, which were published. The published statements were declared in yield per acre of the principal crops per year. Sometime the standard yield submitted was erroneous and sometime showed downward trends. This disparity was due to the inaccuracy present.[97] For example in the table that follows, the two important crops of Malvan saw sizable changes in their Standard yields and their prices. Kulith the premier crop of Malvan occupied about 4,590 acres in 1901 saw its yield decline from 27 *seers* 1 *chataks* in 1884-85 to 13 *seers* 4 *chataks* in 1911.Cocoanuts over the same period saw it's the rise from Rs. 2 annas 8 to Rs.4 annas 15. A.W.Heston was the first to focus on the several errors in the agricultural statistics. The statement given below gives an overall view of the prices prevalent in the Malvan Taluka from 1884-85 to 1911.[98] But it is difficult to determine whether these changes mirrored the real changes in output over time or were the result of a more precise knowledge of the yields.[99]

Table 4.22

Year	Seers of 80 Tolas and Chatakas of 5 Totals Per Rupee					Per 100
	Rice in Husk	Rice in Cleaned	Nachni	Kulith	Seasame	Coconut
	S. Ch	S. Ch	S. Ch	S. Ch	S. Ch	Rs. a. p.
1884-85	19.10	—	22.12	27.01	18.11	2.8.0
1885-86	20.03	—	18.14	22.06	17.08	3.0.0
1886-87	20.07	8.14	22.12	27.01	19.14	3.3.2
1887-88	21.15	09.07	25.10	27.01	19.01	2.8.0
1888-89	20.12	08.08	21.02	25.09	14.09	2.9.9
1889-90	19.10	08.06	22.00	21.10	16.01	3.8.8
1890-91	19.06	07.06	20.03	18.15	15.04	3.0.5
1891-92	18.11	08.06	18.09	19.09	15.06	3.7.7
1892-93	17.12	11.00	18.12	18.02	12.07	3.14.1
1893-94	16.10	11.12	16.15	18.10	12.07	2.14.8
1894-95	19.05	11.01	19.10	19.05	11.02	3.7.3
1895	21.12	08.14	20.10	21.01	09.03	3.12.11
1896	20.09	10.05	19.05	20.00	09.15	3.11.0
1897	15.03	10.14	13.14	13.10	08.09	3.12.2
1898	17.12	10.12	15.09	16.15	10.09	3.1.11
1899	17.13	11.05	16.04	17.12	11.05	2.13.8
1900	15.09	12.02	13.07	12.02	08.14	3.10.0
1901	16.10	10.03	16.02	13.03	08.09	3.14.2
1902	18.12	11.04	17.06	11.05	09.05	3.1.4
1903	18.08	10.10	18.03	19.15	09.15	3.4.8
1904	18.02	09.01	20.14	19.13	12.14	3.12.0
1905	16.06	08.06	18.02	18.09	09.07	4.5.0
1906	14.07	08.02	12.07	16.06	07.04	5.3.4
1907	13.14	10.04	13.08	—	06.13	4.0.9
1908	13.03	10.03	11.12	—	06.03	4.1.0
1909	15.05	09.00	12.15	14.06	07.01	4.14.8
1910	16.09		13.12	13.04	07.14	4.15.0
1911	15.03		14.11		07.04	

The exports of Malvan besides its own produce, included items procured from different parts of Ratnagiri. The articles imported into Malvan came from Bombay, Karwar, Goa, Cochin, Calicut, and Mangalore. The trade was carried on through local merchants like *vanis, Bhandaris, Shenvis, Gujars.* Besides the ones shown in the figure below, the other articles of trade were salt, kernel, wood, coir, betelnut, sugar, black pepper, ginger, turmeric, almond, dry fruits. These articles were subject to land customs. Cloves, nutmeg, mace, silk, leads, copper, iron was subject to 3% custom duty. The above-mentioned items were land customs, while duty on commodities exported and imported by waterways was charged at 2% of the valuation or normally upon the market value of goods of the Malvan town. It is surprising to learn that the import duty of Bombay salt was higher than the export duty on Malvan salt. The main aim of such a high tarriff on the imports of salt was to protect the salt industry of Malvan. Luxury items like sandalwood, salt petre, tobbaco, jaggery, chilly were imported into Malvan and were subject to high rate.[100]

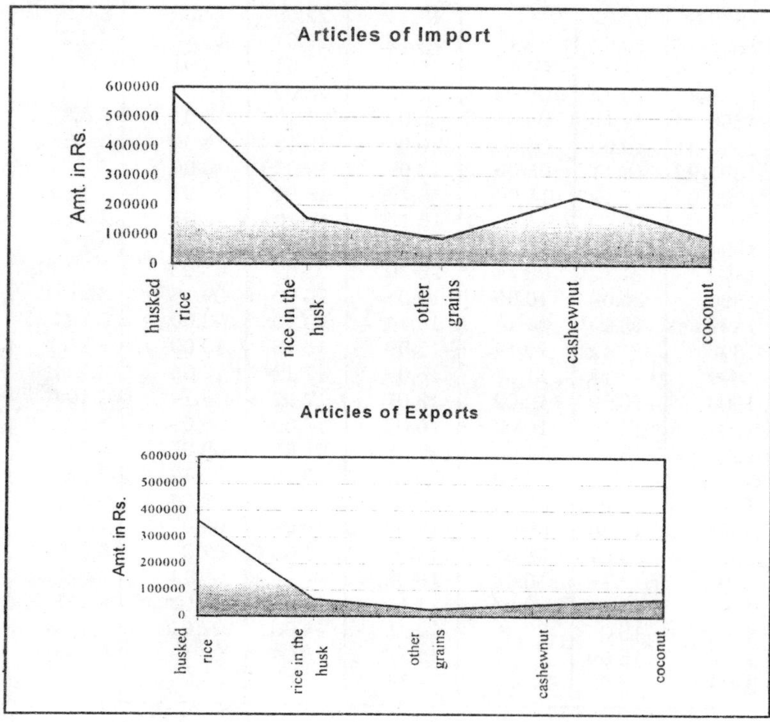

Fig. 4.7

Fishing and & Fish curing yards: Apart from agriculture, fishing also was an important industry in Malvan Taluka. The fishermen manufactured large quantities of fishing nets and ropes from coir and the same was exported to Kanara and Malabar. In fact Malvan rope acquired a good reputation for good quality fishing nets and ropes.[101]

In 1887, the fishermen of Malvan requested that a fish-curing yard to be opened at that place, but the government did not yield to their request on the ground that a yard at Malvan would draw customs away from the Vengurla yard. It was suggested that the yard at Vengurla could be conveniently used by the people of Malvan. But the fishermen at Malvan renewed their request and the Collector strongly favoured the request of the fishermen. He wrote, *'Now that a duty has been imposed on salt fish it may be expected that a great stimulus will be given to the fish curing industry in British territory, since it will compete on more equal terms with the industry so largely carried on in Goa, I have no doubt that there is room for yards both at Malvan and Vengurla and that a flourishing business may be maintained at both places.'*

His proposal was accepted, as the government was convinced about the advantages of opening a yard at Malvan. He was instructed to give the details of the land required, the establishment and the materials along with expenses that would go into the construction of the fish-curing yard.[102]

On 14 August 1894, the Collector of Ratnagiri was instructed to acquire under the Act I of 1894, the land required for the establishment of a fish curing yard at Malvan which was sanctioned in the Government Resolution No.2653, dated 16th April 1894.[103] It was declared that the land was required to be taken by the government at the public expense for a public use, viz a fish curing yard, at Malvan in the Malvan taluka and the land below was acquired within the town of Malvan.[104]

Table 4.23

Names of the Holders	Area	Boundaries			
		East	South	West	North
Ganesh Mahadev Bhikaji Bhandarkar Ramkrishna Gopal Atmaram Ladko Raghunath Vithal Raoji Ganesh and Atmaram Ladko and Raghunath Vithal and Vishnu Bhikaji Bhandarkar	Survey No.956, Plot Ni1, Vada Vairi, in Malvan some portion of the plot no. 6 of Survey No. 956 ditto total area measuring 1 acre 37 Gunthas and 7 Annas, and Assessed at 10 annas per acre.	Survey No.680, plot No. 1	Survey No 956, Pot No.2	The Sea	Survey No.680, plot No.1 and portion of pot No.6 of survey no 956.

The fishing industry was found between the creeks of Vijaydurg, Achra and Devbag, near Malvan. The annual catch of fish in Achra and Malvan in 1912 was estimated at 71,500 maunds that was almost a quarter district's output and at this time the fisher folk of the taluka was about 6,000. The port of Malvan was famous for the availability of the oyster variety of shellfish. This variety was in demand because of its taste and food value.[105] There was a local market for fresh fish and the surplus was either dried and sold for use as manure, salted and dried and sold for consumption as food. The curing was done in government fish-curing yards at Devgad, Achra and Malvan where the salt was supplied free of duty.[106] The cured fish was sold at in weekly bazaars at Kankavli, Kharepatan, and Kudal and taken from there up to the ghats by road. Cured fish was also sent by sea to Mangalore and from Mangalore up to Burma. The total catch was estimated at Rs. 1,46,000. In 1912, fishing boats with an aggregate tonnage of 2,972 tons of fish were registered from Achra and Malvan for export.[107]

Fishermen usually helped one another in the smooth conduct of this trade. Twenty-five to thirty people contributed towards the initial preparations and spreading of a net, which cost them about Rs. 1,500 to Rs. 2,000. They shared the profits of the big catch among themselves.

Besides co-operating in this activity, each fisherman had his own boat and fishing net. Thus the fishermen worked both individually and in teams depending upon the situation. By and large the selling of the fish was done by the women folk who were supposed to be good at it. This trade was carried on for almost all year through except during the rainy season. During these two months, the fishermen were busy making new nets repairing old ones either for themselves or for selling them.[108]

Salt Manufacturing: In 1858, when the British Government took over power from the East India Company, It found that the salt trade flourished in the coastal shores of the Konkan in general and Malvan in particular. In 1863, the balance of salt in store in the Malvan was 47,434 Indian maunds.[109] W.A.Pelly, 1st Assistant Commissioner of Customs, Salt and Opium was employed in June 1864 to investigate all cases of smuggling and other irregular transactions by visiting several *bundars,* salt works and *nakas.* The visits were mainly to Malvan, Vengurla, Ratnagiri, Shiroda, Vijaydurg and other smaller places. He informed that salt was generally sold at Rs 1.4 and total increase in collections amounted to Rs.1,649.3.10.[110] Considering Ratnagiri, and Malvan & Vengurla, there was an overall increase in salt amounting to Rs. 3,83,880.33 Indian Maunds between 1864-65.[111]

The salt under the British Government was conveniently classified under three heads. They were the Bhagra salt, Sea salt, imported salt. The Bhagra salt was manufactured from salt brine at the Government Salt Works that was called as 'Pritchad Salt Works'. At Malvan and other talukas of Konkan, the salt works, the property of the government was leased to private individuals. Imported salt was mainly produced at the salt works in Portuguese India.

There were a number of salt works at the coastal parts of the Malvan and many of the government lands were leased out to private individuals. Salt used to be stored at the storehouses. The quantity stored and produced in 1869 was 66,034 Indian maunds 26 *seers* and the balance of salt in store in the same year was 84,840 Indian maunds and 5 *Seers.* Despite the large trade, the duty collected was disappointing. The decrease of duty in the Malvan taluka was perceived by low prices prevailing throughout the year.

It was also because larger quantities were removed from the works.[112] The average amount of duty collected from 1867-72 shows a decrease as given in the following table.

Table 4.24

Year	Amount in Rs		
1867-68	67,232	1	9
1868-69	1,07,222	0	3
1869-70	89,741	13	4
1870-71	1,07,846	12	8
1871-72	1,60,461	9	3
Total	5,32,504	5	3
Average [1872-73]	1, 01 160	13	3
Decrease	5340	0	7

Salt trade was affected by variations in demand, rise and fall in prices depending upon situation. The causes were sometimes natural and sometimes artificial. The sale of one market affected the other. The increase in the salt production and storage in 1870 was attributed to the increase of trade in general, traders having brought large quantities of grain and cotton from the other side of the ghats to Malvan and taken larger quantities of salt in their return trip. Malvan was affected in 1904 by the salt famine owing to the cyclone of May 1903 followed by a burst of rains. The usual imports not having arrived, salt from the fish curing yards had to be removed leading to variations in prices.[113]

Other trading articles: After the Konkan Co-operative societies started working in Malvan, changes could be seen in various fields. There were intelligent and skilled people among the artisans. The nib making factories, manufacturing of penknives, aluminium ornament making, cashew baking testified the skill they had in Malvan. Near Ramgad, in the Malvan Taluka, a porous rough slate stone was found which was utilized for making ornamental stoneware for house hold purposes. After 1920, there was political unrest in India and this indirectly affected the trade. Simultaneously, Bombay was growing. Many young people started migrating to Bombay and this also hampered the business of Malvan.

There were a large number of kaju trees in Malvan and therefore Malvan found a profitable occupation in the preparation of kaju nuts.[115] Malvan had heavy rains during the months of September and during this period most of the labour of Malvan was devoted to the preparation of kaju nuts to send to Bombay markets. These nuts were also brought from the neighbouring regions. Nuts were also brought from Goa and Savantwadi to Malvan during the months of April and May. The nuts thus imported, were roasted and sent to Bombay markets. This profit giving industry of Malvan had a deleterious effect on the public health. It had a bad effect on the lungs and led to Asthama because of the acrid vapours that were emitted during the roasting process.[116]

Yet in 1933, cashews after being roasted and shelled were exported to America. Cashew nuts were imported from Goa and Africa. It was only Malvan that was importing cashew nuts in considerable quantities from Goa and Africa because of its favorable condition for baking operation of nuts. This was reported by Rao Bahadur Palekar, who was the Deputy Collector of Ratnagiri in 1926.The annual turn over of cashew nuts in the Malvan factory in the early nineteen thirties rose from 11,17,580 to 1932-33 was Rs. 9,46,619. Along with large industry, there was also salt trade in Malvan though it was not on a large scale like Vengurla.[117]

There were other industries like coconut oil pressing, coir and rope making, spinning of pineapple fibre. There were one or two merchants who manufactured cutlery, nibs and button on a small scale but they did not provide work for many employees. Potters were found in various parts of Malvan.[118] There were also petty iron works. There were four floor mills in Malvan in 1919-20.[119]

The Alfonoso mangoes found their place in the London market in the early twentieth century. But the mango sale societies for Malvan Taluka were not able to make finance available to the farmers. As a result, very little business was possible. It so happened that the mango growers were ready to mortgage their lands, gardens and houses to the society. Or the growers of mangoes borrowed funds mainly from brokers either locally or from Bombay directly. Often they borrowed from the sub-brokers on the clear understanding that they would sell their mangoes only through such brokers or sub brokers. But the Co-operative societies that were established decades ago, to help the farmers, took little interest in making finance available to them. As a result the growers could do very little business.

Another problem the mango growers faced was that they entirely depended on the good will of the steam ship Companies to carry their goods. Often the mango parcels reached the destination so late that they were not in fit condition for sale. To add to the woes of the growers, they had to part with high freight charges for the mango parcels, pay high conveyance charges for loading and unloading, finally end up giving exhorbitant charges for carrying the parcels from ferry wharfs in Bombay to the markets, only to find the mangoes not fit for sale.

The exports of Malvan Taluka were mainly sea borne, though few commodities like dried fish, coconuts went via roads too. Sea going traffic touched at three principal ports of Malvan taluka. They were Malvan, Sarjekot, and Achra. There was considerable trade that went on from these ports. The following figure gives the number and tonnage of sailing vessels at these ports.

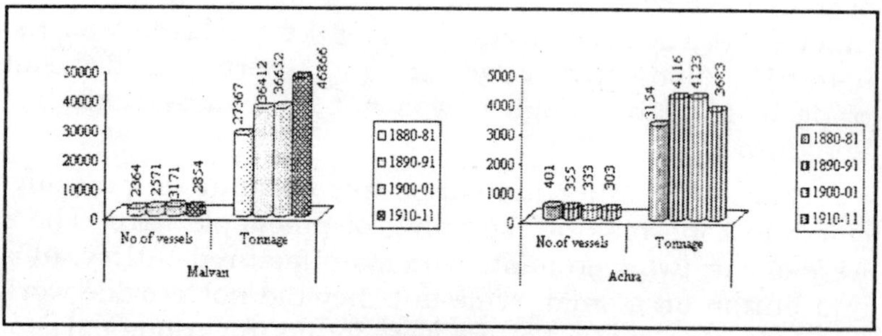

Fig. 4.8

The local sailing crafts were the *shibadi*, the *phatemari*, the *mhangari*, the *machva*, the *padav* and the *balav*. The owners of these sailing crafts were Bhatiyas, Gujars, Muslims, Parsis. There were also fishermen who belonged to *Gabit*, *Koli* and *karvi* classes of Hindus. Similarly the vessels were also owned by Daldi and Konkani classes of Muslims.[120] Very often the Brahmins also were involved in this business, but they either owned the ships or lent money to the fishermen. The taluka was also served by the steamers of the Bombay Steam Navigation Company. This Company had a daily service, but they were purely to carry passengers. As a result of the volume of traffic, Malvan became a shipbuilding center. The teak wood was used for shipbuilding and it was called the 'Oak of India' by the Europeans.[121] When the teak stock of Konkan was exhausted, it was imported from the Malabar. Besides teak, ships were built of the local woods of Nana, Jack and mango trees. A number of ships were built weighing between 10 and 100 tons while it can be noticed from the following table that there were almost no vessels built between 100 and 300 tons. There were no vessels 10 and 100 tons by the end of 1930.[122]

Table 4.25

Year	Vessels	10-100 Tons	100-300 Tons
1909-10-1913-14	16	101	— —
1914-15-1918-19	68	89	— —
1919-20-1923-24	45	40	— —
1924-25-1928-29		— —	— —

Below is given the statistics of the sea borne trade of the Malvan Taluka furnished by the Customs Department. The figures given below were compiled and recorded in the office of the Sarkarkun at Malvan till 1905-06. Thereafter, the Department was re-organised and the records were transferred to the office of the Records General in Bombay. As a result, figures derived sometimes were vague. The combined figures for the Customs Taluka were given and they included the port of Devgad also. However the records lacks uniformity in the figures given below.[123]

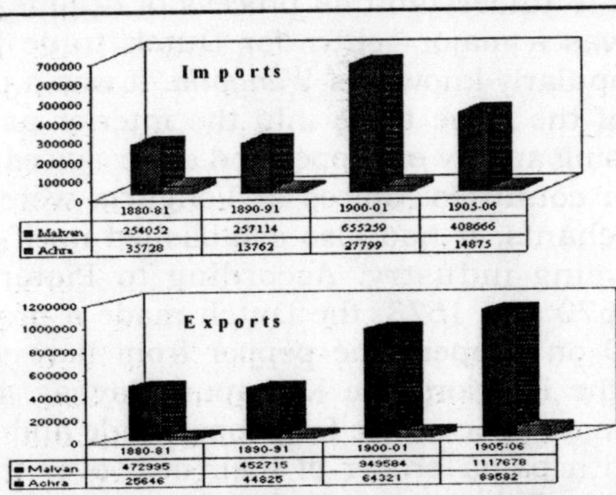

Fig.4.9

Malvan due to a combination of high taxation, low prices, bad communication, traditional society witnessed an overall decline in the economy. It showed that despite the efforts taken by the government and the Co-operative societies trade of Malvan showed downward trend between 1910-1913. Thus, although trade went on in this part of Konkan, still one could see the disintegration of the old coastal society. The port of Malvan no more remained a big centre of trade as before. It also declined because of the absence of proper development of its harbours.[124]

Table 4.26

Year	1900-01	1909-10	1910-11	1920-21	1930-31	1940-41	1945-46	1947-48
Inward	...	13,75,499	15,03,869	32,39,087	25,17,248	...	...	...
Outward	...	8,47,431	8,61,599	12,58,199	13,34,333	...	...	...

Vengurla Petha of Ratnagiri Collectorate

Vengurla in 1860 was a sub-division of the Malvan taluka in the Ratnagiri Collectorate. Situated at the southern extremity of the Ratnagiri Collectorate, it was bounded on the north by the Karli River, which separated it from the subha division of the Malvan taluka, on the east by the Sawantwadi State, on the south by the Portuguese territory of Goa and on the west by the Arabian Sea. Its greatest length from north to south was about 22 miles and its breadth was about 5 miles. The area was nearly 66 square miles.[125]

A brief sketch of the importance of Vengurla is imperative to understand its process of decline in the later years. It was a major centre for Dutch trade in the 17th century popularly known as *Wengorla.* It was a point for the diffusion of the spice trade into the interior as a result of the increasing supply of pepper and other spices from South East Asian countries. Spices at Vengurla were bought by Surat merchants. It had also established itself as a centre for the dyeing industry. According to Pieter Van Dam between 1670 and 1673, the Dutch made a profit of about Rs. 36,200 on pepper. The pepper from here was sent to places in the interiors like Kolhapur, Raybag, Burhanpur. Raybag was a major centre for pepper trade and the English maintained a bania broker of their own over there. In the year 1647, the British volume of trade went so high that they had to borrow about 10,720 pagodas at 13.5.% interest

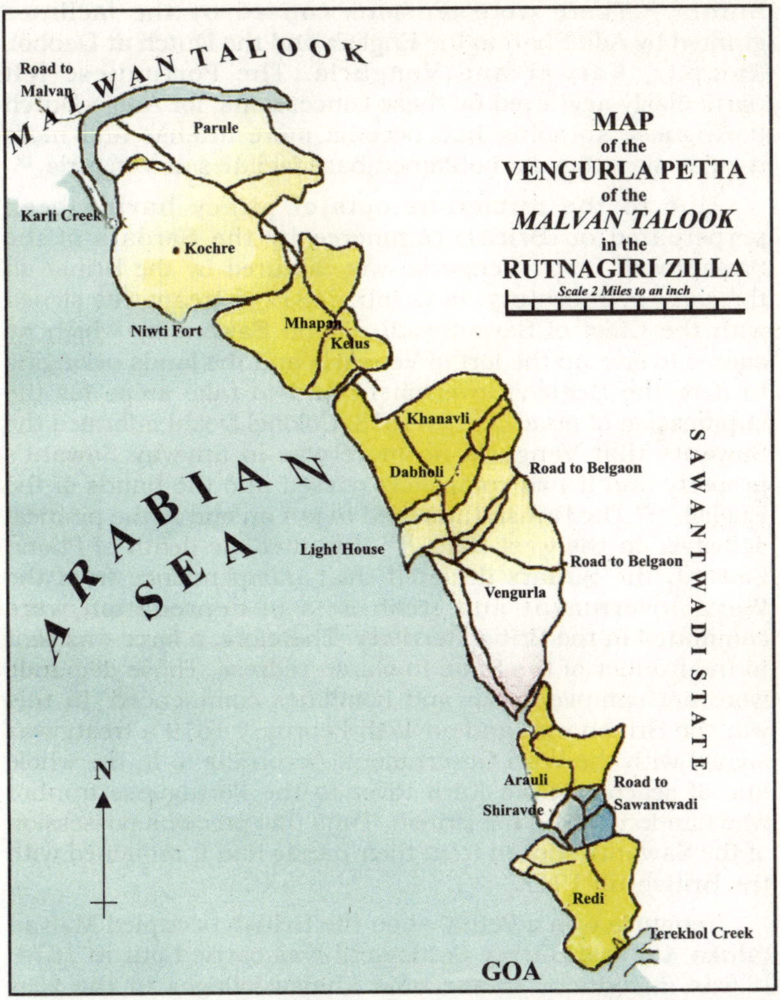

Source : MSA, Revenue Department, Vol. No. 715/1875.

because, they wanted to invest in mercandise to be sent to Surat.[126] There were tensions caused by the facilities granted by Adil Shah to the English and the Dutch at Dabhol, Rajapur, Karwar and Vengurla. The Portuguese felt particularly aggrieved by these concessions, for Anlgo-Dutch Portuguese shipping had become more intense and more regular after they had obtained base facilities at Vengurla.[127]

Due to the numerous acts of piracy having been perpetuated on British commerce by the Sardars of the Sawantwadi State, Vengurla was captured by the British in the early 19th century. In October 1812, a treaty was signed with the Chief of Sawantwadi, Phond Sawant by which he agreed to give up the fort of Vengurla and the lands belonging to it to the British Government and to take steps for the suppression of piracy.[128] By 1813, Colonel Doshi informed the Sawants that Vengurla no more was in anyway Sawant's property and it had completely passed into the hands of the English.[129] The British thus tried to put an end to the piratical activities on the west coast.[130] But after the death of Phond Sawant, the Sirdars declared their independence from the Wari Government and fresh acts of depredation were committed in the British territory. Therefore, a force was sent to the frontier of the State to obtain redress. Those demands were not compiled with and hostilities commenced. In this war the British won and on 17th February 1819 a treaty was signed with the Wari Government. According to it, the whole line of seacoast from Karli River to the Portuguese frontier was handed over to the British. Thus this precious possession of the Sawants slipped from their hands and it remained with the British till 1947.

Vengurla was a Petha when the British occupied Malvan taluka. Its first Survey Settlement was carried out in 1874. It was introduced in the nine khalsa villages in the year 1885 and was to be guaranteed for thirty years from 10th March 1885 till the year 1904-05. The Settlement was introduced in Mhapan on 13th May 1885.

At that time, Vengurla comprised of 10 villages out of which nine were khalsa. (government) They were Vengurla, Parul, Kochra, Kelus, khankavli, Dabholi, Aravali, Rairee, and Shiravde.[131] The tenth village, Mhapan was shirakti *Inam*. The *Inam* share was 10 annas and 3 pies. Even in the late nineteenth century, some of the villages belonged to the Sawantwadi State. The land that belonged to Sawantwadi

State was only 673 acres and was assessed at Rs 1,496. This land was at last brought under the survey Settlement in 1888.

Thus, the area of Vengurla Petha was approximately 41,119 acres or 65.86 Square miles after excluding the land belonging to the Sawantwadi State and 66 after including it. At that time, Vengurla formed a Petha of the Malvan taluka. But in 1879, it was changed to the status of a taluka according to the Government Resolution No.3958 of 1879.[132]

Out of the total area of approximately 41,119 acres, only 16,200 or 40% was under cultivation. The percentage of land under the different crops was as follows:[133] The percentage of rice grown was the highest and occupied about 41.47%.

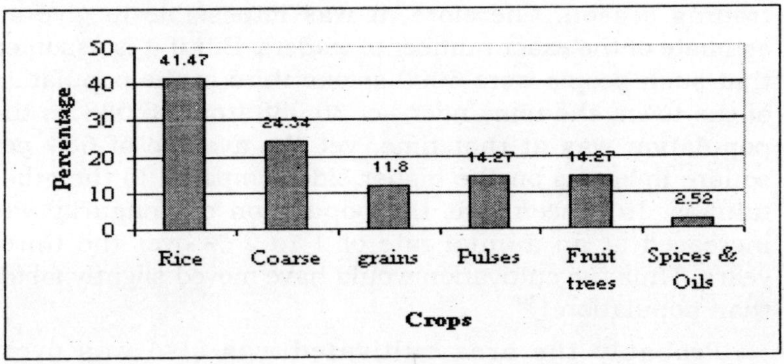

Fig. 4.10

G.W. Vidal who toured the taluka from 24th February 1880 to 27th February 1880 stated that the arable land was 11,817 acres.[134] The arable area was 1 acre and 4 gunthas in 1882 according to N. M. Mint, the Assessment Officer. But Assessment does not seems very accurate.[135] While in 1885, it was reported that the total area in square miles of the taluka was 64.7 square miles with a population of 34,769.[136] According to the report, the cultivated land had increased from 22,440 in 1883-84 to 23,907 in 1884-85. This showed an increase of 2,467 acres.

Between 1875-76 and 1901-02 the total cultivated area rose by 46.69% or from 11,817 acres to 25,306 acres. But the collection of revenue increased only by 8 % from 32, 975 to Rs. 33,879.[137] The population of the taluka in 1872 was 35,088 and in 1901 it was 44,863. In 1912-12 the area was reported to be 27,353. If the population was 35,088 or 532 persons to a square mile and it was 44,863 i.e. 679 per square mile then during a period of thirty years the population had increased by nearly 28% And the prices rose during this time by 1 to 2. These numbers (532 per square mile) were higher than the northern talukas of the Collectorate.[138] For instance in the Lanje Petha, there were only 286 inhabitants to the square mile of the cultivable area. In the chiplun Taluka, the population was 266 per square mile. The numbers were increased due to the trading activities carried on at Vengurla town. The number of persons engaged in trade in that town, properly speaking did not belong to the taluka. They used to arrive in the trading season. Therefore, it was impossible to give an estimate of the exact number of traders. But if it is assumed that such people were 5000 or one third of the population of the town, the remainder i.e. 30,088 from 35,088 as the population was at that time, yet the average of 684 per square mile was on the higher side compared to the other talukas. It is seen that the population of Vengurla was increased at an annual rate of 1 to 2 % over the thirty years. Thus the cultivation would have moved slightly faster than population.[139]

Probably the area cultivated was also was over-estimated or there may be an error largely in the assessment or due to the encroachments on roads, paths and various grounds. On the other hand, an upward bias is due to the fact that additions to government land between 1872 and 1902 was not deducted because of the cessions, lapses and the activities of the *Inam* commission.

Chief Products

The products of the taluka were mainly rice, nachni, kulith, hurrik, and vari, til, coconut, supari. Rice occupied 41.47% of the area, coarse grains 24.34%, pulses 11.80% fruit trees 14.27% spices 2.52% and oils and others 5.60%. There were 1,281 wells. Out of them 174 wells were useful. Water from these wells was used for irrigational and drinking purposes. When a survey of Vengurla was done in 1874 there were 1,033 wells used for drinking purposes.[140]

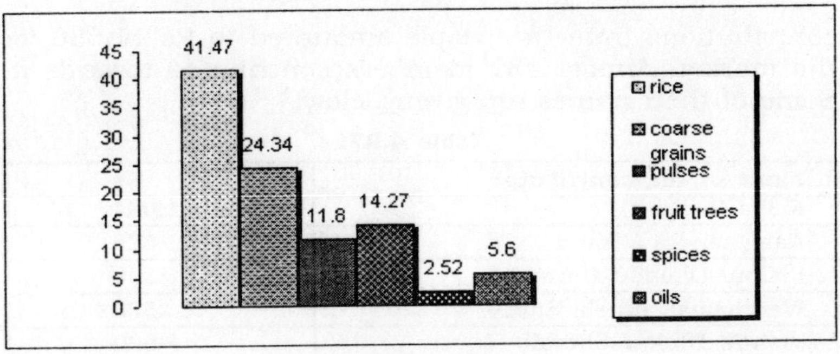

Fig. 4.11

The chief crop of the taluka was rice. There were two classes namely *halwa* and *gurva*. The halwa rice ripened by the end of September or early October and was grown where the soil was shallow. Gurva rice was grown in the low lying areas, where the soil remained moist until the end of November or beginning of December. Nagli was most important crop being 12 to15 % of the produce. It was sown about the middle of June and the crop ripened about the beginning of October. The next in importance were harik, kulith each of which formed 6 to 25 & of the total cultivation. Irrigational facilities were given. For example the Pendur tank was strengthened and the amount spent was Rs. 6,033.[141] But such irrigational facilities did little to improve the agricultural conditions.

Like Malvan and Ratnagiri, Vengurla Petha was a succession of high lying rocky plains and narrow valleys. Most parts consisted of laterite rocks. The sides of the valleys were steep but the upper slopes were well covered with brushwood and kajoo trees. The lower slopes were full of coconut and betelnut palms. The soil was fertile at the foot of the hills. Wherever the streams supplied with ample water, there were rice fields found. The southern part of the taluka was more open. It was here that rice and garden fields were found in plenty. One could see a belt of coconut plantations that extended from Vengurla to Rairee.[142]

The chief market was Vengurla, a large town on the seacoast, which had a considerable import and export trade and from where produce could be easily disposed of. In fact it was the largest town in the Ratnagiri Collectorate., the population being 15,000. So much was the enthusiasm of the local people to trade that they contributed in the building of good market facilities. One such market was built with great rapidity in the year of 1878 and the contributions from the people amounted to Rs 11,686 for the market. Almost 189 members contributed towards it. Some of their names are given below:[143]

Table 4.27

Name of the contributor	Rs
Kalba Gadekar	1,004
Ramchandra Vishnu	526
Vishnu Dhondu Gurayre	500
Wardhaman prushi Shet	500
Vishnu Dinkar Shewde	500
Diwan Kedar Dewji Shet	400
Babaji Baloji Shewade	400
Total	3,830

A daily bazaar was held at Vengurla. The most important articles sold were rice, coconut, salt, ghee, oil and rock oil. People from neighbouring villages came here to buy the products. A lot of trade went on even in salt.

At Shiroda a weekly bazaar was held on Sundays rice, coconut, salt and fish formed the chief objects of trade. However, the entire trade centered around Vengurla. Although the size of the port town was small, it could boast of having about 383 shops for the sale of cloth, grains and miscellaneous articles. That the bazaar had assorted articles for sale is obvious from the table given below[144]

Table 4.28

(A) Bazar held daily (1906)

Articles	Amt. in Rs.	Articles	Amt. in Rs.	Articles	Amt. in Rs.
Rice	58,333	Coconut Oil	2,874	Pepper	20
Coconut	500	Rock Oil	5,000	Tamarind	9
Pigeon Pea	300	Horse Gram	60	Ambsole	2
Field Pea	70	Black Gram	120	Betel Leaves	16
Gram	250	Sesame	60	Pots	10
Wheat	146	Sunflower Seed	10	Betelnuts	41
Ragi (Nagli)	150	Salt	1,100	Fish	80
Gul	625	Green Gram	15	Goat	25
Ghee	3.438	Lentil	13	Poultry	10
Sugar	1,250	Fruiteddolichos	10	Eggs	7
Onion	312	Jowari	20	Liquor	560
Chillies	410	Bajri	80	Baskets	8
Coriander	105	Oil Cake	500	Firewood	50
Sweet Oil	625	Turmerie	15	Vegetables	20
Tobacco	625	English Cloth	600	Rice	250
Fodder	4	Fire Works	125		
Shahapuri Cloth	800	Rice In Husk	1,000		

(B) Bazar held on Sundays (1906)

Articles	Amt. in Rs.	Articles	Amt. in Rs.	Articles	Amt. in Rs.
Coconut	300	Sesame	5	Vegetables	10
Pigeon Pea	10	Safflower Seed	5	Tobacco	15
Field Pea	10	Salt	11,750	Fodder	5
Gram	10	Green Gram	5	Shahapuri Cloth	200
Wheat	12	Lentil	5	English Cloth	300
Ragi (Nagli)	10	Fruiteddolichos	5	Black Pepper	20
Gul	75	Jowari	5	Tamarind	2
Ghee	10	Bajri	2	Ambsole	1
Sugar	25	Oil Cake	10	Betel Leaves	5
Onion	15	Turmerie	3	Earthen Pots	5
Chillies	15	Fish	100	Betelnuts	2
Coriander	5	Goat	10	Rock Oil	30
Sweet Oil	20	Poultry	5	Horse Gram	5
Coconut Oil	25	Eggs	1	Black Gram	5
Liquor	40	Baskets Etc,	3		
Fibre	50	Firewood	20		

The agricultural societies, with the help of the local people, were started in Vengurla in the early twentieth century. The Committee visited the place and started an enquiry with the help of the locals to probe into the needs and problems of the people. The list of persons who gave oral or written evidences before the Committee were as follows:[145]

Table 4.29

List of Persons
The Mamlatdar.
Mr. Ghurye, Land lord.Mr. Athavale, pleader.
K. A. Parab, cultivator.
Govind pandurang, cultivator.
G.D. Anjarlekar, cultivator.
A. N. Prabhugaonkar, cultivator.
U. A. Prabhugaonkar.
R.A.Gavandi.
B.A.Parab of Shiravda.
G.A.Ajgaonkar.
P.N.Varde.

The Agricultural Department had limited success with crops. By the beginning of the twentieth century, land started losing its value. The picture that was emerging, was one of stagnant agriculture, unable to increase the area cultivated or the productivity of the land. A great deal of research was involved for which the British Government neither had the inclination nor the care in it and this port which once was an important commercial center saw its decline by about 1930.

The introduction of the railways and telegraphs by the British though initially were beneficial soon followed by a negative impact. As soon as the new systems were started many business communities like the Banias, Gujarathis, Marwadis came from nearby regions like Rajapur and Chiplun to settle in Vengurla. But very soon, the construction of railways changed the scene of Vengurla port. Railways and roadways took the goods to Bombay. The use of the ports had became minimum. The Gujarathi and Bania community that had settled here migrated to Bombay and other cities for better prospects. Vengurla was reduced to a small port, from where goods were carried to only nearby places.[146] Even the average price per maund of some of the principal articles of trade like paddy, rice, nagli, and kulith hardly showed any remarkable change in prices.[147]

Table 4.30

Period	Average Price per Maund			
	Paddy Rs. A.P.	Cleaned Rice Rs. A..P.	Nagli Rs. A..P.	Kulith Rs. A..P.
1888-1895	2. 1.0	3.12	1.15.4.	2.4.2.
1896-1902	2.5.2.	5.4.	2.11.7	2.12.8

The slight increase in prices during the second period was most probably the effect of the famines that affected this area in 1876. The Assistant Collector-In-Charge of Vengurla while submitting the Famine Report of the year 1876, gave the following figures as representing the average price of grain in that taluka during October, November and December during the six years ending with 1875. This was the period immediately preceding the introduction of the survey. Despite the demand for coconuts, the average price for coconuts for more than ten years from 1878 practically remained the same, the cost being Rs. 3½ per hundred in 1876 to Rs. 3.6.4 after almost ten or more years. But generally the price of rice was Rs. 12, nagli Rs. 12, wari Rs. 10 and harik was Rs. 12.[148]

Vengurla as a trading center

Before the Colonial rule the location of the taluka was more important than the products of the region. It was recognized as a trading center than a place which could yield revenue from land. The trade of Vengurla passed through sea, roads and creeks. As far as the sea trade was concerned, the Vengurla bay was sheltered from the northwest winds. Until the advent of the Southern Maratha Railway, practically the whole of the trade between Bombay and the district of Belgaum and Dharwar passed through Vengurla port.

However, road transport was probably equal or more important there. There was a brisk trade at Vengurla, which was known as the emporium of Belgaum, Shahapur and other inland trading centers.[149] It chiefly consisted of cotton, piece goods of Indian manufacture. A road entered the taluka from Vengurla Bunder to Belgaum by the way of Sawant Wadi and the Parpoli ghat. The opening of the Parpoli ghat road in 1869 gave an impetus to the traffic. As a result, between the years 1872-73, the average import of goods at the Vengurla bunder increased to Rs. 38,37,500.[150]

It was stated by the then collector, A.J.Crawford in his report thus, *'Vengurla is of course a richer and more prosperous town and its population is nearly four times as large as that of Rajapur. The Vengurla merchants too are very bustling and energetic people.'*[151]

Salt: One of the most important articles of trade was salt. Salt was produced only at Shiroda in Vengurla. The government lands were leased to the private individuals on contract.[152] These saltpans at Shiroda produced an annual turnover of almost 89,000 maunds of salt a year. The Shiroda salt works was an industry worth mentioning with

27 licensed owners of saltpans employing about 250 men. In the year 1865 the balance of salt in Vengurla port was 20,001 Indian *Maunds* and 2 *seers.*[153] Usually the saltpans were the property of the government but were leased out to private individuals for a period of five years.

The Statement showing the names of Government Saltpans in Shiroda together with the produce of each during the years 1886-1890 is shown below:[154]

Table 4.31

Names	Produce				
	1886 Maunds	1887 Maunds	1888 Maunds	1889 Maunds	1890 Maunds
Ramacha	1843	2082	1391	1546	1698
Vithogi	2649	2932	2591	2921	1828
Kashibai	1378	1342	954	1205	1108
Naira Desai	1935	3923	3596	3803	3665
Jooma Desai	2113	4053	2746	2747	2197
Wadaiha	988	1431	1365	1126	1171
Dadasaheb	1577	2883	2165	2219	1884
Durgabai	1632	2123	1933	1724	1516
Jayvanti Bai	1456	1692	1420	1255	1271
Total	**15571**	**22461**	**18161**	**18546**	**16338**

Price fluctuations were distinct in all the talukas and more so in the Vengurla taluka. In the Malvan taluka the stock in 1868-69 was 1,67,043 and the sale was only 71,481 Indian *maunds.* In the year 1869-70 the stock was 1,50.874 Indian *maunds,* while the sale was only 53,863 Indian *maunds.* In the Vengurla taluka the stock in the year 1868-69 was 76,275 Indian *maunds* and in the year 1869-70 it was 86,375 Indian *maunds.* The sale in Vengurla for the year 1868-69 was 71,481 Indian *maunds* and the sale for 1869-70 was 50,252 Indian *maunds.* This showed an increase of 994 Indian *maunds* in the year 1869-70.

There were several causes for the variations. Although it is difficult to give an exact cause for it, it can be conveniently said that sometimes the decrease was due to the decrease in the wadi collection in the tolls in the Ramghat road. The increase of Indian *maunds* 4,243 and *seers* 13 was partly due to the heavy fall of rain in the

Malvan taluka and partly due to the fault of the owners of the salt heaps in the Vengurla who neglected to thatch them properly. The sale of one market often affected the sale of the other. The decrease was also brought about owing to the smaller quantity of salt being removed on payment of full excise for home consumption within the Presidency while exporting it free or at a nominal amount of excise to foreign countries. The increase in salt excise in the Malvan taluka was attributable to the increase of trade in general, traders having brought larger quantities of grain and cotton from over the ghats and having taken larger quantities of salt for the return trip.[155]

Besides manufacturing salt at the salt works, the Government imported it from Belgaum, Goa and stored it for further trade. The custom duty collected on salt showed an increase in revenue. This would give revenue to the government as the salt brought would be exported to other parts of the country as well as to foreign countries. It would be used in the fish curing yards to dry the fish with the help of salt. The revenue derived from the imports from Goa and Belgaum was as follows:[156]

Table 4.32

Years	Rupees	Annas	Paise
1867-68	73,226	14	2
1868-69	73,887	8	7
1869-70	84,895	11	5
1870-71	1,25,723	9	0
1871-72	66,304	11	9
Total	4,24,035	53	23
Average	84,807	10	6
1872-73	89,926	9	7
Increase	4,818	15	1

There were a number of disputes as to the leasing out of the farms to the individuals. There were also ups and downs in the prices. Moreover, Shiroda was the only place where salt was produced. The amount of salt stored in comparison with the production of salt in the other parts of the Presidency was very little in the mammoth trade of salt of the Presidency.

The Ramacha salt work had no platform and its salt was stored on the platform of a neighbouring Government Salt Work called Vittoji Platform.[157] Moreover, traders preferred Goa salt to Shiroda as they were able to obtain the former, after it had dried. The opening of a new salt work at Shiroda since the Government Salt Works were based in 1886 had contributed to lower the prices.[158] At one time, Belgaum district obtained its main supply of salt from Shiroda but since the opening of the Southern Maratha Railway, Goa salt was available at cheaper price and reached the destination speedily by rail. This superseded the demand for Shiroda Salt.[159] All the three causes combined together to reduce the value of salt works at Shiroda.

Secondly, the trade was affected by the political fluctuations. There was an Anglo-Portuguese Treaty signed in 1885 with regard to the saltpans, which were leased out to the British. These lands were further leased out to the individuals, according to the Government Resolution No.6079 dated 27 July 1885 for a term of five years. This treaty expired on 31st December 1890. But the government was not sure whether the treaty would be renewed. Therefore, it could not lease out the lands to the individuals working the saltpans. Whatever the outcome of the treaty, it was found not very convenient to lease out the saltpans as they gave little profit as compared to the others in the Presidency.[160]

Other articles of trade

Manganese ore was discovered in Vengurla and the Malvan taluka by Messers Shaw Wallace and Co. of Bombay, to whom two exploring licenses were granted. This seemed to be a promising industry.[161] But nothing was heard about it later.

Toddy brewing and distillation was yet another important industry of the taluka. A large portion of the population eked out a living by toddy drawing. From the many licenses issued at Vengurla for the right to sell toddy in shops, the occupation must have been a good one.[162]

Although Vengurla was acquired by the British for its strategic point, it started declining by the end of nineteenth century. As early as 1885, the Collector wrote *'the trade of Vengurla is steadily declining. The receipts from octroi have declined from Rs 6,894.9.9 in 1884-85 to Rs 5,377.14.8 in 1885-86. In the year 1883-84 the octroi received was Rs 8,314.15.1'*. He further wrote that he was struck by the absence of large quantities of bales of cotton, which he used to see in the carts and warehouse in 1884 and 1885. But by 1902-03 the imports decreased to Rs. 19,83,300. The value of the exports increased to Rs. 40,24,100 and it decreased in 1902-03 to Rs 14,05,500. A comparison of the chief articles imported and exported in these years showed that the chief falling of the imports was under cloth, silk and yarn. The fall in exports was under cotton, coconut, and oil from Goa, cloth and kerosene from Bombay. The auction price of the farm of the toll bar at Vengurla on the Parpoli ghat, which once was a principal place, fell from Rs 13,000 in 1878-79 to Rs 9,610 in 1879-80 and thus reduced by Rs 3,390.

One of the most important reasons for the decrease in trade may be attributed to the negligence of the government to the repairs of the roads. It is seen from the letter given below.

'Considerable salt traffic passes over this road and it is the salt Department that is really benefited by it. It passes over six miles of sandy soil, and one pair of bullocks cannot draw a fully laden cart. Pack bullocks also experience considerable difficulty in going over this road. The salt Department ought in fairness undertake the construction of a good road along this tract...'[163]

Even the most prominent road like the Ram Ghat Road connecting Vengurla with Belgaum was not taken care of. The reporter of the Belgaum Samachar wrote a strong letter complaining of the negligence of the government in the following words. *'The road from Belgaum to Vengurla generally known by the name of Ramghat Road is in a very bad condition, owing to want of repairs. It is to be generally regretted that a road much frequented and used for the purpose of trade and commerce should be neglected. People are consequently obliged to pay double hire for carts in addition to tolls...'*[164]

Although Vengurla had a seaboard and was used for the trade purposes, yet it can be seen from the information given below that the hardly any vessels were built over here. If any vessels were constructed then they were very small in size.[165]

Table 4.33

Year	Vessels	10-100 tons	100-300 tons
1909-10 1913-14	— —	— —	— —
1914-15 1918-19	— —	— —	— —
1919-20 1923-24	— 7	1 1	— —
1924-25 1928-29	— 1	1 4	— —
1929-30 1933-34	— —	— —	— —

This small but historic region of South Konkan witnessed many ups and downs in the political field as well. When the British took it, it was a part of the Malvan Taluka called as Petha or Mahal. It was converted into a taluka owing to its importance as a trading center and a halting station for troops on the line of march to and from the Southern Maratha Country.[166]

The pay sanctioned for the Mamlatdar at that time was only Rs 10 with a permanent travelling allowance of Rs 20. In 1909 when the feasibility of reconverting it into a Mahal was considered, the then Collector admitted that Vengurla did not possess the importance as it did when it was raised from a Mahal into a Taluka, but he did not recommend its reduction to a Mahal, as substituting a Mahalkari for a *Mamlatdar* would cause no appreciable saving. Moreover, the isolated position of Vengurla required an officer of superior status at the head of its administration. The Commissioner thus approved this and the government decided in Government Resolution, Revenue Department No. 6893 dated 2nd August 1910 that Vengurla should be maintained as a taluka. When this decision was passed *Mahalkaris* were in the grades of Rs. 100 and 125.[167]

But by 1922, they were placed in the grade of Rs 150-5-200 with an average pay of Rs 183 1/2 per month. Therefore, they were better placed than they were formerly placed with a pay, which was higher than the *Mamlatdars* in the old lower grades of salaries. Therefore, the Taluka could be converted into a Mahal with a sub-treasury. This also resulted in an average monthly saving of Rs. 972/3 in pay and Rs 15 in permanent travelling allowance.

Thus, on the instructions of the government, Vengurla was once again reduced to the position of a Mahal in 1922.[168] The orders were as follows: *'In exercise of the powers conferred by section 7 of the Bombay Land Revenue Code, 1879 (Bombay V of 1879), and of all other powers enabling him in this behalf, the Governor in Council is pleased to direct that the Vengurla Taluka of the Ratnagiri District, constituted by the Government Notification in the Revenue Department No. 3958, dated 30 July 1879, shall with effect from the first day of November be converted into a Mahal to be called the Vengurla Mahal in the Malvan Taluka of the said district.'*

A number of surveys were done by the British in this region, but no extensive steps were taken to improve the existing conditions. On the contrary, with the rise of Bombay as a port of call in North Konkan, Vengurla declined in its importance.

This small but an important port town declined much before Ratnagiri or Malvan in the British Era. The evolution of the British rule in Vengurla gradually dispelled all illusions that some class of people might have had about the benevolent nature of British Policies. Though the Company because of its strategic importance acquired Vengurla, they strove little to develop it. In the first fifty years of the British rule, the pace of development of the rural economy was quite slow but there was a definite trend towards stagnation in the years to come. By the mid twentieth century, the volume of trade had almost come to standstill. The following table shows the volume of trade in the Vengurla port from 1872-73 to 1947-48.[169]

Table 4.34

Trade	1872-73	1909-10	1920-21	1930-31	1940-41	1945-46	1947-48
Inward	—	14,49,081	32,59,972	18,43,608	—	—	—
Outward	—	14,62,533	22,39,531	15,36,759	—	—	—

References

1. A.F.Maconochie, Collector of Ratnagiri, to the Commissioner, Southern Division, Ratnagiri, dated 26 September 1907, MSA, Revenue Department Vol No.30/ 1908(hereafter R.D.), p.13.
2. F.S.Chapman,Chief Secretary to Government, Bombay Castle, dated 15 March, 1869, Papers Relating to the Second Revision Settlement of Ratnagiri Taluka, BGS, New Series No.DLXXIV, Bombay, Government Central Press, 1914, p.76. (hereafter BGS)
3. L.Ashburner, Acting Revenue Commissioner, Re: Statement Showing When and by Whom the Settlement In the Southern Division was made during the year 1866-67, MSA, R.D.Vol No.3/1869, p.22.
4. *Ibid*, p.240.
5. F.S.Chapman Chief Secretary to Government, Bombay Castle, dated 15 March 1869, Papers Relating to the Second Revision Settlement of Ratnagiri Taluka, BGS, New Series No.DLXXIV, 1914, *op.cit.*, p.76.
6. J.L. Lushington, Superintendent of Land Record and Agriculture to the Collector of Ratnagiri, dated 30 March 1897, MSA, *Ibid*, p.1.
7. *Ibid*.
8. Maharashtra State Gazetteer, Ratnagiri District (Revised), Vol X, Bombay, Directorate of Government Printing, Stationery, Publications, Maharashtra State, 1962, p.1.
9. *Ibid*, p.2.
10. J.A.Madan, Assistant Settlement Officer, Ratnagiri to the Collector of Ratnagiri, MSA, Papers Relating to the Second Revision Settlement of Ratnagiri Taluka, BGS, New Series No.DLXXIV, 1914, *op.cit.*, p.1.
11. *Ibid*, p.12.
12. *Ibid*.
13. J.Francis, Survey and Settlement Commissioner through the Collector of Ratnagiri and Revenue Commissioner, Letter No.354 of 1867, Camp Khed, dated 29 April 1867, MSA, BGS, No.CCCLXXVII-New Series, 1898, *op.cit.*, p.69.
14. E.L.Chapel, Director, Land Records and Agriculture, to T.D Mackenzie, Chief Secretary to Government, Re: Report by A.T.M. Jackson, Assistant Collector Re: Analysis of Crop Experiment, dated 31 December 1892, MSA, R.D.Vol No.81/1893, pp.143-4.

15. W.Dhimbode, for Director of Agriculture to the under Secretary to the Government, MSA, Revenue Department Bombay, dated 10 August 1887, R.D. Vol No- 250/1887, p.245.
16. W.Raymonds, Assistant Director of Agriculture, to the Acting Secretary to the Government, Appendix 'A', 1MSA, R.D. Vol No.250/1887, p.256.
17. A.F.Maconochie, Collector of Ratnagiri, to the Commissioner, Southern Division, Ratnagiri, dated 26 September 1909, MSA, R.D. Vol No.30/1909, p.237.
18. Papers Relating To The Revision Survey Settlement Of The Ratnagiri Taluka Of The Ratnagiri Collectorate, BGS No.DLXXIV -New Series, Bombay, 1914, *op.cit.*, p.5.
19. The Bombay Co-operative Quarterly, December 1923, Gokhale Institute of Politics and Economics, (hereafter GIPE), pp.192-93.
20. H.H Mann & S.R. Paranjape, Department of Agriculture, Bombay, Bulletin No.89 of 1918, 'Artificial Manures, Experiments on their Value for Crops in Western India' No.II, Paranjape, Poona, Yerwada Prison Press, 1919, GIPE, pp.13-14.
21. *Ibid*
22. *Ibid*,1928, p.329.
23. Leaflet No. 4 of 1920, 'Cultivation of Onion In Konkan' Department of Agriculture, Season And Crop, Reports of the Province of Bombay, (1904-1920), Government Central Press, Bombay, 1920, Poona, GIPE, pp.l-3. (hereafter DASCR)
24. *Ibid* .
25. The Bombay Co-operative Quarterly, 'the Konkan Co-operative Enquiry Committee', Report on the Ratnagiri District, December 1923, Government Central Press, GIPE, pp.192-200.
26. The Bombay Co-operative Quarterly, June 1929, Progress of Co-operation in India-Bombay, Government Central Press, pp. 167-68.
27. C.B.Joshi, 'The Ratnagiri Taluka, Land Use and Settlements', *Bombay Geographical Magazine,* Mumbai., p.56.
28. Bulletin No. 103 of 1920, *'The Book of Mango'* by W. Burns & S. H. Prayag, DASCR, Bombay Government Central Press, 1921, GIPE, p.70.
29. *Ibid*, p.70.
30. *Ibid*, p.74.

31. *Ibid*, pp.13-16.
32. H.H. Mann, 'Fodder Crops of Western India' Bulletin No.100 of 1920, DASCR, Government Central Press, 1921, GIPE, p.1.
33. *Ibid*, pp.160-61.
34. L.B.Kulkarni, Assistant Economic Botanist, Bombay, Bulletin No. 112 of 1923, 'Improvement of Grazing Areas In Poona', DASCR, 1923, GIPE, p.5.
35. L.S.Potnis, *The Bombay Co-operative Quarterly*, 'Fishermen and Co-operation', dated 21 March 1921, Poona, fGIPE, pp.34-35.
36. G.Inverarity, Commissioner of Customs, Salt and Opium, Bombay, Office of Commissioner of Customs, Salt fand Opium, dated 15 November 1867, MSA, R.D.Vol No. 38/ 1865, p.33.
37. A.Taylor, Deputy Commissioner of Customs, Salt and Opium, Ratnagiri, Office of Assistant Commissioner of lCustoms, Salt and Opium, dated 27 October 1869, MSA, R.D. Vol No.44/1870, p.251.
38. A.F.Maconochie, Collector of Ratnagiri to the Commissioner, Southern Division, Ratnagiri, dated 26 September 1909, MSA, R.D. Vol No.23/1909, p.63.
39. Co-operative Farming in Bombay Province, Bombay, Government Central Press, 1947, GIPE, p.38.(Obtainable from the Superintendent Government Printing and Stationery, Bombay or through the High Commissioner of India House, Aldwych, London, 1947, p.33.
40. A.F. Maconochie, Collector of Ratnagiri to the Commissioner, Southern Division, Ratnagiri, dated 26 September 1909, MSA, R.D.Vol No.34/1909, p.63.
41. *Ibid*, p.40.
42. Deputy Collector, Ratnagiri Collector's Secretary office, dated 1 April 1873 to Bombay Castle, MSA, General Department Vol No.65/1873(hereafter G.D.), pp.479-80.
43. Papers Relating To The Revision Survey Settlement Of The Ratnagiri Taluka Of The Ratnagiri Collectorate,BGS, No.DLXXIV- New Series, Bombay, Government Central Press, 1914, p.38.
44. DASCR, Province of Bombay, *op.cit.*,1937-38, GIPE, p.7.
45. Papers Relating To The Revision Survey Settlement Of 131 Villages Of The Ratnagiri Taluka Of The Ratnagiri Collectorate, BGS, No.CCCLXXVII - New Series, Bombay, Government Central Press, 1914, p.3.

46. DASCR, Final Report on the Sann Hemp Research Scheme, Bombay Province Ratnagiri District, Bombay Government Central Press, 1940, GIPE, p.1.
47. A.F.Manocochie, Collector of Ratnagiri, to the Commissioner, Southern Division, Ratnagiri, dated 26 September 1907, MSA, R.D. Vol No. 30/1908, p.10.
48. Gazetteer of the Bombay Presidency, Vol No.X-B, *op.cit.*, p.10.
49. *Ibid*, p.3.
50. *Ibid.*
51. W.Hope, Officiating Secretary to the Government of India, to the Secretary to the Government of Bombay, dSimla, dated 13 August, 1882, MSA, R.D. Vol No.169/1882, p.363.
52. J.A.Madan, Assistant Settlement Officer, Ratnagiri, to the Collector of Ratnagiri, dated 11 September 1914, Papers Relating To The Revision Survey Settlement Of The Ratnagiri Taluka Of The Ratnagiri Collectorate, MSA, BGS, No.DLXXIV- New Series, Bombay, Government Central Press, 1914, pp.5-6.
53. J. Elphinstone, Collector of Ratnagiri, Memorandum Re: Ferries to the Revenue Commissioner, General Department S.D. no 3550 dated 28 September 1874, MSA, R.D. Vol No.20/1874, p.633.
54. H.Porteous, Acting Collector of Salt Revenue, Government of India, Department of Finance and Commerce to J.Monteal, Under Secretary to Government, dated 20 July 1882, MSA, R.D. Vol No.53/1882, p.304.
55. J.A.Madan, Assistant Settlement officer, Ratnagiri, to the Collector of Ratnagiri, Ratnagiri, dated 11 September 1914, Papers Relating To The Revision Survey Settlement Of The Ratnagiri Taluka Of The Ratnagiri Collectorate, MSA, BGS, No.DLXXIV- New Series, Bombay, Government Central Press, 1914, pp.5-6.
56. W.A.Marriet, Lieut. Colonel, Secretary to Government to Marine Department, Bombay Castle, dated 3 April 1864, MSA, R.D. Vol No.121/1862 & 64, p.278.
57. D.J.Kennelly, Assistant Dock Master, to Capt J.W.Young, Superintendent of Marine, Bombay, dated 9 April 1864, MSA, *Ibid*, pp.232-3.
58. Trade and Navigation Reports of Bombay Presidency for the Respective Years, The Statistics for the period 1909-10 to 1936-37 were taken from the Department of Commercial Intelligence and Statistics, Government of India., p.88.

59. *Ibid*, pp.29-30.
60. K.B.Vaidya, Shipping Agent to the Bombay Steam Navigation Company Ltd, "Ratnagiri, Kaybee'secretary Indian Shipping Annual Reports", Ports No. 1950, Bombay, 1951, pp.117-18.
61. *Ibid*.
62. *Ibid*, (A Sailing Vessel is one carrying sufficient area of sail to provide adequate means of propulsion and engaged in coastal trade of India or with adjacent countries whether equipped or auxiliary engine or not.)
63. *Ibid*, p.15.
64. Trade and Navigation Reports of the Bombay Presidency for the respective years, (The Statistics for the period 1909-10 to 1936-37 was taken from the Department of Commercial Intelligence and Statistics, Government of India, the Statistics relating to the Sea Borne and Air Borne Trade in India for the respective years).
65. *Ibid*, p.10.
66. Arthur Crawford, Collector of Ratnagiri, Ratnagiri Collector's Office, to the Secretary, Revenue Department, Bombay, dated 29 July 1878, MSA, R.D.Vol No.16/1878, p.31.
67. W.G.Harrison, Acting Superintendent, to T.H.Stewart, Survey & Settlement Commissioner, Koorun, dated 23 January 1882, MSA, R.D.Vol No.28/1882, p.8.
68. Jagan Mitra, REPORT ON THE NATIVE PAPERS For the Week ending with Jan-Dec 1871, New Secretariat Office, Bombay, dated 30 October 1871, p.14 .
69. Department of Commercial Intelligence and Statistics, Government of India, Trade and Navigation Reports of the lBombay Presidency for the years 1872-73 to 1826-27; Department of Commercial Intelligence and Statistics, lGovernment of India, Statement relating to the Sea and Air Borne Trade in India, Bombay Ports Committee, lGovernment of Bombay, Bombay, 1939, p.99.
70. Papers Relating To The Revision Survey Settlement Of Malwan Taluka Of The Ratnagiri Collectorate, BGS, No.DXXVIII -New Series, Bombay, the Government Central Press, 1915, p.1.
71. *Ibid*, p.1.
72. A.K.Nairne.,*History of Konkan*, Asian Educational Services, New Delhi, 1988, p.130.
73. *Ibid*.

74. H.M.Grant, Acting Superintendent, Revenue Survey and Assessment to Lieut.Colonet.J.T. Francis, Survey and Settlement Commissioner, Konchulee,dated 20 December1869, MSA, R.D. Vol No.38/1870, p.340.
75. J.Gibson, Deputy Superintendent to the Collector of Ratnagiri, Akeri, dated 12 April 1888,Papers Relating To The Original Survey Settlement Of The Malvan Taluka Of The Ratnagiri Collectorate, MSA, BGS, No. CCLXXII-New Series, Malvan Taluka of Ratnagiri Collectorate, Government Central Press, 1893, p.1.
76. W.Doderet, Assistant Collector and Magistrate, Ratnagiri to R.E.Candy, Collector and District Magistrate, of Ratnagiri, dated 15 July 1885, MSA, R.D. Vol No.29/1885, p.425.
77. A.W.G. Chuckerbutty, Assistant Collector to the Collector of Ratnagiri, dated 31 July 1895, MSA, R.D. Vol No.34/ 1896, p.360.
78. J.K.Kabraji, Acting Collector, Ratnagiri to the Commissioner Southern Division, Ratnagiri, dated 1 October 1904, MSA, R.D.Vol No. 26/1905, p.173.
79. Sumit Guha, *The Agrarian Economy of the Bombay Deccan 1818-1914,* New Delhi, Oxford University Press, Bombay, 1985, p.52.
80. Census of the Bombay Presidency, 1872, General Report and Tables of the Population, Houses in the Bombay Presidency, part II, Bombay, Government Central press, 1875, p.12.
81. Papers Relating To The Original Survey Settlement Of The Malvan Taluka Of The Ratnagiri Collectorate, MSA, BGS, No. CCLXXII-New Series, Malvan Taluka of Ratnagiri Collectorate, Government Central Press, p.38&6; Census Report of 1881,1891,1901,1911;also J.Muie Mackenzie, Assistant Collector and Magistrate, Ratnagiri, dated 17 July 1880, R.D. Vol No.20/188, p.225.
82. I.Nugent, Notification, R.D., Bombay Castle, dated 21 January 1884, MSA, R.D. Vol No.280/1884, p.33.
83. J.Gibson Survey and Settlement Commissioner, To the Collector of Ratnagiri and Revenue Commissioner, lLetter No.354 of 1867, Camp Khed, dated 29 April 1867 Papers Relating To The Original Survey Settlement lOf The Malvan Taluka Of The Ratnagiri Collectorate, MSA, BGS, No. CCLXXII-New Series, Bombay, lGovernment Central Press, 1893, p.2.

84. Papers Relating To The Revision Survey Settlement Of Malwan Taluka Of The Ratnagiri Collectorate, MSA, BGS, No.DXXVIII -New Series Bombay, Government Central Press, 1915, p.6.
85. A.R.Bonus, Collector of the Ratnagiri to the Settlement Commissioner and Director of Land Records, Poona, Camp Devrukh, dated 10 April 1913, SA, R.D. Compilation No. 903 of 1913, p.530.
86. Collector of the Ratnagiri to the Secretary, Revenue Department, Bombay, dated 29 July 1878, MSA, R.D.Vol No.16/1878, p.31.
87. Papers Relating to the Original Survey Settlement of Malvan Taluka of the Ratnagiri Collectorate, MSA, BGS, No.CCLXXII -New Series Bombay, Government Central Press, 1893, p.8.
88. Collector of the Ratnagiri to the Secretary, Revenue Department, Bombay , dated 29 July 1878, MSA, R.D.Vol No.16/1878, p.24.
89. Papers Relating To The Original Survey Settlement Of Malwan Taluka Of The Ratnagiri Collectorate, MSA, IBGS, No.CCLXXII -New Series Bombay, Government Central Press, 1893, p.8.
90. *Ibid*, p.223.
91. *Ibid*, pp.8 and 16.
92. *Ibid*.
93. The Bombay Co-operative Quarterly, December 1923, Government Central Press, Bombay, GIPE, p.208.
94. *Ibid*.
95. Papers Relating To The Revision Survey Settlement Of Malwan Taluka Of The Ratnagiri Collectorate, Appendix 'C' BGS, No.DXXVIII -New Series, Bombay, Government Central Press, 1915, p.22.
96. Bombay Revenue Proceedings, (hereafter BRP) India office Record, Lands,Vol No.6944 of 1904, p.534.
97. Returns of the Yield per acre of the Principal Crops, 1892 p.17; also BRP, India Office Records, Lands, Vol No.6944 of 1896-97, p.5.
98. A.W.Heston, 'Official Yields Per Acres In India, 1886 -1947', *Indian Economic and Social History Review* (hereafter *IESHR),* Vol No.X ,No-4,1973, p.304.
99. Papers Relating To The Revision Survey Settlement Of Malwan Taluka Of The Ratnagiri Collectorate, BGS, No.DXXVIII -New Series, Bombay, Government Central Press, 1915, p.8.

100. Papers Relating To The Revision Survey Settlement Of Malwan Taluka Of The Ratnagiri Collectorate, BGS, No.DXXVIII -New Series, Bombay, Government Central Press, 1915, p.5.
101. Report, MSA, Bombay Ports Committee, Government of Bombay, Bombay 1873, p.987.
102. W.L. Harvey, Under Secretary to Government, Memorandum-Land-Acquisition Under Act I of 1894, Bombay Castle, Revenue Department, dated 14 August 1894, MSA, R.D. Vol No.244/1894, p.217.
103. *Ibid.*
104. G.W. Vidal, Acting Chief Secretary to Government, Declaration as per the Act I of 189, MSA, Revenue Department, Bombay Castle, dated 14 August 1894, R.D. Vol No.244/1894, p.219.
105. A.R. Kulkarni, *Medieval Maratha Country,* Books and Books Publication, New Delhi, 1996, p.208.
106. The Bombay Co-operative Quarterly, *op.cit.*, GIPE, p.204.
107. Papers Relating To The Revision Survey Settlement Of Malwan Taluka Of The Ratnagiri Collectorate, BGS, No.DXXVIII -New Series Bombay, Government Central Press, 1915, p.4.
108. The Bombay Co-operative Quarterly, *op.cit.*, GIPE, p.215.
109. G.Inverarity, Commissioner of Customs, Salt and Opium, Bombay office of Commerce of Customs, Salt and Opium, Re: Annual Statement of Salt for Local Produce in Store in 1863-64, sold & imported, dated 15 November 1864, MSA, R.D. Vol No.38/1865, p.63.
110. W.H.Pelly 1st Assistant Commissioner of Customs, Salt and Opium to W.H. Payne, Deputy Commissioner of Customs, Salt and Opium, Ratnagiri office of Assistant Commissioner of Customs dated 22 October 1864, Re: Revenue Realization of Salt Department Ending 30 April 1864, MSA, R.D. Vol No38/1865, p.100.
111. W.H Payne, Deputy Commissioner of Customs, Salt and Opium to George Inverarity, Commissioner of Customs, Salt and Opium, Thane, Deputy Commissioner office, dated 20 October 1864, Re:Revenue realization of Salt Department ending 30 April 1864, MSA, R.D. Vol No.38/ 1865, p.227.
112. G.B.Spring, Assistant Commissioner of Custom, Salt and Opium Ratnagiri Range, to A.Taylor, Deputy l llCommissioner, Southern Division, Ratnagiri, dated 12 July 1873, MSA, R.D. Vol No.109/1874, p.98.

113. J.K.N. Kabraji, Acting collector, Ratnagiri, to the Commissioner, Southern Division, Ratnagiri 1904, MSA, lR.D.Vol No.26/1905, p.177.
114. Papers Relating To The Revision Survey Settlement Of The Malvan Taluka Of The Ratnagiri Collectorate, lMSA,BGS, No.DXXVIII -New Series, Bombay, Government Central Press, 1915, p.5.
115. J.H.Garett, Assistant Collector to the Collector of Ratnagiri, dated 15 August 1907, MSA, R.D. Vol No. 30/ 1908, p.137.
116. *Ibid.*
117. R.D.Choksey, *Economic Life in the Bombay Konkan(1818-1939)*, Asia Publishing House, Bombay,1960, p.197.
118. J.H.Gerett, Assistant Commissioner to the Commissioner, Ratnagiri, dated 15 August 1907, MSA, R.D. Vol No. 30/1908, p.137.
119. Report on the Administration of the Bombay Presidency for the years 1920-21, Government Central Press, 1922, p.78.
120. D.G. Dhabbu, *Kulabkar Anger Sarkhel*(Marathi), Bombay 1939, p.416.
121. B.G.Paranjape, *English Records on Shivaji,* Poona, Shivaji tercentenary Memorial Series,Vol No. II &VI,1931,Letter No.10.
122. Trade and Navigation Reports of the Bombay Presidency for the respective years; also P.V.Kulkarni, 'Industrial Development of Konkan', unpublished thesis,1961,Bombay University, p.981.
123. Papers Relating To The Revision Survey Settlement Of Malwan Taluka Of The Ratnagiri Collectorate, BGS, No.DXXVIII -New Series, Bombay, Government Central Press, 1915, p.35.
124. Department of Commercial Intelligence and Statistics, Government of India, Trade and Navigation Reports of Bombay Presidency for the year 1909-1937; Department of Commercial Intelligence and Statistics, Government of India, Statement Relating to the Sea Borne and Air Borne Trade of India, Bombay Ports Committee, Government of Bombay, Bombay, 1939.
125. Papers Relating To The Revision Survey Settlement Of Vengurla Taluka Of The Ratnagiri Collectorate, BGS, No.CCCCXLII-New Series, Bombay, Government Central Press, 1906, p.1.
126. Peter Mundy, The Travels of Peter Mundy, Vol II, Nedein/ Ziechtenstein, 1967, p.47.

127. Teotonio R De Souza, *Medieval Goa, A Socio-Economic History*, Concept Pub. House, New Delhi, 1979,lp.33.
128. A.R.Kulkarni, *op.cit.*,p.204.
129. V.Marathe, *Ratnagiri Jillahyatil Vengurla Mahal Va Parisar*, Vengurla Mitra Mandal, Mumbai,1961, pp.12-13.
130. Bombay Gazetteer, *op.cit.*, p.198.
131. Papers Relating To The Revision Survey Settlement Of Vengurla Taluka Of The Ratnagiri Collectorate, BGS, No. CCCCXLII -New Series, Bombay, Government Central Press, 1906, p.30.
132. J.Gibson, Superintendent, Ratnagiri Survey to the Collector of Ratnagiri, Dapoli, dated 21 October 1874, MSA, R.D. No. 115/1875, pp.237-8.
133. Papers Relating To The Revision Survey Settlement Of Vengurla Taluka Of The Ratnagiri Collectorate, MSA, BGS, No.CCCCXLII -New Series, Bombay, Government Central Press, 1906, p.6.
134. J.Muir Mackenzie, Assistant Collector and Magistrate, Ratnagiri to Government, Wilson, Collector and District Magistrate, Ratnagiri, dated 17 July 1880, R.D.Vol No. 20/ 1880, p.227.
135. A.Cumine, 2nd Assistant Collector and Magistrate to the Collector of Ratnagiri, dated 14 July 1882, MSA, R.D.Vol No.21/1882, p.188.
136. R.E.Candy, Collector of Ratnagiri, Ratnagiri, to the Secretary to Government, Bombay, dated 9 August 1886, MSA, R.D. Vol No.23/1887, p.29.
137. J.K.N.Kabraji, Acting Collector of Ratnagiri, to the Commissioner, Southern Division, dated 10 October 1904, lMSA,R.D. Vol No.26/1905, p.230.
138. J.Gibson, Superintendent, Ratnagiri Survey to the Collector of Ratnagiri, Dapoli, dated 21 October 1874, MSA, R.D. No. 115/1875, p.250.
139. Census of India 1872,1881,1891,1901,1911; A.Cumine 2nd Assistant Collector and Magistrate, First Class to the Collector District Magistrate, Ratnagiri dated 14 July 1882, R.D. Vol No. 21/1882, p.177; R.E.Candy, Collector of Ratnagiri to the Secretary to Government, dated 9 Aug 1886,MSA, R.D. Vol No. 29/1885, p.425.
140. Papers Relating To The Revision Survey Settlement Of Vengurla Taluka Of The Ratnagiri Collectorate, BGS, No.CCCCXLII -New Series, Bombay, Government Central Press, 1906, p.30.

141. W.Woodward, 1st Assistant Collector and Magistrate, First Class, Ratnagiri, dated 17 July1878, MSA, R.D. Vol No.16/1878, p 31.
142. Papers Relating To The Revision Survey Settlement Of Vengurla Taluka Of The Ratnagiri Collectorate, BGS, No.CCCCXLII -New Series, Bombay, Government Central Press, 1906; p.1.
143. W.Woodward, 1st Assistant Collector and Magistrate, First Class, Ratnagiri, dated 17 July 1878, MSA, R.D. Vol No.16/1878, p.33.
144. Papers Relating To The Revision Survey Settlement Of Vengurla Taluka Of The Ratnagiri Collectorate, BGS, No.CCCCXLII -New Series, Bombay, Government Central Press, 1906, p.3.
145. The Bombay Co-operative Quarterly, The Konkan Co-operative Enquiry Committee, December 1923, *op.cit.*, IGIPE, pp.192-200.
146. Anant Vasudev Marathe, *Vengurla Mahal Va Parisar*, Vengurla Mitra Mandal, Mumbai, 1961, p.30.
147. Papers Relating To The Revision Survey Settlement Of Vengurla Taluka Of The Ratnagiri Collectorate, BGS, lNo.CCCCXLII -New Series, Bombay, Government Central Press, 1906, p.5.
148. R.E. Candy, Collector of Ratnagiri to the Secretary to Government, Bombay, dated 9 August, MSA, R.D. Vol llNo. 23/1887, p. 37.
149. W.Woodward, Assistant Collector to the Secretary to Government, Revenue Department, Bombay, dated 21 ll July 1875, MSA, R.D. Vol No. 7/1875, p.259.
150. *Ibid.*
151. A.J.Crawford, Collector and Magistrate, Ratnagiri to R.B.Worthington, dated 17 July 1878, MSA, R.D. Vol No. 16/1878, p.144.
152. R.E.Candy, Collector of Ratnagiri to the Secretary to Government, Bombay, dated 9 August, MSA, R.D. Vol No.23/1887, p.43.
153. G. Inverarity, Commissioner of Customs, Salt and Opium, Bombay office of Commissioner of Customs, Salt and Opium, dated 15 November 1864-A Statement, MSA, R.D.Vol No. 38/1865, p.33.
154. J.H.Dickinson, Assistant Collector of Ratnagiri Range, to I.M. Potgrane, Deputy Collector of Ratnagiri, dated 9 September 1891, MSA, R.D.Vol No. 193/1891, p.165.
155. G.B. Spring, Assistant Commissioner of Customs, Salt

and Opium, Vengurla Range to A. Taylor, Deputy Commissioner of Customs, Salt and Opium, Ratnagiri, Office of Assistant Commissioner of Customs, Salt and Opium, dated 27 October 1869, MSA, R.D. Vol No. 44/1870, pp. 250-1 and 227.

156. G.B.Spring, Assistant Commissioner of Customs, Salt and Opium, Ratnagiri Range to A.Taylor, Deputy Commissioner of Customs, Salt and Opium, Southern Division, Ratnagiri Commissioners office, dated 12 July 1873, MSA, R.D. Vol No. 109/1874, p.79.

157. E.P.Clare, Assistant Collector of Salt Revenue, Ratnagiri Range to J.M.Potgrane, Deputy Collector of Salt Revenue, dated 2 July 1890, MSA, R.D.Vol No. 203/1890, p.259.

158. *Ibid*, p.261.

159. *Ibid*, p.260.

160. Chief Secretary to Government, Memorandum From the Commissioner of Customs, Salt and Opium, Re:Salt Works in Shiroda of the Ratnagiri Taluka of the Ratnagiri Collectorate-Leasing of, Bombay Castle, dated 4 September 1890, MSA, R.D. Vol No.203/1890, p.255. also R.D. Vol No.193/1891, p.161.

161. A.F.Maconochie, Collector of Ratnagiri to the Commissioner, Southern Division, Ratnagiri, dated 26 September 1907, MSA, R.D. Vol No.30/7/1908, p.11.

162. Administrative Report for the year 1898-99, MSA, R.D. Vol No. 24/1900, pp.53-89.

163. J.Elphinstone, Collector to the Survey Settlement officer, Ratnagiri Collectors office, dated 15 January 1875, MSA, R.D. Vol No. No. 105 of 1875, p.39.

164. Dnyanodaya, Report on the Native Papers, 1891, Jan to Dec For the Week ending 16 September 1891, Bombay Education Society's Press, Byculla, Bombay, p.6.

165. Trade and Navigation Reports of the Bombay Presidency For the Respective Years Also, P.V.Kulkarni, *op.cit.*, p.981.

166. S.D.Mankar, Under Secretary to Government to the Commissioner Re:Vengurla Taluka-Conversion into Taluka, by the Government Resolution, R.D. No. 3958, dated 30 July 1879, MSA, R.D. File no - 4968-B/'A' Class, 1921, p.76.

167. *Ibid.*

168. A.R. Dalal, Deputy Secretary to Government to the Commissioner, Re:Conversion of Vengurla Taluka into Mahal, R.D. No.4968, dated 21 June 1922, MSA, R.D. File no 4968-B/'A' class, 1922, p.20.

169. Department of Commercial Intelligence and Statistics, Government of India, Trade and Navigation Reports of the Bombay Presidency for the years 1872-73 to 1826-27; Department of Commercial Intelligence and Statistics, Government of India, Statement relating to the Sea and Air Borne Trade in India, Bombay Ports Committee, Government of Bombay, Bombay, 1939, p.99.

CHAPTER 5

MIGRATION, REMITTANCES AND THEIR EFFECTS ON THE RATNAGIRI COLLECTORATE [1818-1920]

Migration is a phenomenon caused by a variety of factors, like the pull of the city life and the push from rural areas. It leads to the exodus of migrants from the rural areas to the urban areas. The push factors are very often operative in cityward migration.[1] Migration also has consequences often having a lasting impact on the economy and society from the place where migration occurs. Migration in general is any movement of people from one permanent residence to another or less permanent residence for a significant period of time. In the most general sense, 'migration is ordinarily defined as a relatively permanent movement of persons over a significant distance.'[2] In this sense migration means change of residence. The impact of British rule resulted in a type of mass migration springing up with the phase of industrialisation. The most dominant pattern of migration witnessed in the period of industrialisation was migration from the rural to urban areas. This type of modern migration under Colonial rule was characterised by the growth of urbanisation on the one hand and labour migration with a seasonal nature on the other hand.

At this juncture, it is imperative to differentiate labour migration from the general idea of migration. 'Workers who move about systematically, seeking and engaging in seasonal and temporary employment without becoming residents of the areas in which they work, are called migrant labourers'[3] Physical strength and lowering of oneself to earn a living is called for in the case of migrant labourers. As a result, Migrant labour is often called as 'Stoop Labour'. They stoop not to conquer but to be exploited.[4]

Immigration into Konkan

During the early centuries from 1st to 17th, the concept of migrant labour was almost absent and if it existed it was negligent. But migration and inter-action with other communities was not a new concept to Ratnagiri Collectorate. An important feature is that both immigration and emigration took place in Konkan because of commercial activities. Many people came and either settled here for trade purposes or visited the ports often. A witness to this fact is the epigraphic reference of 1008 A.D of Silaharas. It gives information about the ships from Cemulya or Chaul coming to Balipattana, a port in South Konkan. There was a convergence of vessels and confluence of people from different parts on the coast. The port of Balipattana is identified as Kharepatanam in the Ratnagiri district.[5] The trend witnessed in this period continued over centuries. These trading activities though not synonymous with migration did indirectly promote both movement of people to and from South Konkan.

The leading South Konkan ports like Ratnagiri, Malvan, Rajapur, Vengurla and others were connected to the Deccan through the mountain passes which acted as east-west access roads to the main routes. A road network served as the north-south arterial route connecting major towns such as Nasik, Poona, Satara and Kolhapur. A number of traders engaged themselves in carrying grain and other commodities along the coasts.

The trading community of Ratnagiri comprised of classes like the Vanis, Jains, Lingayats, Gujars, Bhatiyas, Marwadis along with the local communities like the Brahmins, Prabhus, Saraswats and others. The above-mentioned trading communities were not original inhabitants of the region but were encouraged by their ancestors to settle in the South Konkan because of the better commercial prospects.[6]

A General Study of the Population Statistics of Ratnagiri Collectorate

To understand the out migration areas of Ratnagiri Collectorate as an impact of the British rule, the Data used are Census Reports, Gazetteers published by Colonial rulers, and birth and death reports. It is difficult to get a correct picture of the outflow in the first few decades of the British rule in Konkan. However the latter part of the nineteenth century helps in furnishing the figures regarding population in the Ratnagiri Collectorate.

Immediately after the conquest of the Konkan, there were several attempts to estimate the population of the newly acquired territory, perhaps the best of it was made by W.H. Sykes as early as 1826. A census of 1846 was also undertaken. However the censuses of 1846 followed by 1851 were mainly conducted by village accountants. The Revolt of 1857 resulted in the postponement of scheduled Census. No estimates seem to have taken till 1872. It was in this year that a specially formed and supervised agency was appointed whose estimates are considered more accurate than the earlier estimates.[7] The Konkan division was divided into five districts one among them being the city of Bombay. They were Kanara, Ratnagiri, Kolaba, Thana and Bombay city. Kanara being the largest of the towns shows maximum density of population. The area of Kanara was 4,235 square miles with a density of 94.04 per square mile. Ratnagiri had the largest number per square mile and it was 268.97 in an area of 3,789 square miles. Tanna (Thana) had 4,052 square miles area while its density was 209.14 square miles. Thana took the second place while Kolaba was the least. The area of Kolaba was 1,482 square miles and its density was 236.44 per square mile. The city of Bombay was one ninth of the Presidency area with an area of 18.64 square miles while its density was 34,571per square mile.[8]

Table 5.1

Districts	Area in Sq.miles	Density per Sq.mile	Percentage on total area of division
Kanara	4,235	94.04	31.19
Ratnagiri	3,789	268.97	27.90
Kolaba	1,482	236.44	10.92
Bombay City	18.64	34,571,01	.14
Tanna	4,052	209.14	29.85

Urban and Rural population

Ratnagiri Collectorate had more number of villages than towns. The number of towns decreased from 1872 to 1921 as seen from the following figure. At the same time it is seen that the total area of the Ratnagiri District had increased from 3,789 square miles to 3,989 square miles by the year 1901-02. It had about 7,744 villages in all between 1872 and 1921 and during the same period the number of towns were 37. The number of towns decreased from 1901-1921. It is seen in the figure given below. There was a steady decrease in the number of villages also.[9]

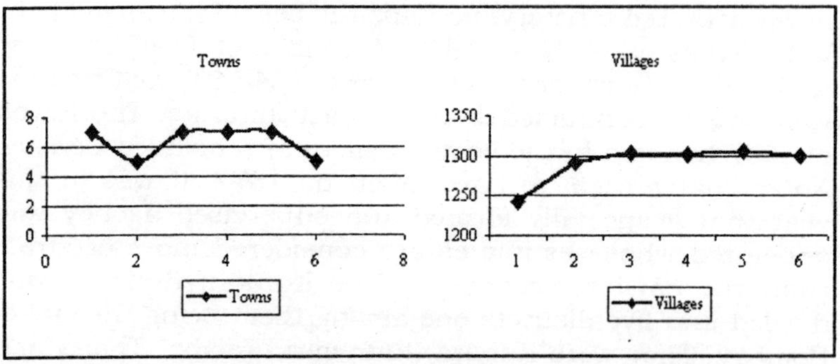

Fig. 5.1

In 1901 Ratnagiri had 2,65,776 acres in square miles but had only one town and 1,447 villages. Malvan covered an area of 1,52,258 acres in square miles but had one town and 58 villages. Vengurla had 41, 451 acres in square miles and had 1 town and 9 villages.[10] The villages at large showed an unstable trend from one decade to another. The proportion of urban to rural population was quite low and lay between 1:13 and 1:15 during the sixty years from 1872 to 1921.

The majority of the population lived in the rural areas. It was quite low as compared to the urban rural ratio of Thana district, which was 1:4 and 1:9 during the same period. The urban population of Ratnagiri district showed a steady number. The rural population on the other hand increased although the number was nominal. Lack of commercial activities in rural areas, on the one hand and a rapid pace of industrialisation in the urban areas created a smooth passage for urbanisation in the Konkan.

The Rural and Urban Population in Thousands

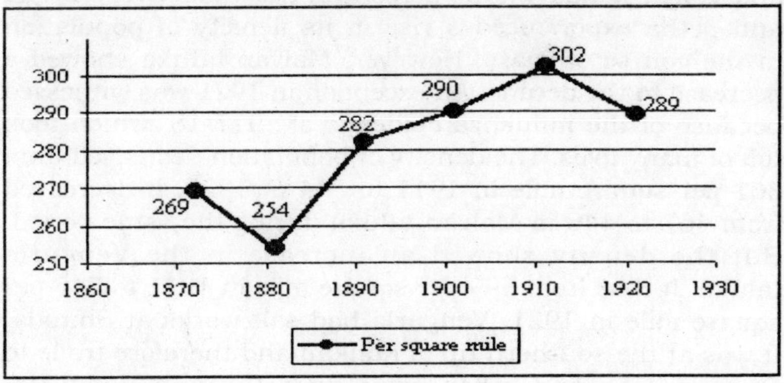

Fig. 5.2

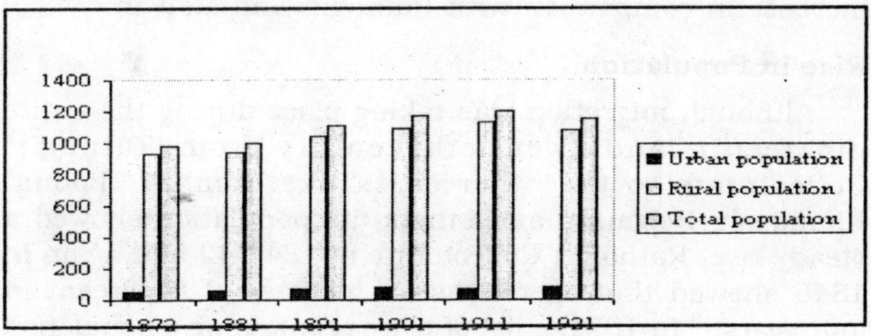

Fig. 5.3

Density of Population

Along with the rise in population, the density of population in Ratnagiri Collectorate had been on the increase in all decades with the exception of 1821. Every petha or taluka experienced a rise in the density of population in the early 20th century. The density of population of the Ratnagiri taluka in 1911 was 361 and increased to 344 in 1921. The density in Malvan was 467 in 1911 but decreased to 446 in 1921. Vengurla had a density of 699 per square mile and it showed a steep increase in 1921 to 745.[11] An overall increase in the density of the Ratnagiri Collectorate is observed from the following figure.

The three towns in the Ratnagiri district had a population ranging from 10,000 to 15,000 in 1872. The population of Ratnagiri was 10,614. At Malvan it was 13,955 and Vengurla had 14,966 persons at this time. Every taluka and petha experienced a rise in its density of population in the course of years. However, Malvan taluka showed a decrease in the decade. An exception in 1921 was witnessed because of the influenza epidemic of 1917-18, which took toll of many lives. The density of population decreased from 361 per square mile in 1911 to 344 in 1921. It decreased from 467 to 446 in Malvan taluka during the same period. But the density showed an increase in the Vengurla taluka. It rose from 699 per square mile in 1911 to 745 per square mile in 1921. Vengurla had salt works at Shiroda. It was at the southern tip of Konkan and therefore trade to Deccan, Goa and other parts pass through Vengurla. Therefore density of population at Vengurla showed higher increase in comparison with Ratnagiri and Malvan.

Rise in Population

Although migration was taking place during the entire nineteenth and twentieth century from Ratnagiri Collectorate to the other cities like Bombay, Poona, Khandesh, Belgaum, and others, its population showed a steady rise. Ratnagiri Collectorate in 1841-42 and again in 1846 showed that there was an increase of 8 percent in four years.[12] In 1874, a list of places containing a population of more than 3000 persons in the Ratnagiri Collectorate was given. It was as follows:[13]

Table 5.2

Names of Places	Population
Mouje Malvan	13,955
Kusba Massure	7,308
Mauje Kundalgaon	3,401
Mouje Pednur	4,487
Mauje Talgao	3,081
Kusba Achre	4,507
Mouje Chinder	3,183
Mauje Parooli	4,253
Bunder Vengurla	14,996
Mouje Shiravde	3,056

[contd...]

Table 5.2 *[contd...]*

Names of Places	Population
Kasba Rajapur	5,368
Mauje Sagwe	3,054
Kusba Neore	3,336
Ratnagiri	10,614
Kusba Sangameshwar	3,172
Kasbe Chiploon	6,071
Mauje Gowal	3,439
Kasba Gohaghar	3,445
Kasba Khed	3,817
Kasba Dabhol	3,980
Mouje Harnai	6,193
Mauje Weshwee	3,346
Kasba Velas	3,767
Kasba Kelshi	3,291

A letter dated 28 August 1874 with the number 2,755 person was forwarded by the Collector of Ratnagiri recommending that the towns of Malvan, Vengurla, Rajapur, Ratnagiri and Chiplun be constituted into Municipal districts as these areas had a population of more than 3000 persons. His proposal was approved by the government on 16 September 1874.[14]

The above table shows that the most populated areas in the Ratnagiri Collectorate were Ratnagiri, Malvan and Vengurla. Ratnagiri had a population of 10,614, Malvan had 13,995 and Vengurla had 14,996 in 1874. Amongst the three regions, Vengurla had the least area but had the highest population. The total area of the Vengurla petha itself was 65.86 square miles which was less than Malvan taluka, which had an area of 238 square miles, and Ratnagiri taluka with an area of 413 square miles. This is indicative of Vengurla's importance as a trading center.

By the year 1901, the population of the district had gone upto 11,67,927. Between 1901 and 1911 the population increased to 12,03,638 or by 2.53 %. But in the year 1918, the influenza epidemic took toll of many lives and the population decreased temporarily by about 4.24 %. It however shot up in 1821 to 11,54,244 or decreased by 49,394 persons. However, in 1931 the population showed an increase to 15,34,540, which were more than 12. 68 %. The cause for this sudden increase was probably due to the closing of many mills in Bombay as a result of the Economic Depression.[15]

The following figure shows comparative statistics of the rising population in the Konkan from 1842 to 1921.

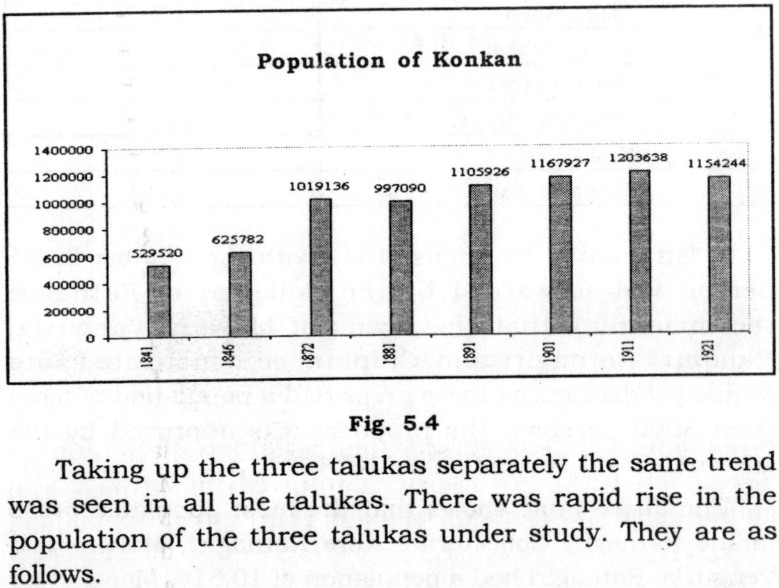

Fig. 5.4

Taking up the three talukas separately the same trend was seen in all the talukas. There was rapid rise in the population of the three talukas under study. They are as follows.

Ratnagiri Taluka

The earliest Census record of the Ratnagiri taluka produced was in 1824 and the population was stated to be 72,967.[16] At the Original Revenue Settlement in 1866, the population was 86,424. The general Census of 1891 showed that the total population was 1,26,330. This showed an increase of 40,000 persons or 46% of increase during the three decades. The density of population which was 242 rose to 354 per square mile. 63% of the population was dependent on agriculture, of which 26.5% were the owners of the lands while 33% were the co-tenants or co-sharers of the lands that belonged to someone else. The remaining population consisted of farm servants, field labourers and crop watchers. About 37% of the population was non-agricultural. 86% of the population were Hindus, 13% Muslims and 10% hardly made up of other sects.[17] The Census of 1911 showed that there were 17,637 Bhandaris, 12,029 Brahmins, 50,735 Kunbis, 10,057 Mahars, 12,979 Marathas, 3,834 Teli s, and 23,997 others.[18]

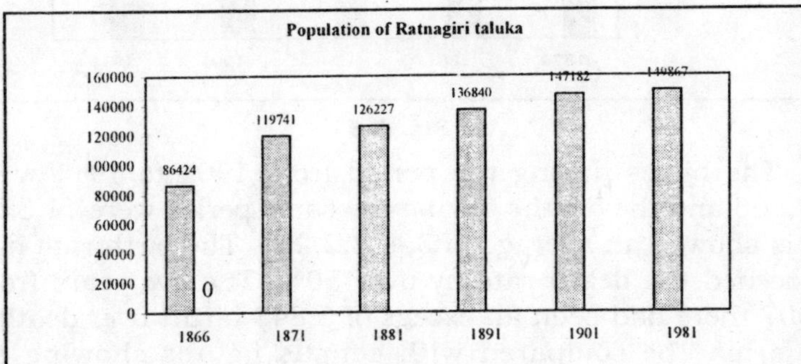

Figure 5.5

Malvan taluka

The first record of the Census taken in the Malvan taluka including Vengurla that was a part Malvan taluka was in 1813. If any Census was taken before this it has not been available. The total population of the taluka was about 4,486.[19] A comparatively reliable record of Malvan taluka was received according to the Census of 1872 and the population was 88,185. Of this number 3,50,784 depended on agriculture 7,547 partly on agriculture and partly other activities, 45,564 totally on non-agricultural activities. The total area of the taluka was 238 square miles and the arable inland was 163.10 square miles. The total number of inhabitants per square mile of the total area was 373.67 and the density of population per square mile was 540.64. The number of persons in each house was 6.26. The number considerably exceeded the average for the Ratnagiri Collectorate, generally, which was 4.53.[20]

The figures supplied by the Provincial Superintendent of the Census operations showed a steady increase in the population in the Malvan taluka throughout the settlement period.

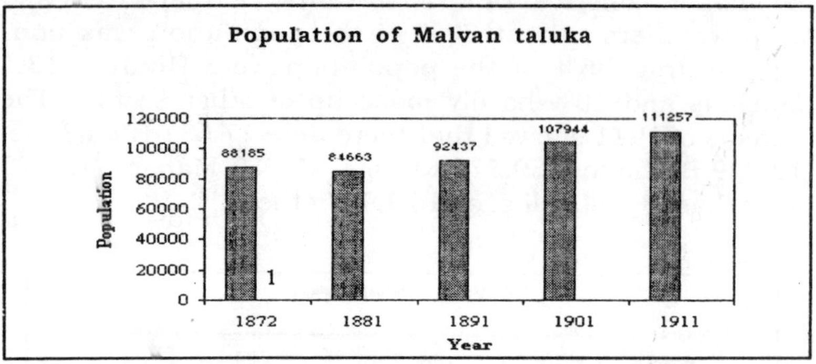

Fig. 5.6

The births during the period from 1901 to 1911 were 17,165 and the deaths during the same period were 11,323. This showed an average of 3,433:2,264. The birth rate had exceeded the death rate by over 50%. The five years from 1907 there had been an excess of 5,843 births over deaths. This may be compared with census figures showing an increase in population of only 3,313 from 1901 to 1911. An explanation to this discrepancy may be sought in the fact that there was the plague epidemic in Malvan in 1901. It drove the people to their home towns. It could also be due to the annual migration to Bombay in search of work.[21] Malvan taluka had a population comprising of various castes and communities. The total number of persons belonging to Hindu and Jain religion according to the Census of 1911 was 1,08,494, Muslim religion was 1,791 Christian religion was 1,962 and others it was 10%.[22]

Vengurla taluka

The earliest Census taken in Vengurla was in 1835. It was a Petha at that time and its population was reported to be about 23,491. The total area of the taluka including Vengurla was 65.86 Square miles and the cultivated area was 43.94 square miles. The returns of the Petha were much inflated by the large number of persons engaged in trade in the town of Vengurla, who properly speaking did not belong to the district, as they resided there only during trading seasons. It was impossible to estimate the number exactly. But assuming it to be 5000 (one third of the population) the reminder still gave a large average of 684 per square mile for the rest of the district. If any Census was taken in 1818-19 no record has been found. However from the Census taken in 1835, it appeared that the population of the Petha was 23,491. The increase was 11,597, or 49.36%. The increase chiefly owed to the rise in the trade of Vengurla. Showing the rise in the number of inhabitants from 9,800 in the year 1835 to 15,000 in the year 1872.

In 1872, the population of the petha was 2,35,088 or 532 persons to the square mile. The Census of 1901 proved that it restored to 44,863 or 679 persons per square mile. During the thirty years of the settlement from 1875-76 the population increased by nearly 28%. In the same period, the population of Vengurla (including the suburbs outside municipal limits) increased from 14,996 to 19,018 i.e. by nearly 27%.

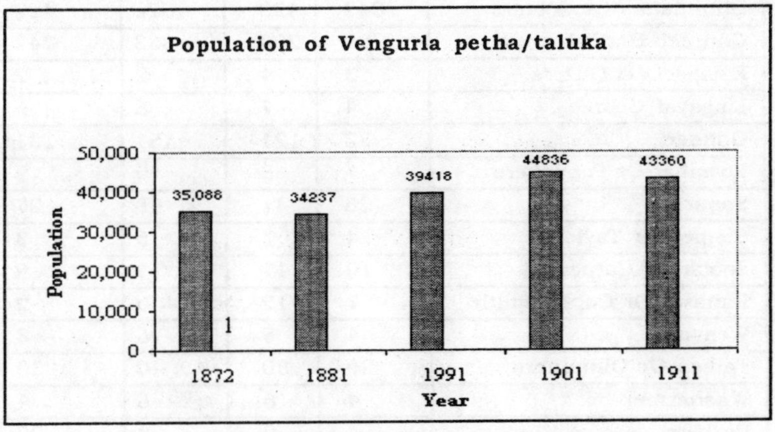

Fig. 5.7

In view of the diminution of trade that was shown to have occurred during the fifteen years, it was noticeable that there had been no falling off in the rate increase of the population. Of the population 56% were working on land, 23% were craftsmen, 21% as unskilled labourers and others. As regards the castes, Bhandaris numbered 15,488 or 35% of the entire population. There were 5,791 Brahmins, 4,466 gabits, 1,776 Christians. Only 850 Muslims were to be found in the Petha.[23]

Migration by Classes in Ratnagiri Collectorate

The Important characteristics of the socio-economic structure of South Konkan or Ratnagiri Collectorate at the end the Peshwa rule and the beginning of the British rule in 1818-20 was the existence of various castes and communities involved in various professions.

Table 5.3

Population by Classes[24]				
Class	**Houses**	**Men**	**Women**	**Children**
Chitapavan & Karahade	22	29	30	32
Sasteker Brahmins	27	33	45	40
Sinoy Brahmins	16	28	41	38
Koodaules Brahmins	18	26	40	33
Bardesker Brahmins	20	25	26	30
Wanee Or Trader	30	5	61	51
Maharattas	197	236	267	220
Bhundaries Or Sootars	347	423	578	422
Gauptee Or Fishermen	209	290	333	247
Rajapoots & Guzers	3	4	2	2
Lingayat Gooree	4	7	8	6
Gondee	83	121	151	131
Koombar Or Potmakera	7	8	9	9
Sonar	26	41	48	27
Simpee Or Taylor	4	7	6	3
Sootar Or Carpenter	10	17	19	9
Kaussor Or Coppersmith	7	12	8	2
Weavers	4	5	6	8
Tallies Or Oilmoners	20	30	40	30
Washermen	4	6	8	4
Barbers	4	9	9	20
Kalawuant	14	2	15	17
Davellie (?)	26	33	43	40
Mussalman	5	10	9	10
Christians Or Canaries	14	11	14	19
Paravaries	6	5	7	8
Chumars	7	9	10	8

The Brahmins consisted of twelve divisions, namely, Chitapavan, Deshasta, Devrukh, Golak or Govardhan, Javal or Khot, Karhade, Kast, Kirvant, Palshikar, Samvedi, Savashe, Tirgul.[25] They enjoyed the advantage of the new era of the British rule because of their formal learning. It helped them to secure entry into government service, which proved to be lucrative and help them to move towards cities.[26]

Ratnagiri taluka: Brahmins were found in large numbers in the Ratnagiri taluka. According to the Census of 1823, there were 13,403 Chitapavans, 3,458 Karahades, 852 Shenvis, 1,253 Devrukhs in the Ratnagiri taluka alone.[27]

Malvan taluka: The Census of Malvan taluka of 1824 showed that there were about 6,795 Chitapavans, 290 Karahades, 310 Shenvis, 609 Kudaldeshkars.[28]

The Chitapavan Brahmins: The first trend in migration from their original area of settlement along the coast in north Central Ratnagiri district appeared to have been south within this district before Colonial rule. The second migratory trend began in the first quarter of the 18th century within the political context on the Chitapavan Peshwai. This was from 1713-1818. The steady spread was out of Ratnagiri then to the Desh, followed by Poona and other political and administrative centres of Western Maharashtra. The third phase of migration was in the nineteenth century after the defeat of the Peshwa by the British in 1818 and was closely related with the pressures and benefits of English education. The fourth phase of migration took place as members of this caste progressed, as a direct consequence of education into the clerical and administrative positions under the British. Such motivation in the wake of increased employment opportunities brought about a radical change in the residential pattern of the chitapavans. Thus, if in the year 1700 practically 100% of chitapavans lived in the Ratnagiri district, by the year 1931 Census, only 20% stayed behind in their place of birth.[29]

When Mountstuart Elphinstone introduced English education, the class that benefitted most was the Brahmin class. 'Compared to the other castes of Maharashtra, Chitapavans took great advantage of the facilities for gaining education...the effect of this was they left all other fields and set themselves in the goal of gaining knowledge for government service. Leaving their homeland and their agriculture, they first came to the Desh and found many new ways to earn money through commerce'. However, the Parsis, Gujarathis, Bohras and others seized the business opportunities. So all the intelligent Chitapavans went into government service and did extremely well in it.[30]

Saraswats: The Saraswats also called as Goud Saraswats or shenvis, were found chiefly in Ratnagiri and Sawantwadi. The Ratnagiri taluka had 852 shenvi Brahmins in 1823 while there were 310 shenvis in the Malvan taluka in 1824.[31] They were landlords, bankers, government servants, pleaders, and doctors. Many of them were hereditary village accountants called Kulkarnis.[32]

The 1820 Census reported that there were 2,099 Shenoys mostly employed as accountants.[33] The Census of Bombay in 1780 lists the Goud Saraswats as a majority among the Brahmins of Bombay, a lead that they appeared to have maintained until the 1923 Census when the last Census was undertaken. The details of the estimate of population taken in 1780 showed that the Rigvedic Brahmins numbered 147, Palse 189, Gujarathi 145, while Shenvis were largest in number and it was 409.[34]

The Goud Sarawat Brahmins took to English education early. They excelled over the other Brahmin classes in Bombay. An example of this an article in GSB caste monthly namely Mahrashtra Sarawat showing their excellence in education and their progress in various fields taking them ahead of the other Brahmin castes. This data appeared in the July 1946 monthly and is given below:[35]

Table 5.4

Name	Year	Occupation in 1843
Atmarama K. Bhandare	1827	Owner, United Service Gazette Part Owner, Darpana, first Marathi Newspaper
Sakharam Keshav	1827	Head Accountant, Messrs.Grey and Co.
Gopinath Narayana	1828	Teacher, Wilson High School, and soon Auctioneer, Secretarial office of the Bombay Government
Narayana K. Lad	1830	Partner, Messrs.Hood and Co Editor, Aine Shikandar
Keroba Ramchandra	1834	A Manager in Messrs.Forbes and Co
Govind Narayana	1834	Teacher, Wilson High School
Atmarama Antoba	1836	A Job in Messrs.Forbes and Co
Anadrao Kashinath	1836	A Job in the Registrar's Office of the Bombay Government
Vonoba Bapu	1836	Merchant
Raghunath Narayana	1842	A Job in Messrs. Griffth and Co
Raghunath Nagannath	1843	Teacher, English Private School
Moroba Ramchandra	1843	Civil Auditor's Office

They had close relation with the Gujarathi Banias and Parsis. The American civil war resulted in the boom in the cotton trade of India. Many Saraswats grabbed the opportunity to make money. Mulgaokar, a GSB, was the first Indian to be the proprietor of a textile mill in Bombay in 1865 along with the Parsis.[36] In the political sphere, the shenvis were supporters of the British. As a result, they turned out to be one of the elite groups of Bombay in the last quarter of the nineteenth century.

Among the four graduates of the University of Bombay to be awarded the degree of the Bachelor of Arts in 1862 were two GSBs, R.G.Bhandarkar and B.M. Wagle.[37] The English Mayor's court was hampered by the difficulty of knowing the various languages spoken by the different communities. A Goud Sarawat Brahmin, Bhika Sinay was appointed by the Government as 'Linguist' on Rs 8 a month.[38]

The shenvis migrated to place like Kolhapur also. Both the mills namely ground nut crushing and oil pressing mills in Kolhapur with 26 employees belonged to a Sarawat in 1921.[39]

The other Brahmins were the Karhades who were intelligent, hardworking, hospitable and well behaved. They occupied mostly the southern part of the Ratnagiri Collectorate. Devrukhs had their original home at Sangameshwar. They were spread in the northern parts of the Ratnagiri district.[40]

Marathas : Next in large numbers were the Marathas who were either cultivators or soldiers and according to the Census Report of 1820, they numbered 2,48,356 in the entire Collectorate. They were respectable, unassuming race of men. But few were literate. Many of the Marathas were khots. This explained why their villages were managed badly in comparison with villages under the Brahmins.[41]

Muslims: Muslims were immigrants or other descendants who came to the western coast from the eighth century onwards.[42] The Bojgars, Vatlas, Chharas, Chudiwalas, Chundaigiras, Dalals, Darveshis, Dhavads, were some of the sections of the Muslim community. The daldis were fishermen who were chiefly found in the Ratnagiri taluka of the Ratnagiri Collectorate.[43] According to T.B.Jervis, they were a race of people who descended from the Arabian colonies who settled on the west coast in the seventh or the eighth centuries. They corresponded with the Moplas of Malabar. They made and sold nets and ropes of all sorts and most of those in Ratnagiri were fishermen differing little from Hindus in their ways of fishing.[44] The bhusarees or daldees raised hemp. Others navigated the coasting vessels.[45]

The Kunbis : The Kunbis appeared weak in body. The Kunbis, the name commonly derived from kulambi or kutumbika and was a Marathi term. It meant a husbandman. The deshmukhs and others who were in good service were well off but they generally were poor. They were good husbandmen, and had a fair knowledge of farming. Their womenfolk and children assisted them. The Konkani Kunbis were mainly found in northern talukas of the Ratnagiri Collectorate and were known as tilori Kunbis.[46] Most of them cultivators, steady and industrious. But they were poor because the soil was infertile. Many made up the balance and earned enough to meet marriage and other costs by looking for employment in Bombay working as carriers, labourers, garden or house servants or by working in the steam and spinning mills.[47] Many Kunbis settled in Bombay for salt manufacturing industry. In the early eighteenth century, the Kunbis joined the service of the East India Company as sepoys. They were relieved of their duties as sepoys whenever the occasion demanded, so that they went back to their former occupation of manuring salt grounds and manufacture salt.[48]

The Bhandaris: The origin of the caste Bhandari seems to have its beginning in Adil Shah's time. They mostly settled in areas close to the sea. Their main occupation was drawing toddy from coconut trees and distilling it at their homes. Some of them were agriculturists, while others were good at shipbuilding. They also navigated small vessels.[49]

The Bhandaris were an active community and by nature courageous. Many of them also excelled as musicians, actors, and sculptors. They received lands in the form of inams near Rajapur and Deogad for their excellence during the time of the Peshwas.[50]

There were Parsis, Jains, Christian, and other communities who lived in South Konkan. Encouragement was given to talented workers, weavers, and artisans to establish themselves in Bombay.[51] Many were attracted to the new lucrative government jobs. These jobs opened new avenues for the educated class. The local trading communities like the Saraswats, Prabhus, Vanis often worked in partnership with the Bania merchants in the coastal trade.[52] The elite among the commercial community were the Marwari vanis and came from a township of Vambori in Ahmednagar district. They established a monopoly over the business of money lending. The vanis also provided capital to the Kunbis to cultivate lands. The Portuguese settlements of Goa banked on the rice convoys from the Konkan-Kanara unit.[53] Rice was the principal item of trade with the Portuguese Goa.[54] The Saraswats and Konkani traders who went and settled in Goa thrived during the heyday of the Portuguese rule just on the grain trade.[55] The trade was carried on along the coast namely Konkan-Kanara-Malabar and was mainly in the hands of the Konkani Sarawat traders. The Shenoy Brahmins, such as the Sinays, Kamats had started residing in Bombay from the end of eighteenth century to carry on their trade activities. These traders although Brahmins by caste, did not suffer much from caste restrictions on sea travel.[56] Thus, it was not only trade that brought about migration but all classes of people migrated to Bombay.

In general the population religion wise in the Ratnagiri Collectorate was a mixed group having Hindus, Muslims, Jains, Zoroastrians, Christians, Jews, Parsis, and others. The Hindus formed the majority. Roughly they made ninety percent of the total population in it. The next group comprised of Muslims, which could be said to share about four percent of the total inhabitants. The remaining population belonged to various communities.

The following table show the religion wise population of the Ratnagiri Collectorate between 1881-1921.[57]

Table 5.5

Religion	**1881**	**1891**	**1901**	**1911**	**1921**
Hindu	9,21,046	10,19,943	10,77,747	11,10,594	10,65,119
Muslim	71,051	79,673	8,2825	85303	80,991
Jain	1,699	2,054	2,328	1913	1,640
Zoroastrian	-	-	29	46	36
Christian	2,375	4,206	4,981	5714	6,431
Jew	1	-	-	5	1
Parsi	16	15	-	-	-
Others	2	35	17	63	26

Education and Migration

Literacy had a direct impact on migration and increased the movement of population from the Konkan to cities especially in Bombay. Konkan in general seemed to have made good strides in the province of literacy. The improvement appeared to be gradual but in a definite direction. The beginning of primary schools was made as early as 1824 when the Native Education Society decided to start 'Vernacular schools' with the object of teaching western education to the people. The first two Marathi schools were started in 1826 and the schools were under the charge of T.B. Jervis.[58] A fairly satisfactory picture of the indigenous schools in the early nineteenth century is obtained mainly from the report of the State of Education in South Konkan submitted to the government by T.B. Jervis an officer employed by the government of Bombay for a Statistical Survey of South Konkan. He joined his duties in 1890 as statistical surveyor and started collecting statistics of schools in 1820. He was the first officer under the British rule to collect such statistics on indigenous in schools and therefore deserve special mention in the history of modern education.[59]

T.B. Jervis established the Native School Society of south Konkan which was the first society for the promotion of education of the people. In this venture the local people also helped and within two years four schools were opened. The Government of Bombay granted cash and books to these schools.

T.B. Jervis himself styles his Report as ' Report on the State of Education in India'. He has given in this report a full distinct and impartial review of the State and system of education amongst the natives and of the causes to which the chief detects therein are to be attributed and present condition of their literature and Sciences.[60]

From 1826 and 1855, eighteen more schools were opened. These schools were started from the commencement of the Board of Education to the creation of the Department of Education. The first of these was opened at Malvan followed by Vengurla and Ratnagiri and other parts of Konkan.[61] In 1837 the British Government found it necessary to appoint somebody to inspect and supervise vernacular school. Capt Candy was appointed as Superintendent of school in Deccan and Southern Konkan. It was three years later that a semi government body called Board of Education was created consisting of 7 members of whom 4 were appointed by the government and 3 by the Bombay Native Education Society.[62]

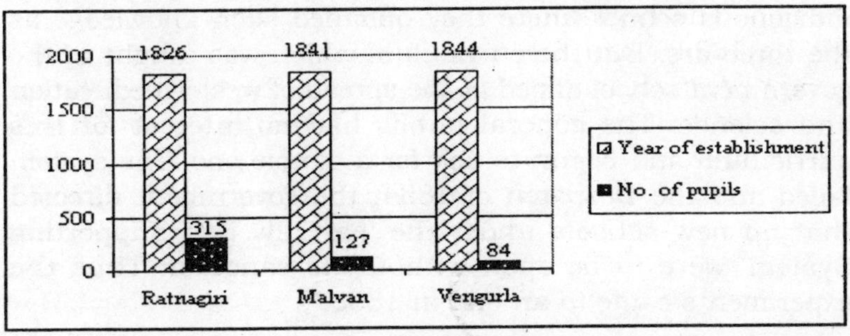

Fig. 5.8

One of the inspectors who visited the schools remarked 'The best schools in the division are those at Ratnagiri No I and II, Chiplun, Vengurla and Malvan in the Ratnagiri Collectorate.' He further remarked that, *'The Ratnagiri School No. I fully maintains the high character it has borne for so many years. It continues under the able management of Gangadhar Ramchandra, (father of Balgangadhar Tilak, India's leading Social cum Political reformer) an excellent teacher, talented, well informed and industrious.'*[63] This shows the employment opportunities provided by the British for the public. By and large the better class of Brahmins found openings in the government service. These well-to-do comprised of the higher-class group and were employed in administrative fields be it educational, military or civil. This elite group enjoyed an advantage in the new era of British rule because of their interest in formal learning introduced by the administrators. It helped them to secure entry into government services, which proved to be rewarding and helped them to shift towards cities.

The new scheme called 'Partially Self Supporting System' was introduced after 1855 all over Bombay province. The government embarked on establishment of schools if the people gave aid more than half the expenditure. Such schools were started at Achre in Malwan, Shiroda in Vengurla between 1855-57. The school at Malvan had 84 students and the school at Shiroda had 93.[64] It appears that the people of southern part of Ratnagiri namely Malvan and Vengurla talukas took advantage of schools under ' Partially Self Supporting System' under the notification of 1854. However, it was difficult to collect subscription from people as the masses preferred to send their children to the indigenous school where they obtained such knowledge as the three hrs. But the curriculum which was taught in the government school aimed at the spread of western education and science. The general public had no interest for this curriculum and begun to ask for a simple one. The system failed and the Despatch of 1854, the government directed that no new schools under the 'Partially Self Supporting System' were to be open without its sanction. Thus the experiments came to an end in 1858.[65]

Generally people had became aware of their rights and took interest in education. In Malvan, Bhandari Education Society High School was established in 1890, Anant Shivaji Desai Topiwalla High School was established in 1911, New English School at Achra was established in 1916, Waradkar High School was established in 1926. Some of the schools established at Vengurla were Vengurla High School, 1912, R.K.Patkar high school 1913, Tutorial High School, Shiroda 1915. The education in the district regardless of some drawbacks like want of funds, prevalence of epidemics, superstitions certainly benefited the general public.

Yet there was some sluggishness in the entire course of action. Ratnagiri had a number of schools established but many of them closed by the beginning of the twentieth century. For example the Anglo Vernacular School, which was established in 1868-69, was closed in a period of five years. Ratnagiri Private English school started in 1886 was redundant in 1922. Theodore Carter Royal A.V. School established in 1911 became non-functional within a decade.[66] Anglo Vernacular School at Masure was started in 1886 but was closed within two years. Konkan Education Society's School at Achre closed within a year of its opening in 1909. Vengurla also had defunct schools. English school at Vengurla started in 1868 and closed in 1871. Private new English school was established in 1914 but stopped functioning in 1921. Shiroda English school at Shiroda was established in 1920 and became non-operational in 1922.

There were instances when the local people protested against the closure of schools. At some instances schools would closed for insignificant reasons. A fitting example may be cited here to substantiate the fact that the government wished to close down a school to replace it by a government office. A report in the newspaper called Vengurla Vritta showed its regret at the hasty action of the government in closing Vernacular School No.1 at Malvan because the place was to be allotted to the establishment of a municipality. The report further stated that this had placed the boys of the school at a disadvantage.[67] The municipality office could have undeniably been established elsewhere.

The number of scholars also decreased during the years from 1872 to 1879.

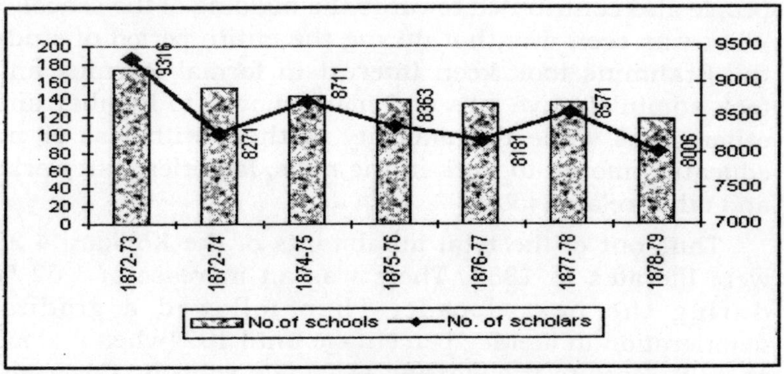

Fig. 5.9

The Mamlatdars complained that the number of schools had decreased from 174-110 in the Collectorate while the number of scholars had increased from 53.5% to 70.3 % with new applications increasing as time went. In fact the local people assisted the local municipality contributions towards schools and its development by collection of local funds. It was requested that the government take personal interest and prevent the closing of schools. It was brought to the notice of the government that many schools at Malvan and Vengurla had been closed down for want of funds. The demand was also made to open schools of industry so that it could help people to seek direct employment.[68]

The Jagan Mitra of the 13th July advocated the opening

of schools of industry for teaching useful crafts and professions to the people. It was stated that the agricultural and manufacturing classes did not appreciate book instruction given in existing schools and consequently did not send their children to them. But the school of industry would prove beneficial to them and to the country at large.[69]

Education in the initial years of the British rule, nonetheless, benefited the higher class of people who became aware of the benefits of education. They took active participation in helping the government in various educational activities. Lieut. Stowell, Secretary to Ratnagiri Collector office requested J.G.Lumsden, Secretary to Government to pay Rs.500 to complete a school building. What causes the attention to this letter is that the local people also contributed towards the building of the school.[70] What was seen was that during the entire period of study the Brahmins took keen interest in formal learning and took administrative jobs and many moved to Bombay and other cities while the majority of them with less or no education moved to work in the mills, factories, salt works and other related jobs.

Thus out of the total inhabitants of the Konkan, 4.28 were literates in 1881. There was an increase of 1.62 % during the next decade. Then followed a gradual deterioration in literacy percentage until 1921when it stood at 5.08. Despite the starting of female schools, the plight of the female literacy in Konkan in general was a miserable one.

Growing Need of Human Resources in Bombay

An economist Ravenste, scholar in the 'Laws of Migration', proposes the theoretical explanation of rural-urban migration. According to it the migrants move from areas of low opportunity to the areas of high opportunity and the choice of destination is regulated by distance. The positive effect from such a transfer as surplus labour is absorbed in a rapidly growing, more productive, urban industrial sector.[71]

In the late eighties and early nineties of eighteenth century, Bombay was not yet an significant port and lay outside the usual route network.[72] But its supremacy on the urban scene, in Western India was steadily but slowly established by mid nineteenth century. Many cities in western India concentrated in any one or two functions, such as Surat in textiles industries, Poona as a seat of administration. But Bombay was a major stronghold of the British. It had a combination of commercial, industrial, administrative, educational transportation functions.[73] Ratnagiri district became a major supplier of human resources to this fast developing city.

The English traders of the East India Company offered Bombay its due opportunity as early as 1668. They planned to make it a trade mart in Western India and shifted their headquarters from Surat to the island of Bombay during that year. The acquisition of Bankot in 1755 destroyed the piracy at Vijaydurg. The capture of the forts of Malvan and Redi in 1759 and 1765 were further steps taken in the interest of trade. The same period witnessed the opening of the two new docks at Bombay one completed in 1750 and another in 1762. This increased the number of vessels.

Thus as far as Bombay's commercial growth was concerned, there were distinctive trends noticed. The Company regulated the trade of the Konkan. Its enormous potential for capital from Parsis and Gujarathis was a boon. The merchants from whichever part with ability to help in the growth of Bombay were given assurance of enhanced convoy services. Bombay's growing demands opened new avenues for the trading contractors. Supply of cheap labour was available from the Konkan. Raw materials were brought from Gujarat, Khandesh and other nearby places. The relations of the entrepreneurs with the Company stood them in good stead for the prospects.

Thus by 1750s Bombay started having a steady inflow of migrants. It began to participate in the Surat-West Asia trade activity.[74] Thus population from Konkan started moving towards Bombay for trade.

At this time, the famine of 1803 drove a number of people from Konkan to Bombay. Bombay's beginning as an industrial city was initiated with the appearance of modern methods used in the construction of mills, roadways and railways.[75]

The very purpose of beginning cotton mills in Bombay was creating a private Indian venture employing local capital and imported British technology to confront 'Manchester with her own weapons'.[76] A cotton mill was started in 1854 here and within a span of twenty years, the number rose to almost 15 employing about 11,000 workers on a daily basis.[77] Another reason for this boom in the cotton industry between 1861 and 1865 was the outbreak of the civil war in America. The supply of the American cotton suddenly cut off, Lancashire turned largely to Bombay as a substitute. It poured more than 81 million sterling for their cotton into the pockets of the mercantile community.[78]

Simultaneously, the first railway track in India was laid down from the center of Bombay city northeast to the twenty-mile distant town of Thana in 1853. Ten years later, railway was extended to Poona through the mountainous terrain. Soon an extensive railway network joined Bombay with other major cities.[79] Between 1872 and 1881 railways extended in the interior and steam navigation along the coast.

Bombay's harbour was developed. Ship building industry was given impetus. Lowjee Nussurwanjee, a foreman and carpenter of ships built at Surat, started this industry in 1735. He was persuaded by the East India Company to migrate to Bombay to work for their shipbuilding yard at Bombay. This was an important event in the history of the Bombay Presidency. Lowjee and his successors brought many other carpenters, bricklayers, apprentices from Surat.[80] The Bombay Steam Shipping Navigation Company, a joint Parsi British concern was founded in 1845. It was floated with a capital of Rs. 10,00,000 . Its aim was to run services of Bombay both southwards to Sri Lanka, calling at ports like Ratnagiri, Vengurla, Goa, Cannanore, Cochin and northwards to Gujarat.[81] It was taken over by an English partnership that was created by J.H.Shepherd. Along with this, native crafts also continued though a slow decline in their use was noticed.[82]

When the island of Bombay came in possession of Great Britain in the year 1664, the population was estimated at 10,000 persons.[83] There is a reference to another Census in 1716 the population was about 16,000. A third was taken during 1814-15 and the population recorded was 2,21,550. The next two Censuses in 1872 and 1881 were recorded as 6,44,000 and 7,73,000.[84] By the beginning of 1880, Bombay city towered over the other larger cities and had a population of 7,73,196 in 1881. This number was six times greater than Poona with a population of 1,29,751 or almost thirteen times larger than Sholapur which had a population of 61,281.[85] The population grew at a slow pace in the early twentieth century. The reason probably was the influenza epidemic of 1917-18.[86] But such incidence of epidemic was temporary.

Ratnagiri population accounted for more than 45% in Bombay.[87] Parel, Byculla, Chinchpokli, Nagpada had expanded through the industrial enterprise into the populous dwelling places of a large immigrant population. A large influx of Konkan labourers who worked in mills and docks and lived in these parts took place between 1860 and 1890.[88]

Pattern of Migration, Labour Potential and Remittances

Having taken a survey of the class, castes and professions in the Ratnagiri Collectorate, it is seen that there were four categories of population termed as well-to-do (usually referred to professional and administrative personnel be it civil or military), traders, people engaged in specialised occupations, and labourers (usually agricultural labourers) who migrated to Bombay and other cities.[89] These terms were generally translated as gentlemen, traders and merchants, artisans and day labourers and beggars.[90]

In 1824 when the British captured all the territories of the South Konkan, Jonathan A. Dunlop made a strange but factual statement. He wrote about the disadvantage which the South Konkan Country suffered from the change of administration. He said, '*the domestic habits of natives led to large supplies of money flowing to the Konkan from all parts of the Late Peshwa's dominions, where its natives were employed, these have all ceased and instead of consignments of treasure from Poona, for the support of the garrisons, a considerable part of the revenue is now remitted to Bombay.*'[91]

This showed the impact of British rule, which laid great importance to the development of Bombay as a commercial center. The fact that Konkan or Poona was losing ground both as commercial and administrative centres was obvious by the statement made by Jonathan Duncun.

This *Elite group* enjoyed an advantage in the new era of the British rule because they adopted English education. This habit stood them in good stead in the early days of the British rule. It also helped them to secure entry into government service which proved to be lucrative and move towards cities. Almost 80% of the Brahmins were covered under the well to do category and 10% as traders and another 10% as others. The educated Brahmins found service in government while Muslims, Marathas and Mahars joined the army. It was said that Ratnagiri was the nursery of the Bombay Army. As A.K.Nairne observed, *'Until the accession of the British Government, the population had always distinctly war-like character and the South Konkan still supplies so great a number of recruits to the Bombay army that there are many military pensioners in this district as in the whole of the rest of the Presidency.'*[92]

The *traders or the business community,* during the course of nineteenth century were drawn by the economic forces towards the cities. They gained economic power and influence and grabbed the opportunity of this power and went hand in hand with the British. The other trading community consisted of specialised artisans like rope makers, milkmen, thatchers, goldsmiths, silversmiths, barbers, and others.[93]

The third and the most important class were skilled workers who were also *mill workers.* Majority of them belonged to Bankot and Malvan. They saved large sums which they took back home and spent most of the savings on marriages and other family events. Improved communications helped the ones with modern ideas to go as far as Aden and Mauritius. It is seen that those who opted to go far were generally the Muslims, Kunbis and Mahars.[94] Almost all Mahars took service as sweepers in the municipal streets of Bombay and carried their savings to remit to their hometowns.

The Fourth category of people, which migrated in large numbers, was the *Agricultural Labour Class.* The labour class also were in mills besides a number of odd jobs that they took up in Bombay and other parts. Konkan had an agricultural economy. The numbers of persons supported by agriculture in the Ratnagiri Collectorate were as follows:[95]

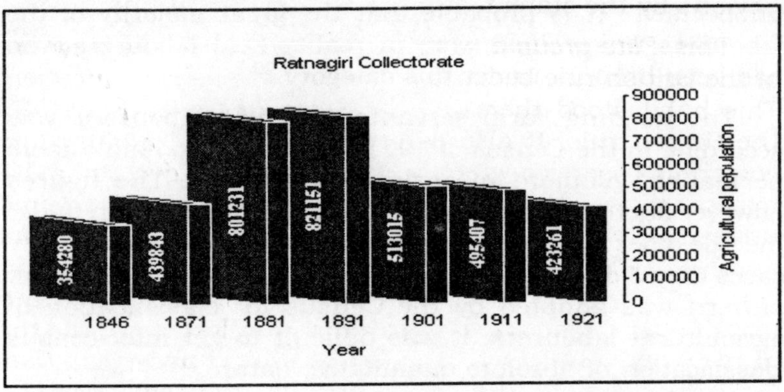

Fig. 5.10

Agriculture provided a large section of population in the Konkan. The ratio of employment of agricultural to that in non-agricultural pursuits was roughly 3:1 in 1881. The agricultural labourers consisted of three categories namely field labourers, ordinary labourers and skilled labourers. Ploughmen, reapers, sowers, transplantors fell under the category of field labourers. Ordinary labourers comprised of embankment workers, well diggers, canal cleaners and such other jobs. Skilled labourers included carpenters, masons, blacksmiths, and leather workers. Out of the three categories, the first one represented labour of seasonal character.[96]

Agricultural labourers were divided into different types. They were permanent, semi-permanent and casual. Those who belonged to the permanent labour category came from families of landless labour class, while employment as semi permanent or as casual labourers was sought by all classes of rural labour.[97]

The Census of India of 1901 adopted a different classification for agricultural labourers. Agricultural labour was divided into three groups namely, farm servants field labourers and Jhum or taungya cultivators who lived by the wasteful form of shifting cultivation. Most unskilled labourers depended on fieldwork for their subsistence.

When there was less fieldwork than usual, they temporarily migrated to seek some other kind of labour.[98]

The Census of 1911 brought all farm servants and field labourers under one head and entered them as 'Labourers unspecified'. It is probable that the great majority of the labourers unspecified were in reality field labourers who had been brought under this category.[99]

The heading 'farm servants and field labourers' was according to the Census of 1921 intended to contain a more permanent element of agricultural labour. The figures however fluctuated considerably from the figures given under the title other labourers and labourers unspecified. In majority cases they did not differ from the others. Thus as no uniform pattern was adopted by the Census for classification of agricultural labourers, it was difficult to get inter-census classification of absolute quantitative nature.[100]

The constant changes in the classification also made it difficult to determine accurately the extent of disguised unemployment that prevailed. But that there was abject poverty among all the classes in the Ratnagiri Collectorate in general and the agricultural class in particular was definite.[101] However, the figures give the proportion which agricultural population bore to the total agricultural population from time to time and with its help an explanation may be possible as to the extent of rise and decline of agricultural labourers vis-à-vis agricultural population in the Konkan in general.

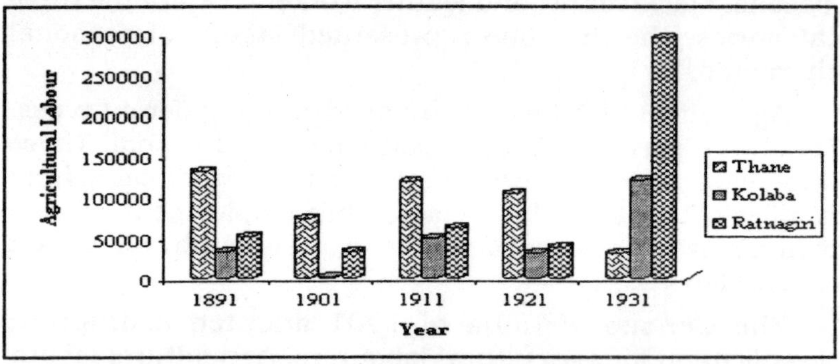

Fig. 5.11

It is important to note that although all categories of migration took place from Ratnagiri Collectorate to Bombay and other parts most of it was the labour force. The Konkan in general supplied its labour for economic purposes. It wielded a good influence in respect of labour which it supplied to the adjoining cities particularly the metropolitan city Bombay. The Bombay Provincial Enquiry Committee of the Government of Bombay observed, *'Konkan has become an important recruiting ground for labour required for the trade and industry of Bombay.'*[102]

Similarly the labour investigation of the Government of India noticed that of the city's resources of labour supply from the Province of Bombay, the Ratnagiri district is by far the most important. Out of 616 persons coming from various districts of the Province, 316 or 51.3 % come from Ratnagiri district alone.[103] Out of the five persons born in Ratnagiri, one was compelled under economic pressure to eke out a living in the city of Bombay. Economic pressure alone drove the rural population to leave the healthier conditions of village and migrate to cities and live in the slums and unsanitary conditions.[104]

Emigration began growing in the 1830s. The expansion of mills and factories in Bombay caused a rapidly escalating exodus of labour from Ratnagiri Collectorate from the middle of the nineteenth century. By the seventies and eighties, bands of husbandmen and field labourers, numbering altogether not less than 1,00,000 some by foot, others by sea to Bombay.[105] By 1845 both emigration and immigration took place though emigration exceeded immigration. There were three types of immigration found. From other talukas of each Collectorate, from other Collectorate and from beyond the Company's territories. There were males, females who immigrated. It was the case with the emigration. But in both cases males exceeded the females.[106]

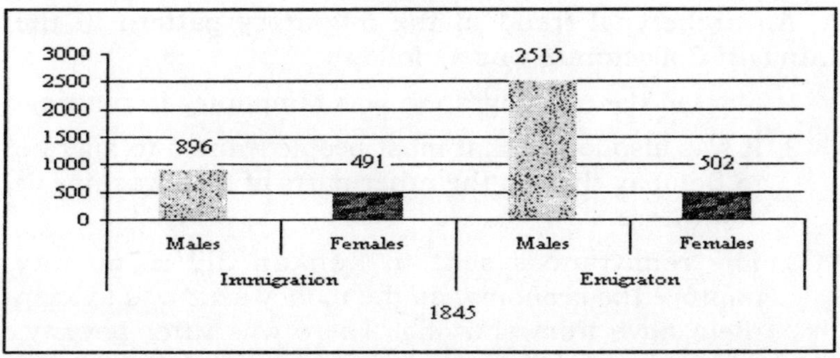

Fig. 5.12

The bulk of factory employment was concentrated in and around Bombay city especially in the cotton textile mills. The Collector of Ratnagiri reported in 1881 that every new mill drew much of its labour from the district and a great number of mills established in the few years from 1875 showed a decrease in the population. The population according to the Census showed a decrease of 26835 or 2.2% on the population 10,19,136 of 1872.[107] This was due to the temporary emigration for work from the district to Bombay. This also showed that more than half the mill hands came from the Konkan region. In 1926 on an average 3,82,255 workers were employed daily in the Presidency as a whole.[108] A study of the agricultural labourers shows that the Deccan provided a small proportion of workers in the cotton mill industry in comparison with the Konkan region.[109]

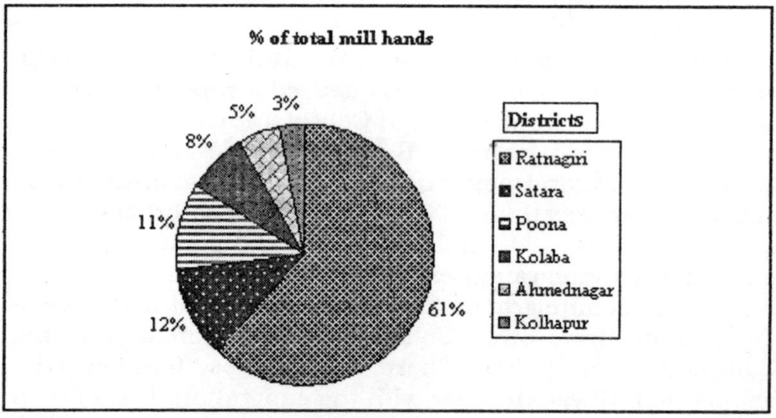

Fig. 5.13

An archetypal trend in the migratory pattern in the Ratnagiri Collectorate was as follows:

1. Most of the out-migration was temporary in nature.
2. It was also found that most people wanted to migrate to Bombay than to the other parts of Maharashtra or elsewhere.
3. The remittances sent to Konkan did in no way improve the economy, as the money sent was to keep them alive from starving. There was utter poverty, which dragged the people to the cities to eke out a living.

Temporary Migration and Remittances:

The migration was temporary in nature was clear from the various reports made by various officers of the Ratnagiri Collectorate from time to time. A.K.Nairne observed that *'All castes of the South Konkan are much more in the habit of seeking their living abroad than the natives of the other parts, though they almost invariably return home to end their days.'*[110]

W. Wilson, Assistant Collector wrote about the love of the people of the land that always brought them back home. He wrote, *'there is no local trade extensive enough to give employment to all and the tenacity with which they cling to their country makes them blind to the advantages of emigration. It is true that a large number of men from every class of society go abroad for employment, but they very seldom settle there and nearly always eventually return home.'*[111]

Besides the agricultural group, which went to Bombay, there were many who went and joined the army. The annual report of the year 1882 described that whenever a man was seen with a silver ornament, it was sure that he was an army pensioner. For so strong was the love of country among the people that nothing not even the offer of free land and free houses in the North Konkan would induce them to emigrate permanently and they always returned with their savings to end their days in their own villages. In fact if it were not for those savings brought from elsewhere and for the lakhs of pensions and family remittances poured into the district every year it was difficult to gauge how the people would get along at all.[112]

The British Government was aware of the human resources available in the South Konkan. Keeping this in mind education was also imparted to them. That the British tried to persuade local people to migrate for better prospects is seen from the following statement given by an W. Wilson, an assistant officer in 1875, *'Nothing but emigration will better their condition and I mean to make strong efforts next travelling season to induce some of the ryuts to avail themselves of the liberal terms on which government propose to grant lands in Khandesh.'*[113]

Their reluctance to migrate was reported by an officer in the following words: ' The only real means of improving the material condition of the people and raising their standards of comfort would be a system of permanent emigration, but as long as the Hindoo law of inheritance remains unchanged there is little hope of this. None of them will give up the few square yards of land that their birth entails them to. Much is always said as to benefit conferred on the districts by the mills and docks in Bombay. But they do not stick to their work regularly and let those at home enjoy the land but come back every year or two to quarrel with their brothers about it and spend half of their savings on lawyers'.[114]

But it was not easy to induce the people to go and settle in Khandesh or any place. The Ratnagiri records given by W.Wilson showed that no efforts were spared by the government from time to time to induce the people to settle permanently in Khandesh, The Mauritius and other places by giving lands at a low rate or some similar concessions but at the same time he brought to the notice of the government that at least 1,00,000 Ratnagiri labourers migrated to Bombay as temporarily.[115] The people preferred to go to Bombay because Bombay to a great extent stood to them in place of factories as far as surplus labour population was concerned. For every year tens of thousands of people went up from there to Bombay to get work. Although some of them stayed back, most of them returned to their homes for the rains.[116]

This proved that the people were well aware of the benefits of emigration, still the inherent love for his homestead would lead them to put up with misery before they decided to go. Lakhs of rupees poured in to the Collectorate as pensions and family remittances.[117]

Construction of Railways and Decline of the Port Towns

The once busy ports and the towns showed a declining trend after the construction of railways above the ghats. A.Cumine mentioned the poor state of affairs of the county caused by this development. He said, that the coast the Bhandaris and the whole of Malvan, Vengurla talukas were fairly well off. But in the center and east of the district the kulwadis, Mahars and mass of people were decidedly poor. The pressure of population on the land was so great that these people can never be well off. But he suggested that something had to be done to open out the district a little more. According to him Ratnagiri was the most backward district in the Presidency so far as communications were concerned. And the opening of the new railways above the ghat had seriously diverted the course of trade and left her even more out of the world than before. The railway to Bombay parallel to the coast, he said would probably never be able to compete with the steamers. And the engineering difficulties would be formidable. The natural course of the trade was not parallel to the coast but at right angles to it. The rivers also ran at right angles to the coast and their banks afforded comparatively level and easy tracks for railways. The Southern Maratha line passed along not very far from our boundary. And so A.Cumine suggested that a very light railway laid down from some point on the southern part of Konkan it would benefit the country.[118]

Regarding the construction of railways, L.N.Brown, Collector of Ratnagiri felt that the construction of railway would not help in improving the conditions of the country. He wrote that 'the railway at present is extended only as far as Dasgaon in the Kolaba district. (119 miles by road from Ratnagiri). I understand that if that stretch of line pays the railway may be extended as far as Chiplun. (60 miles by road from Ratnagiri). From Chiplun it might be extended up to Ratnagiri'. He further brought to the notice of the government the difficulties in constructing a railways. He said that the difficulties of extending the railway over the hilly country of Konkan south of Mahad across its numerous rivers and creeks were considerable, and the likely hood of such a railway paying was remote. Even if the railways were built, the distance by railway to Bombay would hardly be less than Rs. 3.14.6. The distance by sea however was only Rs.3. There could be no doubt that very few passengers who then travelled to intermediate ports in that district would prefer to travel by land. The distance by road to Bombay was 235 miles. Ratnagiri was 82 miles from Kolhapur and Kolhapur was 309 by railway from Bombay. The III class fare from Kolhapur was Rs 5.11.0 and two changes were involved. Travelling by steamers by the lowest cost was preferred. It would always be cheaper to travel by Ratnagiri, Malvan and Vengurla by sea rather than land.[119]

Regular steamers existed but were not satisfactory. While returning from Kaira, W. Wilson, the Acting Collector of Ratnagiri was struck with the bareness of Ratnagiri and poverty of the people but the demand for labour in Bombay was brisk. Traveling to and from Bombay was becoming difficult. The fairly high level of local wages, 9 annas 4 paise for skilled and 3 annas and 10 paise for unskilled labour in 1880 did not seem to point out any over stocking of local labour market.[120]

If railways were, according to the reports of the British not feasible because of the existence of the ports, the steamers should have been taken care of. Unfortunately, the steamers which, carried men and goods witnessed a declining stage. The ports needed repairs from time to time. Boring operations had to be performed. Boring operations were performed in the Ratnagiri harbour in 1915. Drilling machines and oil engines used for the work were stored in Rajapur.[121] But these jobs were not satisfactory and very little attention was paid to the improvement of landing facilities. A Committee was created to examine the feasibility of building a pier and provide an estimate of the cost. It consisted of H.Moreland, Deputy Director, B.E.Vaccha, Marine Engineer T.J.Walke, Superintendent of Lights and B.R.Nanal, MLC.[122]

The Committee considered that it was impossible to build a pier that was serviceable all year round. The estimated cost of the project amounted to approximately Rs.9,00,000, which included the cost of approach road. The paying capacity of the passengers and the traders was limited and therefore such a project would not yield any profit.[123]

It was reported by the Committee that there were several more bunders of nearly equal importance to Ratnagiri in point of passenger traffic. The question of constructing a big ferry wharf therefore would have to be in abeyance. It was necessary to take up only such works, which would give relief to greater population on the Konkan line with as little expenditure as possible. Smaller schemes were more economically viable than spending on the construction of a Ferry Wharf, which would lead to expenses and further taxation.[124]

Not only the Ratnagiri port but most port and creeks of Ratnagiri Collectorate had considerably silted up. The nature of silt varied from coarse sand to gravel three inches diameter. Lower down several bars had been formed by material varing from coarse sand to gravel three inches diameter. Boats of 80 tons with a draft of 5 feet could only pass the bars at high tied and thus they very often took 2 to 4 days to cover a distance of 20-30 miles. Transport charges had naturally increased and ruined the trade.

Swamp at Ramghat Road

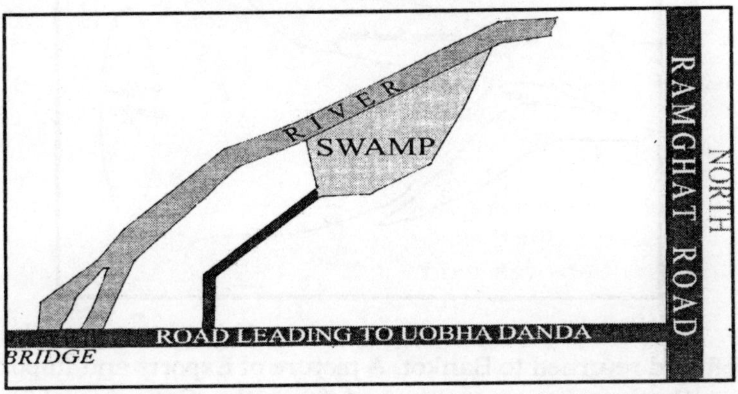

The declining utilization of ports was a stumbling block in the progress of the Ratnagiri Collectorate. The sea-boards, namely Bankot, Dabhol, Jaygad, Jaitapur, Vijaydurg, Malvan were getting more and more unapproachable on account of the increasing bars at the mouths of the creeks mention above.[125] For example Bankot had a bar at the mouth of the river which was dangerous for the navigation. An inquiry by Shepherd's steamers showed that the boats touched Bankot almost till 1902-1903. In that year the position of the bar at the mouth of the creek considerably changed. The channel instead of running west to east opened about 2-3 miles away in south westerly direction and it was difficult for the steamers to enter the port. It was that after the rains the bar had change the position. The buoys were refixed in October following the change. But the main question that was of concern for the British was whether the money should be spent on removing present bar or whether it would be preferably to have new entrance made. The following sketch was given to show the probable consequence to new entrance.

Sketch showing the probable position of the bar and the Sand-banks

After a cut is made at A

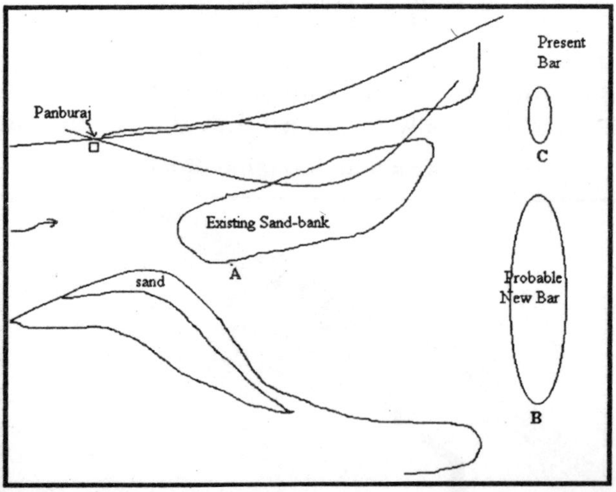

It was stated that nearly a hundred passengers daily left and returned to Bankot. A picture of Exports and Imports for three years was obtained from the Collector of Salt Revenue.[126]

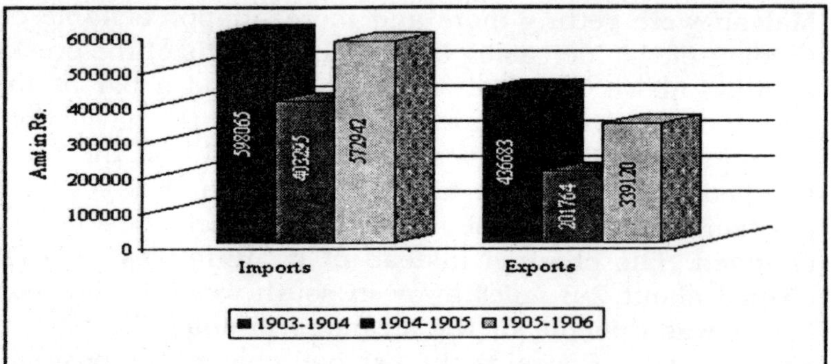

Fig. 5.14

It was observed that the traffic by this route was not

negligible and that something had to be done to improve communication by navigation, especially as there were no railway facilities nearby and the bunder did not possess telegraphic communication and worse still there was not even a road or cart track between Bankot and Mahaparal.

However, the cost of new road from Bankot to Mahaparal would cost the Government Rs,80,000 without bridges and the cost of the repairs for that portion would be Rs 3,000 per annum. It was probable that an annual expenditure of about Rs.200 would be required to keep the channels at the bars in proper working order. Therefore it was seen that it was more economical to dredge out silt an improve navigation that construct new road.[127]

Trade within the country was already on the decline. As early as 1898-99, an administrative report described, how an agent of the Southern Maratha Railway at Rajapur was trying to induce the merchants in that town to send their goods as far as Kathaiwad and Gujarat by rail instead of by country craft.. The commodity he was trying to trade in was gul (Jaggery) from Kolhapur. This trade route earlier to this was the road to Goa, and then the ports of Konkan sent gul from where it was transported by the Messers Shepherd and Co.'s boats to Porbunder. The completion of the Southern Maratha Railway tended to divert trade from the chief towns of the district. The Collector suggested that some compensating element had to be introduced if Ratnagiri could be connected by rail with Kolhapur.[128]

The declining of trade and a floating population acted as brakes to the overall development of the Ratnagiri Collectorate. The number of people who left Ratnagiri in search of work was so large every year that it did not give stability to the country. The changing pattern in numbers depended upon various factors such as like the plague in Bombay, famines, locusts' ravage and such others.[129] The people who migrated to work in mills, shops, clerk's professional jobs like lawyers and as domestic servants numbered to 1,44,734 in 1911. In 1921 the Konkan sent 2,93,533 people to Bombay, of which Ratnagiri Collectorate alone contributed 2,35,556.[130]

Since 1911, their proportion declined. The decline was

not due to an absolute decrease but due to the relative increase in the number of migrants from other areas to Bombay.[131] A quantitative dimension of the number of migrants from Ratnagiri district to Bombay and their contribution to the population of Bombay is given in the following table. Between 1881 and 1931, migrants from here contributed an increasing proportion of the population of Bombay.

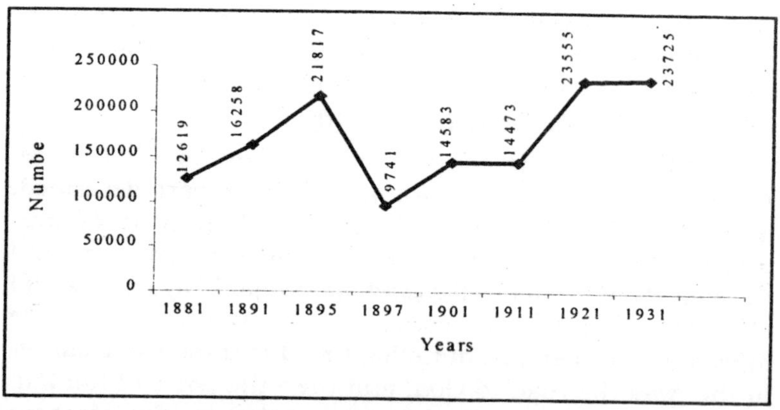

Fig. 5.15

Increase in Transportation Fares

There were two important steamships Companies namely, The Indian Co-operative Navigation and Trading Company Limited and The Bombay Steam Navigation Company. These steamship Companies carried passengers from and to Bombay. There were a number of complaints by the local people about the mismanagement of the owners of the ships. All the newspapers of Ratnagiri namely the Bakul, the Satyashodhak and the Jaganmitra in their respective issues of the 29th and the 30th December drew the attention of the port and district authorities of that station to the recklessness and rudeness of the men in charge of the boats plying there to carry passengers to and from the steamers in the Ratnagiri harbour that resulted in a few deaths and injury to others.[132]

Complaint was also registered about the delay in the coming of ships to the coast and the people had to wait for hours on end before they got into it. The agent according to the report was that the agent of the Indian Steam Navigation Company issued tickets to intending passengers for many days before a steamer was expected and then detained them all that time by informing them that it may arrive at any moment. The passengers thus were put to great inconvenience.[133] It also mentioned the suffering of the people while embarking and disembarking from the steamers and the negligence of the Messers Shepherd and Company in these matters. A suggestion was made that since most of the steamers had more than one gangway on each side, they ought to be opened, one for embarking and the other for disembarking.[134]

The end number of difficulties faced by the local people did not stop the traffic because this was the cheapest mode of transport available for the population to go towards Bombay. The following tables show the statement of the number of passengers who traveled from Malvan to Bombay and back during the years 1911-12.[135]

Table 5.6

Year/ Month	Malvan To Bombay				Bombay To Malvan			
	I	II	III	Total	I	II	III	Total
1911								
Oct	1	327	2235	2563	3	504	2168	2675
Nov	0	375	2613	2988	1	548	2179	2728
Dec	4	418	3268	3690	4	523	2111	2638
1912								
Jan	0	415	2456	2871	4	444	2714	3162
Feb	0	269	1764	2033	4	646	8127	8777
Mar	3	561	3051	3615	1	771	2410	3182
Apr	3	638	2211	2852	7	839	2510	3356
May	6	800	1685	2491	9	624	1983	2616

Thus in all 40,636 passengers left the taluka for Bombay and 38,745 returned giving a net emigration of 1893 for the year. The prosperity of the migrants is suggested by the larger proportion of the first and second-class passengers on the homeward going boats. The heavy traffic to Malvan in the month of February and March was due to the festival of Shimga, and the marriage season and in may the return of cultivators to their villages for agricultural operations.

The following statement has been compiled from the information supplied by the Steamship Company who went to and returned from Bombay to Ratnagiri from October 1913 to May 1914.

Table 5.7

Year/ Month	From Ports in the Ratnagiri Taluka to Bombay				From Bombay to the Ports in the Ratnagiri Taluka			
	I	II	III	Total	I	II	III	Total
1913								
Oct	37	1781	6404	8222	32	2146	3051	5229
Nov	30	1962	6673	8665	46	2505	4334	6885
Dec	42	2056	8805	10903	27	2599	5393	8019
1914								
Jan	34	2054	7675	9763	32	2072	6593	8697
Feb	22	1507	5097	6626	29	2177	5714	7920
Mar	45	1883	5845	7773	77	4794	8981	13852
Apr	45	2362	6326	8733	52	3265	7674	10991
May	86	4082	5255	9423	89	4140	10136	14365

Thus in all 70,117 passengers left Ratnagiri for Bombay and 75,975 returned from Bombay to Ratnagiri thus giving a net immigration of 5,857 for the year The following were the fares on the three ports of Ratnagiri, Malvan and Vengurla on the Konkan coast.[137]

Table 5.8

Ratnagiri Port									
Years	Class								
	I			II			III		
	Rs	A	P	Rs	A	P	Rs	A	P
1913-14	5	0	0	1	0	0	0	10	0
1914-15	5	0	0	1	10	0	1	0	0
1915-16	5	0	0	1	10	0	1	0	0
1916-17	6	0	0	2	8	0	1	8	0
1917-18	6	9	0	2	11	0	2	1	0
1918-19	6	15	0	3	1	0	2	7	0
1919-20	8	12	0	3	12	0	2	8	0
1920-21	9	12	0	4	12	0	3	0	0

Table 5.9

Malvan Port									
Years	**Class**								
	I			**II**			**III**		
	Rs	**A**	**P**	**Rs**	**A**	**P**	**Rs**	**A**	**P**
1913-14	5	0	0	1	2	0	0	10	0
1914-15	5	0	0	2	4	0	1	8	0
1915-16	5	0	0	2	4	0	1	6	0
1916-17	6	0	0	2	12	0	1	14	0
1917-18	7	9	0	3	11	0	2	13	0
1918-19	8	1	0	4	3	0	3	3	0
1919-20	9	14	0	4	14	0	3	4	0
1920-21	11	2	0	6	2	0	4	0	0

Table 5.10

Vengurla Port									
Years	**Class**								
	I			**II**			**III**		
	Rs	**A**	**P**	**Rs**	**A**	**P**	**Rs**	**A**	**P**
1913-14	5	0	0	1	2	0	0	10	0
1914-15	5	0	0	2	6	0	1	10	0
1915-16	5	0	0	2	6	0	1	8	0
1916-17	6	0	0	2	14	0	2	0	0
1917-18	7	13	0	3	13	0	2	15	0
1918-19	8	5	0	4	5	0	3	5	0
1919-20	10	2	0	5	2	0	3	6	0
1920-21	11	6	0	6	6	0	4	2	0

Besides Bombay, migration took place to Kolhapur, Belgaum and other nearby Deccan regions. The goldsmith industry was found to engage persons belonging to various castes and communities such as Sonars, Marathas, Brahmins, Jains, Muslims, Lohars. Although there were traditional local goldsmiths, majority of them engaged in this industry came from outside. The percentage of outsiders to the total number of shops in the city was specified as 34. Many of them came to the city from the Konkan.[138] Passengers came by motorbuses from Konkan to the city of Kolhapur to work as silver and bead makers, rold gold ornament makers, and coppersmiths. They got jobs in the bakeries, flour mills and iron works.[139] The population of the Kolhapur city increased by 140% during the period of seventy years from 1872 to 1941. In the year 1872, a bridge on the Panchaganga River was constructed which connected Konkan and Kolhapur. This resulted in the growth of trade and traffic into and through Kolhapur. This town came to call as the Gateway to the Konkan. The population in 1911 of the people born in Ratnagiri Collectorate and settled in Kolhapur was 1984, it was 1277 in 1921 and it rose to 1586 in 1931.[140] A few went to Karachi. Some more went to the East and South Africa.[141]

Chief Features of Migrating Population

The most characteristic feature of the population of the Ratnagiri Collectorate was the large proportion of people who temporarily migrated. One man in almost every family whether he belonged to the cultivating class or was petty landlord usually was away for the major part of the year out of his home. He, as a general rule, was a young and competent person in the family. This left the weaker members of the family to look after the fields. Women and children were mostly left behind. If one would peep into cause of migration of this sort it will be noticed that the produce of the land cultivated by an average family was not enough to keep the family going for more than three or four months a year. In other words, agriculture was not the main but considered as a subsidiary industry with majority of the cultivating classes.

On the other hand, there was a constantly increasing demand for all kinds of labour in and around Bombay. The jobs that these migrants took up generally were as factory workers, domestic servants, postal peons, police, and coolies in government and business offices, gardeners, carpenters, and dockworkers. The educated people worked as clerks in government offices, factories, business houses, schoolmasters and professors, lawyers.

There was hardly any immigration to these parts. A large number of kulwadis and Mahars went to Bombay to seek employment.[142] Malvan, Vengurla which had brisk trade in the earlier years became places of no importance. Ratnagiri eked out the deficiency of her food supply not by manufactures but by sending its young men to Bombay and elsewhere. Remittances came from there making it a money order economy. Money came even from South Africa. A number of Rajapur Muslims who settled in South Africa sent money home but these remittances were not really in large amounts.[143]

During the year 1907, revenue received by money orders amounted to Rupees 9,270. This mode of remittance continued to be more popular year after year.[144] The total amount of revenue of all kinds received by postal money orders during 1909 was Rupees 10,624 and in 1910 it was Rupees 14,027.[145] In spite of the large amount of money that came to the Collectorate in the form of pensions, in spite of nearly a quarter of the entire population annually spending the best part of the year in earning livelihood in Bombay or elsewhere and sending money home, the people still lived under below poverty line.[146]

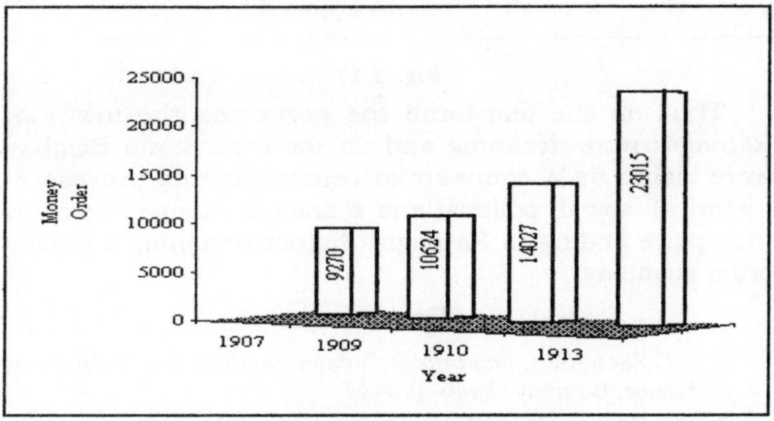

Fig. 5.16

The remittances through money orders did not improve the economy in any way because the money was consumed to feed the family. The remittances also were used for marriage of relatives, repairing houses, purchasing lands, for gifts during festivals, funerals or to pay the lawyer settle property disputes. They also contracted debts for agricultural purposes and waste on marriage expenses.[147] About ¼ of the population were bound to go to enable the khot his ardhil or tirdhil.[148] The proportion of income remitted was also quite low though exact figures were not available. That the poverty of the Konkan was phenomenal is evident from the per capita Income of this region given by L.J. Sedwick in the Census of India. The table shows the per capita income of the whole of Konkan. Ratnagiri had a lower rate than the other parts of Konkan. This explains why there was so much of migration from here.

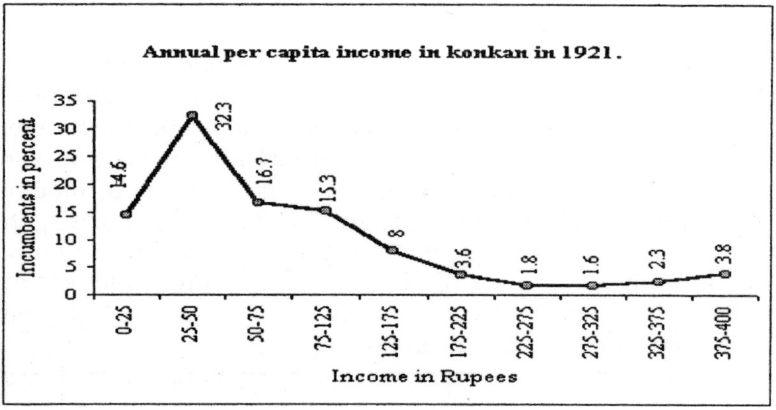

Fig. 5.17

Thus on the one hand the ports and the towns of Ratnagiri were declining and on the other hand Bombay were rising as a commercial center. In this process of historical, social, political and economic change migration took place ending in Ratnagiri district becoming a money order economy.

References

1. K.C.Zachariah, *Migrants in Greater Bombay,* Asia Publishing House, Bombay, 1966, p.341.
2. R.A.Edwin, Ed, JNU, Encyclopaedia of Social Sciences,Vol No. IX, The Macmillan Co., New york,1957, Migration: Social Aspects, pp.420-422.
3. David L.Sills, JNU, International Encyclopaedia of the Social Sciences, Vol No.X, The Macmillan Co. and The Free Press, 1968, Migrant Labour, p.286.
4. Vidyut Joshi, *Migrant Labour and Related Issues,* Mohan Oprimlani for Oxford & IBH Co. Pvt Ltd., Bombay, 1987, p.12.
5. V.V.Mirasi, Ed., *Corpus Inscriptionum Indicarum,* Vol No.VI, New Delhi, 1978, pp.17-28, Verses 31-32.

6. Gazetteer of the Bombay Presidency, Kolaba and Janjira, Vol XI, Government Central Press, Maharashtra State, 1883, pp.43-45; also Gazetteer of the Bombay Presidency, Vol-X, Ratnagiri and Savantwadi, Government Central Press, Maharashtra State, 1880, pp.114-15.
7. Census of the Bombay Presidency 1872, General Report and Tables of the Population, Houses in the Bombay Presidency, part II, Bombay, Government Central Press, 1875, p.12. [GIPE]
8. *Ibid.*
9. GIPE, Census of India, Census of the Bombay Presidency of 1872, General Report & Tables of the Population, Houses in The Bombay Presidency, Bombay Government Central Press, 1875; Census of India 1881,Operations and the Results in the Presidency of Bombay Including Sind, Vol No.II, Tables, Bombay, 1882; Census of India 1891 Bombay and its Feudatories, Imperial Tables, Part II, Vol No.VIII, Bombay 1892; Census of India 1901, Bombay Provincial Tables, Part III, Vol No.IX-B, Bombay 1902; Census of India 1911, Bombay Imperial Tables, Part II, Table VII, Bombay 1912; Census of India 1921, Imperial and Provincial Tables, Bombay Presidency, Part II, Vol No.VIII, Bombay 1922.(hereafter Census)
10. Census of India, *op.cit.*,1901.
11. Census of India, *op.cit.*,1911, 1921.
12. W.Courtney, Acting Secretary to Government to E.H.Townsend, Revenue Commissioner, Southern Division, Census, *op.cit.*, p.17. [GIPE]
13. Jonathan Elphinstone, Collector of Ratnagiri, Ratnagiri Collector's Office, to the Secretary to Government, Revenue Department, Bombay, dated 28 August 1874, MSA, General Department Vol No.40/1874, pp.87-88.(hereafter G.D.)
14. *Ibid*, p.91.
15. *Jillah Janganana Nirdesha Grantha*, Ratnagiri, Bharatiya Janganana 1961, Maharashtra Janganana Karyalaya, l(Marathi), Mumbai, 1965, p.13.
16. G.Elliot, Collector, Ratnagiri to Thomas Williamson, Revenue Commissioner, dated 26 September 1833, MSA, Revenue Department Vol. No. 41/663/1835, pp.86-87.(hereafter R.D.)
17. Papers Relating To The Revision Survey Settlement Of The Ratnagiri Taluka Of The Ratnagiri Collectorate, BGS, Vol No.CCCLXXVII- New Series, Bombay, Government Central Press, 1898, p.5.

18. Papers Relating To The Revision Survey Settlement Of The Ratnagiri Taluka Of The Ratnagiri Collectorate, BGS, Vol No.DXVIII- New Series, Bombay, Government Central Press, 1915, Appendix D, p.24.
19. R.D.Choskey, Ed, L.Smith to Sir Evan Napean, Re: Remarks on the Ceded Territories, dated 4 December 1813, *Malwan Residency, Select Documents from the Ratnagiri Collection's Files* (Peshwa Daftar), The Sangam Press, Poona, 1956, p.18.
20. Papers Relating To The Revision Survey Settlement Of The Malwan Taluka Of The Ratnagiri Collectorate, llBGS, Vol No.DXXVIII- New Series, Bombay, Government Central Press, 1915, pp.6, 23 and 24.
21. Papers Relating To The Revision Survey Settlement Of The Malwan Taluka Of The Ratnagiri Collectorate, llBGS, Vol No.CCLXXII- New Series, Bombay, Government Central Press, 1893, p.4.
22. *Ibid*, No. DXXVIII- New Series, Appendix E, p.23.
23. Census of India, *op.cit.*, 1872, 1881, 1891,1901,1911,1921.
24. *Ibid*, p. 18.
25. R.E.Enthoven, *The Tribes and Castes of Bombay*, Vol No.I, Asia Educational Services, New Delhi, 1990, p.241.
26. J.H.Pelly, Collector of Ratnagiri, to Francis Warden, Chief Secretary to Government, Bombay, dated 18 December 1820, MSA, R.D. Vol No. 16/1821, pp.468-70.
27. Census Report, R.D.Vol No. 41/663/1835, p.83.
28. Report on towns, villages and population, R.D. Vol No.41/ 663/ 1835, p.86.
29. Maureen P. Patterson, 'Changing Patterns of Occupation among Chitapavan Brahmins', University of Chicago, *Indian Economic and Social History Review*,(hereafter *IESHR)*, Vol No.VII, 3 September 1970, pp.376-7.
30. G.V.Bhave, *Bhave Kula Vrittanta*, (Marathi), G.V. Bhave Publications, Poona, 1940, p.69.
31. Census Report, R.D. Vol No.41/663/1835, p.83.
32. R.E.Enthoven, *op.cit.*, pp.249-50.
33. 1 lJ.H.Pelly, Collector of Ratnagiri, to Francis Warden, Secretary to Government, dated 18 December 1820, MSA, R.D. Vol No.16/16/1821, p.470.
34. S.M.Edwardes, *Rise of Bombay, A Retrospect*, Reprint from the Vol I of the Census of India series, Times of India Press, Bombay, 1902, p.210.
35. N.K.Wagle, 'The History and Social Organisation of the

Gauda Sarawata Brahmanas of the West Coast of India', *Journal of Indian History,* Vol No.XLVIII, part III, April-December 1970, Published by University of Kerala, Trivandrum, p.316.

36. N.K.Wagle, *op.cit.*, p.316.
37. *Ibid,* p.316; S.R.Dongerkery, A History of the University of Bombay,1857-1957, Bombay, University of Bombay, 1957, p.17.
38. G.W.Forrest, Selections from the letters, dispatches and other papers in the Bombay Secretariat, Vol No.II, Government Central Press, Bombay, 1885, p.364.
39. Dr. Balkrishna, *The Commercial Survey of Kolhapur City in 1926*, Mumbai,1928, p.1.
40. Ratnagiri District Gazetteer, 1880, *op.cit.*, p.13.
41. W.W.Dowell, Lieut. and Assisstant Class, Survey Department, dated 1 November 1829, MSA, R.D. Vol No.225/1851, pp.272-3.
42. R.E.Enthoven, *op.cit.*, p.72.
43. *Ibid,* p.103.
44. T.B.Jervis, *Statistics of Western India,* Bombay, pp.14-5.
45. MSA, W.W.Dowell, Lieut. and Assisstant Class, Survey Department, dated 1 November 1829, R.D.Vol No.225/1851, pp.272-3.
46. R.E.Enthoven, *op.cit.*, pp. 310-11.
47. Ratnagiri District Gazetteer, *op.cit.*, 1880, p.128.
48. *Ibid.*
49. G.Guriyale, Superintendent to E.H. Townsend, Revenue Commissioner, dated 13 January 1850, MSA, R.D.Vol No.557/1851, p.78.
50. Narayan Ganesh Musale, *Ratnagiri Zillah Kal Aaj va Udya,* Abhinav Prakashan, Mumbai, 1958, p.60.
51. M.D.David, 'The Beginning of Bombay's Economic Development,' 1661-1708, *Journal of Indian History,* lp.224.
52. Consultation, MSA, Public Department Diary(hereafter Pub.D.), Vol No.15 C of 1742, dated 3 September 1742, lp.88.
53. Anthony Disney, *Twilight of the Pepper Empire,* Harvard University Press, 1978, p.95.
54. *Ibid.*
55. M. N. Pearson, *Wealth and Power, Indian groups in the Portuguese Indian economy,* South Asia, Vol No. III 1973, lp.34.

56. Consultation, Pub.D. No.19 A of 1746, dated 4 November 1746; G. W. Forrest (ed) *Selections from letters, despatches, and other State papers preserved in the Bombay Secretariat Maratha series,* Vol No.I, Part 1, Government Central Press, Bombay, 1885, see introduction.
57. Census of India, *op.cit.*, 1881,1891,1901,1911,1921.
58. R.V.Parulkar and C.L.Bakshi, Selections from the Educational Records, Bombay, Part II, (1815-1840), Published by the Indian Institute of Education, Bombay, 1955, p.88.
59. R.V.Parulekar, Ed, Survey of Indigenous Education in the Province of Bombay (1820-30), Published by Indian Institute of Education, Bombay, 1951, p.XV.
60. *Ibid,* p. XV.
61. R.V. Parulekar and C.L.Bakshi, *op.cit.*, p.5.
62. *Ibid.*
63. Report of the Board of Education, *op.cit.*, 1852, pp.74-75.
64. Nurullah Naik, *History of Education in India,* Macmillan & Co. Ltd, Bombay, 1951, p.324.
65. *Ibid,* pp.368-369.
66. M.S.Rege, 'The History and Survey of Education in the Ratnagiri District' Unpublished Ph.D Thesis, 1961, lBombay, pp.325-33.
67. REPORT ON THE NATIVE PAPERS For the Week ending with 6th may 1890, Government Central Press, Bombay, pp.14-15.
68. Aurthur Crawford, Commissioner to John Nugent, Secretary to Government, Poona, dated 28 July 1880, MSA, R.D. Vol No.20/1880, pp.27-28.
69. Reporter, REPORT ON THE NATIVE PAPERS For the Week ending with the week 27 July 1868, Poona, Office of the Director of Public Instruction, p.6.
70. Stowell, Secretary, Board of Education, Ratnagiri Collector office to J.G.Lumsden, Secretary to Government MSA, G.D., Board of Education, Bombay, dated 16 April 1850, R.D. Vol No.30/404/1850, p.9.
71. Jayasri Ray Chaudhuri, 'Migration & Remittances Inter-Urban and Rural-Urban Linkages', *IESHR,* SAGE Publications, New Delhi, 1993, p.24.
72. Meera Kosambi, *Bombay in Transition, the Growth, Social Ecology of a Colonial City, 1880-1980,* Almquist & Wiksell Institute, Stockholm, Sweden, 1986, p.35.
73. K.C.Zachariah, *op.cit.,* p.7.

74. Ashin Das Gupta, *Indian Merchants and the Decline of Surat, 1700-1750,* Franz Steiner Verlag, Wiesbaden, 1979, pp. 3-4; Ashin Das Gupta, 'The Crisis at Surat, 1730-32', *Bengal, Past and Present,* Vol No.86, 1967, p. 148; Ashin Das Gupta, *Indian Merchants and Trade of the Indian Ocean, 1500-1775,* Cambridge Economic History of India, Vol No.I, Forthcoming.
75. Imperial Gazetteer of India, Provincial Series, Bombay Presidency, Vol No.I, Usha publications, New Delhi, pp.219-220.
76. S.M.Edwardes, *op.cit.*, pp. 264-65.
77. Gazetteer of Bombay City and Island, Vol No.I, Government Central Press, Bombay, p.488.
78. Imperial Gazetteer of India, *op.cit.*, p.221.
79. *Ibid*, pp.342-44.
80. N.C.Parkinson, *Trade in Eastern Seas*, 1793-1813, Cambridge University Press, Manchester, 1961, p.330.
81. Andrew Pope, ' British Steam Shipping and the Indian Coastal Trade 1870-1915', IESHR, Vol No.XXXII, No. 1, SAGE, New Delhi, 1995, p.11.
82. *Ibid*, p.16.
83. Census of the Island of Bombay, 1864, Education Society's Press, Byculla, Bombay, p.9.
84. Census Reports of 1872 and 1881.
85. Meera Kosambi, *op.cit.*, p.50.
86. K.C.Zachariah, *op.cit.*, p.14.
87. Heather and Vijay Joshi, *Surplus Labour and the City, A Study of Bombay*, Oxford University Press, 1976, Bombay, p.19.
88. Imperial Gazetteer of India, *op.cit.*, p. 228.
89. D.R.Gadgil, GIPE, *A socio-Economic Survey*, part II, Publication No 25, Poona, 1952, p.32.
90. M.R.Montogomery Martion, *Possessions of the East India Company,* 1837, p.33.
91. John.A.Dunlop, Collector of South konkan, Collector's Office to the Secretary to Government, dated 15 August 1824, R.D. Vol No.11/1825, part-III, p.78.
92. A.K.Nairne, *History of Konkan,* Gazetteer of the Bombay Presidency, Vol No.I, Part II, Bombay, 1894, p.12.
93. M.R.Montogomery Martion, *op.cit.*, p.33.
94. Gazetteer of the Bombay Presidency Vol No.X-B, Ratnagiri and Sawantwadi, Government Central Press, Bombay, 1904, p.143.

95. Census of India, *op.cit.*, 1872,1881, 1891, 1901, 1911, 1921.
96. M.B. Nanavati, J.J.Anjaria, *The Indian Rural Problem,* Bombay, Indian Society of Agricultural Economics, lBombay Vora and Co., 1951, p.15; also Census Reports.
97. W.B.Donde, 'Rural Labourers in konkan', Unpublished Ph.D Thesis, Bombay University, 1950, p.10.
98. H.H.Risley and E.A Gait, Census of India, 1901, *op.cit.*, 1903, p.206.
99. E.A. Gait, Census of India, 1911, *op.cit.*,1913, pp.413-14.
100. J.T.Martin, Census of India, 1921, *op.cit.*,1924, p.246.
101. P.A.Wadia and K.T.Merchant, *Our Economic Problems,* Bombay, 1954, pp.341-2.
102. The Bombay Provincial Enquiry Committee of the Government of Bombay, Government of India, Report, 1929-30, Vol No.I, 1930, p.8.
103. The Labour Investigation Committee, Report, Government of India, 1929-30, Vol No.I, 1930, p.8.
104. P.A.Wadia, *Natural Resources and Population of India,* Bombay, 1959, pp.38-9.
105. Gazetteer of the Bombay Presidency Vol No.X-B, Ratnagiri and Savantwadi, Government Central Press, Bombay, 1904, p.143.
106. E.H.Townsend, Revenue Commissioner, Sholapur District, Revenue Commissioner's Camp, 24 December 1846, to The Secretary to Bombay Government, Papers relating to the Revision Survey Settlement of the Ratnagiri Taluka of the Ratnagiri Collectorate, MSA, BGS, No-CCCLXVII- New Series, Bombay, Government Central Press, 1898, p.12; also R.D. Vol No.194/1898, p.133.
107. The Collector of Ratnagiri to the Secretary to Government, Bombay, dated 18 July 1881, MSA, R.D.Vol No.20/1881, p.3.
108. Sunanda Krishnamurthy, 'Agricultural Labourers in the Bombay Deccan, 1874-1922', *IESHR,* Vol No.XXVI, lNo I, SAGE Publication, 1987, p.92.
109. Morris David Morris, *Emergence of an Industrial Labour Force in India: A Study of the Bombay Cotton Mills 1854-1947,* Bombay, 1965, p.63.
110. A.K.Nairne, op.cit., p.12.
111. W.Woodward, 1st Assistant Collector, Ratnagiri Collector's Office to the Secretary to Government, dated 21 July 1875, MSA, R.D. Vol No.7/1875, p.262.
112. A.Cumine, Assistant Collector to the Secretary to

Government, Ratnagiri Collector's Office, dated 19 July 1882, MSA, R.D. Vol No.116 /1882, p.37.

113. W.Wilson, 1st Assistant Collector, Ratnagiri Collector's Office to the Secretary to Government, dated 21 July 1875, R.D. Vol No.7/1875, p.262.
114. R.E.Candy Collector to N. Pratt, the Commissioner, dated 21 March 1894, MSA, R.D. Vol No.34/1896, p.34.
115. Aurthur Crawford, Commissioner to John Nugent, Secretary to Government, Poona, dated 28 July 1880, MSA, R.D. Vol No.20/1880, p.21.
116. R.E.Candy, Collector of Ratnagiri to the commissioner, dated 9 August 1886, MSA, R.D. Vol No.16/1886, p.45.
117. R.E.Candy, Collector of Ratnagiri to the Commissioner, dated 9 August 1886, MSA, R.D. Vol No.16/1886, p.38.
118. A.Cumine, Acting Collector of Ratnagiri to the Commissioner, Ratnagiri, dated 9 August 1892, MSA, R.D. Vol No.26/1893, pp.28-9.
119. L.N.Brown, Collector of Ratnagiri to the Commissioner, Ratnagiri, dated 28 February 1915, MSA, R.D.File No. 8528/24, Vol No. II, pp.165-66.
120. W. Wilson, Acting Collector of Ratnagiri, Re: Administrative Report, Bombay Castle, dated 9 November 1880, MSA, R.D. Vol No. 20/1880, p.294.
121. B.E.Vaccha, Executive Engineer in charge of boring works, Nasik to the Superintending Engineer, Southern Circle, dated 30 August1927, Re: Ratnagiri Pier, MSA, R.D.File No. 8528/24,Vol No.I, p.190.
122. *Ibid*, p.73.
123. H.Moreland Director, and the Committee Members, dated 20 August 10928, MSA, R.D.File No. 8528/24, Vol No.III, p.29.
124. Dattatreya Mehendale to Sir Fredrick H.Sykes, Governor of Bombay, dated 17 March 1929, MSA, R.D.File No. 8528/24, Vol No.I, pp.143, 146 and 147.
125. K.K.Desai, Executive Engineers of Ratnagiri and Colaba District to the Chief Secretary to Government, Revenue lDepartment ,dated 15 June 1908, MSA, R.D. Vol No.231/1909, pp.231-32.
126. *Ibid*, p.236.
127. *Ibid*.
128. Administrative Report for the year 1898-99, dated 28 Nov 1899, MSA, and R.D. Vol No.24/1900, pp.49-51.
129. J.K.N.Kabraji, Acting Collector, Ratnagiri, to the

Commissioner, Southern Division, dated 1 October 1904, lMSA, R.D. Vol No.26/1905, p.179.

130. Meera Kosambi, *op.cit.*, p.64.
131. The figures of the migrants from 1881 to 1931 are based on the Census of India, 1931, Vol No.IX, 'The Cities lof Bombay Presidency', p.16.
132. REPORT ON THE NATIVE PAPERS For the Week ending with the Jan to Dec 1890, Office of the Reporter of the Native Press, New Secretariat, Bombay, pp.24, 38 and 59.
133. Indian opinion, REPORT ON THE NATIVE PAPERS For the Week ending with 15 December 1878, Issue of 23 November 1878, Office of the Reporter of the Native Press, New Secretariat, Bombay, p.8
134. Jagan Mitra, Re:Inconveience Caused to the Passengers, REPORT ON THE NATIVE PAPERS For the Week ending with 8 August 1891, Issue of 3 August 1891, Office of the Reporter of the Native Press, New Secretariat, Bombay, p.12.
135. Papers Relating to the Revision Survey Settlement of the Malwan Taluka of the Ratnagiri Collectorate, BGS, No DXVII- New Series, Bombay, Government Central Press, 1915, pp.6-7.
136. Papers Relating to the Revision Survey Settlement of the Ratnagiri Taluka of the Ratnagiri Collectorate, BGS, lNo. DLXXIV- New Series, Bombay, Government Central Press, 1914, p.9.
137. Census of the Bombay Presidency 1921, *op.cit.*,1921, Appendix K, Statement A.
138. Dr. Balkrishna, *op.cit.*, p.22.
139. N.V.Sovani, GIPE, *Social Survey of Kolhapur City- Industry, Trade and Labour,* Vol No.II, Publication No.23, 11951, p.106.
140. *Ibid,* pp.12 and 14.
141. The Konkan Co-operative Enquiry Committee, Report on the Ratnagiri District, Government Central Press, lBombay, GIPE, The Bombay Quarterly, December 1923, p.195.
142. K.V.Joshi, District Deputy Collector to the Collector of Ratnagiri, dated 22 August 1908, MSA, R.D. Vol lNo.26/1909, p.182.
143. J.H. Garett, Assistant Collector to Company, Ratnagiri, to the Collector of Ratnagiri, dated 15 August 1907, MSA, R.D. Vol No.30/1908, pp.137-8.

144. A.F.Maconochie, Collector of Ratnagiri, to the Commissioner, Southern Division, Ratnagiri, dated 24 September 1907, MSA, R.D. Vol No.30/1908, p.44.
145. A.F.Maconochie, Collector of Ratnagiri, to the Commissioner, Southern Division, Ratnagiri, dated 21 September 1909, MSA, R.D. Vol No.23/1910, p.28.
146. J.Ghosal, Collector to the Commissioner, Southern Division, Ratnagiri, dated 26 September 1910, MSA, R.D. Vol No.16/1911, p.37; Papers Relating to the Revision Survey Settlement of the Ratnagiri Taluka of the Ratnagiri Collectorate, BGS, No DLXXIV- New Series, Bombay, Government Central Press, 1914, p.9.
147. Arthur Crawford, Commissioner, Southern Division to John Nugent, Secretary to Government, Poona, dated 26 August 1885, MSA, R.D. Vol No. 29/1885, p. 225.
148. *Ibid.*

CHAPTER 6

CONCLUSION

The chief yardsticks of measuring the prosperity of any place whether it is large or small, is the produce of the region, its transport facilities and the volume of her internal and external trade and its social conditions. Our study of South Konkan is a witness to the fact that Ratnagiri, Malvan and Vengurla, the three coastal towns enjoyed a good degree of prosperity in the long past much before the advent of the foreigners. Having gone through the impact of British on Ratnagiri, Malvan, Vengurla one conclusion can be conveniently drawn that the celebrated ports of Konkan seemed to pale into insignificance by the beginning of the twentieth century.

The British rule witnessed an array of changes- in the administration, in the economy and above all its impact on the society. And this impact was more concrete and more enduring. They were much more severe than the problems of fall in prices or stagnation in cultivation that were visible in the first few years of the British rule. It seemed that the new administrators, wished to move towards changes smoothly and gradually rather than impose any policies rapidly. Even the most conscientious reforms, the new survey system maintained was to be safeguarding and recording customary rights.

The observations of the British rule in the beginning pointed out to Konkan traditional economy adjusting itself to meet the requirements of an administrative system, which was the product of a developed capitalist economy. By mid nineteenth century, however, distinct signs in agricultural revival were seen. An upward trend in cultivated area and nominal rise in prices were also noticed. It is true that the development of new order and the new forces with their new norms and values was a positive aspect of the British occupation of South Konkan. But the impact of the introduction of a totally alien economic system into a traditional base of its economy was baffling and not conducive for its growth and development. The changes seen were illusive. Moreover, South Konkan became part of the periphery of Bombay, the Metropolis did not take too long to decline in its importance. It could not escape the adverse impact of centripetal forces that set in during the growth of the Metropolis Bombay that had emerged as a commercial city under British rule.

The decline of these regions, which has been one of our principal concerns, is explained by a combination of different factors.

To begin with, the new methods of revenue collection, the various settlements made yielded comparatively good revenue yet they were not consistent. A bleak picture was reflected in the Southern Konkan as a whole. It was however, found that despite the efforts taken both by the British and the Indians things did not go the way they were expected to go. The policy of the British was to collect tax, but this made the farmer's condition more miserable. At the same time the prices of food grains fell heavily and the farmers had no money to pay the taxes. Money was difficult to come by. Even in difficult situations of famine like the ones that affected the region they did not relax the policies and forced the people to pay the taxes.

The new administrator's inability to understand and recognize the existing system of the massive property holders of land namely the khots of Ratnagiri and at the same time their passion to grab more lands led to the transformation, de jure of almost all land holders into tenants of the government. The property became more standardized as the watandars or the khots lost ground on the soil that was once their pride and it was no longer for sale. All their gifts, rights, inams, and powers seemed to be slipping out of their hands.

At difficult times also the Mamlatdars used physical force against people to collect taxes. The farmers suffered a great deal during the British rule. Although the British did not snatch the rights of the Mamlatdars or the khots, they did not also give them the authority to reduce the rate of tax. Therefore the Mamlatdars were ready to use any means to collect the taxes. All this had a negative effect on agriculture. Many people were idle. It was not possible for them to show proficiency in this condition. There was one question that found no solution. What was the effect of the British policies about the land and the revenue.? Despite the innumerable Surveys, Experiments and Acts, the condition of the people of Ratnagiri was bad. No sooner than the Company's rule started the Officers of the East India Company began to be responsible slowly but systematically for the downfall of certain parts of South Konkan.

British rule brought about many institutional changes here which influenced its economy and its effects were felt in the long duration. The khots took advantage of their position and tried to get the best, both from the people and the government. The khoti which had been absorbed into the Ratnagiri economic system was not easy to do away with. On the one hand it annoyed the khots who had held a high position for so long and on the other hand it enraged smaller khots because they were neither able to satisfy the ryuts nor the government. In this process they suffered in the hands of the new government.

Thus, the greatest obstacle to the progress in South konkan was insecurity of life and property. The relation between government and the khot and the khot and the tenant had become very unsettled during this period. Numerous theories were advanced as to the relative positions of the Khot and the tenant. This at large determined the mutual rights and obligations of the parties and was hailed with satisfaction both by the khot and the tenant although many difficulties and doubts hampered the smooth running of the revenue administration at times.

The principal crops of the three regions, it should be agreed were not very important from the economic point of view. It is also true that the vagaries of monsoon, capacity of land to give a single crop, absence of irrigational facilities and erosion seemed to rob the region of a profitable cultivation. It was equally true that the cultivator was left with a poor size of the holding. Nevertheless things could have changed for the better with apt government intervention.

To add to the problems, rural indebtedness haunted the agricultural economy of South konkan. It can be assumed that the expansion of cultivation that took place was because of the reduction and equalisation of land tax. But unfortunately the land of the region was of a poor quality. Therefore output did not exceed as much as expected. Meanwhile, the population was increasing. This resulted in the increase of rents. The land labourers were not paid good wages.

As regards the techniques and productivity, it may be conveniently said that they remained fundamentally unchanged over most of the Konkan. Improved seeds or methods did not seem to have been able to prevent the stagnation of the yields in the different belts of the Konkan. Information on crops was scanty and it was difficult to gauge the rise in yield if it rose at all.

But from the point of view of industrialisation the three coastal regions fell into two distinct parts-the hilly tracts and the coastal regions. The former was economically worse off as it did not offer scope for producing crops other than paddy, ragi, nachni, kulith and coarse rice. The latter was much better on account of its capacity to grow paying crops like cocoanuts, areca nuts, bananas and mangoes. Both the hilly parts and the coastal regions had an essentially an agricultural economy. But the fact remains that while the hilly tract depended on the forest resources, the coastal region depended on salt, fisheries and some essential commodities. Thus the industrial development of the three port towns and South konkan as a whole depended on economy of natural wealth, scientific development of salt, improvement of fisheries and modernising of agro-based industries.

It is unfortunate that no special efforts were taken by the government to open new industries, which could thrive in these regions. Even core industries like forestry, fisheries, salt, weaving and similar others were not attended to during the British time. In fact the growth of industries since 1891 seemed to be only intermittent and it cannot be stated that any particular industry had ever had a stable course of progress. If cultivation expanded and more people started experimenting on agriculture, it was not because of better prospects or improved prices or better transportation facilities that were provided. The government did not provide both these facilities to the satisfaction of the people. Vengurla's salt pans, Malvan's cashew and cocoanut production and Ratnagiri's mango production if had been managed by the British on smoother lines, South Konkan's economy would not have been in such a bad shape. Even in the early twenties hardly any expansion or improvement could be seen regardless of the experiments done by the Agricultural department. A few regions like Ratnagiri did show some progress as a result of the experiments done on mangoes, sann and onions yet generally the picture was one of stagnation or decline.

In the growth of the oceanic trade of South Konkan in general no distinct trends were noticeable. The picture of South Konkan at the time of British acquisitions as it appears in the accounts and reports of the various officers in charge is gloomy. Before 1860 many British officials wrote in-depth and to a certain extent reliable accounts of Konkan.

In fact, a reporter on External Commerce has mentioned that there was ' a stagnation in this part of the world.' Further the economic depression of 1830s resulted in the decline of trade. The opening of the new ghat roads in the 1830-40s gave a partial blow to the oceanic trade while activating the external trade of the Konkan coast. However, there was transformation both in the pattern and the quantum of trade.

The fact cannot be ignored that the attitude of the British Government to the South Konkan had been rather step-motherly and if at all attempts were made sometime they were hindered by the difficult topography in the region. Thus most roads were kuccha or unmettled roads that could scarcely be called as roads. The roads were in a bad shape and constantly needed repairs. The local people often complained about the condition of roads to the government.

Almost all the trade for centuries was carried on from minor ports. They may be conveniently called as minor as no port on the Konkan coast could be considered as a major port in the real sense of the term. Ratnagiri, Malvan, Vengurla, may undoubtedly be called minor ports. Even when they were subsidiary members of the cluster surrounding one or larger ports they performed a distinct and an intelligible function in that cluster. In fact it was impossible for steamships to serve hundreds of small ports on economic lines. Sailing vessels alone could meet their need. So sailing vessel traffic required to be economically mobilised.

The bright prospects of these minor ports continuing to handle traffic of about four million tons throughout the latter part of the nineteenth century could have been maintained by the government. The demand for building material, firewood and timber could be increased. The movement of raw materials and food grains could be continued.

Notwithstanding the traffic that was handled by water transport, the ports were in a neglected state. Siltation of creeks was said to be one of the major handicaps that reduced the importance of the ports in the course of years. The Vengurla port was highly silted and navigation was only possible only at high tides. As a result only small boats up to five tons could ply in it and passengers and cargo steamers had to anchor at a distance. The reduced importance was hastened as a result of the deforestation and reclamation of the Khajan (marshy) lands.

The decline of ports was could be because of another different trend that was seen in the trading pattern by the beginning of the twentieth century. While the coastal trade was reducing, roadways sent commodities to other parts. As far as Malvan was concerned it served very little as a shipping port for the over ghat traffic while Ratnagiri had a good deal of over ghat traffic that used to pass through the port of Jaygad. The southern Maratha railway later diverted this traffic. This kind of a diversion affected the traders and the middlemen more than the agriculturists. The commerce by road from Malvan town in the early twentieth century showed that the inward trade was almost 48 lakhs while outward trade was 9 lakhs. Vengurla's inward trade was 69 lakhs and outward trade was 12 lakhs. In general the inward trade exceeded the outward trade. Although there are chances of errors, it can yet safely be said that the proportion of inward trade to outward trade was approximately 3:1.

Although the ports seemed to be in the background there were commercial ties between Bombay and Konkan that constituted an important aspect of the oceanic trade of South Konkan of this period. Even though it was a negligible part of west coast, indeed it had close relations with Bombay. The physical contiguity and the shipping on the same coastal line in general facilitated the commercial links. The ports of South Konkan were trade links between the indigenous interior lands and foreign dependent markets. Bombay being the entre pot of the west coast was the centre through which trade went on between Konkan and the other parts of the country. The increasing trade of Konkan with England was also conducted through the port of Bombay. To be more precise Bombay became the trade link between Konkan and

England, Konkan and other Western Coastal regions like Canara, Malabar, Gujarat and such other larger and smaller ports on western coast of India. It also linked Konkan with a few foreign countries.

The increased export of Mangoes, Betel nuts, rice, sugar, dry grains, coconuts from South Konkan port of Ratnagiri, Malvan, Vengurla to Bombay meant for the English markets gave a boost to the trade of South Konkan after 1840s.This on the one hand cemented commercial ties between Bombay and the nature based ports of South Konkan and on the other hand became instrumental in their regression. This is evident from the dominance of total exports over imports diminishing. M.N.Pearson rightly remarked that the problem of the third world countries lay not in poverty for often they were naturally rich.* The problem was this wealth ended up in metropolis. The three ports of South Konkan were not an exception to this rule.

The picture also reveals that the smaller ports in general conducted the inter-portal trade within the radii of the Konkan and Canara coasts while ports like Mangalore, Bombay, Gujarat carried on commerce on a broader and diversified scale. The vivid dimensions of the coastal trade on the west coast also reflected the mercantile motives along with the administrative interests of the ruling class. Indeed the process of decline in these coastal ports of South Konkan was probably more because of the various factors discussed above rather than silting of the Coasts.

The impact of British rule brought into focus one more factor. The resistance movement that showed up against the changing revenue system resulted in the emergence of a new group of educated people who were in a position to take up the leadership of the ryots in their fight for justice. First of all the economic policies followed by the British were such that they retarded the natural growth of the South Konkan economy and invariably affected the growth and development of various social classes in the society. The possibility of accumulation of wealth in the hands of a few people was remote and limited. The enhancement of land revenue policies could not have helped one section of the Konkan people at the expense of the ryots. Therefore the slightly

---

*M.N.Pearson, '*Wealth and Power, Indian Groups in the Portuguese Indian Economy*', South Asia Publication, lVol No.III, 1973, p.34.

better and affluent among the ryots and village officers were as much affected as the common ryots. That is the reason why they got the support of the large section of local people whenever they refused to pay the enhanced revenues or when they opposed to certain policy decisions as discussed in this chapter earlier. This was seen in the reactions of the people in their writings in the various Native newspaper reports and letters of complaint to the British officers through petitions and objections. The impact of British policies was making the educated class unite to fight for the interests of the South Konkan society.

A periphery of a metropolitan city could not evade the adverse impact of centripetal forces that set in during the growth of a metropolis. Its economy suffered due to the exodus of males and flows of inadequate capital and thereby got transformed into a money order economy. The already existing economy came to a stand still and even declined.

Under such circumstances, one cannot expect a swift development. In fact it has been observed that the region lacks the benefit for self-sustained development. The government involvement in the region therefore becomes vital to improve upon the deteriorating condition.

South Konkan being a part of a periphery of Bombay could not escape the adverse impact of centripetal forces that set in during the growth of metropolis, namely Bombay. The existing economy suffered due to the exodus of males turning it into a money order economy. The already subsistence economy stagnated and even declined. The British Government which had acquired the Southern Konkan territories by 1818, partly for political domination and partly for improving its trade probably fell short of its efforts. By the end of the century, the Government seemed to have lost interest in it.

One more important change under the new regime was the creation of a new class of English educated people in the South Konkan that was quick to grasp the new government jobs. This was the result of the already dominant Brahmin caste that was intelligent to adapt to the changes. If any increase in volume was achieved they were through new practices evolved by the people themselves. The chief castes of the Ratnagiri taluka namely the Brahmins, the Marathas, the Bhadaris, the Kunbis, the Muslims and the Mahars- all felt the impact of British rule. The Brahmin caste being the elite group of the society could afford to get good education. The Kunbis laboured without rest between infancy and old age. The Marathas were respectable race of men and influential. The Muslims who were either daldees or bhusarees mainly depended on fishery, made twine for fishing nets or raised hemp. The Bhandaris employed themselves in drawing toddy and cultivating land.

A number of factors accounted for this. One of the most important factors that accelerated the decline of this region was that South Konkan lay in the shadow area of Bombay. The attention of the British government was diverted to the port of Bombay, which had rapidly developed as a commercial center. In return, Ratnagiri district supplying majority of its people as major source of migrants to Bombay helped in the speedy growth of Bombay. The other cities of attraction were the Desh regions like Dharwar, Kolhapur, Belgaum, and Poona though not as important as Bombay. There were yet others, who went to Mauritius and Aden, and other parts away from their lands to earn money.

From the study based on the available evidence on the agricultural produce, volume of trade, their changes, their pattern, migration and remittances and the impact of British rule on the three ports of Konkan in the above discussion, striking features of South Konkan were experienced under the British rule.

- The three ports Ratnagiri, Malvan and Vengurla were midway points for the international trade.
- They may have been agriculturally poor, but were rich in forests products, salt production, crops like cocoanuts, cashew nuts, mangoes and fisheries, which could yield substantial income if the British had cared to develop. This in turn would have minimised migration.
- The European traders, the Portuguese and the Dutch in the beginning and the English later not only cut into the trade in commodities produced or exchanged by the regions but almost secured a monopoly of the carrying trade
- While it is agreed that the coming of the British meant intrusions it must not forgotten that their arrival and

operations meant fresh infusion of capital into the regions. Only the capital should have been given proper outlet.

- The three ports in general of South Konkan stood in the shadow of three dominant economic regions of India (Gujarat and Malabar and North Konkan coasts.) The commerce of the three ports was small when compared to the volume of goods and amounts involved in the total trade of the other two regions.

Economic, social and political conditions were in cosequence important among the many factors that led to the decline of the Konkan economy making it a money order economy.

The role of the state is vital in the growth or decline of an economy. It is not important whether the area is a periphery or is in the mainstream, it can be developed according its extent and its capability if the government takes identifies its plus and minus points.

Today slow but steady changes are seen in Ratnagiri, Malvan and Vengurla with the construction of Konkan railway. It is a missing link between India's commercial capital, Mumbai and other coastal parts. The 760-kilometer line, which was flagged off on 26 January 1998, connects Maharashtra, Goa and Karnataka. The completion of Konkan railway redeemed in the fiftieth year of India's Independence was a 'tryst with destiny' for many people in the Konkan region. It has already started giving a much-needed impetus to socio-economic development on the western coastline of India transforming the lives of eleven million people who live there. New agricultural and industrial experiments are being undertaken to develop Konkan region while generating employment to people. Roads are being attended to. The beaches are again gaining importance as a result of the efforts of the Tourism Department of Maharashtra. The safe and clean waters with a historical background full of coastal forts and sites have become an attraction even for the foreigners. All these efforts will not only fetch good revenue to the government but also bring back the lost glory of the coastal towns.

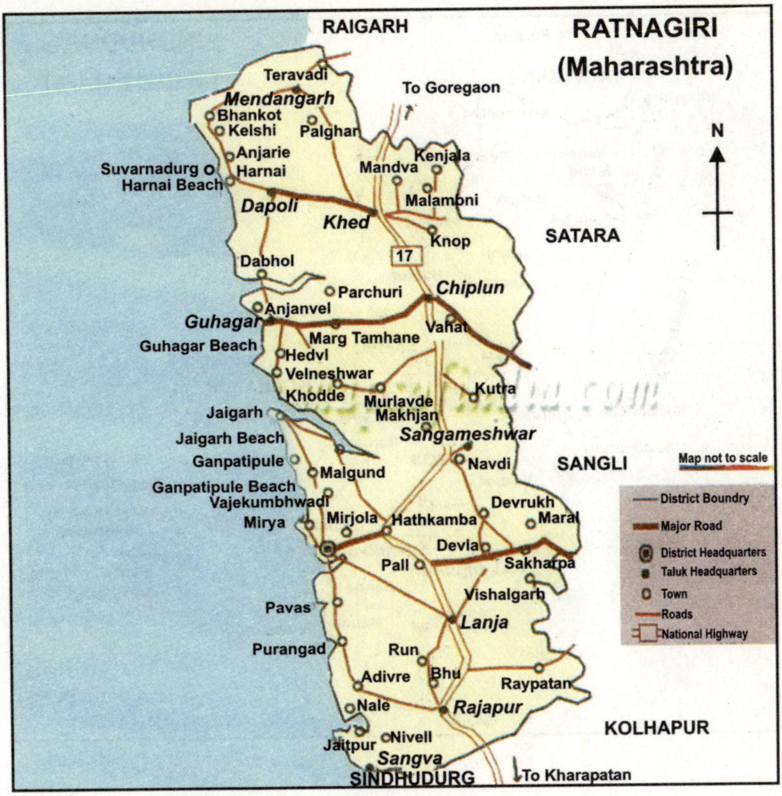

Source : www. mapsofindia.com

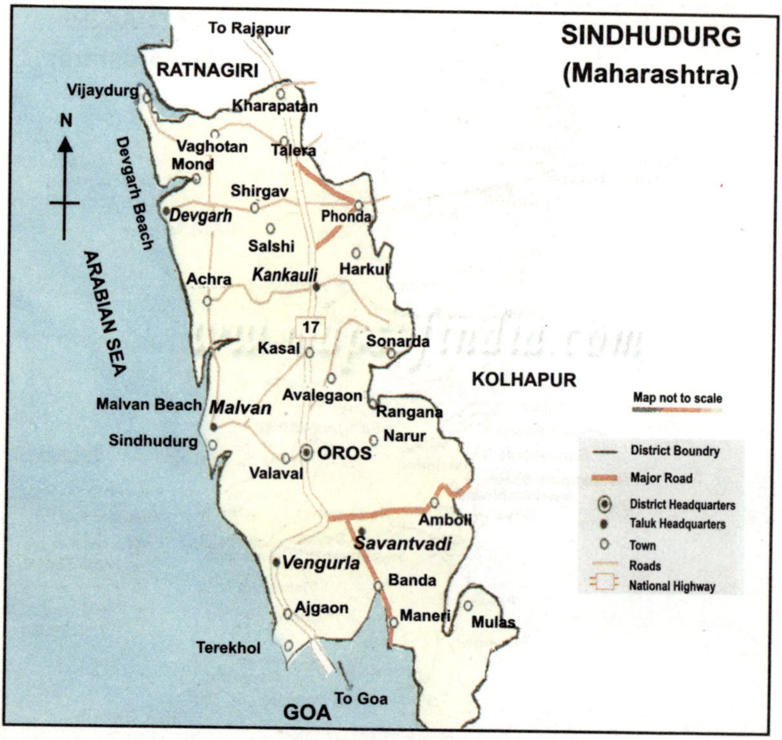

Source : www. mapsofindia.com

APPENDICES

APPENDIX-A

GLOSSARY

Abhavani	Appraisement
Ain	Terminal tomestosa (type of wood)
Ambapoli	A sweet made by Squeezing the juice of mango and drying it
Amboshi	A fruit used in curries
Ambsulpatti	Cess on a typical sour fruit of konkan
Ardhelis	Paying half of one's crop as rent
Asana	Ariedelia retusa (type of wood)
Asthadikar	Right of the khot over the eight officers of the village
Ath veth or varsai	Forced labour
Bagal kotee	Type of coins in circulation in early 19th century
Bajri	A millet
Bamboo	A type of wood
Bangdiya	Bangles (a variety of sugarcane)
Bhat	Cooked rice in husk
Bhatle	Level arable
Bhatta	Dearness allowance
Bhonsa	A kind of reed grown in Ratnagiri
Bhurrad	Strong land

Borshe	A kind of mango fruit
Casurina	A type of wood
Chinchori	Type of coins in circulation in early 19th century
Chouthelis	A cultivator or tenant paying one fourth of crop share
Dahi handi	Pots of curds
Deshmukhs	Village servants' dues in kind
Deshpande	Hereditary executive official of a pargana
Devdevasaki	Right of the khot in the duties connected to the worship
Dhara	Assessment; land liable to pay assessment
Dharekari	Dhara holding
Dharekari karkoon patti	Dharekari labour cess
Dhatee	A kind of flower used for medicinal purpose
Dhep	Ingot
Donghur	Steep part of the hill
Fadfarmas	Standing crops and fruits
Faida farmas	Right of the khot to take part of produce
Faski	A toll of palmful of grain per maund exacted by the collector of grain
Gair dasti	Improper use of taxable land
Galbat	War vessel having a mast
Gaon Karch	Village expenditure
Gavki	The right of the khot to collect land revenue
Gayal	Deserted land
Gharpatti	Cess on house
Gool	Jaggery

Goorcheer	Grazing jungle
GSB	Goud Saraswat Brahmin
Hakka	Right or privilege of khot to collect fees, fine; Legitimate due
Hing	Asafoetida
Holi poli	The right of the khot to be chief guest at festival
Hulad	Turmeric
Inam	Grant
Jama	Extra collection
Jamabandi	The fixing of the land revenue to be levied during the year
Jambala	Violet
Jambhul	Eugenia jambolana (type of fruit)
Kabuliyat	Formal agreements by the khot with the tenant in fixing revenue
Kala	Black
Kanne	A pest (black smut)
Kannon kayade	Right of acquiring
Kanvathi	Wood apple
Karpa	A disease in rice crop
Karsai	Impost of fodder, fruits
Kasba	Town
Kath	Coir
Kathi	Staff to major land
Katuban	Fixed rent
Khair	Acaciacatechu (type of wood)
Khajan land	Land lying along the shore of the sea or inlets
Kharedi katha	Rope
Kharif	Land producing autumnal harvest
Khichiari	Mixed villages

Khot	A farmer of land or revenue; a contractor or monopolist
Khot wadi	Belonging to the khot
Khoti Faida	Private property in case of foreifiting the land
Khoti Khasgi	Special office or right of the khot
Khoti Nisbat	Entirely in charge of khot
Kinjal	Terminaliaculata (type of wood)
Kowl	Written agreement usually relating to land revenue
Kularag	Land belonging to tenant or cultivator
Kulkarni	Hereditary accountant of a pargana
Laonee	Harvest
Lavajima	Village services from mahar and gurav to the khot
Mamlatdar	Appointed executive head of a taluka
Mamul	Old, customary
Manpan	Honours and presents offered at festive occasion to hereditary officer
Moonim	An examiner(survey of land etc)
Moramba	A sweet pickle made from raw mango {boiled in sugar syrup)
Nachani	Ragi (edible grain)
Nakad	Hard cash
Nangar veth	Labour extracted on plough
Nila	Blue
Nival Khoti	Purely khoti as opposed to khichadi khoti
Pahani	Survey
Pahani kharda	A rough account of a revenue survey of Peshwa's time

Paistha	Gradual slope below the hill
Pand	A land measure equal to 20 square kahtis or rods; 1/20th of beegas
Paragana	Territorial sub-division
Pat	Water courses
Patil	Village headman
Pawte	Edible seeds of pod-bearing plant
Payari Khoont	A kind of mango fruit
Pendhi	Bunch of tied grass
Phatemar	Fast sailer and coaster
Phundia	A kind of sugarcane
Pok	Shark fins
Popoyata	A kind of mango fruit
Pot phani	Detailed field inspection
Quasi Dharekari	Occupancy tenant
Rab	Refuse used for manure
Rapin	A net used for fishing
Ratambi	Carcinia purpurea (type of fruit)
Ryut	Peasant
Sanad	A document
Sheri land	Crown land
Shilotri	Lands embanks and reclaimed from the sea
Shivshv	Black wood
Sicca	Type of coins in circulation in early 19th century
Soomaree	Things taken by number
Ṭag	Hemp
Taluka	Sub-division of a district
Tambada	Red
Tambhut	Grain
Tanka	Assessments fix by Adilshahi on the revenue

Tel	Oil
Theri	Unoccupied lands
Tirdhel	A third of the produce
Toop	Ghee
Undi	Calophyllum (type of tree)
Upari	Shifting tenant having no right of occupancy
Varee	Edible grain
Vartala	Excess arising on certain measurements
Veet	A pest
Vethbegar	Tenant's services offered to the khot without remuneration
Vilayati	Foreign
Warkas	Ground chiefly hilly
Watan	Usually heritable right to office
Watandars	Hereditary officer or one who holds estates
Zillah	District

APPENDIX-B

KONKAN DISTRICTS

Ratnagiri

Name	Sub-division	Description
Achra	Malvan	Port with sea customs and post offices and salt store
Ambaghat	...	Hill-pass
Anaskura	...	Hill-pass
Anjanvel	Chiplun	
Anjarla	Dapoli	Port with sea customs office
Bankot	...	Port with sea customs office and post offices
Bavda	....	Hill-pass
Bavnadi	....	River
Bhatya	...	Tidal river
Borya	Chiplun	Port with sea customs office
Chiplun	Chiplun	Chiplun sub-division head-quarter. Town with sub Judges Court and municipality
Dabhol	Dapoli	Ruined city. Post office
Dapoli	Dapoli	Dapoli sub-division head-quarters. Sub Judges court and civil hospital
Devgad	Devgad	Devgad sub-division head-quarters. Sub judges court, Port with sea customs office
Devgad creek	...	Creek
Dhamapur	Malvan	Lake, post office
Gadnadi	...	River

Name	**Sub-division**	**Description**
Golap	Ratnagiri	Post office
Guhagar	Chiplun	Guhagar petty division head-quarters, with mahalkaris And post office
Harnai	Dapoli	Town and port with sea customs office
Jagbudi	Ratnagiri	River
Jaygad	...	Port with sea customs office
Jaytapur	Rajapur	Port with light house; tidal river
Kajirda	...	Hill-pass
Kalavali	...	Tidal river
Kelshi	Devgad	Port with sea customs office and post offices
Kahrepatan	Devgad	Post office
Khed	Khed	Sub-division head quarters
Kumbharli	...	Hill-pass
Lanja	Rajapur	Lanja petty division head quarters, with mahalkari's post office
Machal	Rajapur	Sanitarium
Malaghat	Malvan	Hill-pass
Malvan	...	Malvan sub-division head quarters. Town and port with Sub judge's court sea customs office and salt store
Mandangad	Dapoli	Mandangad petty division head-quarters, with mahalkari's and Post office
Masura	Malvan	Town with post office
Mirya	Ratnagiri	Hill-pass
Nivti	Malvan	Rock, port with light house and sea customs office
Parsahram	Chiplun	Ancient shrine
Pendur	Malvan	Lake, post office
Phonda	...	Hill-pass
Pule	Ratnagiri	Hindu fair
Purangad	Ratnagiri	Port with sea customs office

Name	**Sub-division**	**Description**
Muchkandi	...	Tidal river
Rajapur	Rajapur	Rajapur sub-division head quarters. Town with sub judges court and muncipality
Ratnagiri	Ratnagiri	Ratnagiri district and sub division head quarters.judge's and assistant judge's courts, sea customs office, port, Salt store and light house
Redi	Malvan	Old fort. Port, sea and land customs office
Sayadri	...	Mountain range
Sangameshwar	Sangameshwar	Sub-division head quarters; sub judge's court
Savitri	...	River
Shastri Jaygad	...	Tidal river
Shiroda	Malvan	Salt store
Terekhol	...	Creek
Tivraghat	...	Hill-pass
Varad	Malvan	Lake
Vasisthi	...	River
Vengurla	Malvan	Vengurla petty division headquarters. Town with Mahalkaris, post, telegraph, sea customs office, sub judge's court, Municipality, civil hospital, salt store, port and light house
Vijaydurg	Rajapur	Old fort, sea customs office
Yashwantgad	Rajapur	Old fort, sea customs office; Tidal river fort

APPENDIX-C

REGULATION OF 1827

REGULATION- II A.D. 1827, ZILLA OF THE SOUTHRN KONKAN

Grounds of the Jurisdiction	Territory	Date when the Jurisdiction Commended
Section I Reg. XI 1814	The fort and island of Sindoodroog in Malvan, and the forts of Puddunghur, Rajkot and Serjeekot, with the villages and lands dependent on the said forts.	1 October 1812
Treaty with the Waree State	The fort of Vingorla, with six hundred (600) yards around.	3 October 1812
Cessions by the Waree State	The rest of the vallery of Vingorla	5 May 1813
	So much of Warar and Muloondee as belonged at the time to the State of Waree	19 January 1814
Section IX and XI Reg. 111 of 1819	The territories of the Paishwa Bajee row, bounded on the north by the Apta River, and on the south by the Karlee or Malvan river, and lying between the ghauts and the sea, with the four (4) following exception: - **1st**-The Oonderee talooka, except the village of Khar Dolvie, which village belongs to the zilla. **2nd**- The three(3) following village in Chawool, viz. Waolee, Karley and Komprolee. **3rd**- The five (5) following warees in Chawool and thuls, viz Pakaree Rumeshwur, Pakaree Bolawee, Ramjee Mahadeo, Vessaje Keshow and Wursolee. **4th**- The Oarts belonging to and situated without the walls of the fort of Rewdunda.	2 September 1818
Regulation III of 1820	The nine (9) following sea coast villages in the turufs Ajgaum and Paut, viz:- **of Ajgaum** — Raree, Arowlee, Seerodse; Dabolee, Kanolee, Keyloos, **of Paut.** — Mahapun, with the adjoining fort of Newtee, Konchuree, Purolen.	17 February 1819
Treaty with the Colaba State	So much of the Toongartun turuf situated south of the Apta river as belonged to the State of Colaba, with the exception of the village of Khuraree Oozoorg. The two (2) villages Wueree and Shetolee, and the four(4) Khars Sonkhar, Dhadur Khar, Khar Dubaba and Dolvie Khar, in the Humrapoor turuf.	6 June 1824

REGULATION- V A.D. 1827, ZILLA OF THE SOUTHRN KONKAN

Regulation or other Aiuthority	Territory	Date when the Jurisdiction Commended
Cession by the Waree State	The actual possessions of the waree state in Wura and Muloondee.	20 January 1815
Regulation III of 1829	*The territories of the Paishwa Bajee row, bounded on the north by the Apta River, and on the south by the Karlee or Malvan river, and lying between the ghauts and the sea, with the four (4) following exception: -* **1st**-The Oonderee talooka, except the village of Khar Dolvie, which village belongs to the zilla. 2nd- The three(3) following village in Chawool, viz. Waolee, Karley and Komprolee. 3rd- The five (5) following warees in Chawool and thuls, viz Pakaree Rumeshwur, Pakaree Bolawee, Ramjee Mahadeo, Vessaje Keshow and Wursolee. 4th- The Oarts belonging to and situated without the walls of the fort of Rewdunda.	2 September 1818
Regulation III of 1820	The nine (9) following sea coast villages in the turufs Ajgaum and Paut, viz:- **of Ajgaum** **of Paut.** Raree Dabolee, Mahapun, with the Arowlee Kanolee, adjoining fort of Newtee, Seerodee Keyloos, Konchuree,Purolen.	17 February 1819
Treaty with the Colaba State	So much of the Toongartun turuf situated south of the Apta river as belonged to the State of Colaba, with the exception of the village of Khuraree Oozoorg. The two (2) villages Wueraee and Shetolee, and the four(4) Khars Sonkhar, Dhadur Khar, Khar Dubaba and Dolvie Khar, in the Humrapoor turuf.	6 June 1824

APPENDIX-D

LIST OF INDIAN PORTS, BOMBAY [1882][1]

Chief Port- Bombay

Achra	Bhatta	Edwan	Karadi
Agashi	Bhiwandi	Gangawali	Karanja
Alibag	Bingi	Gaviyar	Karwar
Alibag Taluka	Borya	Gholwad	Karwar Taluka
Alibag	Broach	Ghorebandar	Bingi
Kihim	**Broach Taluka**	**Ghorebandar Taluka**	Chendia
Mandwa	Broach	Bandora	Karwar
Rewadanda	Hansot	Ghorebandar	Sadashivgad
Rewas	Balsar	Manori	Kasheli
Thal	**Balsar Taluka**	Rayi	Kavi
Anjanwel	Balasar	Utan	Kelsi
Anjanwel Taluka	Dungri	Vesawa	Kelva
Anjanwel	Gudarda	Gogo	Khairna
Borya	Hariya	**Gogo Taluka**	Khun
Anjarla	Kolak	Gudarda	Kihim
Ankola	Kusumba	Hansot	Kirnpani
Ankola Taluka	Poeha	Hariya	Kolak
Ankola	Umarsari	Harnay	Kolibundar
Belikerii	Warli	Honawar	Koramthana
Gangawali	Chendia	**Honawar Taluka**	Kusumba
Tadri	Chirner	Bhatkal	Kudyana
Antora	Chikhli	Coompta	Magadala
Bandora	Coompta	Murdeshwar	Mahul
Bankot	Dahanu	Shirali	Mahim
Bassein	Dantiwara	Jaigarh	Malwan
Bassein Taluka	Degam	Jaitpur	Malwan Taluka
Agashi	Dehej	**Jambusur Taluka**	Achra
Bassein	Deogarh	Degam	Deogarh

Rajpuri Taluka	Tena	Mahul	Viziadurg
Kolibandar	Dholera	Dehej	Malwan
Naughar	**Dholera Taluka**	Kavi	Mandwa
Bauliari	Bauliari	Tankaria	Manori
Belapur	Dholera	Jhaigowda	Maroli
Bhagwa	Khun	Kalai	**Matunga Taluka**
Bhandup	Dumas	Kalyan	Matwad
Bhatkal	Dungari	Kantyajal	Mora
Murdeshwar	Shewa	Nawapur	Vingorla
Murwa	Shirali	Satpati	**Vingorla Taluka**
Nagothna	Surat	Sawata	Nivti
Naughar	**Surat Taluka**	Tarapur	Redi
Nivti	Bhagwas	Usarni	Vingorla
Panwel	Bhatta	Wardrai	Viziadurg
Panwel Taluka	Dumas	Tena	**Viziadurg Or Yeshwantgad Taluka**
Belapur	Gaviyar	Thal	Jaitpur
Chirner	Kantiyajal	Tonka Phansa	Viziadurg
Khaima	Karadi	Trombay	Wadrai
Panwel	Kudyana	Trombay Taluka	**Wari Talulka**
Phakland	Magdala	Bhandup	Kirnpani
Poeha	Matwad	Bhiwandi	Warli
Purngarh	Rander	Kalyan	**Yeshwantgad Or Viziadurg Taluka**
Rajivada	Surat	Kasheli	Jaitpur
Rajpuri Taluka	Tena	Mahul	Viziadurg
Talkhari	**Suverndurg Taluka**	Tanna	**Foreign Konkan (Non-British Indian Ports) Native**
Rander	Anjarla	Trombay	Bordi
Ratnagiri	Bankot	Umarasari	Danda
Ratnagiri Taluka	Harnay	Umbargam	Jambali
Jaigarh	Kelsi	Umbargam Taluka	Kumbhari
Purngarh	Tadri	Gholwad	Murad
Rajivada	Talkhari	Jhaigowda	Nandgaon
Ratnagiri	Tankaria	Kalai	Rajpuri
Rayi	Tanna	Maroli	Shriwardhan
Redi	Tarapur	Sanjan	Non-British Indian Ports [Portuguese]
Rewadanda	Tarapur Taluka	Tonka Phansa	Damaun
Rewas	Dahanu	Umbargam	Diu
Sandashivgad	Dantiwara	Uran Taluka	Goa
Sakse Taluka	Edwan	Karanja	
Antora	Kelva	Mora	
Sanjan	Koramthana	Shewa	
Satpati	Mahim	Usarni	
Sawata	Murwa	Vesawa	

Reference

1. MSA, H.Porteous, Acting Collector, of Salt Revenue, Government of India, Department of Finance and Commerce to J.Monteal, Under Secretary to Government, dated 20 July 1882, Revenue Department Volume No 53/1882, pp.303-304, 308-309.

APPENDIX-E

EAST INDIA (WEIGHTS AND MEAUSRES), A REPORT, 1865

Metal	Present Rupee Coinage	Decimal Rupee Coinage	English Coinage Present	English Coinage Decimal	Weights of Proposed New Decimal Coinage
Copper	Pies 0.96	Cents 0.5	... .	Mil 0.5	Grain Troy 35
	Pies 1.92	Cents 1	Farthing 0.96	Mil 1	Grain Troy 70
	Pies 3.84	Cents 2	Halfpenny 0.96	Mil 2	Grain Troy 140
	Pies 4.76	Cents 3	... .	Mil 3	Grain Troy ....
	Pies 5.68	Cents 4	Penny 0.96	Mil 4	Grain Troy 280
	Pies 7.06	Cents 5	... .	Mil 5	Grain Troy ...
	Annas 1.6	Cents 10	... .	Mil 10	Grains 1.75
Silver	Annas 3.2	Cents 20	... .	Mil 20	Grains 35
	Annas —	Cents 25	Sixpence	... .	Grains ...
	Annas —	Cents 40	Tenpence or Franc	... .	Grains ...
	Annas 8	Cents 50	Shiling	Mil 50	Grains 87.5
	Annas 16	Cents 100	Florin	Mil 100	Grains 175
Gold	... .		Half Sovereign	... .	Grains 61.637
	... .		Sovereign	... .	Grains 123.274

	Grains, Silver	Grains
English Florin Contains	161.645	12.9
English Florin Indian ally	160.419	14.581
New Rupee, English alloy	161.874	13.126
Actual Rupee, Indian ally	165.—	15.—

— The English alloy is said to be 37 silvers to 3 coppers.

— Indian alloy, 11 silver to 1 copper, or 33 silvers to 3 coppers

— The English florin weight 174.545 grains, a legal remedy of 727 grains, so that the rupee or 0.175 grains is within the remedy and for practical purposes considered is identical

Weights and Measures

So far the Indian arrangements of Weights and Measures is as:

80 tolas = 1seer
40 seers= 1 maund

Has been adhered to but a change would be convenient to adopt the English pound as the standard and use the cental instead of the maund, leaving the pound to be sub-divided in to 16 ounces.

The advantage of decimal division is most felt in dealing with large numbers or multiples of pound; the sub multiples are of less importance and may be left to binary scale.

Then 40 toals= 1 seer or pound
100 pounds = 1 cental
20 cental= 1 ton or 2000 lbs

All convenient numbers for calculation and near to those at present in use in England, Viz the CWT and ton of 2,240 lbs.

1 cental = 100 lbs cost rupees 17.27   80 lbs cost 17.25
1 pound = 100 lbs cost rupees 0.175   1 lbs cost 1.727/8 =0.215

In the first place decimal point is shifted and in the second it is divided by 8 or if it is considered preferable to retain seer of 80 tolas or 2 lbs the scale runs thus-

80 tolas = 1 seers = 2 lbs
100 seers= 1 cental = 200 lbs
10 centals= 1 ton =200 lbs

The seer and cental and tons would then resemble the French Kilograms and myrigramme

Dry Measure

The Bengal mun of 8.2286 gallons is so nearly equal to the bushel of 8 gallons that the latter may be adopted without inconvenience

2 pali or gallons = 1 phura or peck
4 phuras = 1 mun or bushel
8 muns = 1 khundi or quarter

Notes

Lieut.Colonel A. Delisle, Re: minutes on proposed new coinage and weights and measures, dated 1 February 1865, East India Weights and Measures, Printed 29 November 1867, Bombay Branch of Royal Asiatic Society, Bombay, pp.31-33.

Ratnagiri Fort

Source: P.K.Ghanekar, *Koknatil Paryatan*, (Marathi), Pune 1997.

Vijaydurg Fort

Source: P.K.Ghanekar, *Koknatil Paryatan*, (Marathi), Pune 1997.

Jaigad Port

Source: P.K.Ghanekar, *Koknatil Paryatan*, (Marathi), Pune 1997.

Malvan Seashore

Source: P.K.Ghanekar, *Koknatil Paryatan*, (Marathi), Pune 1997.

BIBLIOGRAPHY

PRIMARY SOURCES

Government Unpublished Records (Maharashtra State Archives)

1. Revenue Department Volumes (1821-1913)
2. R.D. Compilations (1934-1918)
3. Political Department Diaries (1756-1839)
4. Public Department Diaries (1720-1839)
5. General Department Volumes (1821- 1873)
6. Secret and Political Diaries (1812- 1829)
7. Judicial Department Volumes (1853 -1854)
8. Home Department Special File No.329

Census Reports: (Gokhale Institute of Politics and Economics, Pune)

1. Census of India, 1871, Bombay Presidency, Part III, Bombay, 1872.
2. Census of the Bombay Presidency of 1872, General Report & Tables of the Population, Houses in the Bombay Presidency, Government Central Press, Bombay, 1875.
3. Census of India 1881, Operations and the Results in the Presidency of Bombay including Sind, Volume II, Tables, Bombay, 1882.
4. Census of India 1891, Bombay and its Feudatories, Imperial Tables, Part II, Volume VIII, Bombay 1892.
5. Census of India 1901, Bombay Provincial Tables, Part III, Volume IX B, Bombay, 1902.
6. Census of India 1911, Bombay Imperial Tables, Part II, Table VII, Bombay, 1912.
7. Census of India 1921, Imperial and Provincial Tables, Bombay Presidency, Part II, Volume VIII, Bombay, 1922.

Gazetters:

1. Gazetteer of the Bombay Presidency, Volume X, Ratnagiri and Savantwadi, Government Central Press, Maharashtra State, 1880.

2. Gazetteer of the Bombay Presidency, Kolaba and Janjira, Volume XI, Government Central Press, Maharashtra State, 1883.
3. Gazetteer of the Bombay Presidency, Volume XIII, Part II, Thana, originally Printed in 1882, Government Photo Zincographic Press, Pune, 1986
4. Maharashtra State Gazetteer, Ratnagiri District (Revised), Volume X, Bombay, Directorate of Government Printing, Stationery, Publications, Maharashtra State, 1962.
5. Gazetteer of The Bombay Presidency, Volume I, Part II, History of Konkan, Asian Educational Services, New Delhi, 1988.
6. Maharashtra State Gazetteer, Thane District, Part II, Government of Maharashtra, Bombay, 1982.
7. The Imperial Gazetteer of India, Provincial Series, Bombay Presidency, Volume I, Usha Publications, New Delhi, 1907.
8. Gazetteer of Bombay City and Island, Volume I, Government Central Press, Bombay, 1909.
9. Gazetteer of the Bombay Presidency, Surat and Broach, Government Central Press, Volume No.II, Bombay, 1877.

Official Publications

1. Reports on Native Papers, (1871 1896).
2. Department of Agriculture, Season and Crop Reports of the Province of Bombay, (1904 1920), Government Central Press, Bombay.
3. The Ratnagiri District Congress Committee, Report, Government Central Press, 1938.
4. The Bombay Quarterly Report, Government Central Press, June 1929.
5. The Bombay Quarterly Report, Government Central Press, December 1923.
6. Annual Trade and Navigation Reports of The Bombay Presidency. (1872 1926)
7. Reports of the Bombay Ports Committee, Government Central Press. (1873 1925)
8. The Bombay Provincial Banking Enquiry Committee, Government of India, 4 Volumes, Bombay, 1930.
9. Survey of the Minor Ports of India, Report, Government of India, New Delhi, 1952.
10. East India Papers, Government Central Press, 1867
11. Encyclopedia of Social Science, Vol No.IX,The Macmillan Co., New York,1957.

12. Linguistic Survey of India, Bombay Presidency, Feudatory States,1898.

Selections from the Records of the Bombay Government: (Maharashtra State Archives)

1. 'Papers Relating To The Revision Survey Settlement Of 131 Villages Of The Ratnagiri Taluka Of The Ratnagiri Collectorate', *Selection From The Records Of The Bombay Government* No. CCCLXXVII -New Series, Government Central Press, Bombay, 1898.
2. 'Capt Dowell's Notes On Survey Of Old Ratnagiri Taluka', *Selection From The Records Of The Bombay Government* No.CXCVII -New Series, Government Central Press, Bombay, 1912.
3. 'Papers Relating To The Revision Survey Settlement Of The Ratnagiri Taluka Of The Ratnagiri Collectorate', *Selection From The Records Of The Bombay Government* No.DLXXIV - New Series, Government Central Press, Bombay, 1914.
4. 'Papers Relating To The Revision Survey Settlement Of The Malvan Taluka Of The Ratnagiri Collectorate', *Selection From The Records Of The Bombay Government* No.CCLXXII -New Series, Government Central Press, Bombay, 1893.
5. 'Papers Relating To The Revision Survey Settlement Of The Malvan Taluka Of The Ratnagiri Collectorate', *Selection From The Records Of The Bombay Government* No.DXXVIII -New Series, Government Central Press, Bombay, 1915.
6. 'Papers Relating To The Revision Survey Settlement Of The Vengurla Taluka Of The Ratnagiri Collectorate', *Selection From The Records Of The Bombay Government* No.CCCCXLII-New Series, Government Central Press, Bombay, 1906.

SECONDARY SOURCES

English Works

1. Apte B. K., The *Maratha Navy and Merchantships,* State Board of Literature and Culture, Government of Mahrashtra, Bombay, 1973.
2. Arasaratnam. S., *Maritime India In The Seventeenth Century,* O U P, New Delhi, 1992.
3. Ballhatchet Kenneth., *Social Policy and Social Change in Western India,* Oxford University Press, Londòn, 1961.
4. Banarjee A.C and Ghosh., *Comprehensive History of India, The Maratha Ascendancy (1712 1772),* Volume IX, People's Publishing House, New Delhi,1978.
5. Banga Indu., *Ports And Their Hinterlands In India,* (1700 1950), Manohar Publication, New Delhi, 1992.

6. Barber W. J., *British Economic Thought in India (1600 1858)*, A Study in the History of Developmental Economics, Clarendon Press, Oxford, 1975.
7. Barbosa Duarte., *The Book of Duarte Barbosa, Ed,* M.L. Dames, Volume I, Hakluyt Society, London, 1918.
8. Bidulph C.H., *Pirates Of Malabar And An English Woman In India Two Hundred Years Ago,* Smith Eldee and Co., London, 1907.
9. Birds James., *Medieval Gujarat: its Political and Statistical History, based on Mohd Ali Khan's,'mirat I Ahmadi',* transcribed in 1822 by Narayan Dass, New Delhi,1985.
10. Bound Ford., *Coastwise Shipping and Small Ports of India,* Oxford University Press, New Delhi, 1951.
11. Briggs John., *History of the Rise of Mohemmedan Power in India till the Year A.D.1612, Translation from the Original Persian Mohd Kasim Ferishta,* Volume II, New Delhi, 1981.
12. Candy E.T., *Khoti Tenure,* Selections from Records of Bombay Government, IOC, Bombay, 1873.
13. Chattopadhaya B.D., *Urban Centers in Early Medieval India,* An Overview in Sabyasachi Bhattacharya and Romila Thapar; Ed Situating Indian History for S. Gopal, New Delhi, 1987.
14. Chaudhuri V.P., *The Trading World of Asia and The East India Company,* London, Cambridge University Press, 1978.
15. Chavan V.P., *The Konkan and The Konkani Language,* The British India Press, Mazgaon, Bombay, 1924.
16. Choksey R.D., *Early British Administration* (1817-1836), Selections from the Peshwa Daftar, Poona, 1964.
17. Choksey R.D., *Select Documents from the Ratnagiri Files,* Malvan Residency, The Sangam Press, Poona, 1956.
18. Choksey R.D., *Economic Life in the Bombay Deccan and Karnataka,* Asia Publishing House, Bombay, 1960.
19. Choksey R.D., *Economic Life In The Bombay Konkan* (1818-1939), Asia Publishing House, Bombay, 1960.
20. Copleston W. K., *The Bombay Forests,* Government Central Press, Bombay, 1925.
21. Cotton Evan., *East India Men,* the Batch North Press, London, 1949.
22. Cowell E.B., Jatakas (Translated), Luzac and Company Ltd, London, 1957.
23. Crawford Arthur., *Legends of the Konkan,* Asian Educational Series, Allahabad, 1909.
24. Cunha Da Gerson., *Notes on the History and Antiquities of*

Chaul and Bassein, Thakar Vining and Company, Bombay, 1870.

25. Cunningham A., *The Ancient Geography of India*, Varanasi, Indological Book House, 1963.
26. Das Ashin Gupta., *Indian Merchants and the Decline of Surat*, (1700-1735), Manohar, Mumbai, 1994.
27. Das Ashin Gupta., *Indian Merchants and Trade of The Indian Ocean*, 1500-1775, Cambridge Economic History of India, Volume I, Cambridge, 1979.
28. David M.D., *History of Bombay*, 1661-1708, T.V.Chindambaran Publication, Bombay, 1973.
29. De Souza T.R., *Medieval Goa: A Socio Economic History*, Concept Publishing House, New Delhi, 1979.
30. Desai V.P., *The Khoti Settlement Act I of 1880*, Vakil High Court, Bombay, 1913.
31. Desai Z.A., *Studies in Indian Epigraphy*, Volume I, The Epigraphical Society of India, Geeta Book House, Mysore, 1977.
32. Deshpande C.D., *Western India, A Regional Geography*, R.G.Hukkeri, The Student's Own Book Depot, Dharwar, 1948.
33. Disney Anthony., *Twilight of the Pepper Empire*, Harvard University Press, Harvard, 1978.
34. Douglas James., *Bombay and Western India*, A Series of Stray Paper, Volume I, Sampson Low Marston and Co.Ltd, London, 1893.
35. Dowell H.H., *The Cambridge History of India*, Volume V, British India, Cambridge University Press, London, 1929.
36. Dr. Balkrishna., *The Commercial Survey of Kolhapur City in 1926*, Bombay, 1928.
37. Duff Grant., *History of the Maharattas*, Volume I, London Longman, Ed. S.M.Edwardes, The Times of India, Bombay, 1826.
38. Edwardes S. M., *The Rise of Bombay*, A Retrospect, Reprinted from the Volume I of the Census of India Series, Bombay, The Times of India Press, 1902.
39. Elphinstone, M., *A Report on the Territories Conquered by the Peshwas*, Volume I, Bombay Government Central Press, *Bombay*, 1838.
40. Enthoven R.E., *Folklore Notes Compiled from Materials Collected by A.T.M. Jackson*, Volume II, Konkan, Bombay, 1915.
41. Enthoven R.E, *The Tribes and Castes of Bombay*, Volume I,

Asia Educational Services, New Delhi, 1990.

42. Forrest G.W., *Selections from the Letters, Dispatches and other Papers in the Bombay Secretariat,* Volume I, Government Central Press, Bombay, 1885.
43. Gadgil, D.R., *A Socio Economic Survey of Poona,* Part II, Publication No 25, GIPE, Poona, 1952.
44. Gokhale B.G., *Buddhism in Maharashtra: A History,* Popular Prakashan, Bombay, 1976.
45. Gopalachari K., *Early History of Andhra Country,* G.S.Press, Madras, 1941.
46. Gordon Stewart., *The New Cambridge History of India,* Volume II, No. 4, *The Marathas* 1600- 1818, Cambridge University Press, Cambridge, 1993.
47. Guha Sumit., *The Agrarian Economy of the Bombay Deccan,* 1818-1941, Oxford University Press, London, 1907.
48. Hamilton Walter., *The East India Company Gazetteer,* London, 1815.
49. Heather and Joshi Vijay., *Surplus Labour and the City, A Study of Bombay,* Oxford University Press, Bombay, 1976.
50. Henderson H D., *Colonies and Raw Material (in Oxford Pamphlets on World Affairs),* Oxford University Press, Oxford, 1939.
51. Hourani G.P., *Arab Sea Faring, in The Indian Ocean in Ancient and Early Medieval Times,* Princeton University Press, Princeton, 1951.
52. Hughes Thomas., *Treaties, Agreements and Engagements Between the Hon. East India Company and the Native Princes, Chiefs and States in Western India; the Red Sea; the Persian Gulf;* Bombay Education Society Press, Bombay, 1851.
53. Hunter W. W., *History of British India,* Volume II, Longman Green and Company, London, 1912.
54. Jervis T. B., *Geographical and Statistical Memoir of the Konkan,* Calcutta, 1840.
55. Jervis T.B., *A Report of the Weights and Measures of the Konkan Province,* American Mission Press, Bombay, 1929.
56. Jervis W., *Thomas Best Jervis,* (A Centenary Tribute), London, 1898.
57. Joshi Vidyut, *Migrant Labour and Related Issues,* Mohan Oprimlani for Oxford & IBH Co. Pvt Ltd., Bombay, 1987.
58. K.S. Behera., Ed, *Maritime Heritage of India,* Aryan Books International, New Delhi, 1999.
59. Khobrekar, V.G., *Konkan: From the Earliest Times to 1818 A.D.(A Study in Political and Socio Economic Aspects),* Sneha

Vardhan Publication House, Pune, 2002.

60. Kosambi Meera., *Bombay in Transition, the Growth, Social Ecology of a Colonial City*, 1880-1980, Almquist & Wiksell Institute, Stockholm, Sweden, 1986.

61. Kulkarni A. R., *Medieval Konkan, Its History, Society and Economy*, 56th Session of Indian History Congress, New Delhi, 1996.

62. Kulkarni A.R., *Medieval Maratha Country*, Books and Books, New Delhi, 1996.

63. Maine H.S., *Village Communities in the East and the West, Six Lectures delivered at Oxford*, John Murray, London, 1881.

64. Maity S.K., *Economic Conditions in Northern India in the Gupta Period*, New Delhi, 1970.

65. Majumdar R.C., *The Classical Age*, Bharatiya Vidya Bhavan, Bombay, 1970.

66. Maqbul Ahmed S., *Early Arabic Accounts of India and China (Translations of Accounts of Suleiman and Ibn Khurdabeh)*, Simla, 1989.

67. Mehta Ashok., *Indian Shipping*, N.T. Shroff, Bombay, 1940.

68. Mookerji Radhakumud., *Indian Shipping, A History of the Sea Borne Trade and Maritime Activity of the Indians from Earliest Times*, Longman Green and Company, Bombay, 1912.

69. Morris David Morris., *Emergence of an Industrial Labour Force in India: A Study of the Bombay Cotton mills*, 1854-1947, Bombay, 1965.

70. Naik Nurullah., *History of Education in India*, Macmillan & Co. Ltd, Bombay, 1951.

71. Nairne A. K., *History of Konkan*, Gazetteer of the Bombay Presidency, Volume I, Part II, Bombay, 1894.

72. Nilkantha Shastri K.A., *The Comprehensive History of India*, Volume II, New Delhi Allied Publication, 1991.

73. Pannikar K.M., *India and The Indian Ocean: an Essay on Influence of Sea Power*, Unwin Ltd, 1945.

74. Paranjape B.G., *English Records on Shivaji*, Poona, Shivaji Tercentenary Memorial Series, Volume VI, 1931.

75. Paranjape.V.G., *Collected Works of Sir R.G.Bhandarkar*, Volume III, UPBCW, Bhandarkar Oriental Research Institute,Poona,1927.

76. Patel V.P., *The Land Problem of Reorganized Bombay State*, Tripati Private Ltd, Bombay, 1957.

77. Pearson M. N., *Wealth and Power, Indian Groups in the Portuguese Indian Economy*, South Asia, Volume III, 1973.

78. Pearson M.N., *Before Colonialism: Theories on Asian European Relations,* 1500-1750, Delhi, Oxford University Press, 1988.
79. Philips C.H., *East India Company,* Manchester University Press, Manchester, 1975.
80. Pilot. C.D., *Western Coast of India Pilot Comprising the West Coast of Ceylon of Indian from Colombo to Karachi, also the Maldive and Laccadive Islands, Great Britan Admirality,* Hydongraphy London, 1926.
81. Powell Baden B.H., *Administration of Land Revnue and Territories in the British India,* Ess Ess Publication, New Delhi, 1907.
82. Proes E.M., *Bombay Presidency Motor Guide,* Government Central Press, Government of Bombay, 1923.
83. Rajamanickam Victor & Subbarayalu W., *History of Trditional Navigation,* Sarma's Sanatorium Press, Tamil University, Tanjavur, 1988.
84. Ravinder Kumar., *Western India in the Nineteenth Century,* a study in the Social History of Maharashtra, Routledge and Kegan Paul, London, 1968.
85. Raychaudhari H. C., Geographical Conditions in a Yazdani, Ed 'Early History of the Deccan, Volume I, London, 1960.
86. Roberts James., *Western India, 'Report Addressed to the Chamber of Commerce of Amnchester,* Liverpool, Blackburn and Glasgow by their Commissioner Late. Alexander Mackay Nathanial Cooke', Milkford House, London, 1953.
87. Rogers Alexander., *The Land Revenue of Bombay,* Volume II, Low Price Publication, New Delhi (Reprint), 1993.
88. Schoff W.H., *Periplus of Erythrian Sea,* Longman, Green and Co, London, 1912.
89. Sen S.N., *Administrative System of The Marathas,* Oxford, Calcutta, 1976.
90. Sircar D.C., *Inscriptions of Ashoka,* Publication Division of Information and Broadcasting, Government of India, New Delhi, 1957.
91. Sovani.N.V., *The Social Survey of the Kolhapur City: Population and Fertility* Part I,, Gokhale Institute of Politics and Economics, Poona, 1948.
92. Spate O.H.K., *India and Pakistan, A General and Regional Geography,* Methuen and Co, London, 1954.
93. Sridharan K., *A Maritime History of India,* Publication Division, Ministry of Information and Broadcasting, New Delhi, 1965.
94. Srivastava Balarama., *Trade and Commerce in Anicent India from the Earliest Times to Circa. A.D. 300,* Varanasi,

Chaukhmba Sanskrit Series office, 1968.

95. Sutherland Lucy K.,*The East India Company in Eighteenth Century Politics,* Clarendon Press, Oxford, 1952.

96. Tibetts G.R., *Arab Navigation in The Indian Ocean Before the Coming Portuguese being a tr of Kitab al Fawaid Fi Usul Al Bahr Wal Quwaid by Ahmed B Majid al Najdi together with an introduction of the History of Arab Navigation with Maps and Charts,* Leida, London, 1971.

97. Utgikar N.B. and Vaidya K.B., *Ratnagiri, Kay Bee's Indian Shipping Annual Reports, Naval defence of India, Thakar and Co.,* 1951, Bombay 1951.

98. Varghese, T.C., *'Agrarian Change And Economic Consequence', Land Tenure in Kerala,* 1850-1960, Allied Publication, Bombay, 1970.

99. Vincent William., *Voyage of the Nearchus and the Priplus of the Erythrian Sea,* London, 1880.

100. Wadhwa D.C., *Agrarian Legislation in India,* Volume I, Oriental Longman Limited, Poona, 1973.

101. Wadia R.A., *The Bombay Dockyard and The Wadia Master Builders,* Ruttonjee Ardheshir Publication, Bombay, 1955.

102. Wilson John., *Indian Caste,* Volume I, Deep Publication, New Delhi, 1976.

103. Yanagisawa Haruka., *A Century of Change Caste and Irrigated Land in Tamilnadu,* Manohar Publication, New Delhi, 1996.

104. Yazdani. G., *Early History of the Deccan,* Volume I, Oxford University Press, London, 1960.

105. Zachariah K.C., *Migrants in Greater Bombay,* Asia Publishing House, Bombay, 1966.

Marathi Works

1. Altekar A.S., *Shilharancha Ithihas,* Damodar Savalaram ani Mandali, Bombay, *1935.*
2. *Bhave G.V., Bhave Kula Vrittanta,* G.V. Bhave Publications, Poona, 1940.
3. Dhabbu D.G., *Kulabkar Angre Sarkhel,* Bombay, *1939.*
4. Gadgil D.G., *Hindusthancha Arthik Itihas,* Jambhekar G, Lokshikshan Laghu Grantha Mala, Poona, 1932.
5. *Ghanekar P.K., Koknatil Paryatan,* Snehal Prakashan, Pune 1997.
6. Karve C. G., Maharashtratil *British Rajwatichi Pahili Gadi,* Prasad Publishers, Poona, 1957.
7. Katdhare Murlidhar., *Marathe Kaleen Sarkari Adhikari Ani Tyanche Gair Vartan* Sugava Prakashan, Nanded , 1995.

8. Khobrekar V. G., *Maharashrache Arthik va Samajik Khacchikaran, Maharashtratil Sahastra* Utsav, Bombay, 1958.
9. Kolte V.B., *Maharashtratil Tamrapat va Shilalekh* Maharashtra Rajya Sanskriti Mandal, Bombay, 1987.
10. Lokahitawadi., *Aitihasik Goshti va Upayukta Mahiti,* Volume No.1, Nirnaya Sagar Prakashan, Pune,1908.
11. Marathe Anant Vasudev., *Vengurle Mahal va Parisar, Vengurla,* Mitra Mandal, 2nd Edition, Mumbai, 1961.
12. Musale Narayan Ganesh., *Ratnagiri Jillah, Kal, Aaj Va Udhya,* Abhinav Prakashan, Mumbai, 1958.
13. Pawar A. G. *Jijabai Kalin Kagad Patre,* Kolhapur, 1975.
14. Pissurlencar S., *Portuguese Marathe Sambandha,* Poona, 1967,
15. Shejwalkar.S., *Kokanachya Itihaschi Parshvabhumi,* Bharatiya Itihas Samshodhak Mandal, Poona, 1883.
16. Talwalkar Govind., *Sattankar,* Volume I, Mony Prakashan, Grihamumbai, 1983.

Journals

1. Chakravarti Ranabir., 'Monarchs, Merchants and A Matha in North Konkan' *The Indian Economic and Social History Review,* Volume No 27, No.2, SAGE, Delhi , 1984.
2. Chakravarti Ranabir., 'Merchants of Konkan, Burdhwan University', *The Indian Economic and Social History Review,* Volume 23, No.4, SAGE, Delhi 1986.
3. Chaudhuri J.R., 'Migration & Remittances Inter Urban and Rural Urban Linkages', *The Indian Economic and Social History Review,* SAGE Publications, Volume 23,New Delhi, 1993.
4. Das Ashin Gupta., 'The Crisis at Surat', 1730-32, *Bengal, Past and Present,* Volume 86, 1967.
5. Deloche Jean., 'Geographical Considerations in the Localization of Ancient Seaports of India', *The Indian Economic and Social History Review,* Volume 20, No.4, SAGE, Delhi,1983.
6. Patterson Maureen P.,'Changing Patterns of Occupation among chitapavan Brahmins', University of Chicago, Indian Economic and Social History Review, Volume 7, No. 3, SAGE, Delhi , 1970.
7. Pope Andrew., 'British Steam Shipping and The Indian Coastal Trade 1870-1915', *The Indian Economic and Social History Review,* Volume 32, No.1, SAGE, New Delhi, 1995.
8. Rabitoy N., 'System Vs Expediency:' The Reality of Land Revenue Administration in the Bombay Presidency, 1812-

1820', *Modern Asian Studies* Volume 9, No. 4, 1975.

9. Savur. M., 'Ratnagiri Underdevelopment of an Area of Reserve Labour Force', *Sociological Bulletin*, Volume 31 No.2, 1982.
10. Shri Krishnan., 'Peasant Mobilisation, Political Organisations and Modes of Interaction: the Bombay Country Side', *The Indian Economic and Social History Review*, Volume 36, No 4, SAGE, Delhi , 1995.
11. Sita. K., 'Migration and its effects on urbanization, South Konkan', *The Indian Geographical Journal*, volume 54, No1, June 1979.
12. Subramanyam Lakshmi., 'Bombay and the West Coast in the 1740's' *The Indian Economic and Social History Review*, Volume 8, No.2, SAGE, Delhi 1907.
13. Subramanyam Sanjay., 'The Portuguese, The Port of Basrur and The Rice Trade', (1600-1650) *The Indian Economic and Social History Review*, Volume 21, No 4, SAGE, Delhi , 1984.
14. Sunanda Krishnamurthy, 'Agricultural Labourers in the Bombay Deccan', 1874-1922, *The Indian Economic and Social History Review*, Volume 25, No I, SAGE, New Delhi, 1987.
15. Thosar T.S., 'South Indian Inscriptions and Place Names', Volume XII, Mysore, 1991.
16. Wagle N.K., 'The History and Social Organisation of the Gauda Sarawata Brahmanas of the West Coast of India', *Journal of Indian History*, Volume XLVIII, Part III, April December 1970, University of Kerala, Trivandrum.

Unpublished Thesis

1. Donde. W.B., 'Rural Labourers in Konkan', University of Bombay, 1950.
2. Jagjit Singh., 'History of Bombay (1708-1750)', University of Bombay, 1977.
3. Khobrekar V.G., 'History of Konkan' (1630-1818), University of Bombay, 1985.
4. Manshuramani C.R.,'History of Bombay' (1756-1782), University of Bombay, 1966.
5. Prasad M.A., 'Studies in India's Trade Relations During Ancient Times with Reference to Maharashtra', University of Bombay, 1989.
6. Rege M.S., 'The History and Survey of Education in the Ratnagiri District, University of Bombay, 1961,
7. Shirgaonkar Varsha.,'Conservatism in Maharashtra, Vishvanath Narayan Mandlik', University of Bombay, May 1987.

8. Wagle B. G., 'Geomorphology and Evolution of the Coastal and Offshore Areas of Maharashtra and Goa', University of Goa, March 1987.

INDEX